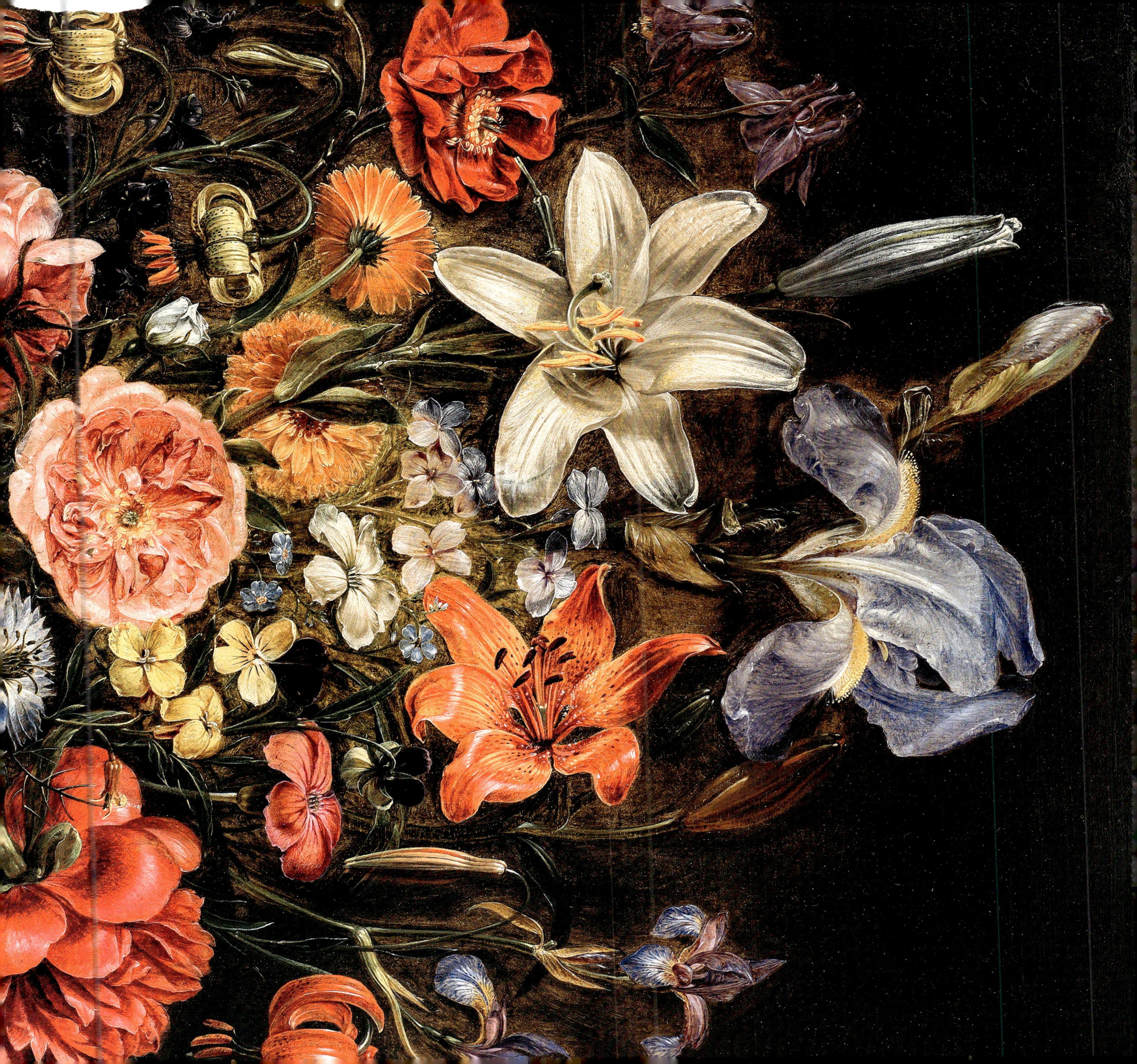

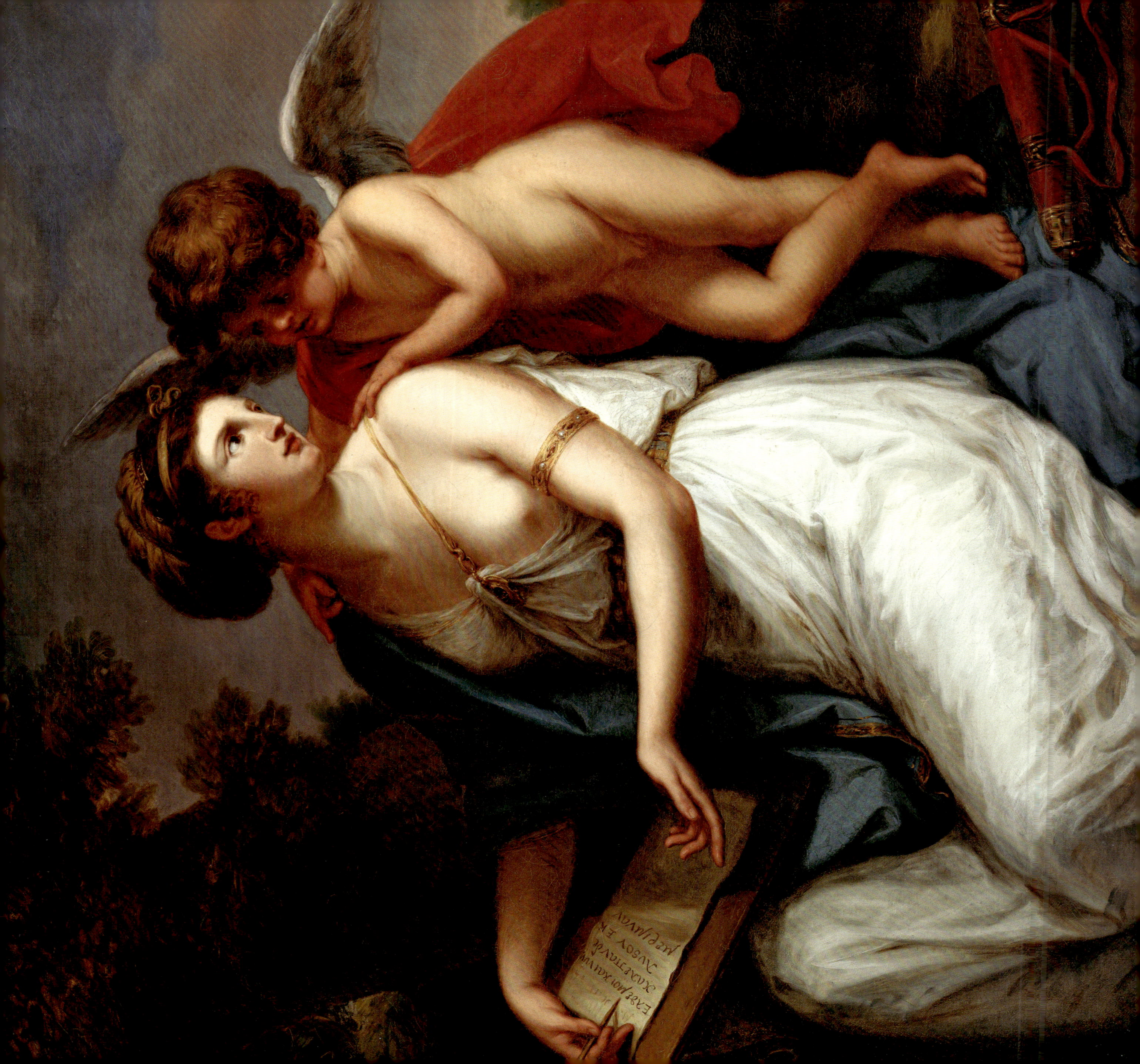

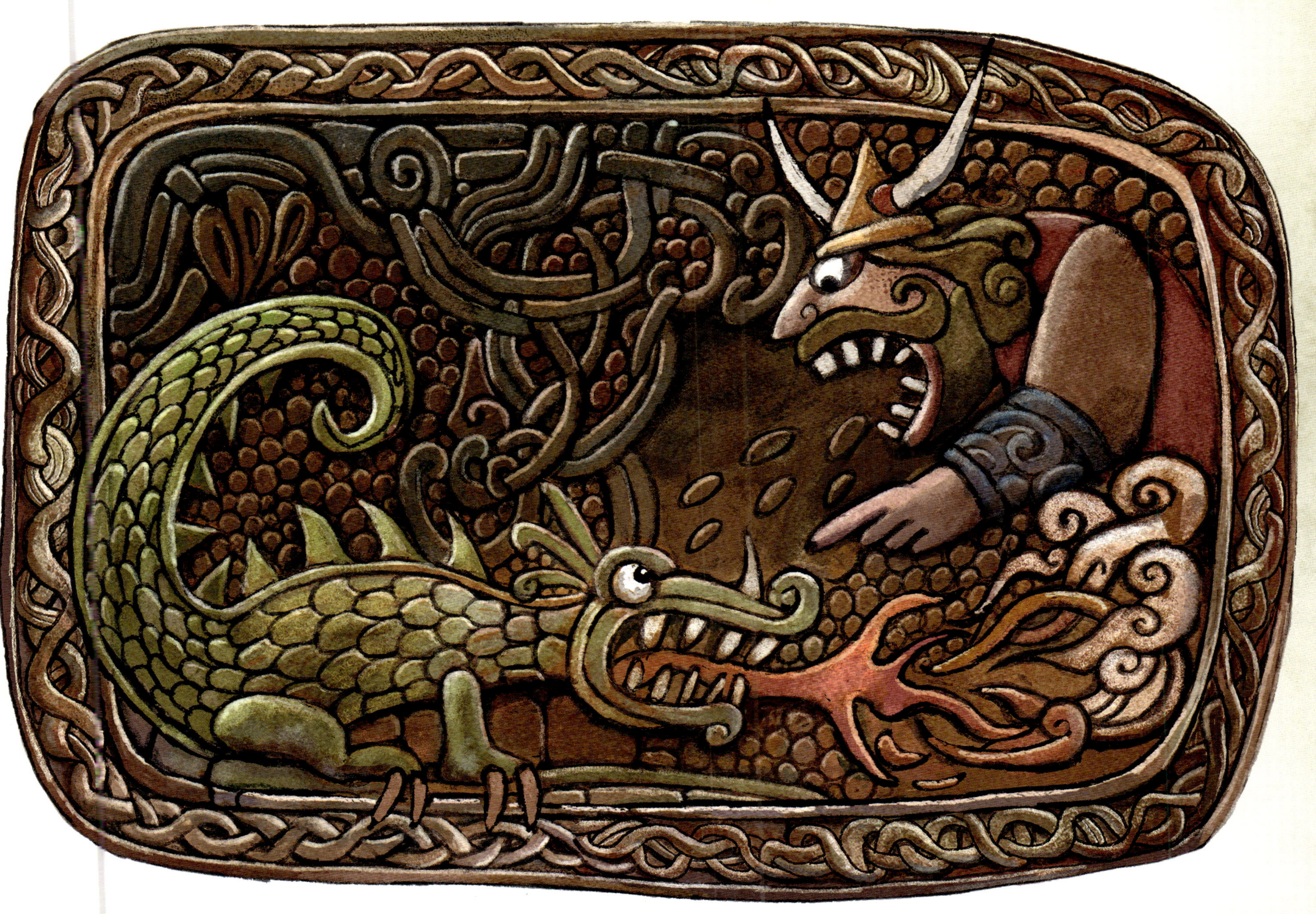

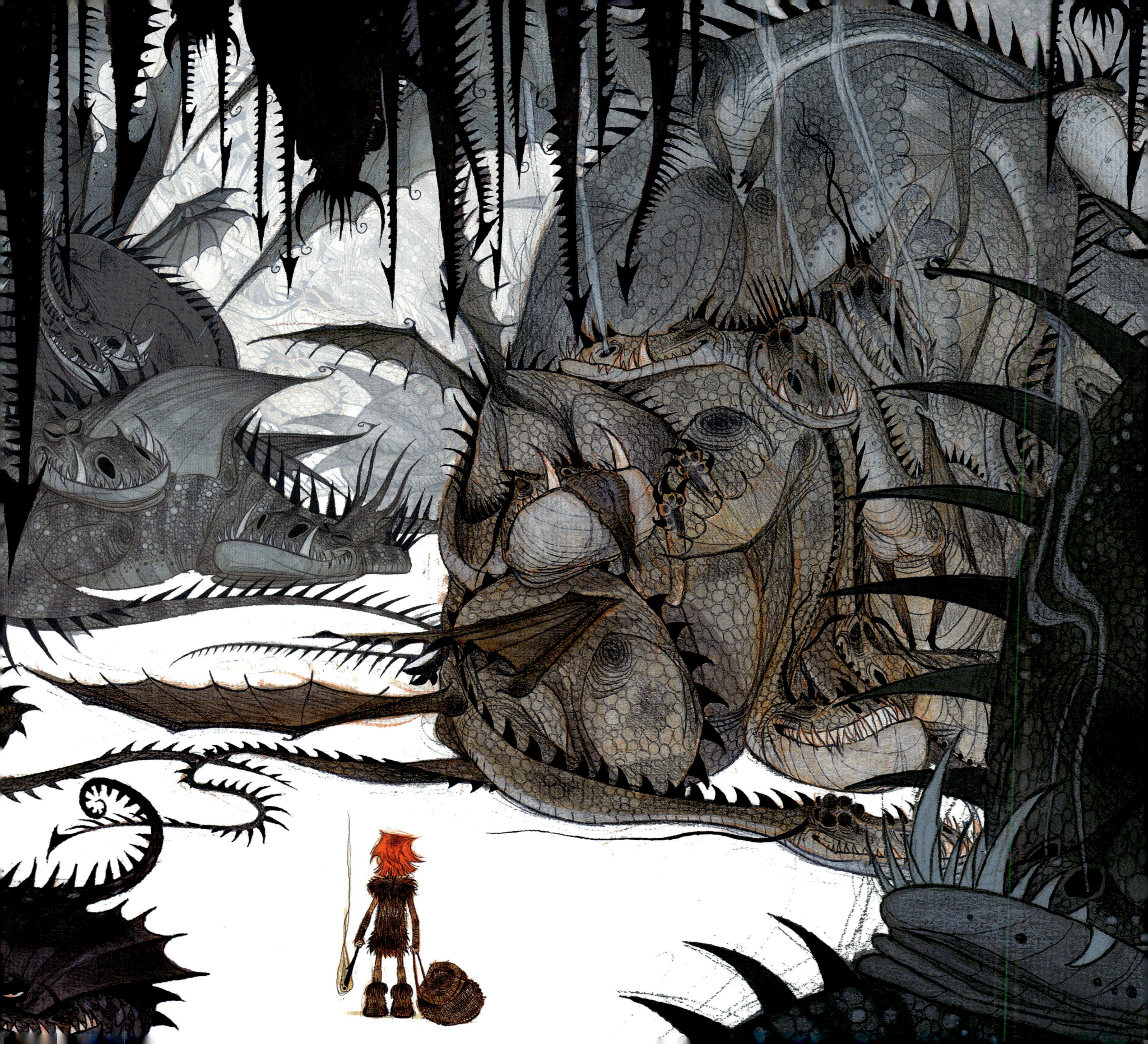

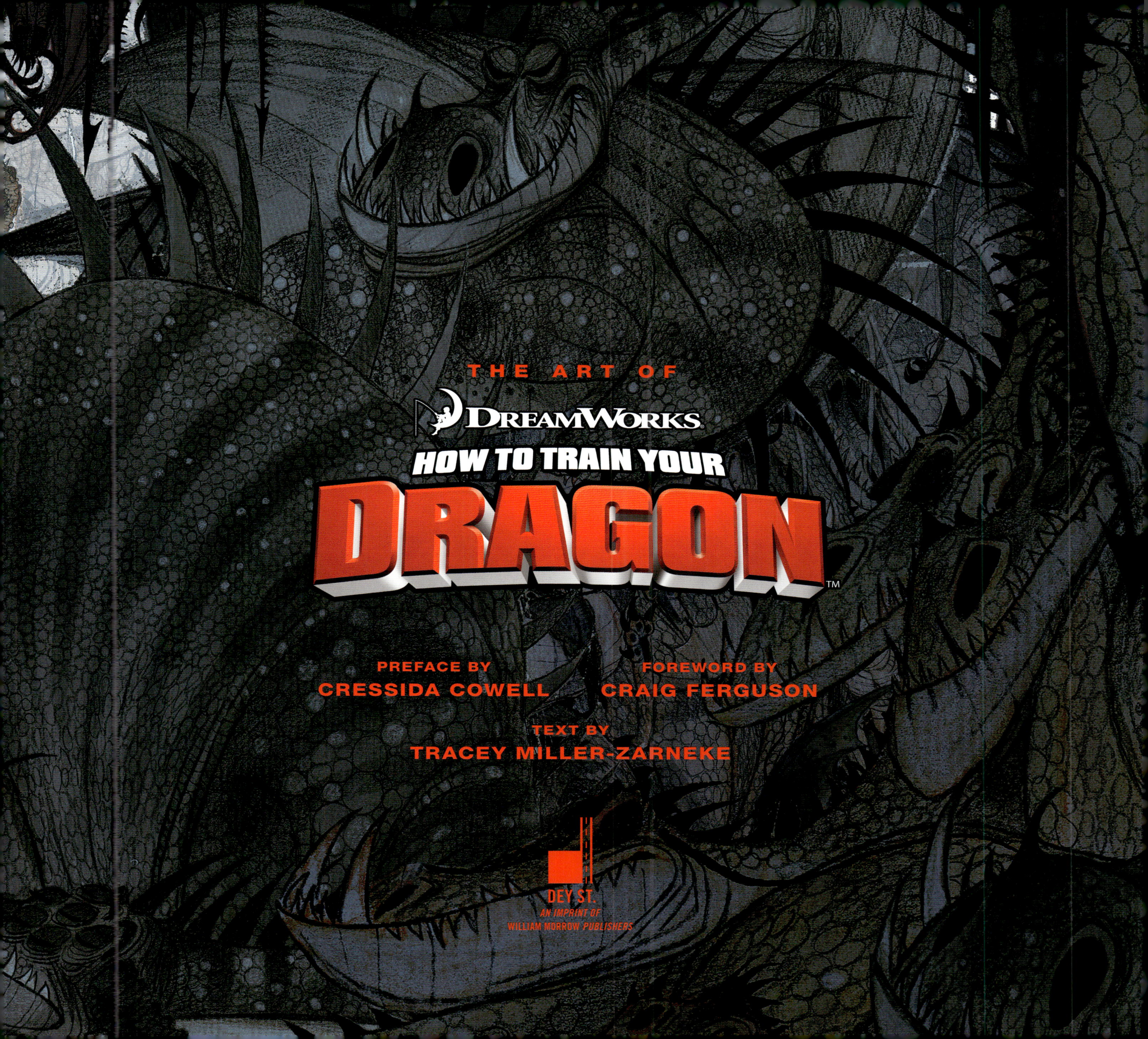

THE ART OF

DREAMWORKS

HOW TO TRAIN YOUR DRAGON™

PREFACE BY
CRESSIDA COWELL

FOREWORD BY
CRAIG FERGUSON

TEXT BY
TRACEY MILLER-ZARNEKE

DEY ST.
AN IMPRINT OF
WILLIAM MORROW PUBLISHERS

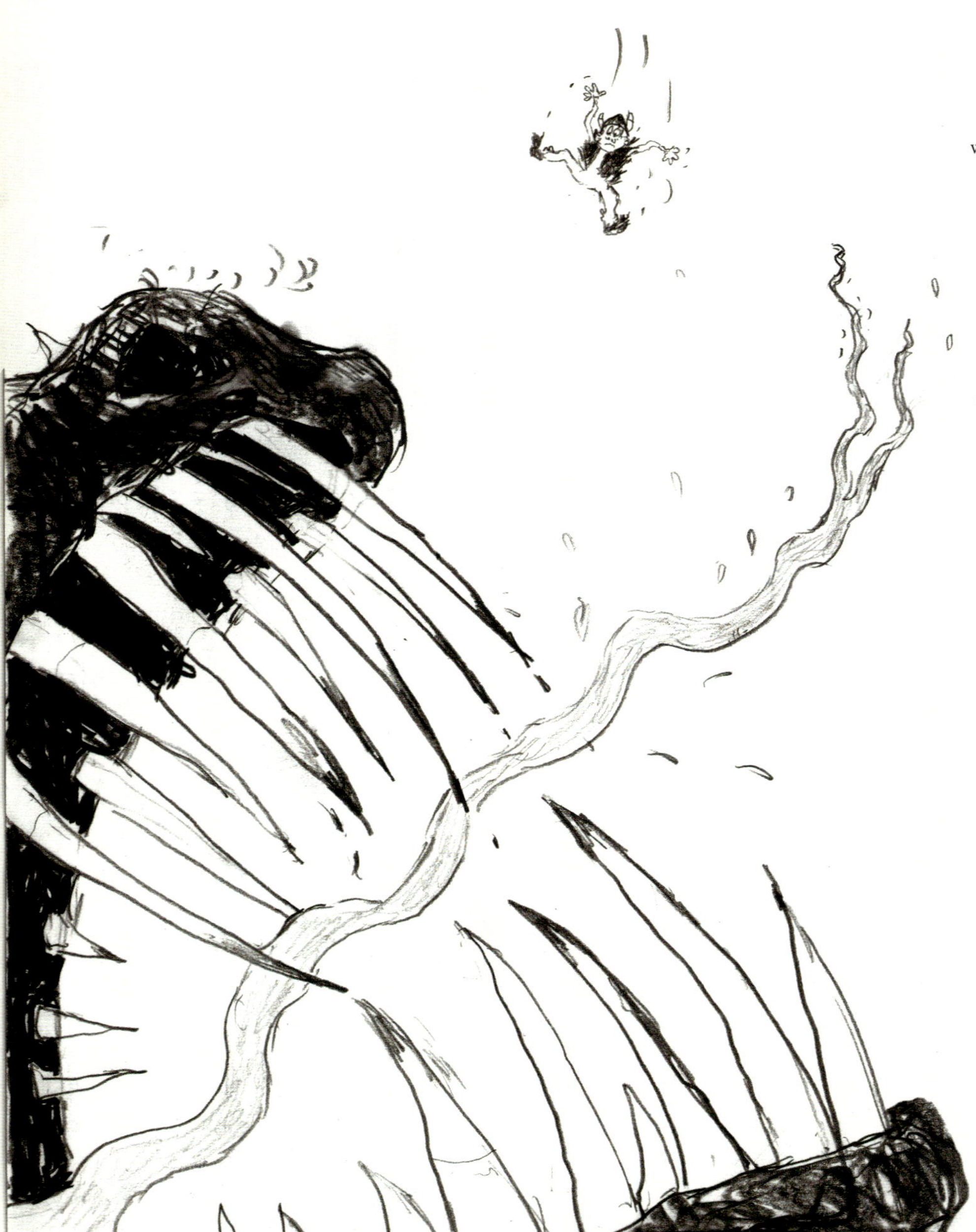

First Edition

25 RRDSEA 16

ISBN: 978-1-55704-863-9 (hardcover)

Library of Congress Catalog-in-Publication Data available upon request.

Quantity Purchases
Companies, professional groups, clubs, and other organizations may qualify for special terms when ordering quantities of this title. For information, email sales@newmarketpress.com or write to Special Sales, Dey St., 195 Broadway, New York, NY10007. call (212) 832-3575 ext. 19 or 1-800-669-3903; FAX (212) 832-3629;.

Manufactured in Vietnam

Special thanks to Writer Tracey Miller-Zarneke and Designer Timothy Shaner (nightanddaydesign.biz).

Produced by Newmarket Press: Esther Margolis, President and Publisher; Frank DeMaio, Production Director; Keith Hollaman, Executive Editor; Paul Sugarman, Digital Supervisor

Other Newmarket Pictorial Moviebooks and Newmarket Insider Film Books include:

Angels and Demons: The Illustrated Movie Companion
The Art of Monsters vs. Aliens
*The Art of The Matrix**
*The Art of X2**
The Art of X-Men: The Last Stand
*Bram Stoker's Dracula: The Film and the Legend**
*Chicago: The Movie and Lyrics**
*Dances with Wolves: The Illustrated Story of the Epic Film**
*E.T. The Extra-Terrestrial: From Concept to Classic**
Gladiator: The Making of the Ridley Scott Epic Film
*Good Night, and Good Luck: The Screenplay and History Behind the Landmark Movie**
*Hotel Rwanda: Bringing the True Story of an African Hero to Film**
The Jaws Log
Memoirs of a Geisha: A Portrait of the Film
Milk: A Pictorial History of Harvey Milk
The Mummy: Tomb of the Dragon Emperor
*Ray: A Tribute to the Movie, the Music, and the Man**
Rescue Me: Uncensored
Rush Hour 1, 2, 3: Lights, Camera, Action!
Saving Private Ryan: The Men, The Mission, The Movie
Schindler's List: Images of the Steven Spielberg Film
*Superbad: The Illustrated Moviebook**
Tim Burton's Corpse Bride: An Invitation to the Wedding

*Includes the screenplay

(half title) **Training Carving** — Kirsten Kawamura — digital paint. *(title spread)* **Hiccup in Cave of Dragons** — Pierre-Olivier Vincent — composition — Nico Marlet — design — pencil & marker.

(above) **Green Death** — Cressida Cowell — pencil. *(right)* **Sheep** — Cressida Cowell — pencil.

Contents

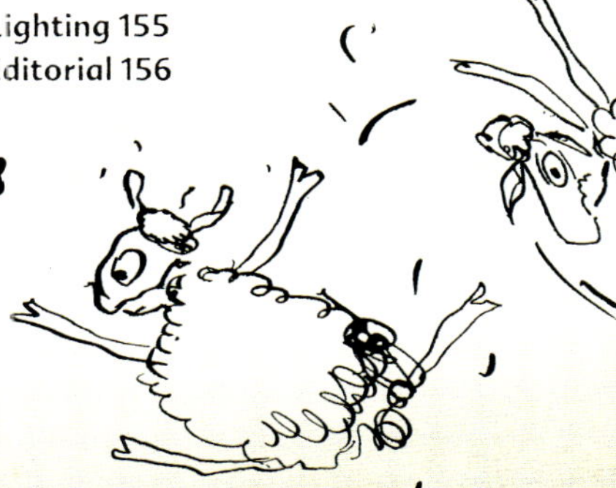

Preface
by Cressida Cowell

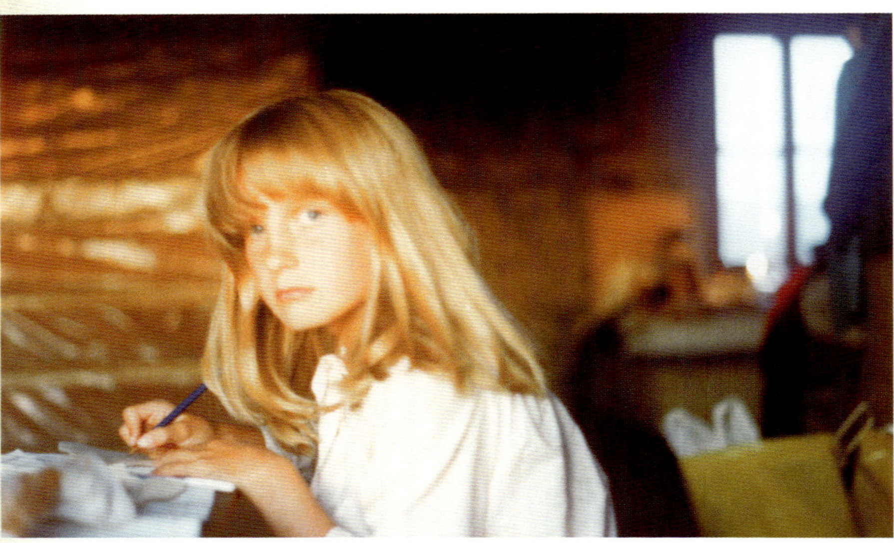

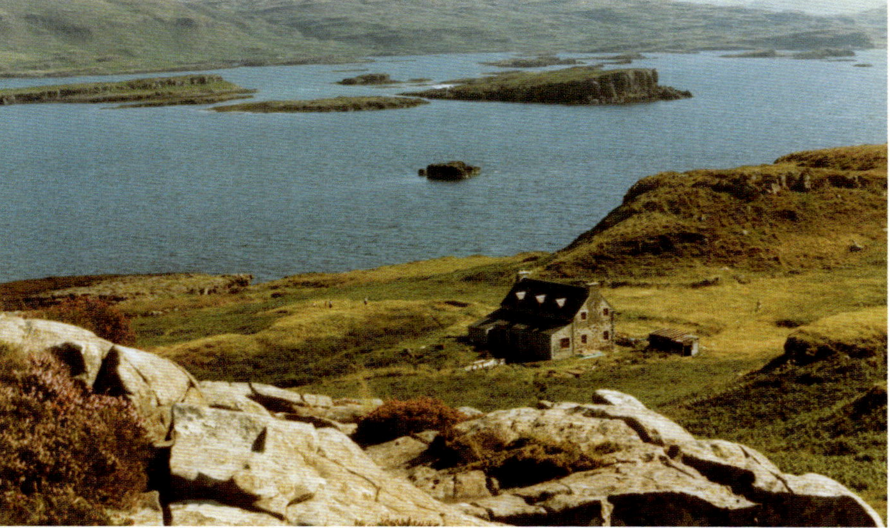

Every year since I was four years old, my family would leave our home in London to spend the summer on a remote, uninhabited island off the west coast of Scotland.

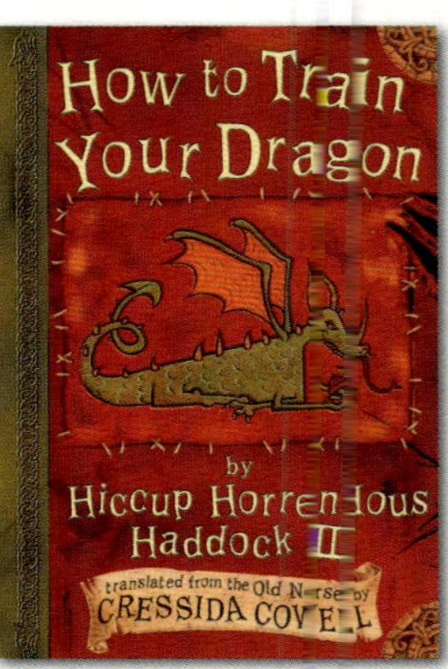

The name of the island is a secret, but it was such a small island that it hardly justified having a name at all. It was so small that when you stood on the top of it you could see ocean all around you. There were no roads, houses, or electricity, just a storm-blown, windy wilderness of sea-birds and heather.

For the first four years we visited the island, my family and I would be dropped off on the island like castaways by a local boatman and picked up again some weeks later.

Even as a child, I felt that this was a little reckless on my parents' part, since they had absolutely no way of contacting the outside world if anyone fell ill or something went wrong. But nonetheless, I knew I was the luckiest child in the world. Imagine having a whole island to yourself to explore. . . .

By the time I was eight, my family had built a small stone house on the island, so we no longer had to camp out in tents, which made life much drier. And my father now had a boat, so we could catch fish, crab, lobsters, and the like to feed the family for the whole summer.

The house was lit by candle-light, and there was no telephone or television, so I spent the whole summer drawing and writing stories. In the evenings my father read us tales of the Vikings who had invaded this Archipelago twelve hundred years before. We listened attentively to the stories of the quarrelsome Tribes, who fought and tricked each other, and of legendary dragons, who were supposed to live in the caves.

It seemed perfectly believable that dragons might live in this wild, stormy place. Once, we hauled up the tangle-nets to find giant prawn-like creatures that had mysteriously grown to the size of small dogs. We asked a local fisherman what they were, and he shook his head. "I've been fishing here for forty years," he said, "and I've never seen such a thing before . . . . "

This confirmed what I had always suspected, that there were things on this earth that even the adults had not yet discovered, nor understood.

So that was how I first began to write the *How to Train Your Dragon* stories, back when I was eight or nine years old. My starting point was, what if dragons really had existed, long ago? Perhaps they once roamed the earth, like dinosaurs, and something had caused them to retreat back into the ocean, where they were hibernating, far from human sight.

The dragons I would write about would not be the rather generalized, big, green things that I had read about in storybooks. What *I* wanted to create was a multiplicity of different dragon species, of all shapes and sizes, adapted to their environment and habitats in the same way as birds or other animals we see today.

The hero of my books, Hiccup, is a Viking, living on an island called Berk that is remarkably like the island where I grew up. In black-and-grey pencil and ink drawings, I can only hint at the wild, glorious beauty of the Archipelago where Hiccup lives.

And now Hiccup and the dragons are moving from the carefully constructed pages of my books to the big screen. I've had a chance to see the development of the movie, and one of the great joys for me is that the genius of the artists at DreamWorks can bring this sea-and-island landscape, and its inhabitants, so stunningly to life.

You can see how beautifully they have done this in the pages that follow.

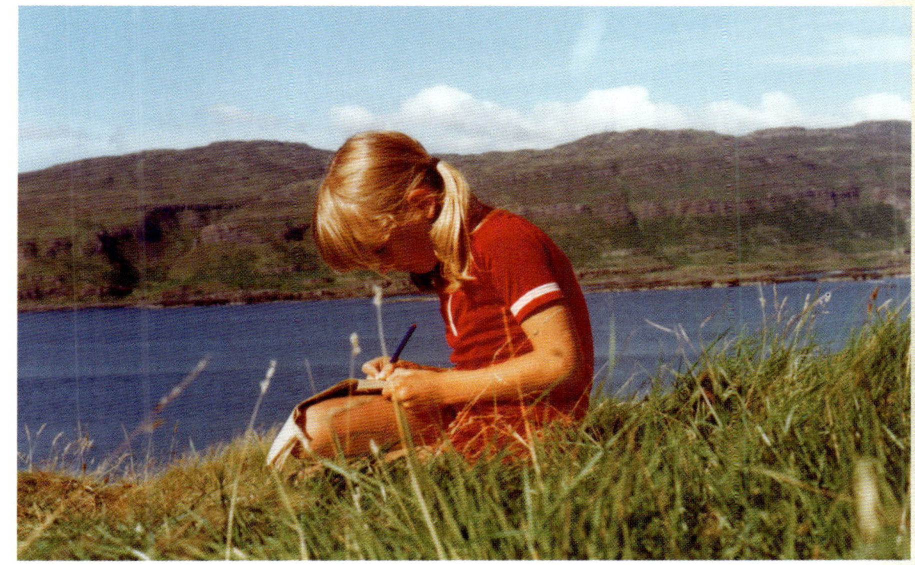

Cressida Cowell's childhood images from her Scottish summers.

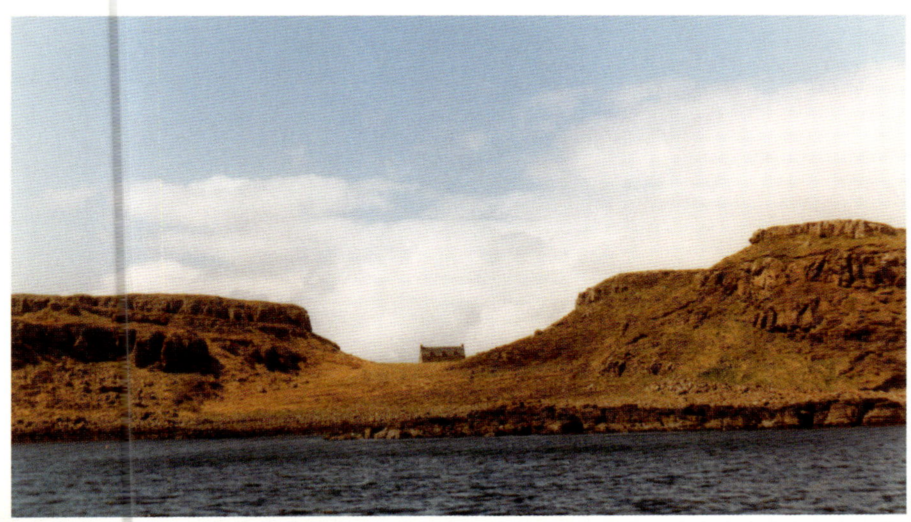

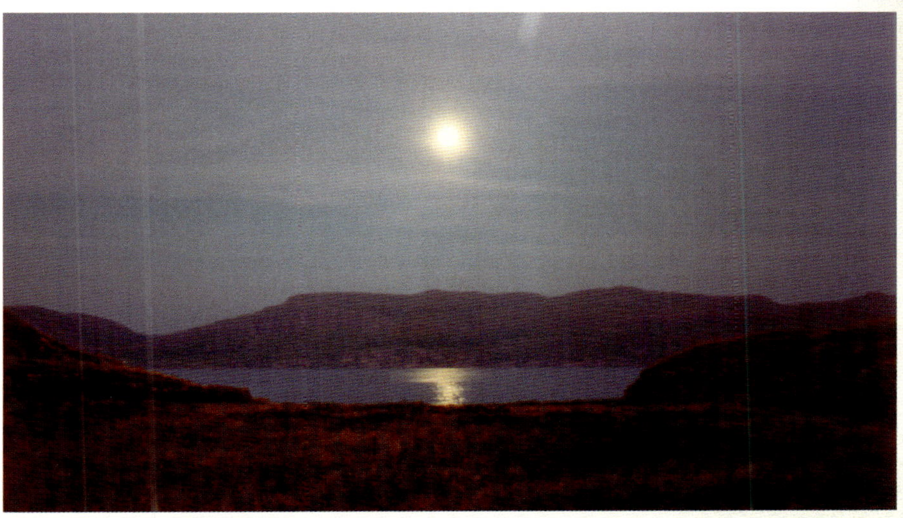

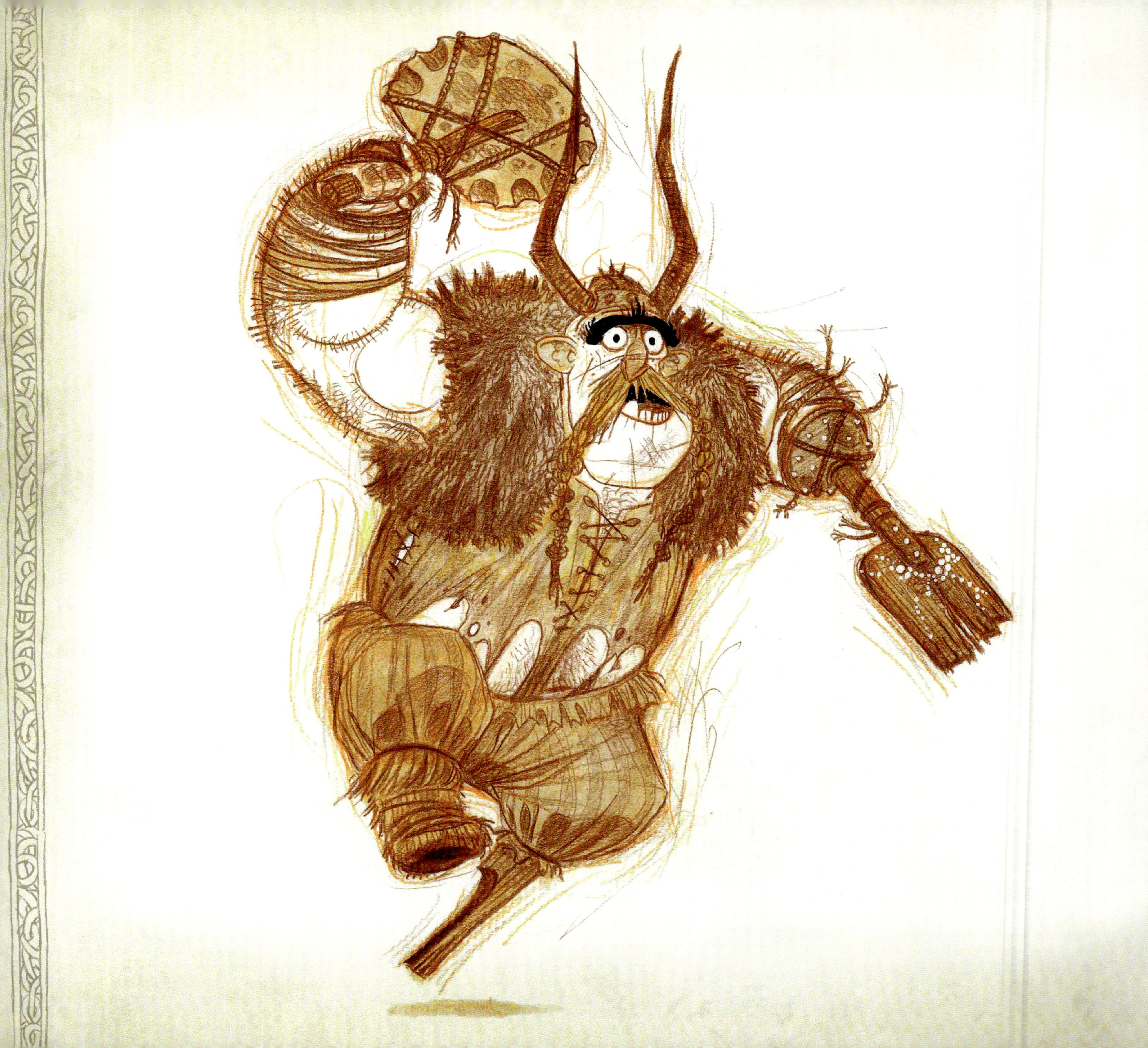

Foreword

by Craig Ferguson

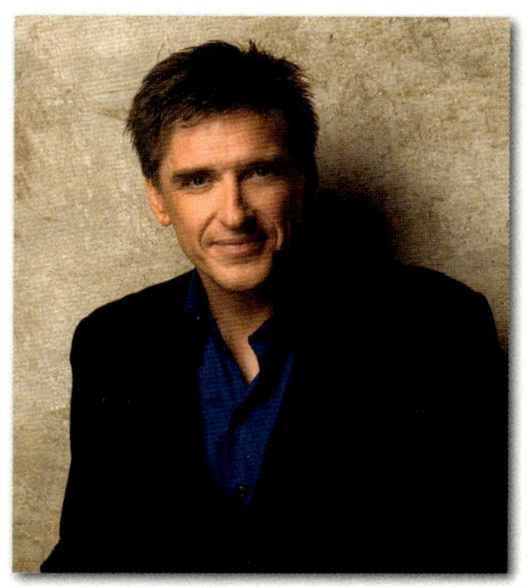

I used to be afraid of flying. Terrified. The slightest bump or rattle had me rigid with fright, my breath shallow and my heart pumping. I had to be sedated to sit on a 747. Given the amount of traveling that is involved in my line of work, this was a horrible inconvenience. I wasted long hours on airplanes grinding my teeth and sweating. Eventually, at the suggestion of my wife, who had seen me suffer terribly on routine trips, I took flying lessons in the hope that if I better understood the process, I would be less afraid of it.

The first few flights in the small training Cessna were hell, but after about fifteen hours or so of training, something strange happened. I was still apprehensive, but I also started to enjoy myself. I began to realize that there was something on the other side of my fear, and it became a mission, almost an obsession, to find out what that was. I flew and flew and flew, and eventually got my pilot's license and bought a small airplane. Now I fly for fun.

I could never really express what had happened, why I fell in love with what I had previously feared, but when I saw the first cut of *How to Train Your Dragon,* I saw it explained to me. There is a scene in the movie where Astrid and Hiccup fly on Toothless's back toward the island of Berk. The animation is intensely real, from the waves on the sea to wisps of wind blowing in the characters' hair. The feeling I get watching that scene is why I fly—just for that feeling.

And that is why I believe the DreamWorks Animation movies are so successful. It's because of how they make you feel—great stories pictured with empathy. They are remarkably detailed of course, sumptuously animated with great thought and precision. The artists I met during the making of this movie at the studios in Glendale, California, take great pride in their work. They have a confidence that they are at work on something that is both beautiful and valuable, and that reflects an optimism that is neither didactic nor rigid. They're funny too; very few eight-year-olds watching the movie will be cognitive of the metaphor of riding the black dragon (which used to terrorize you). It's funny and immediate and entertaining, but if you look closely, the animation is breathtakingly skilled and far more complicated than one viewing would allow your mind and eyes to absorb.

Pause then and enjoy the visual poetry in this book. And I wish you luck rendering your own black dragons toothless.

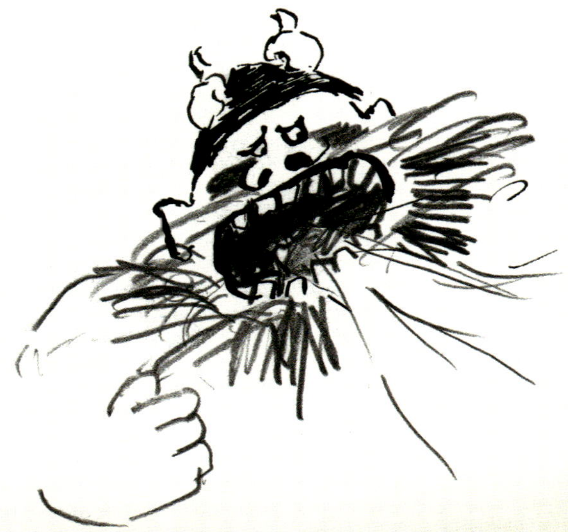

(left) **Gobber Final** — Nico Marlet — pencil & marker. *(above)* **Craig Ferguson** — voice of Gobber. *(right)* **Gobber** — Cressida Cowell — pencil.

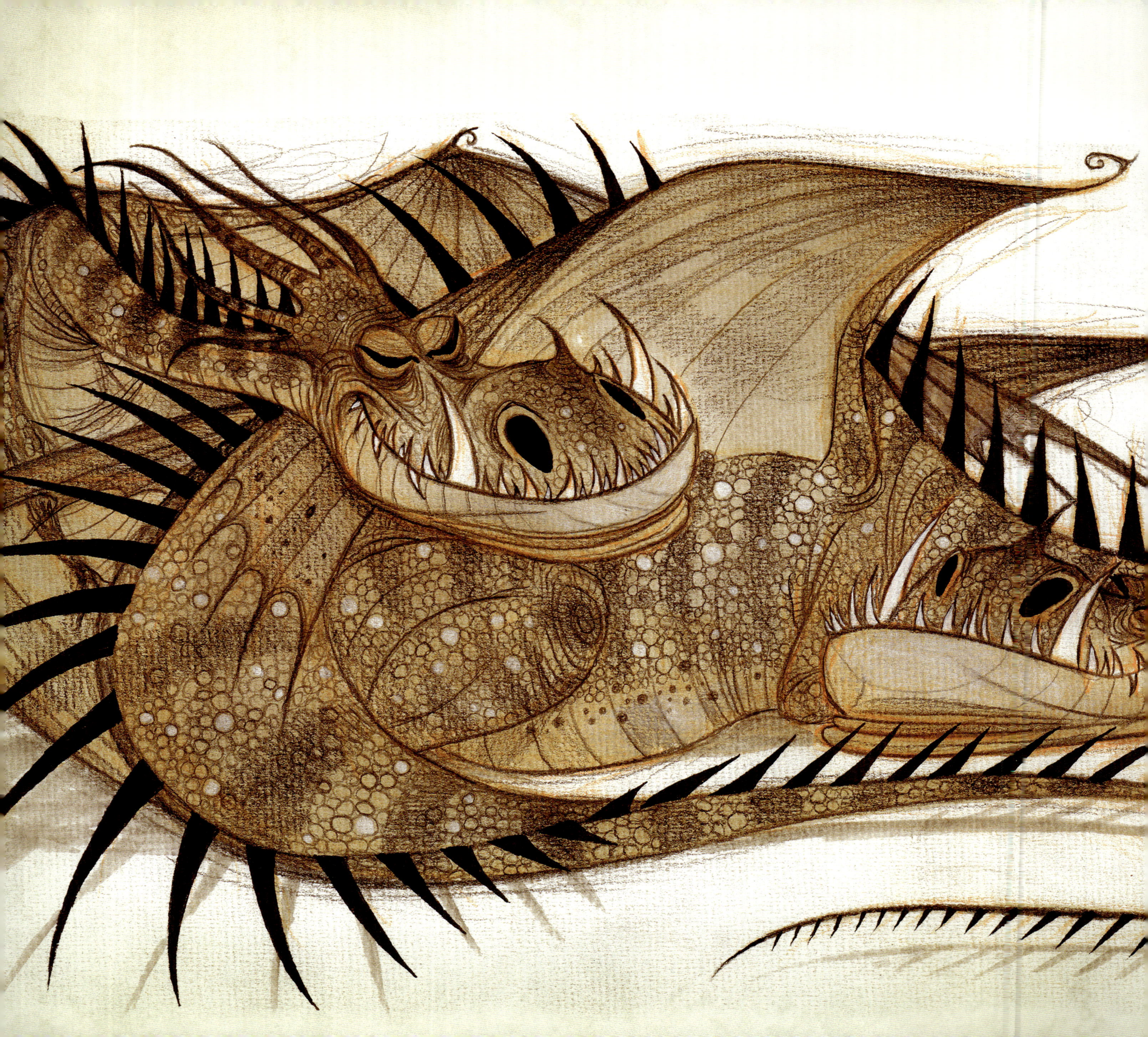

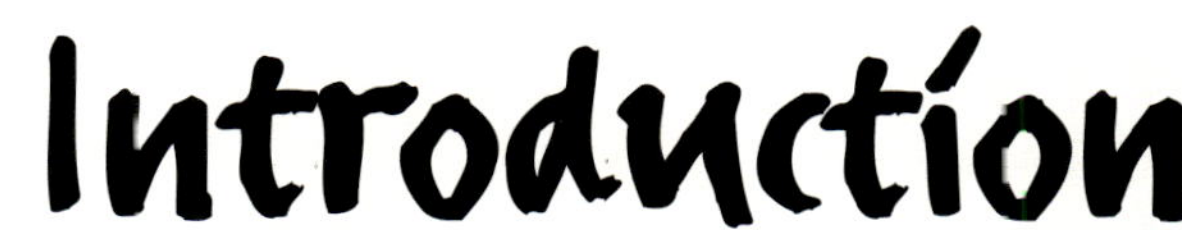

Introduction

One Film, Two Worlds

In traditional folklore, Vikings and Dragons have lived in two distinct and diametrically opposed worlds. But what if it didn't have to be that way? That's the question asked by Hiccup, the main character in the DreamWorks Animation feature film *How to Train Your Dragon*, and it's the central story that the writing and directing duo of Chris Sanders and Dean DeBlois has explored in a movie whose visual magnificence is matched only by its powerful combination of heart and humor.

Launched from the original book by Cressida Cowell, *How to Train Your Dragon* has become a feature-length action film, full of fantastical creatures, spectacular special effects, character-based humor, and heartfelt drama. While many of the landmark locations and names have translated from the pages to the screen, "it was our goal to take the original concept of the story and bring it to the level of some of our favorite fantasy adventure films, with real world stakes, exciting action sequences, and more mature character interactions and themes," explains DeBlois.

The film is almost a prequel to the book, since Dragons and Vikings do not coexist but merely terrorize and antagonize each other in this story—that is, until Hiccup and a legendary dragon encounter one another and introduce a more peaceful existence for the Viking/Dragon relationship.

The Vikings live on the island of Berk where Hiccup is the son of Stoick

(left) **Hiccup** — Nico Marlet — pencil & marker.

the Vast, the imposing chief of the tribe. Being slight and smart compared to his generally brawny and brainless peers, Hiccup has not matured into the true Viking he wants to be—and the powerful, brutish Viking that his father had in mind. The two associate in a mutually frustrating, non-communicative manner, and when Hiccup secretly befriends a dragon he names Toothless, this alliance with the mortal enemy of the Vikings further widens the gap between father and son.

As the story progresses, Hiccup's friendship with the injured dragon enables him to better understand these fearsome creatures and the motivation to change the way Vikings perceive them. This proximity also sparks a very unViking-like compassion for the creature and inspires Hiccup to construct a prosthetic tail system that reestablishes the dragon's ability to fly as Hiccup steers the attached support system. It was this concept that truly energized the story development: "The symbiotic relationship between the dragon that couldn't fly without the boy, and the boy who couldn't be himself without the dragon; they both completed one another," recalls Sanders.

The look of *How to Train Your Dragon* is that of a stylized realism in both character and environment design. "We've applied realistic textures in a shape language that is pushed to the point of caricature but is still believable," notes Production Designer Kathy Altieri. The exaggerated use of scale is especially relevant to this story, considering that the modern-day perception of the Viking people is that they were "larger than life": holding true to that, Stoick stands seven feet two inches tall, while some of the dragon species reach more than 5,000 pounds in weight. "For locations, we had to keep in mind that the real element of fantasy in the story is the dragons, so we established a believable, naturalistic environment to set them off," adds Art

The image of the partially reconstructed dragon struck both of us right away, reminiscent of our favorite creations of Hayao Miyazaki, where early mechanics are coupled with something organic.

—Dean DeBlois, Director

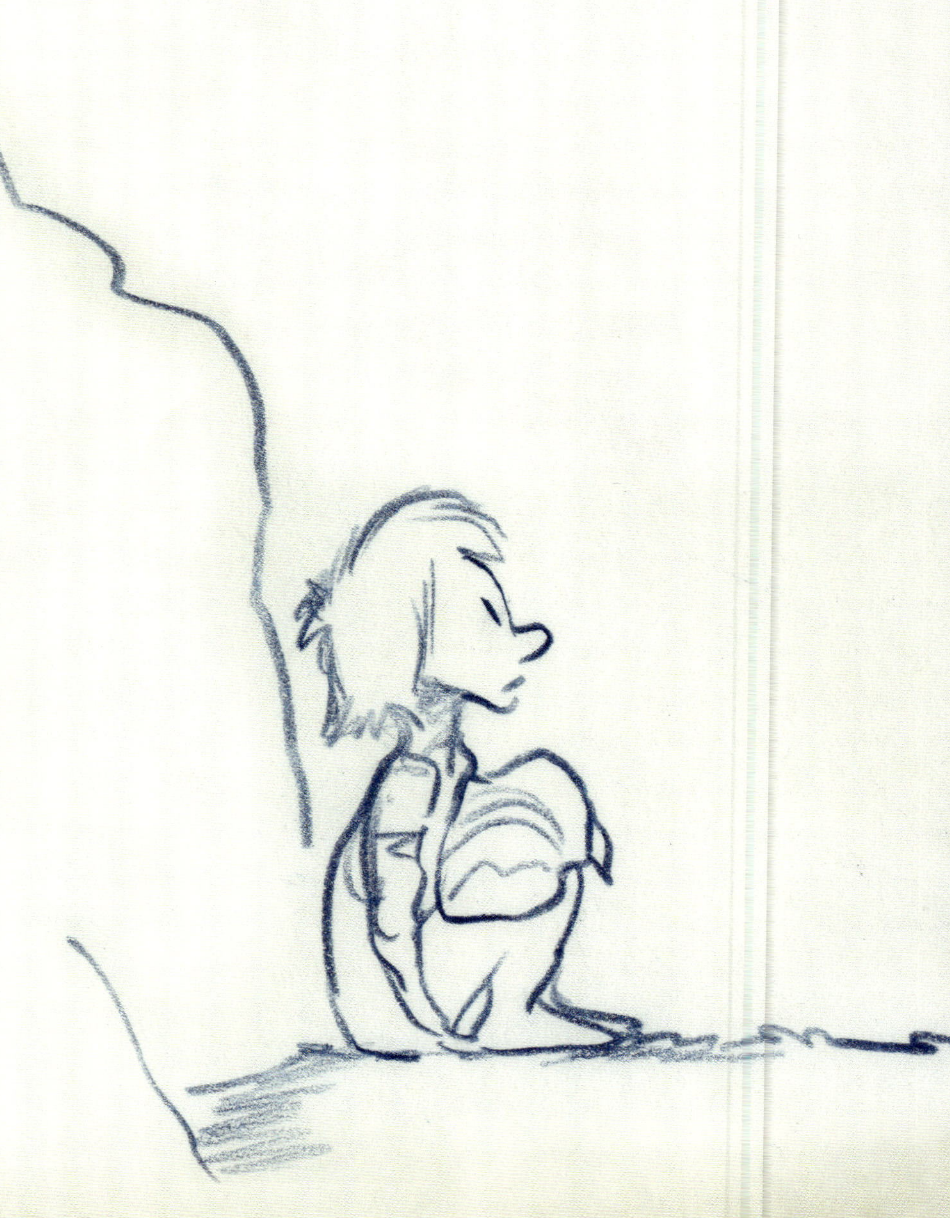

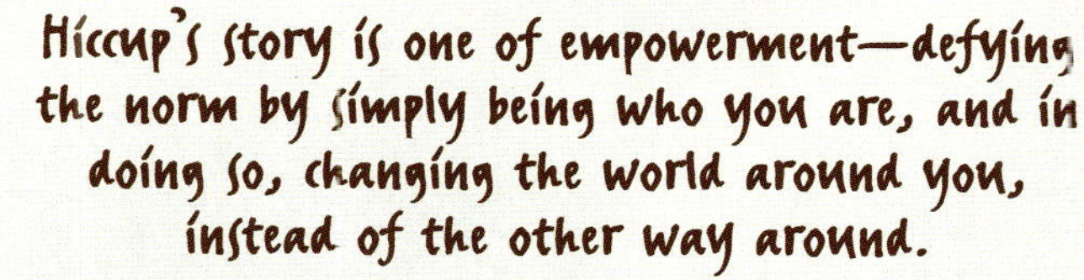

Director Pierre-Olivier Vincent. While developing lands that range from lush greenery to rocky terrain, the production boldly amped up the scale of various details, constructing sixty-foot-tall doors on Meade Hall, the gathering place in the village, and a mountain peak that would dwarf Mt. Everest.

Another key element that adds to the sense of drama and believability in *How to Train Your Dragon* is the theatrical style of lighting. Cinematographer Roger Deakins was brought in as a Visual Consultant, and his influence makes this film stand out. "The atmosphere and mood of the frame are as important if not *more* important than specific details within the frame," says Deakins, so this film does not hesitate to let its characters' faces fall in shadow or background details fade out into total blackness in order to play to the tension of a scene. The color palette complements Deakins' sensibility by incorporating less saturation and higher contrast. This choice in art direction further supports the tone and sophistication of the story.

The collection of art within this book pays tribute to the flames of creativity fanned by the filmmakers of *How to Train Your Dragon*, and it also provides an in-depth look at the process involved with bringing both the Dragon world and the Viking world to life with present-day cinematic energy.

(left) **Forbidden Friendship** — Chris Sanders — pencil.

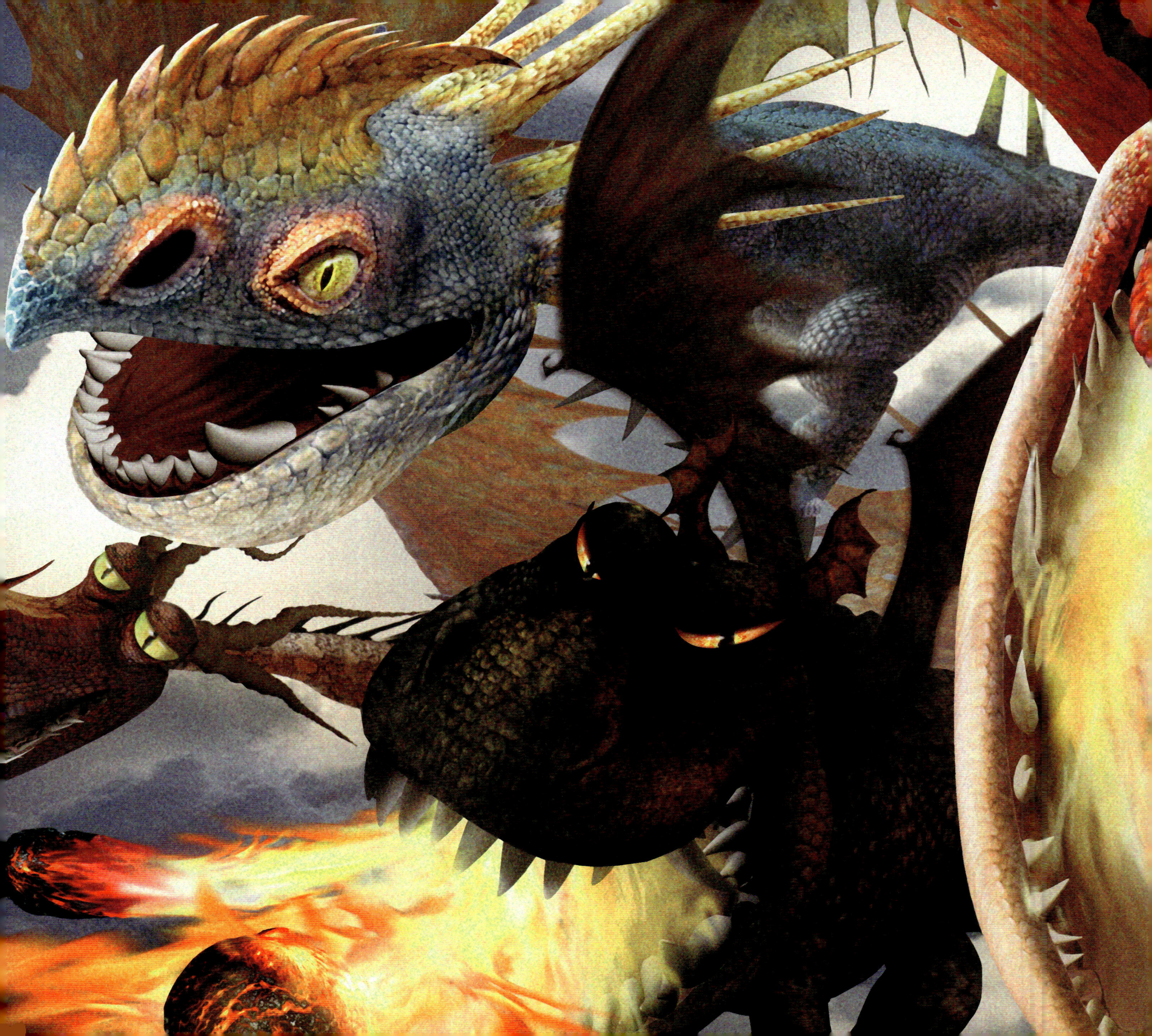

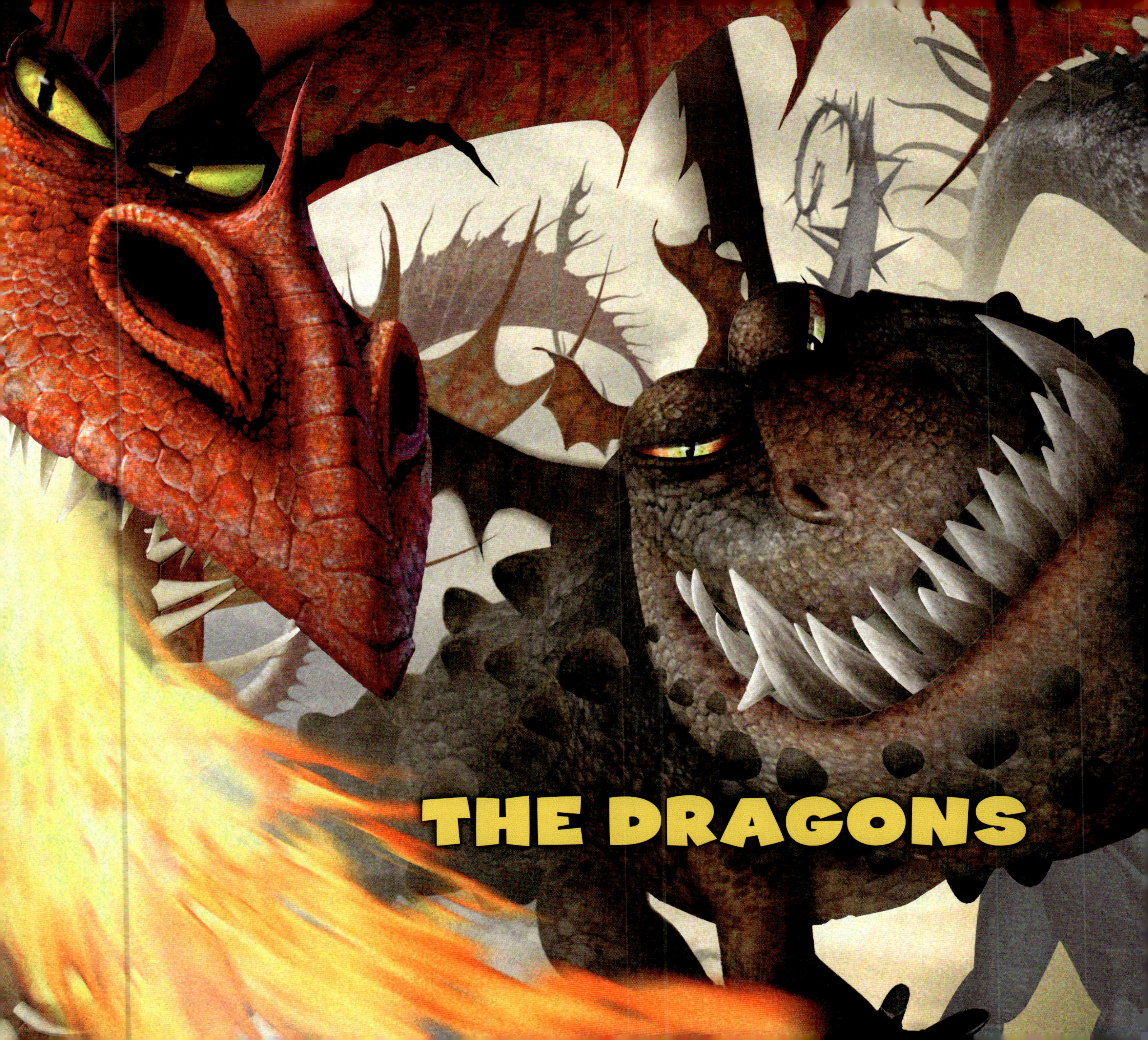

THE DRAGONS

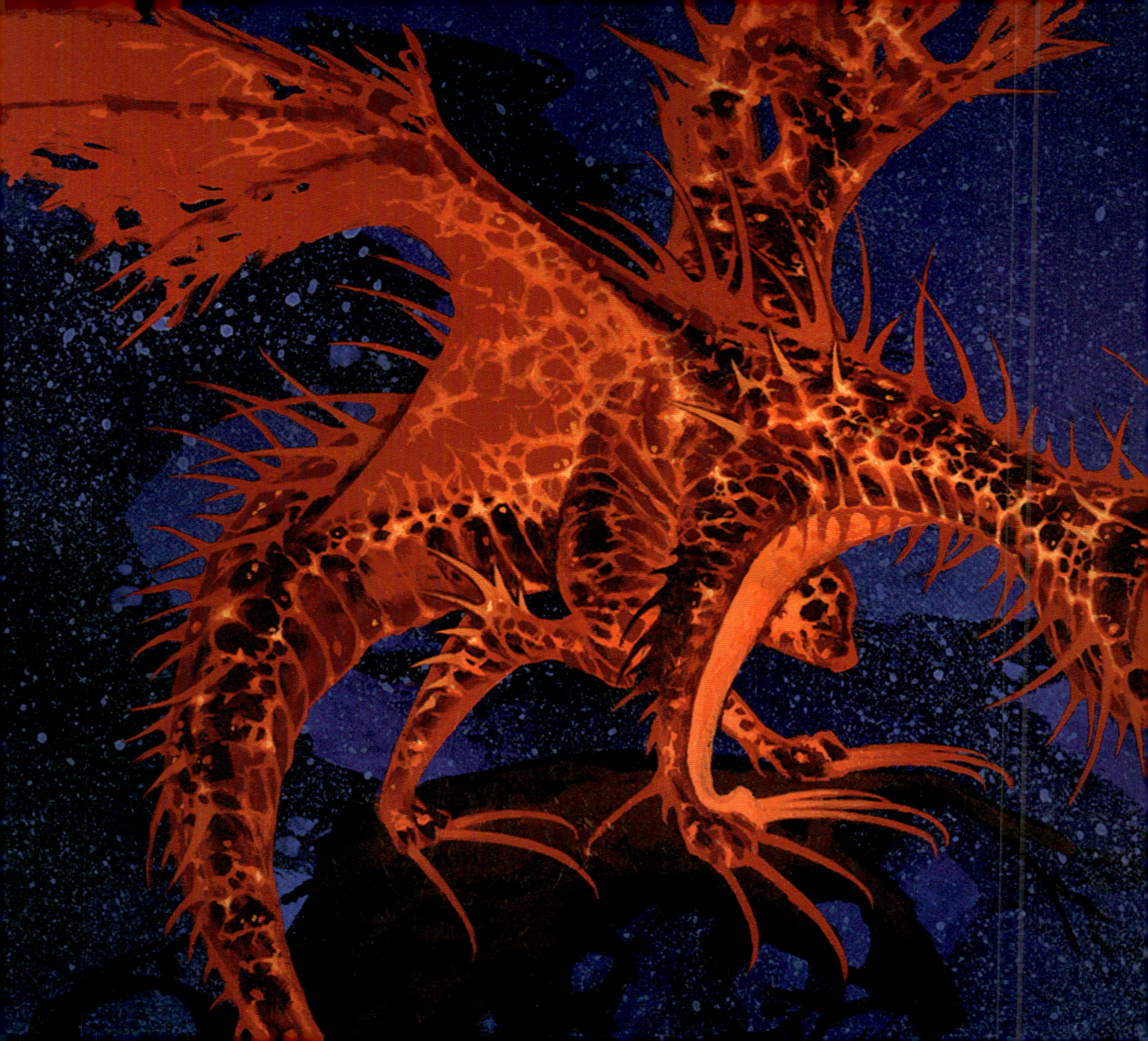

The Fire-Breathing Line-Up of Characters

Everyone has seen them before . . . probably not in real life, but dragons have been ingrained into the collective imagination through various cinematic and literary properties. So how does a film crew go about telling a story that offers a fresh take on dragons? Taking a cue from Cressida Cowell's book, "the first tool in our arsenal was that we had a variety of species with distinct personalities to offer," explains Director Chris Sanders. The production team continued to develop unique traits for each of its six species, including behavioral characteristics and firepowers that vary greatly among the different dragon types.

(previous spread) **Dragon Charge** — Pierre-Olivier Vincent — digital paint.
(left) **Dragon Red** — Jean Francois-Rey — acrylic.

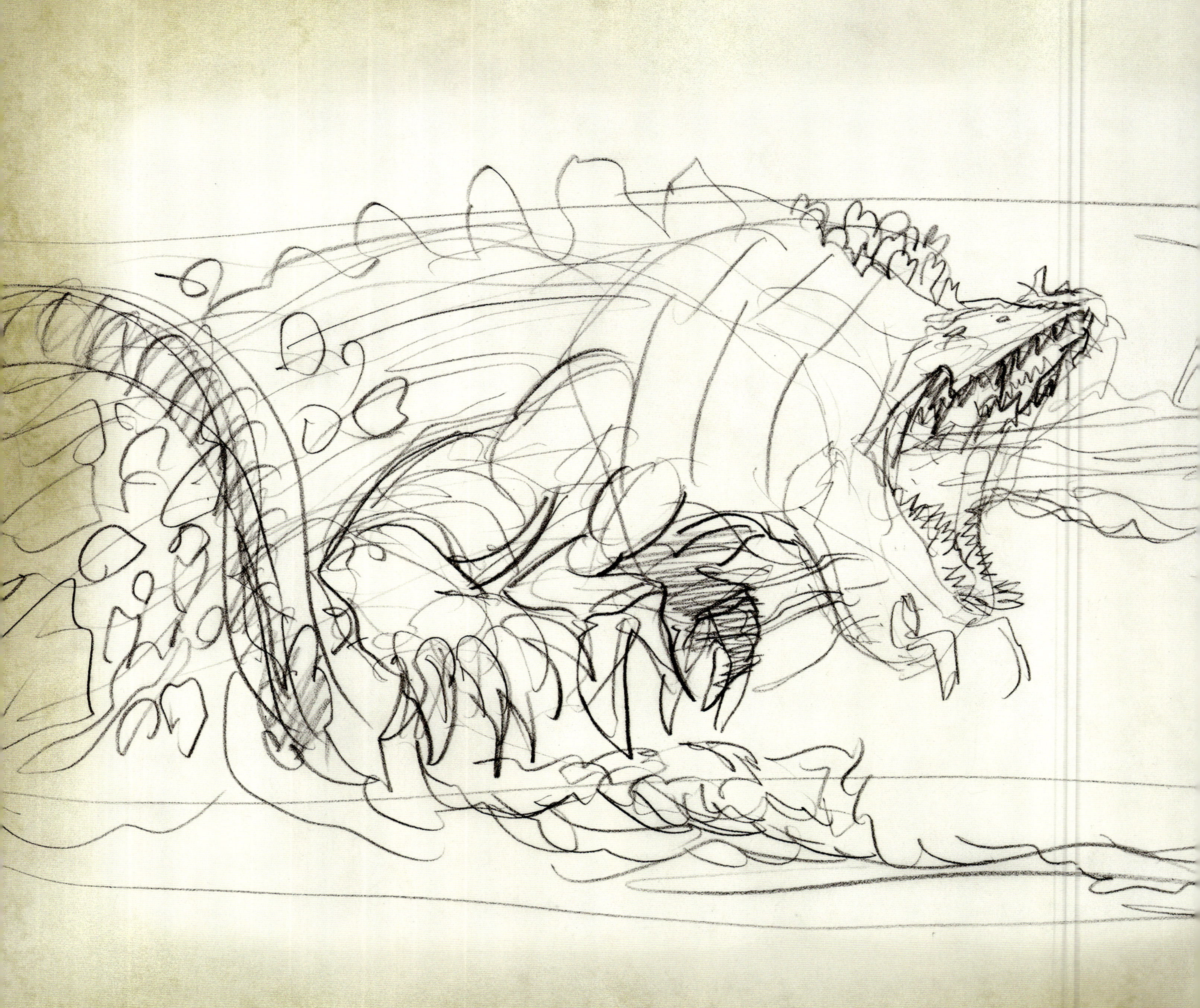

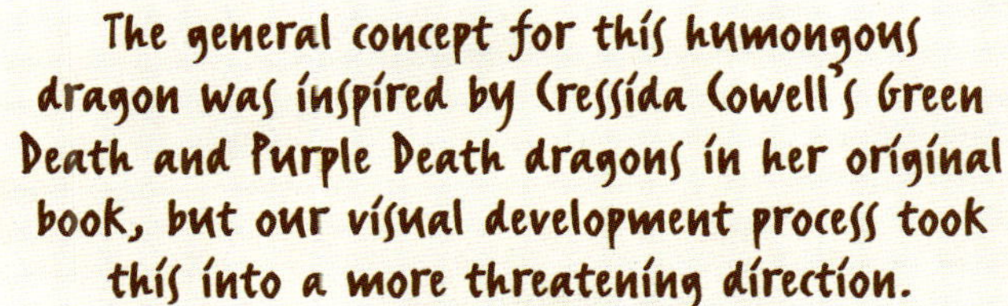

The Red Death

As the Vikings discover once they land upon Dragon Island, the entire society of dragons functions to serve a larger and more hideous creature than they ever could have imagined—the Red Death. This massive dragon is, in fact, a common enemy to both the Vikings and the Dragons. It is quickly apparent that all of the other dragon species are engaged as "workers in service, forced to bring food to their leader in order to sustain their own existence on the island," explains Director Dean DeBlois. "By using the beehive concept of workers serving one master as the paradigm for the dragon's world, we knew our dragons wouldn't need to portray anthropomorphic behavior in order to make their society understandable. Plus, this relationship is a way to build some sympathy toward the dragons, seeing that they are in service to something, and also to hint that if that thing was no longer, then they'd be free."

In its earliest development, this dragon was portrayed as a beast of the sea, for which Character Designer Nicolas Marlet drafted a wondrous creature replete with a jellyfishlike bioluminescence; a coral-shaped mane with stylized tendrils that float like sea plants; and detailed, barnacle-inspired scale designs. "But this was too elegant of a dragon, which made it too hard to want to see it killed," recalls Production Designer Kathy Altieri. The Red Death dwarfs all of the other dragons, measuring a length of 400 feet with a wingspan of 550 feet, sporting 94 teeth and almost 900 spikes. Plus, thanks to the wonders of CG animation, "we are able to scale the Red Death as needed to make it work in some scenes where it might just be too big," notes Visual Effects Supervisor Craig Ring.

(left) **Red Death 016** — Ricardo Delgado — character design — pencil.

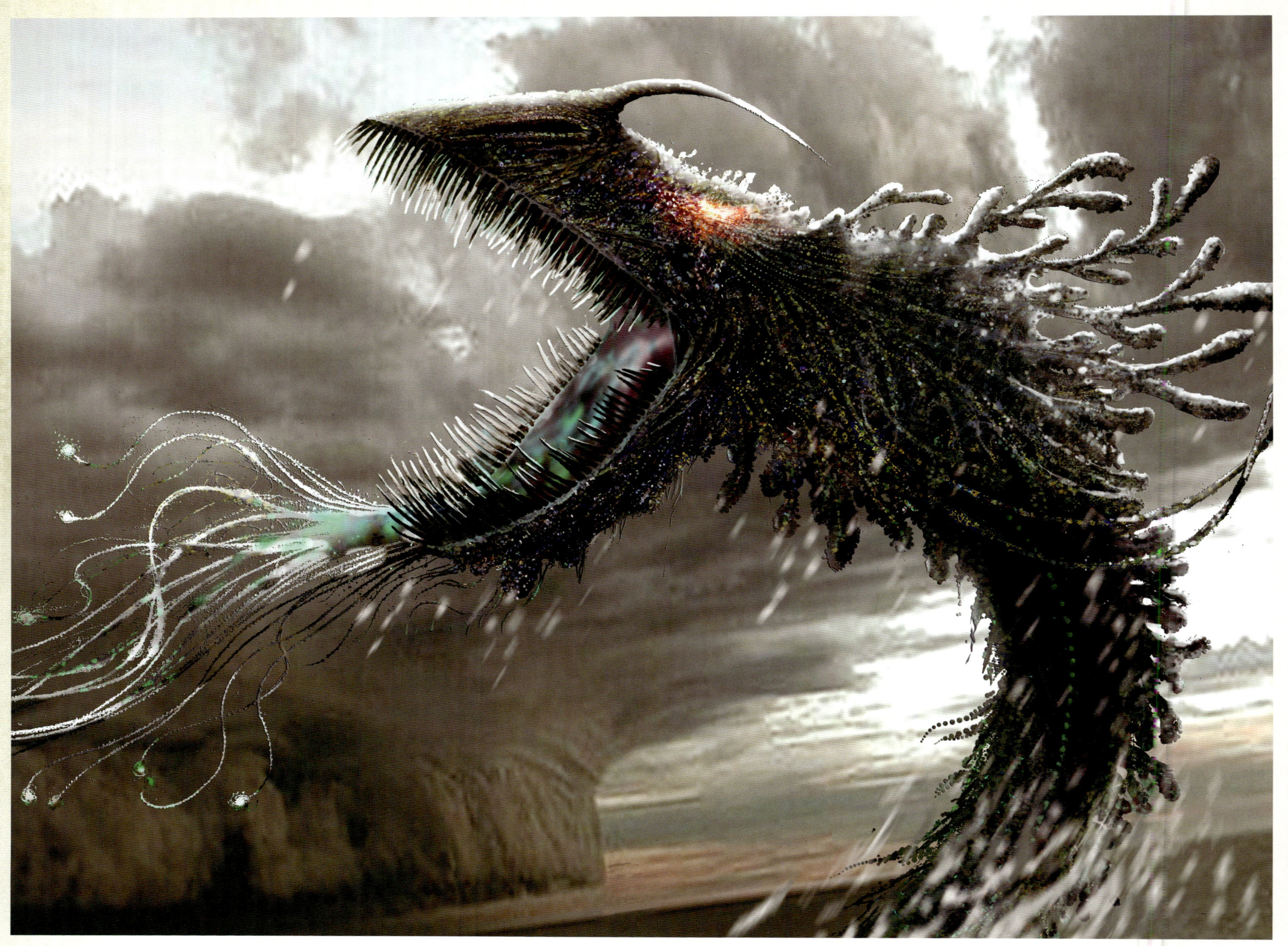

(above) **Red Death Head** — Nico Marlet — character design — Zhaoping Wei — digital paint. *(right)* **Red Death** — Nico Marlet — pencil & marker.

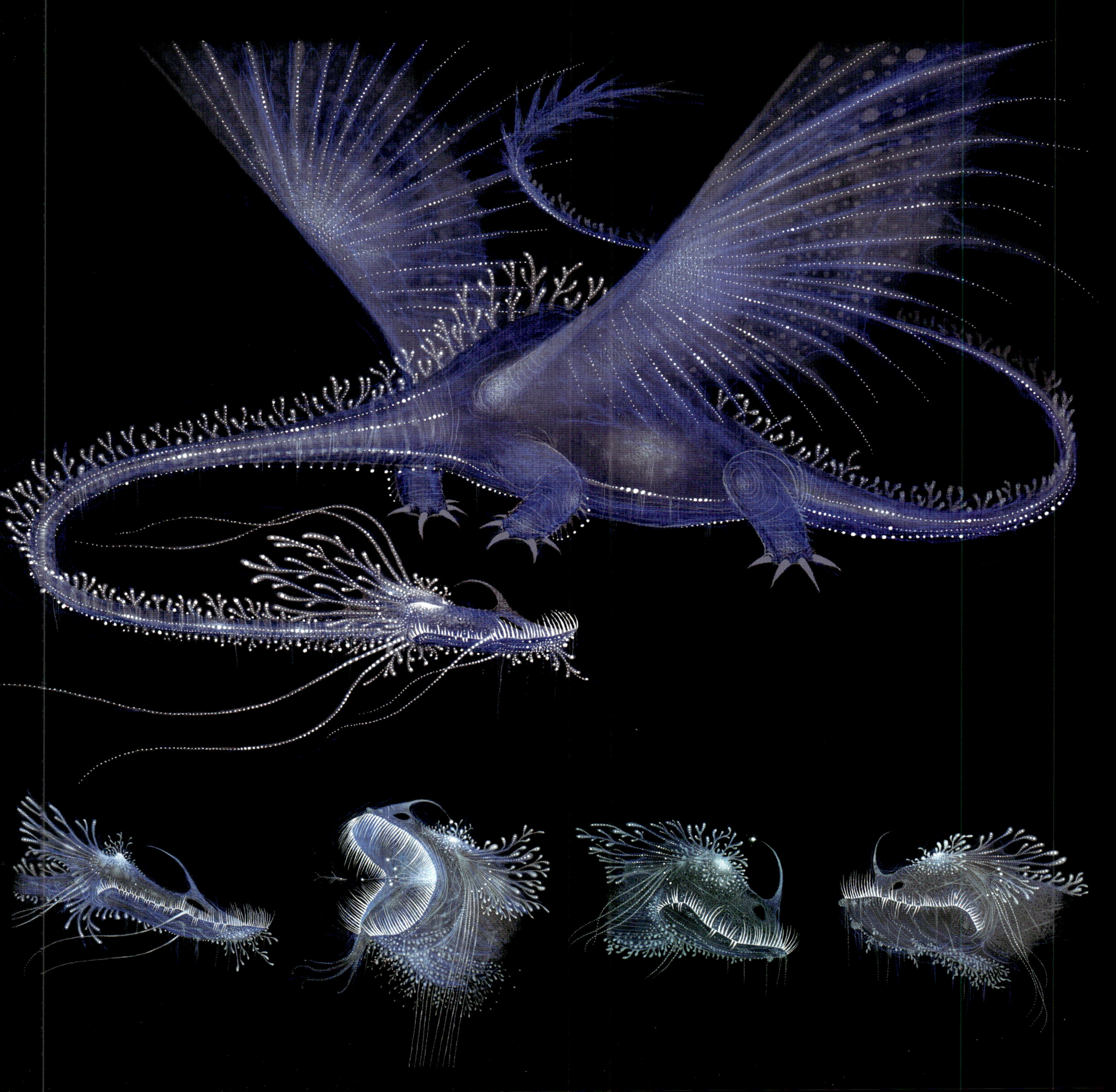

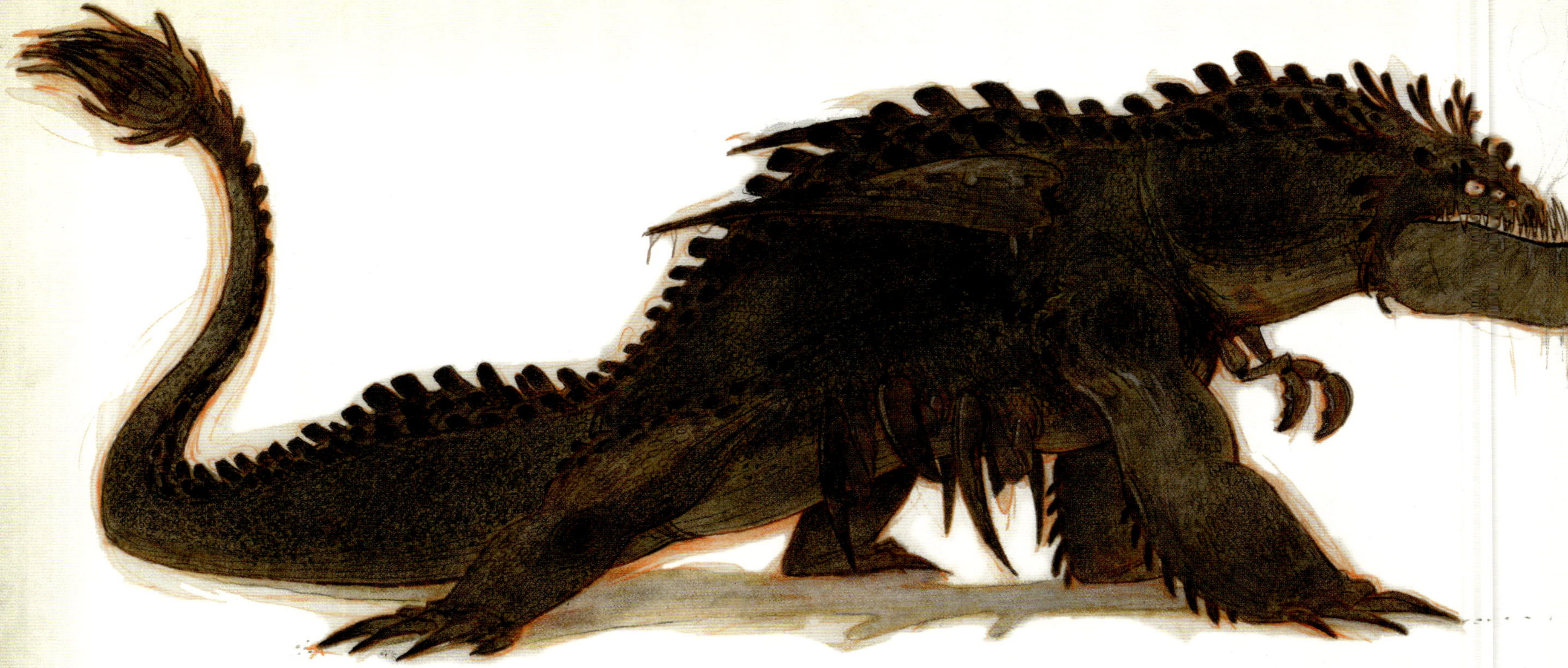

(above) **Red Death Final** — Simon Otto — pencil & marker.

(below left) **Red Death** — Ricardo Delgado — pencil.

(below) **Red Death Heads** — Ricardo Delgado — pencil.

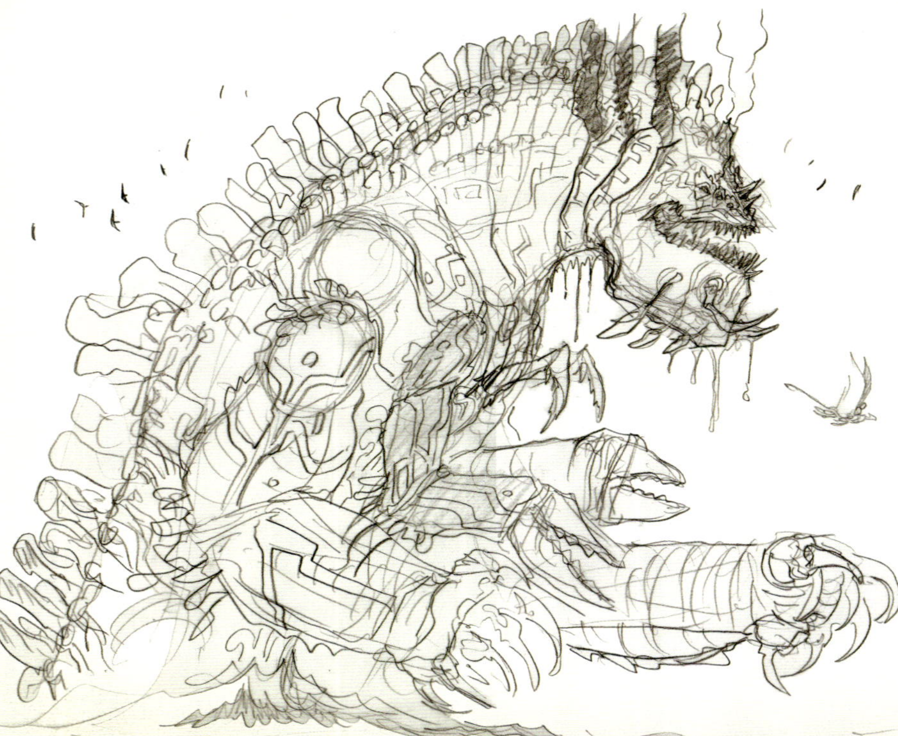

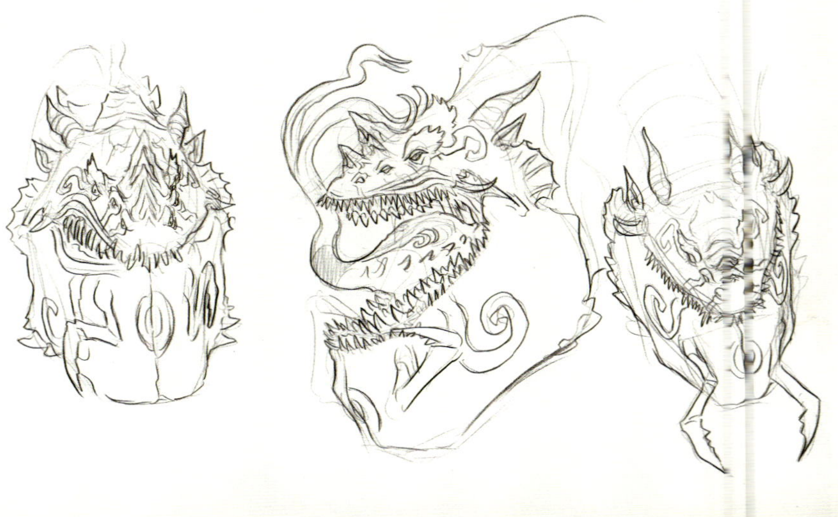

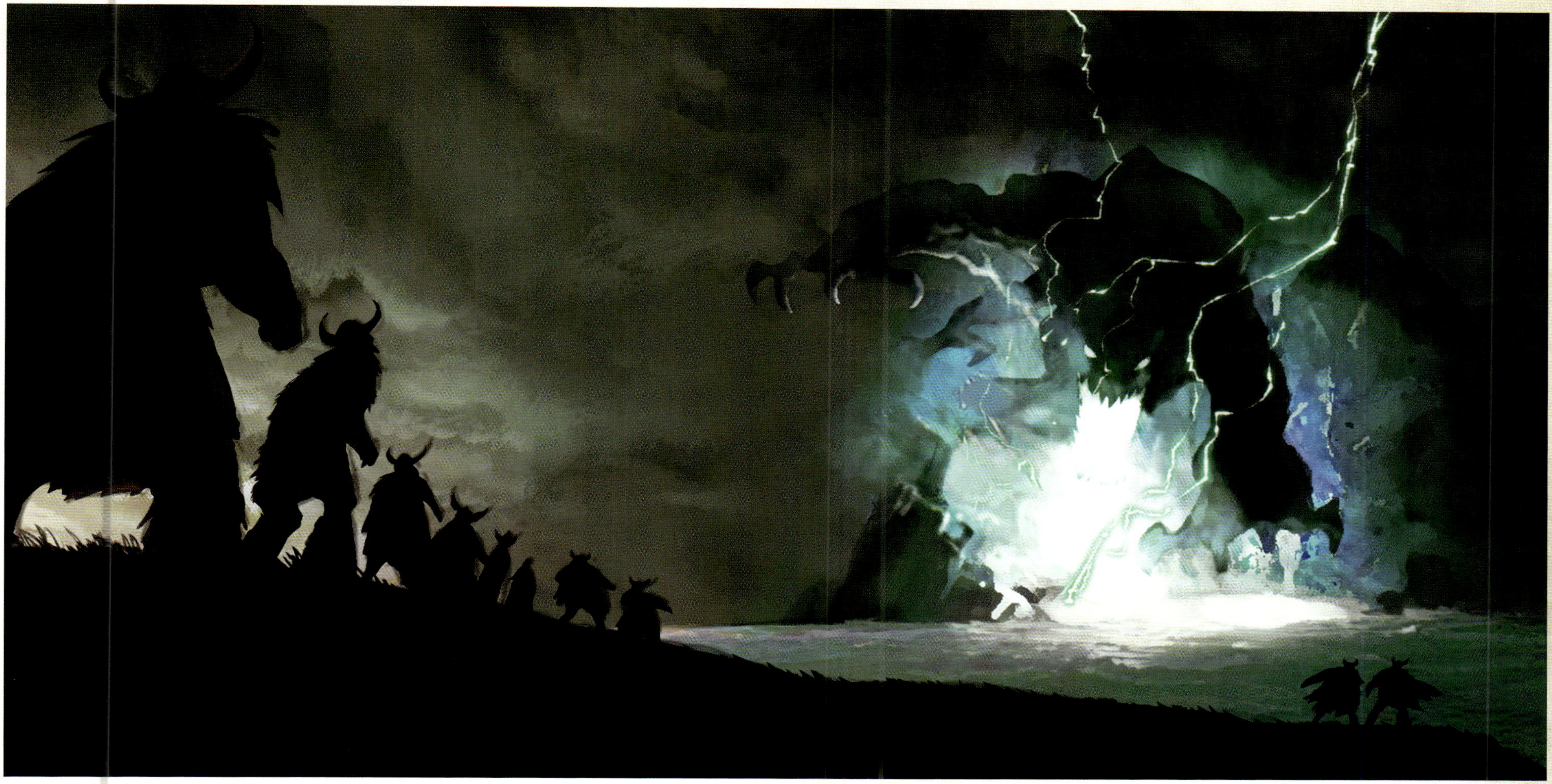

The directors kept telling us to make it more gross, giving notes like "add blisters, sores, cataracts in its eyes, broken teeth, crumbling spikes, and a more decayed look to its skin."

—Sabrina Riegel, Head of Surfacing

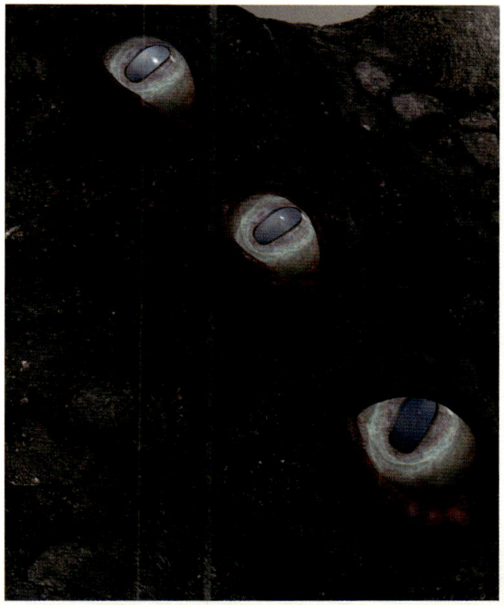

(above) **Red Death Monster Rise** — Jeff Snow — story sketch — Pierre-Olivier Vincent — digital paint.

(right) **Red Death Eyes Three** and **Teeth** — Jeremy Engelman — surfacing

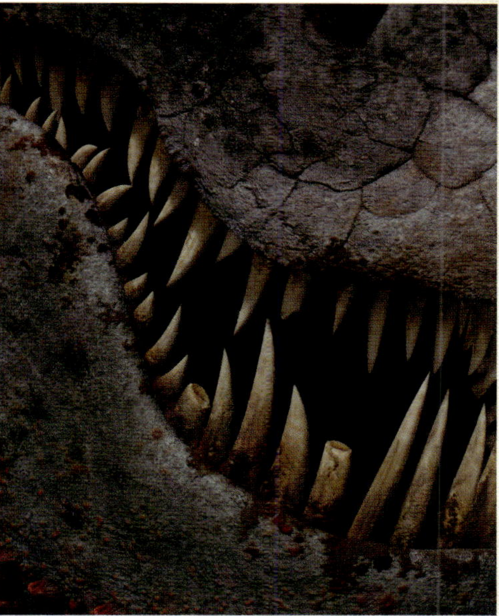

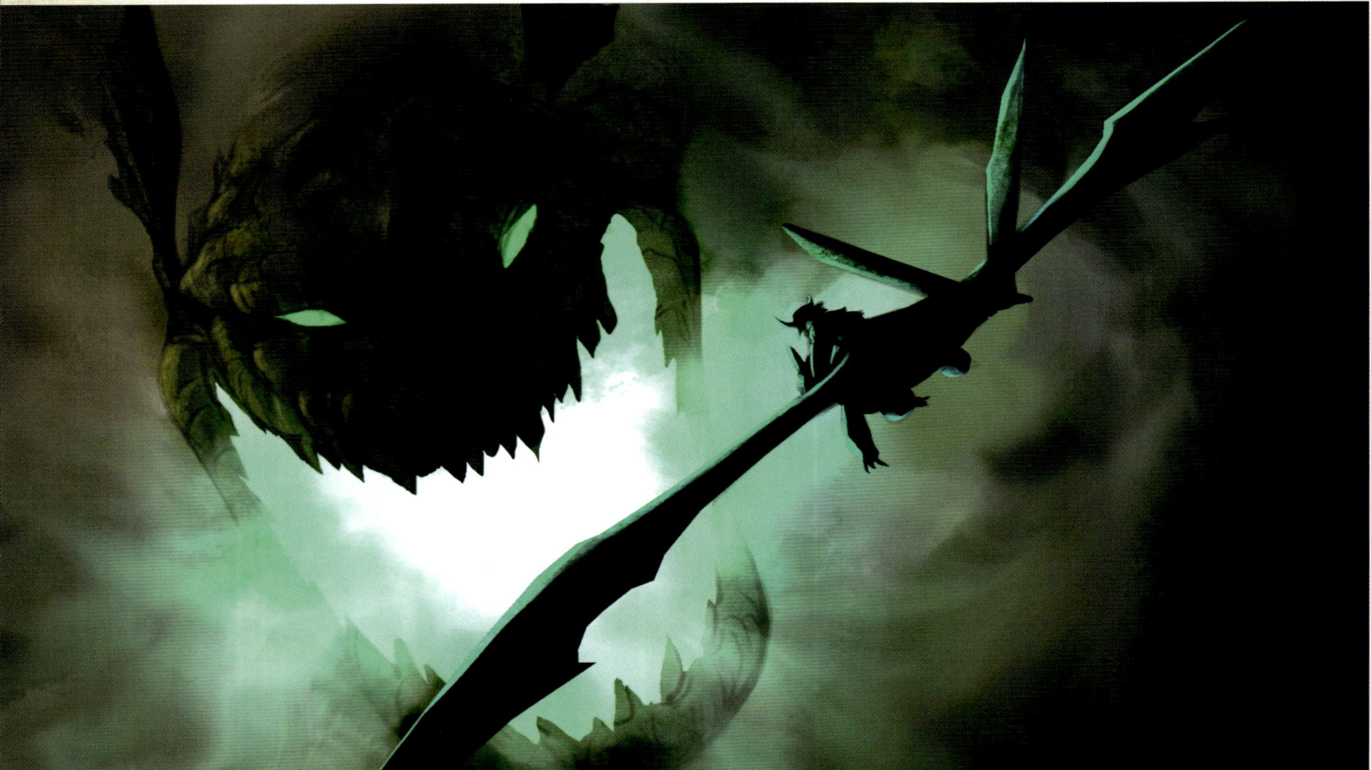

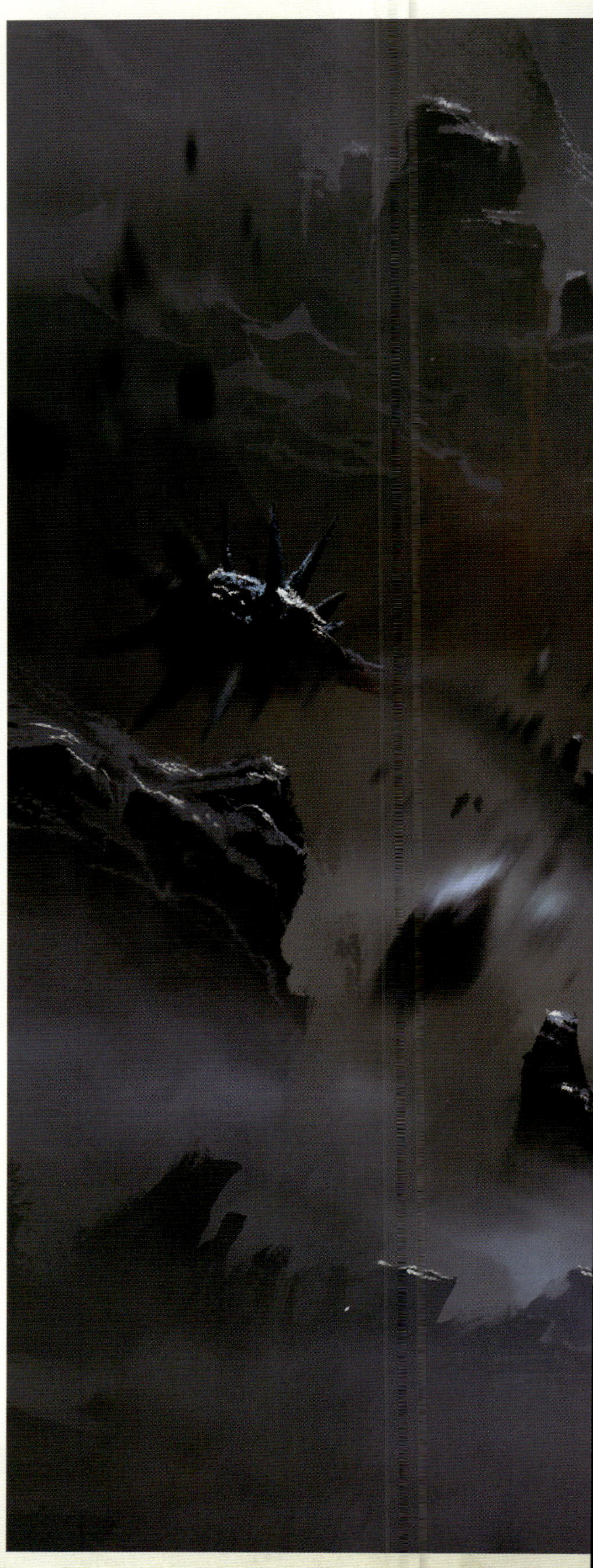

THE RED DEATH emits fire in a jet of flame that can project half a mile, and it's accompanied by dirty smoke that creates a sense of something ancient and dusty. The effects team "created fire strands that animated on a group of curves to create a huge, smoky, fiery element that looks like it is lit from the core, fading to the outside of the smoke," explains Head of Effects Matt Baer. The effects team also built several varieties of fluid simulations to use within these shots, as if 2,600 feet of shooting flame isn't impressive enough.

(above) **Red Death Battle** — Jeff Snow — story sketch — Pierre-Olivier Vincent — digital paint.

(right) **Red Death Texture** — Dominique Louis — digital paint.

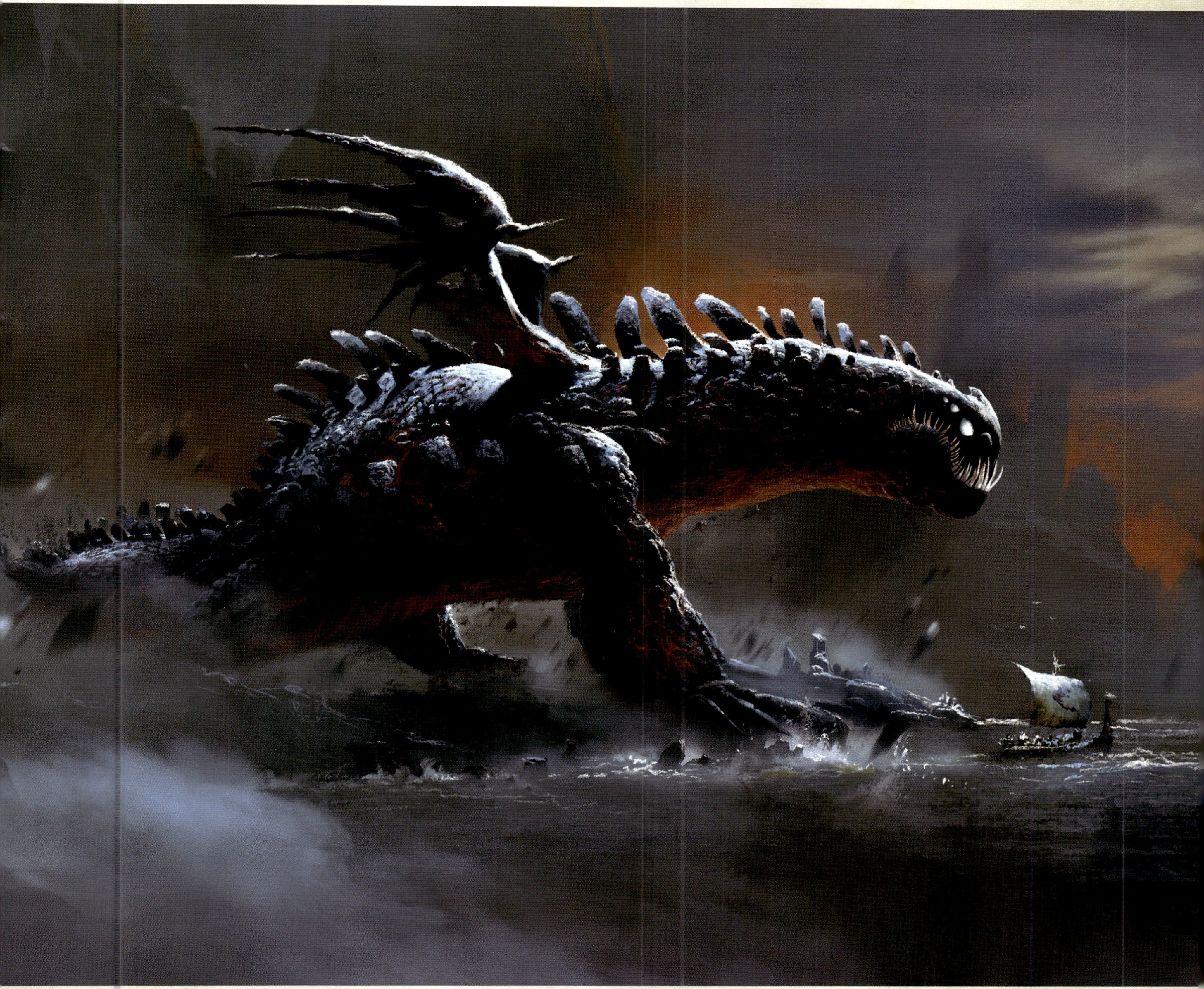

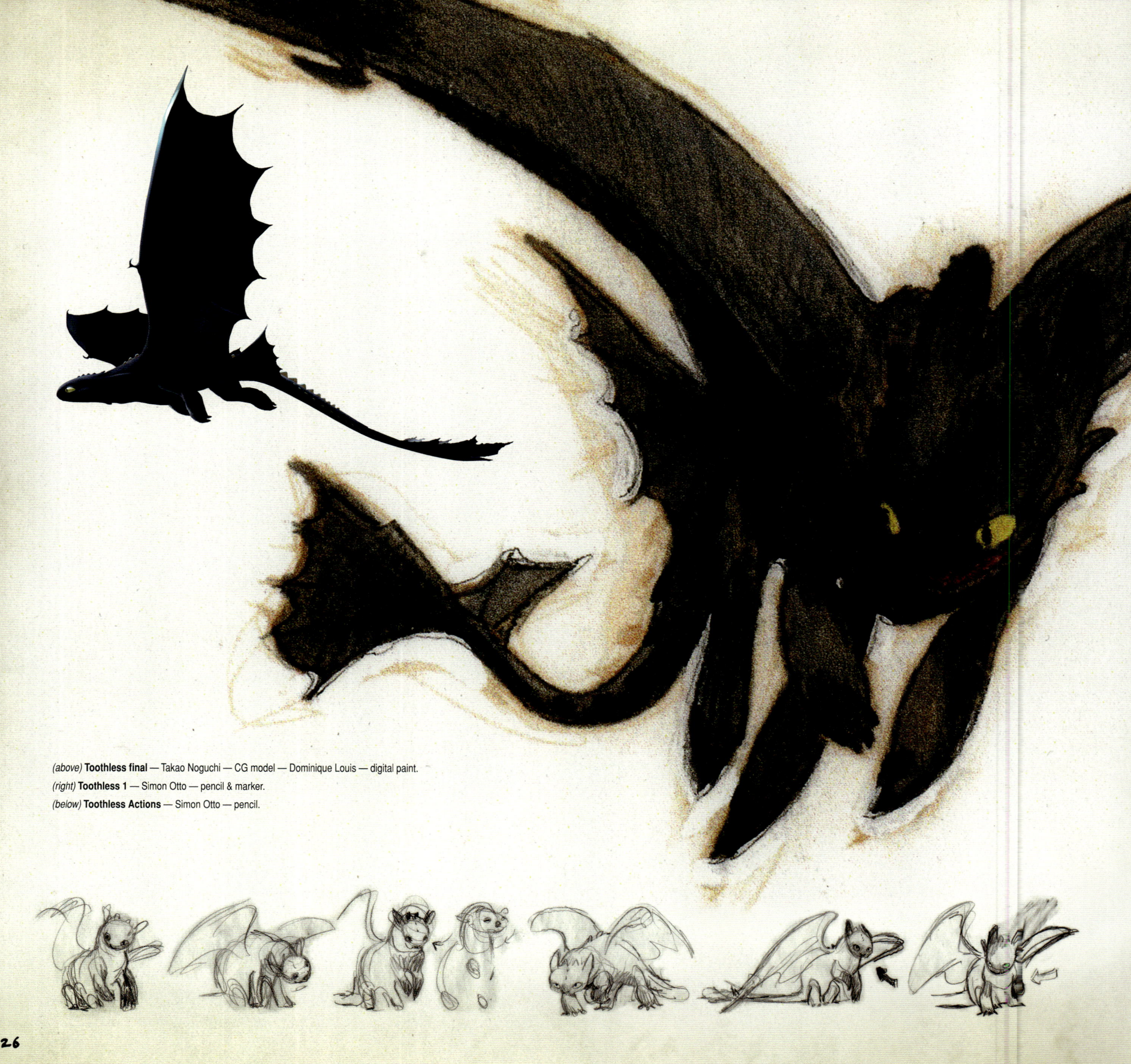

(above) **Toothless final** — Takao Noguchi — CG model — Dominique Louis — digital paint.
(right) **Toothless 1** — Simon Otto — pencil & marker.
(below) **Toothless Actions** — Simon Otto — pencil.

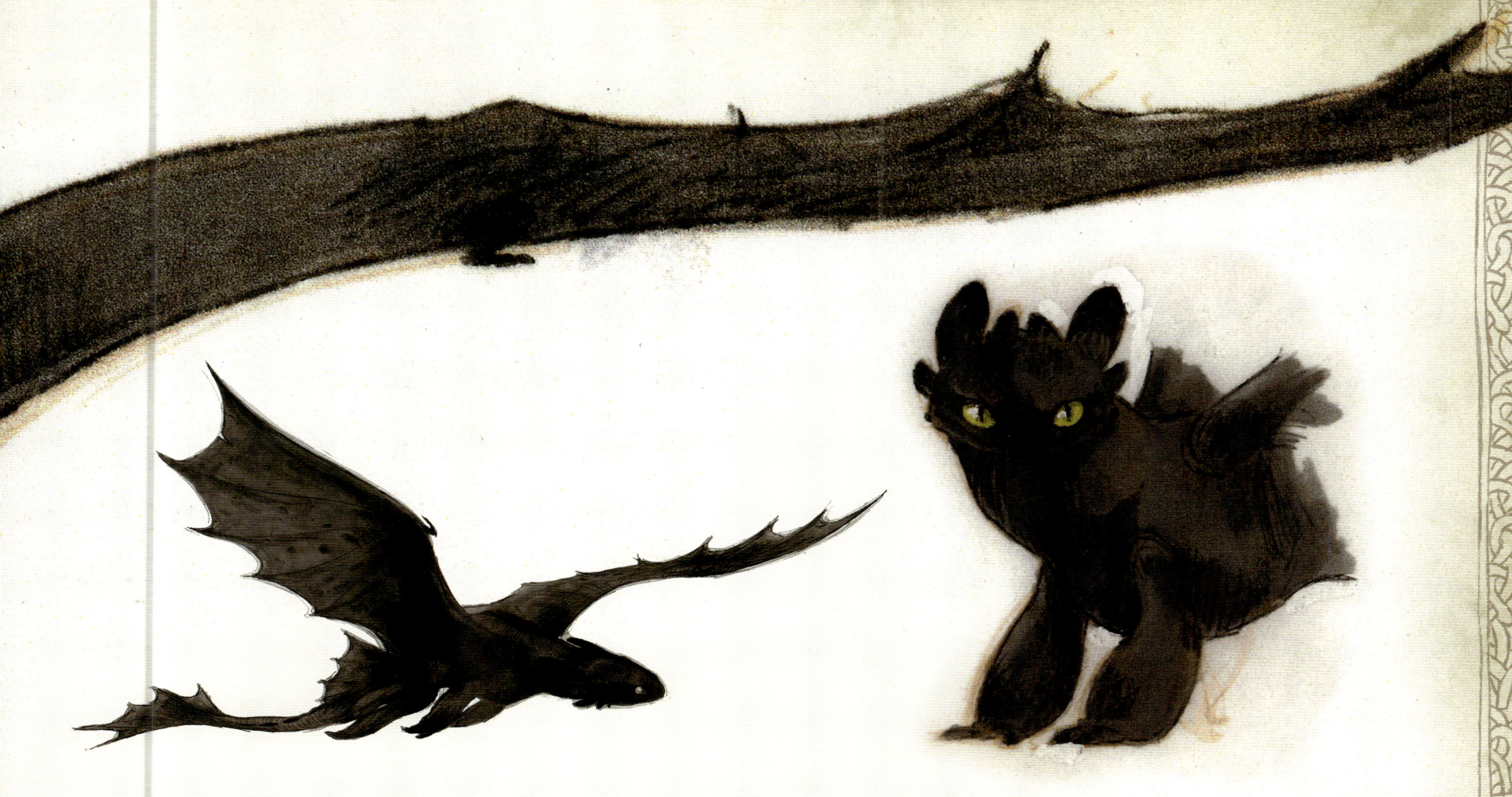

Toothless: The Night Fury

The main dragon character in the film is the Night Fury, a species regarded by the Vikings as the most dangerous due to its reclusive nature and surprising, powerful fire skills. While Toothless may be formidable by virtue of his species, he proves to be an intelligent, emotional creature that just happens to have agile artillery.

"His firepower consists of plasma bolts of explosives that are fired with great accuracy—you hear it coming and then see a blue bolt and shockwave ring. It is a percussive blow which can set things on fire and explode them in a blue-and-white flash of light," explains Visual Effects Supervisor Craig Ring. This makes Hiccup's relationship with the dragon all the more forbidden.

Toothless is designed to be a cleaner, sleeker, stealthier dragon than the others in the film. "We had previously thought of him as wolflike, but then we discovered another big cat worked even better," recalls Director Dean DeBlois. "His color was inspired by a black panther screensaver on one of our story artist's monitors. That image was striking and electrifying, with those eyes staring out from the darkest black face," explains Director Chris Sanders. This desire to give the Night Fury a pure black skin presented unique challenges for the artistic team due to the difficulty in portraying pure black color under a variety of lighting conditions. "We tested specularity and reflectivity to show detail that would read well in everything from crisp moonlight

(left and above) **Toothless** — Simon Otto — pencil & marker.

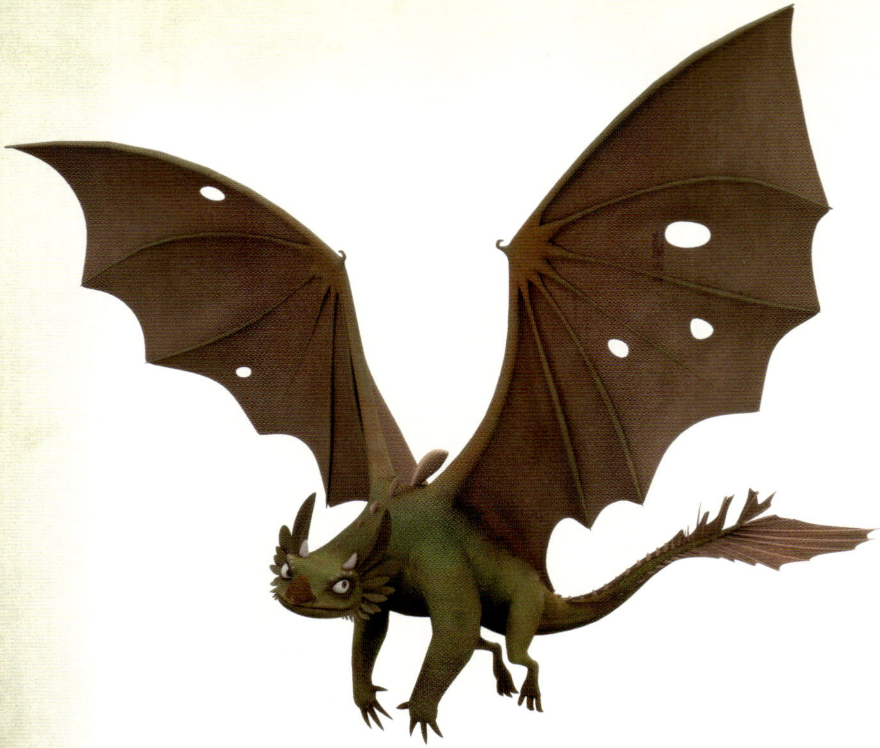

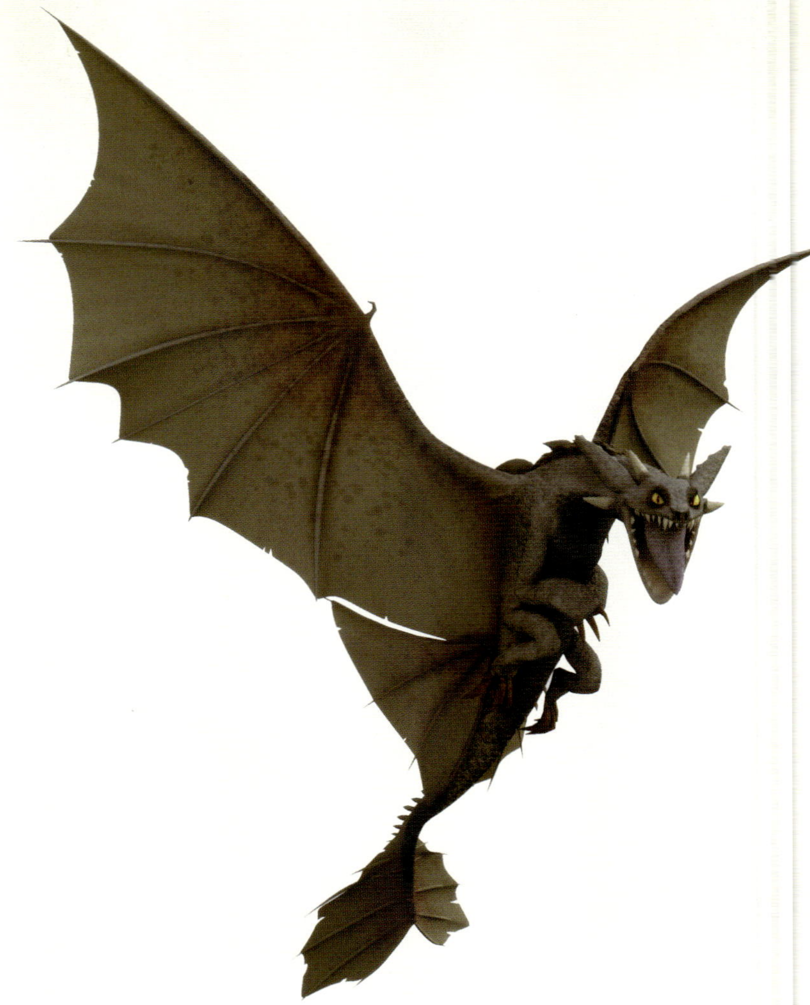

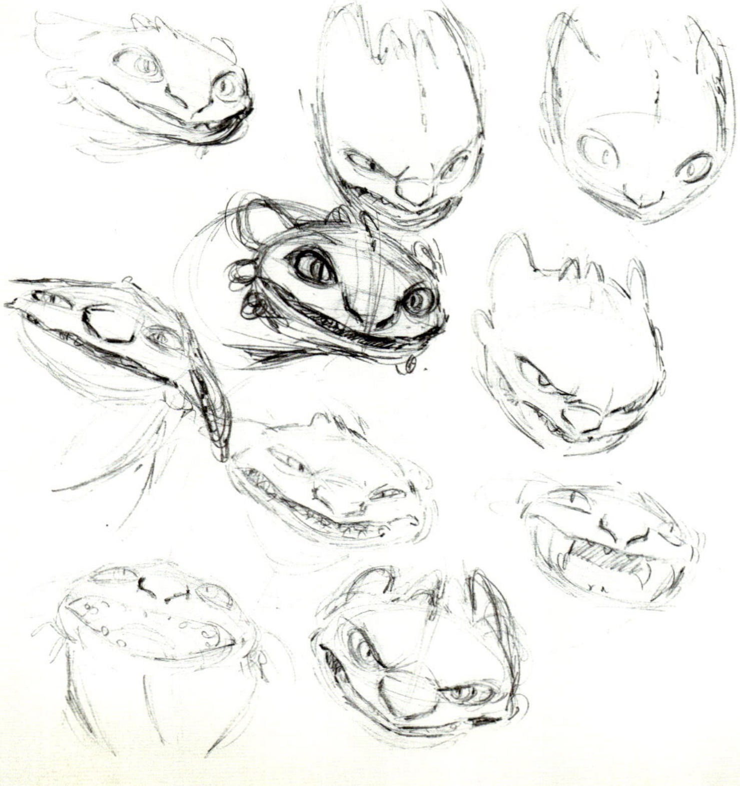

to foggy or smoky scenes. We tried applying a velvetlike texture and iridescence, and we were finally satisfied with a skin that is more like that of a shark or stingray than reptilian," recalls Head of Surfacing Sabrina Riegel.

The audience's acceptance of Toothless as a main character requires a vast shift of perception: He must go from being regarded as an unknown, dangerous threat to a magical, charming creature in order for the story to work. "We wanted to make sure his intelligence and emotional personality came through without anthropomorphizing him," says Executive Producer Kristine Belson. To facilitate his connection to the audience, Toothless exhibits behaviors that a dog, cat, or horse might use when interacting with humans, with the hopes that the viewers will "be touched by their recognition of this bond," according to Head of Character Animation Simon Otto.

(above) **Toothless** — Takao Noguchi — CG models. *(left)* **Toothless Heads** — Gabe Hordos — pencil.
(above right) **Hiccup & Toothless in Clouds** — Tron Mai — digital paint.
(below right) **Toothless in Clouds** — Zhaoping Wei — digital paint.

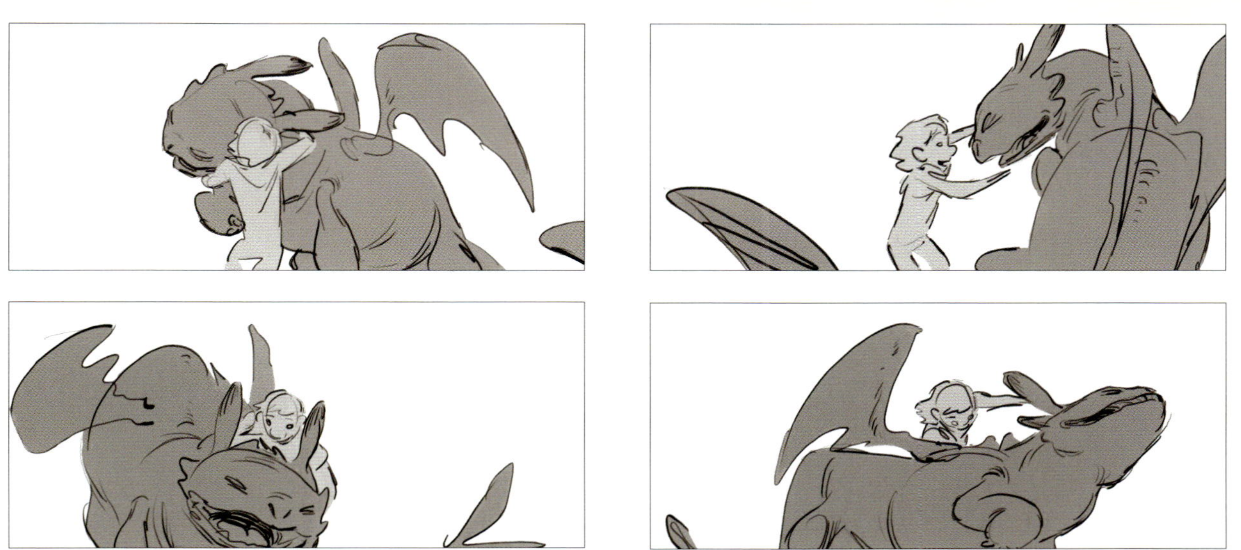

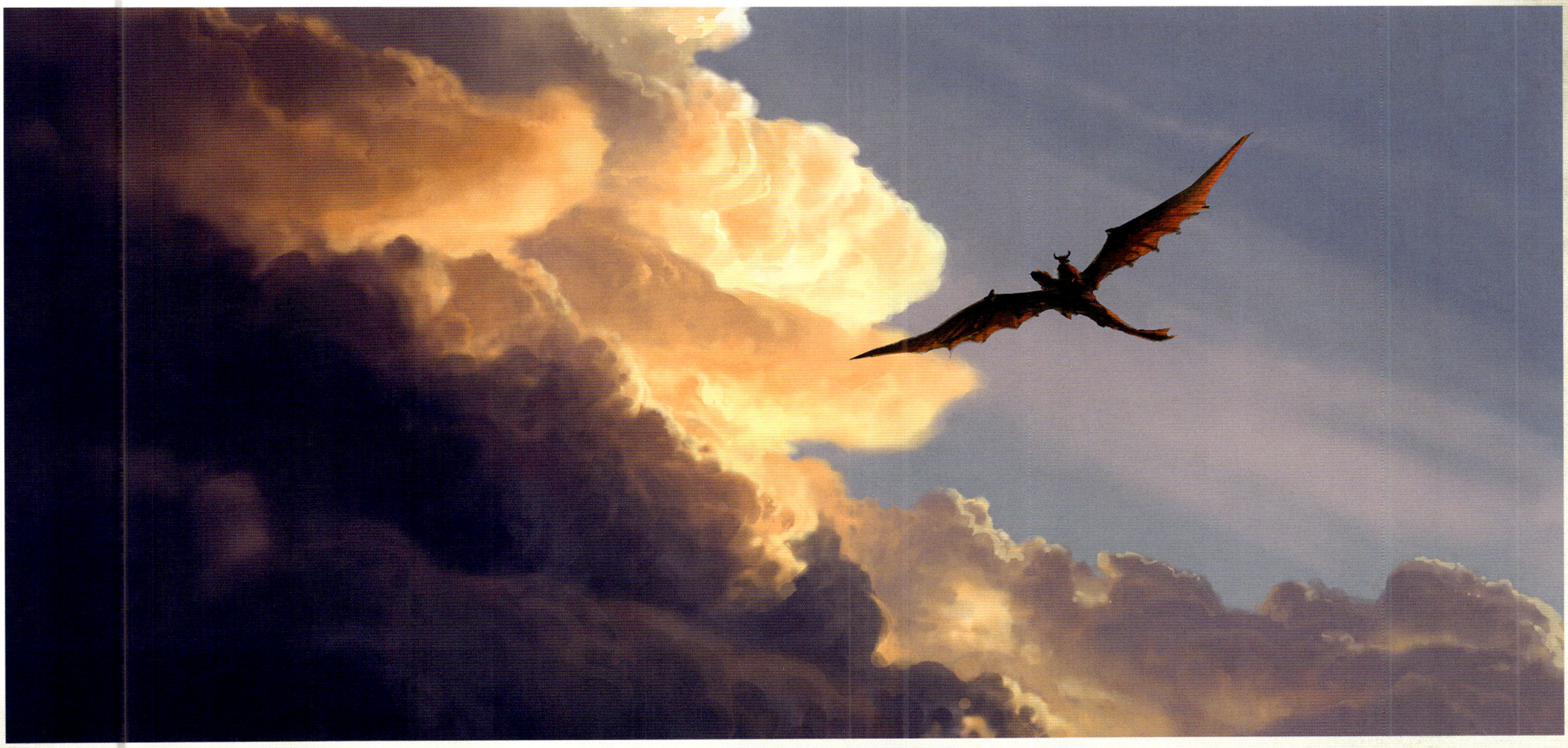

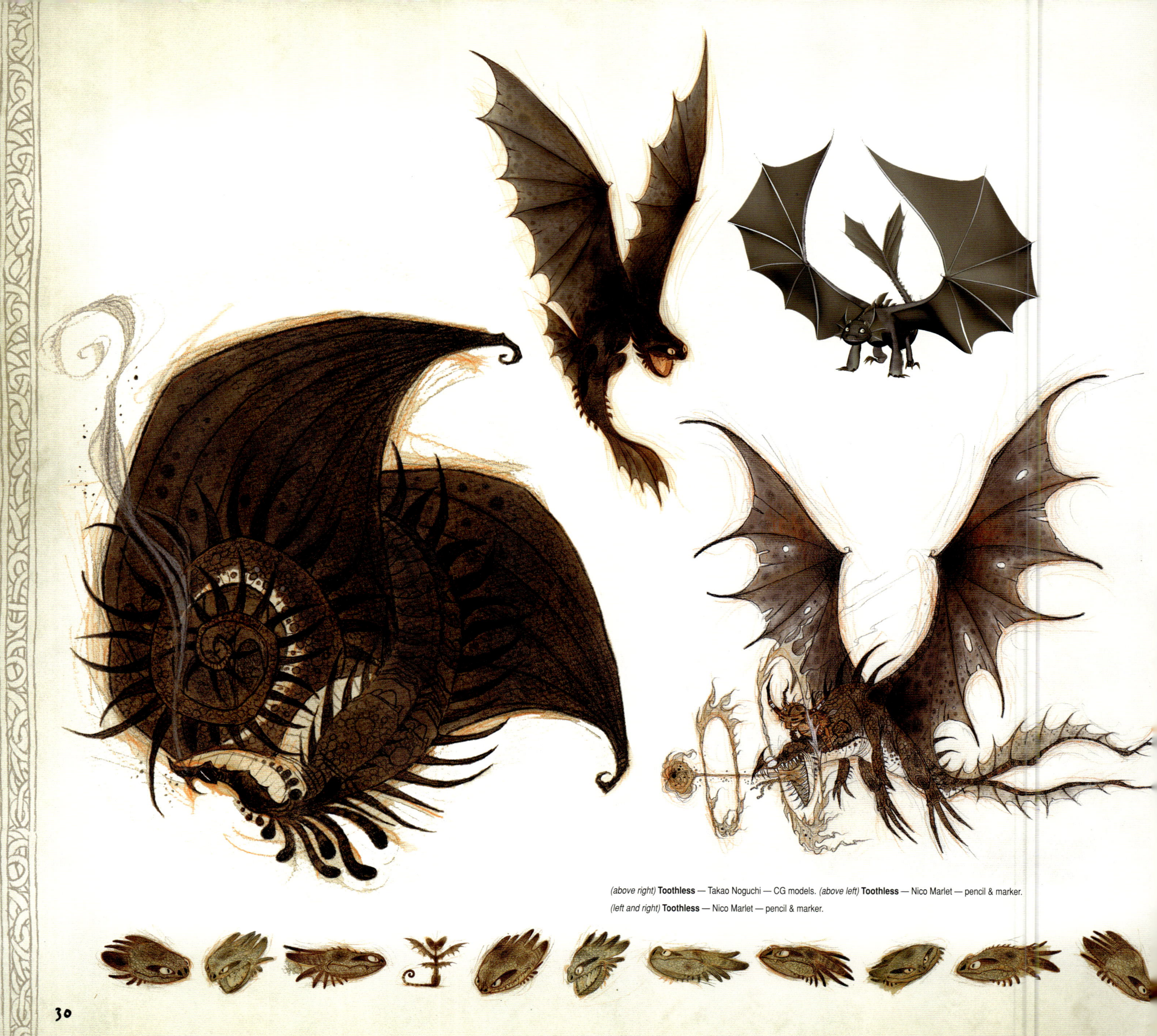

(above right) **Toothless** — Takao Noguchi — CG models. *(above left)* **Toothless** — Nico Marlet — pencil & marker.
(left and right) **Toothless** — Nico Marlet — pencil & marker.

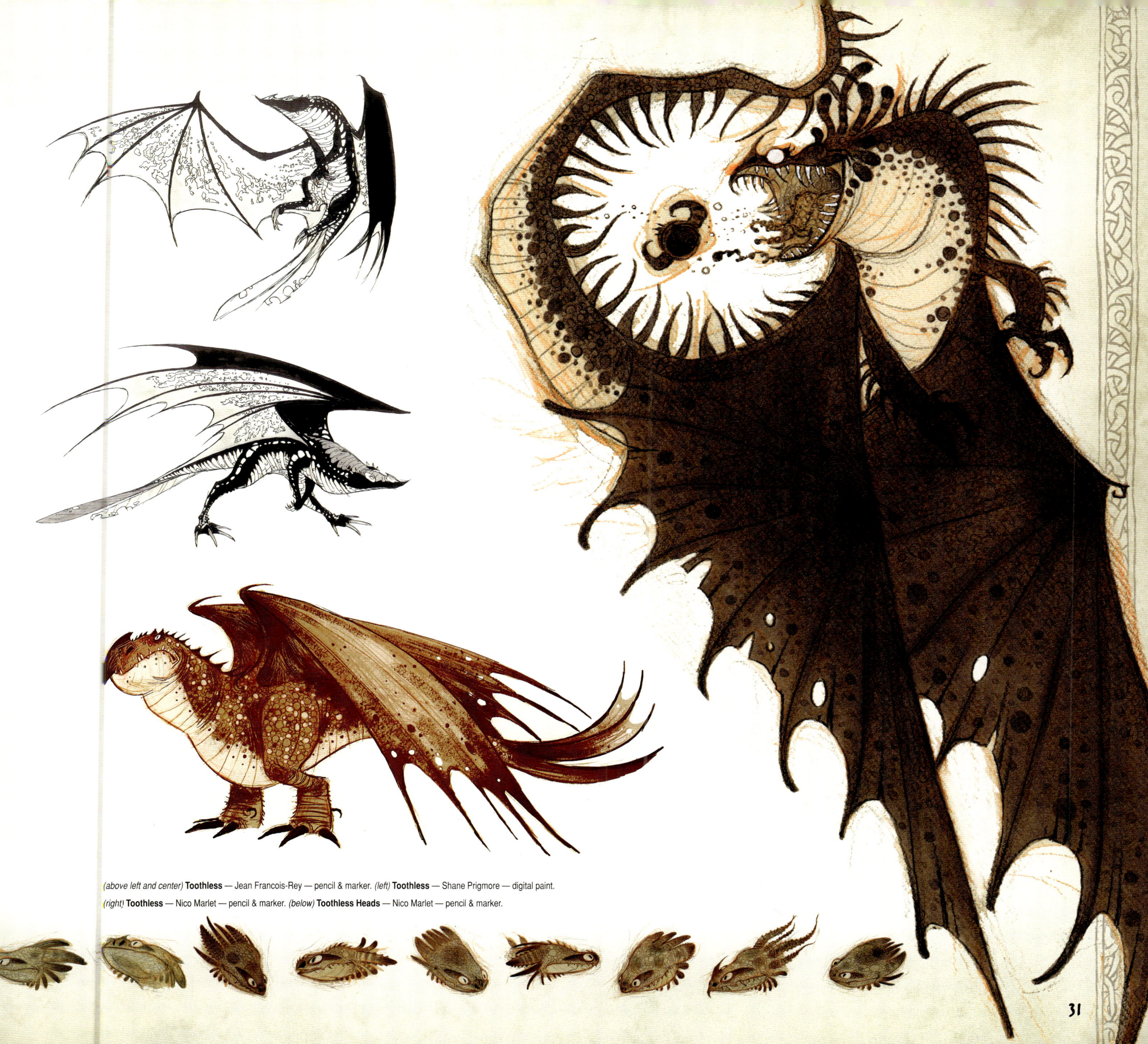

(above left and center) **Toothless** — Jean Francois-Rey — pencil & marker. *(left)* **Toothless** — Shane Prigmore — digital paint.
(right) **Toothless** — Nico Marlet — pencil & marker. *(below)* **Toothless Heads** — Nico Marlet — pencil & marker.

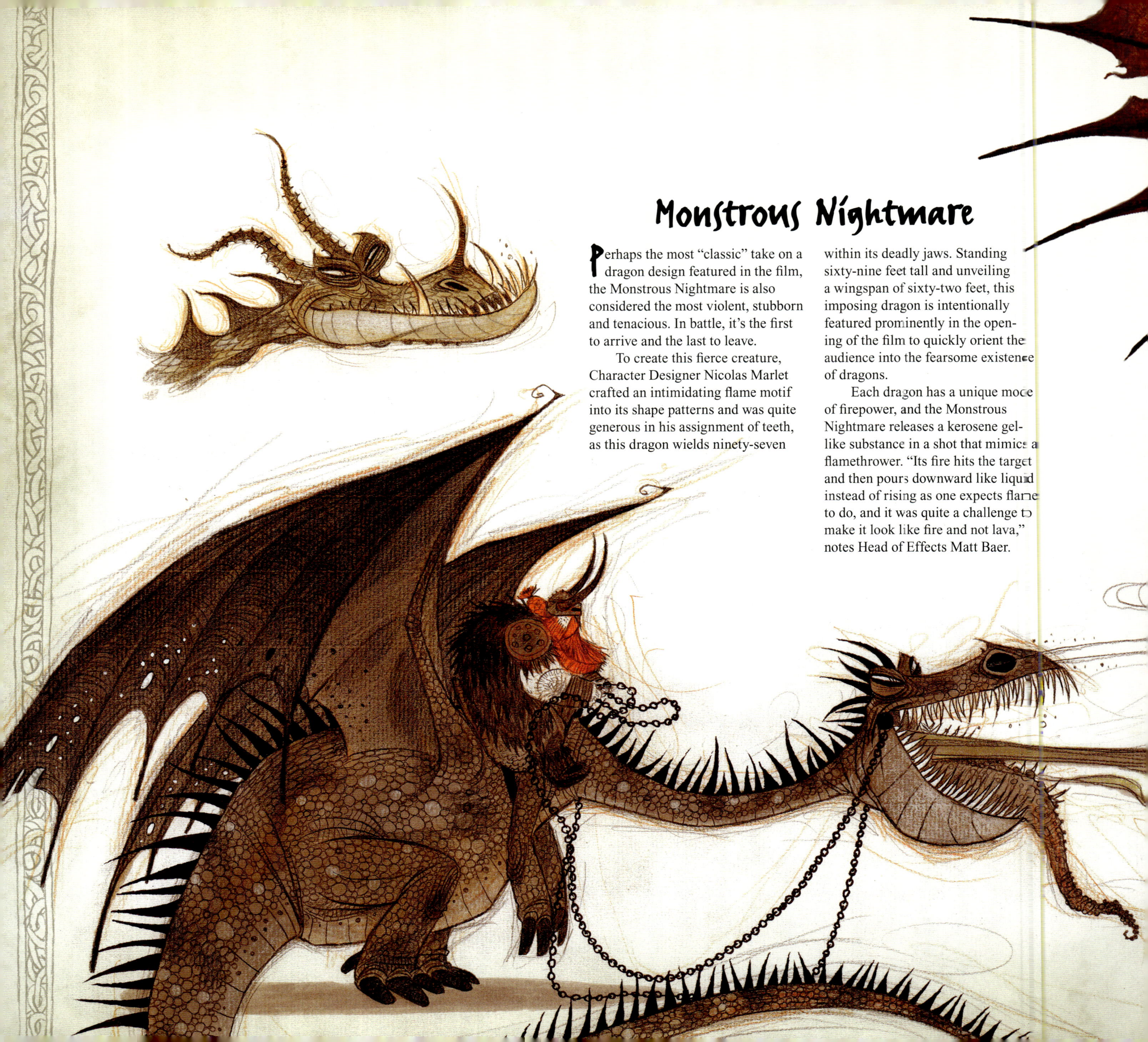

Monstrous Nightmare

Perhaps the most "classic" take on a dragon design featured in the film, the Monstrous Nightmare is also considered the most violent, stubborn and tenacious. In battle, it's the first to arrive and the last to leave.

To create this fierce creature, Character Designer Nicolas Marlet crafted an intimidating flame motif into its shape patterns and was quite generous in his assignment of teeth, as this dragon wields ninety-seven within its deadly jaws. Standing sixty-nine feet tall and unveiling a wingspan of sixty-two feet, this imposing dragon is intentionally featured prominently in the opening of the film to quickly orient the audience into the fearsome existence of dragons.

Each dragon has a unique mode of firepower, and the Monstrous Nightmare releases a kerosene gel-like substance in a shot that mimics a flamethrower. "Its fire hits the target and then pours downward like liquid instead of rising as one expects flame to do, and it was quite a challenge to make it look like fire and not lava," notes Head of Effects Matt Baer.

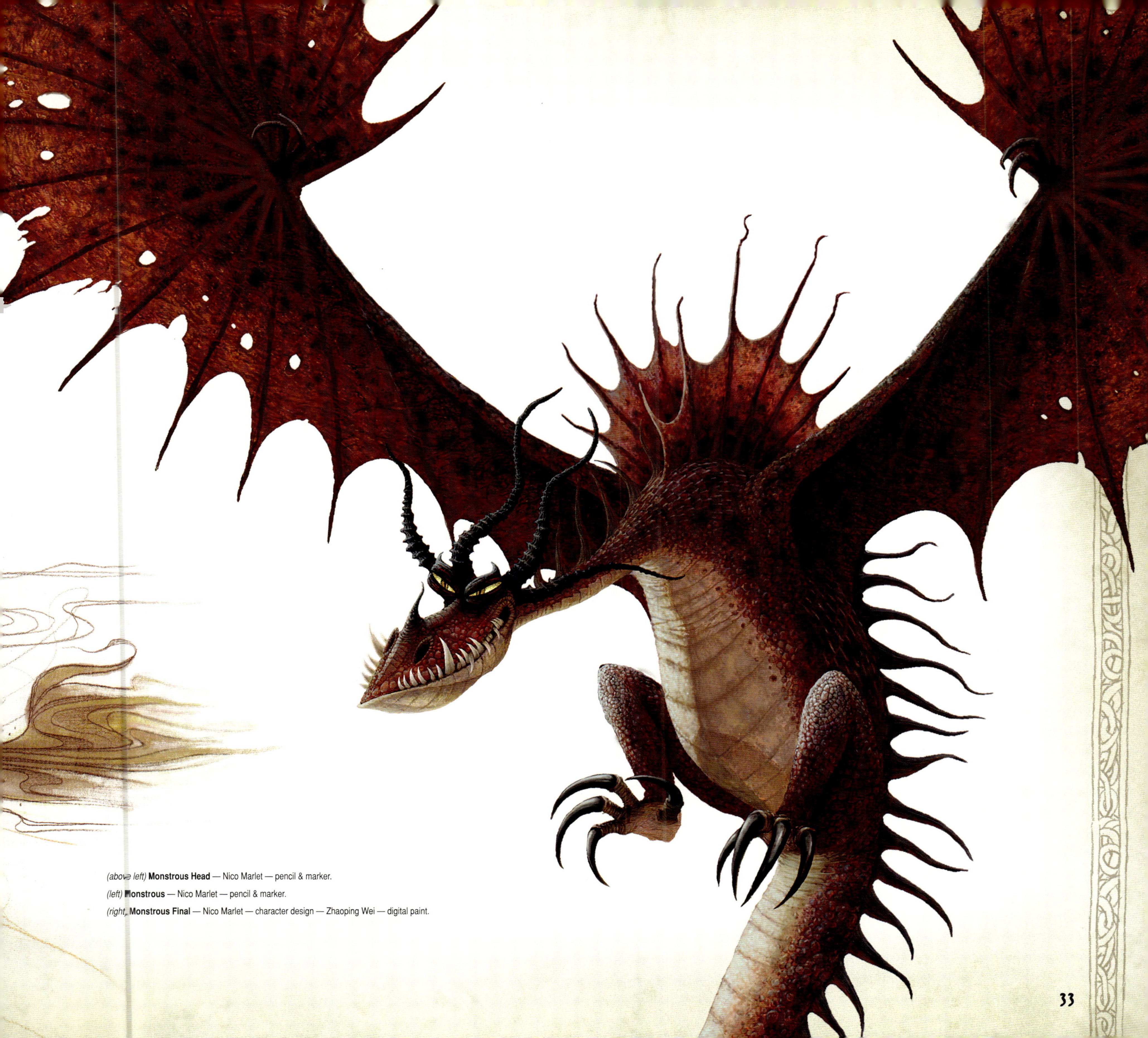

(above left) **Monstrous Head** — Nico Marlet — pencil & marker.

(left) **Monstrous** — Nico Marlet — pencil & marker.

(right) **Monstrous Final** — Nico Marlet — character design — Zhaoping Wei — digital paint.

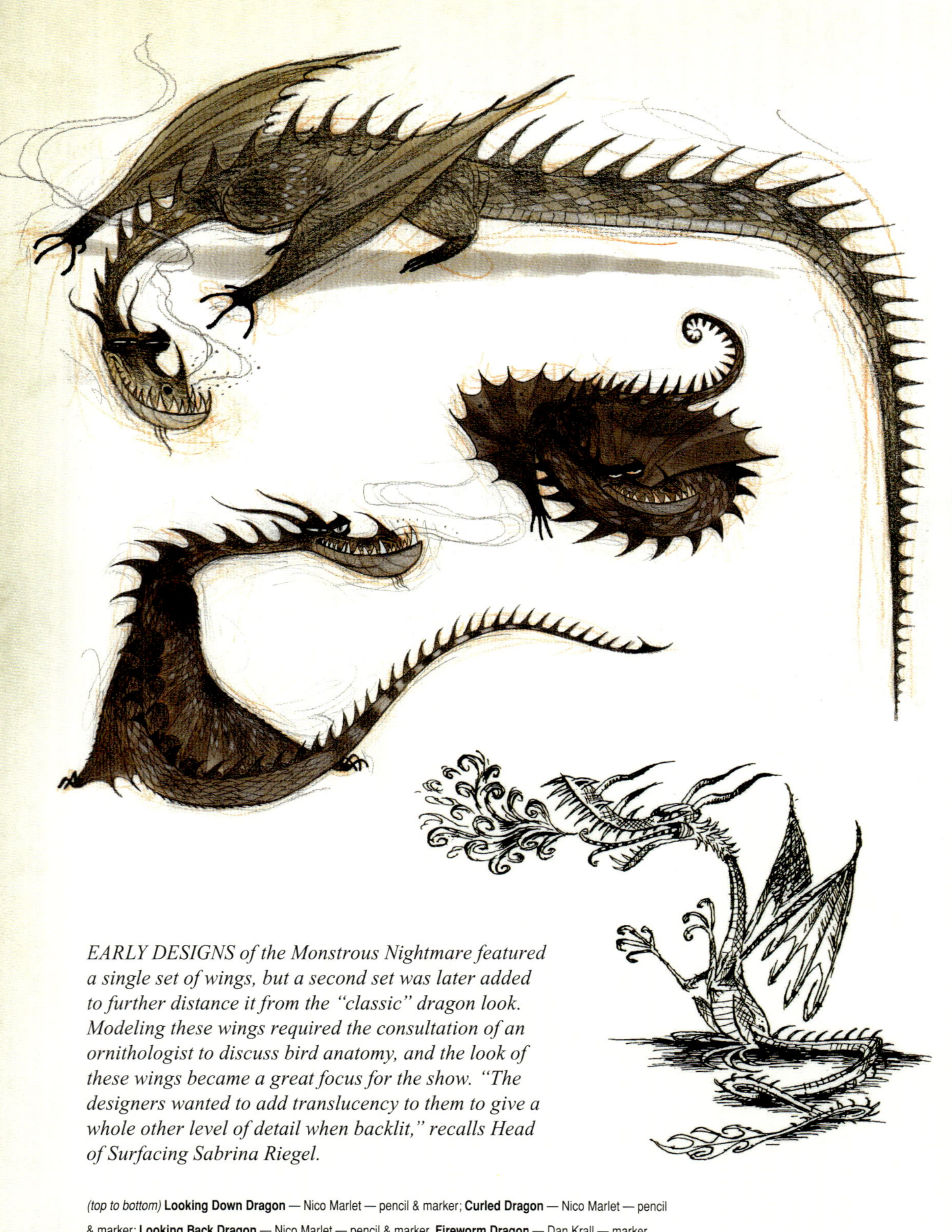

EARLY DESIGNS of the Monstrous Nightmare featured a single set of wings, but a second set was later added to further distance it from the "classic" dragon look. Modeling these wings required the consultation of an ornithologist to discuss bird anatomy, and the look of these wings became a great focus for the show. "The designers wanted to add translucency to them to give a whole other level of detail when backlit," recalls Head of Surfacing Sabrina Riegel.

(top to bottom) **Looking Down Dragon** — Nico Marlet — pencil & marker; **Curled Dragon** — Nico Marlet — pencil & marker; **Looking Back Dragon** — Nico Marlet — pencil & marker, **Fireworm Dragon** — Dan Krall — marker. *(right)* **Dragon of Spring** — Pierre-Olivier Vincent — digital paint.

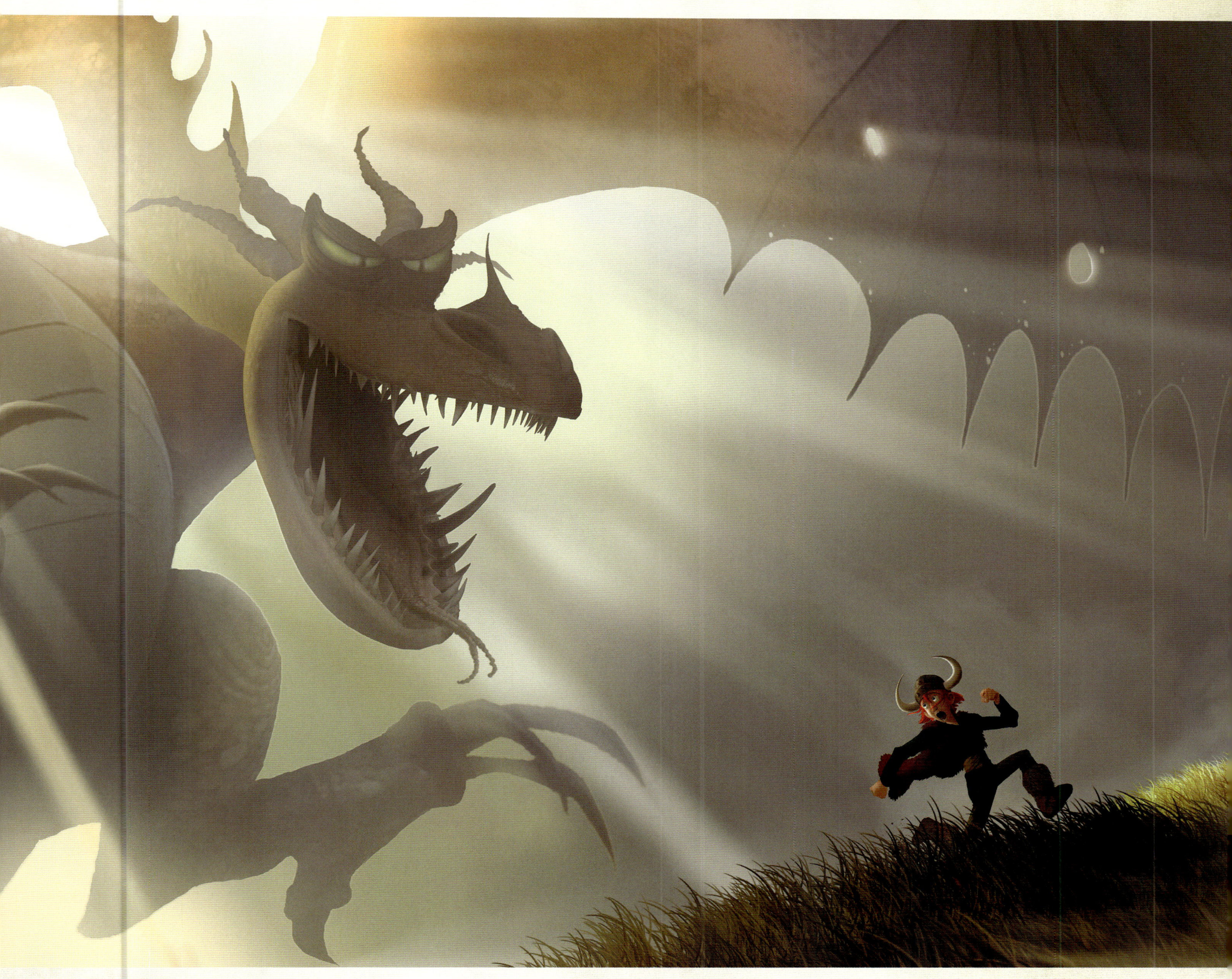

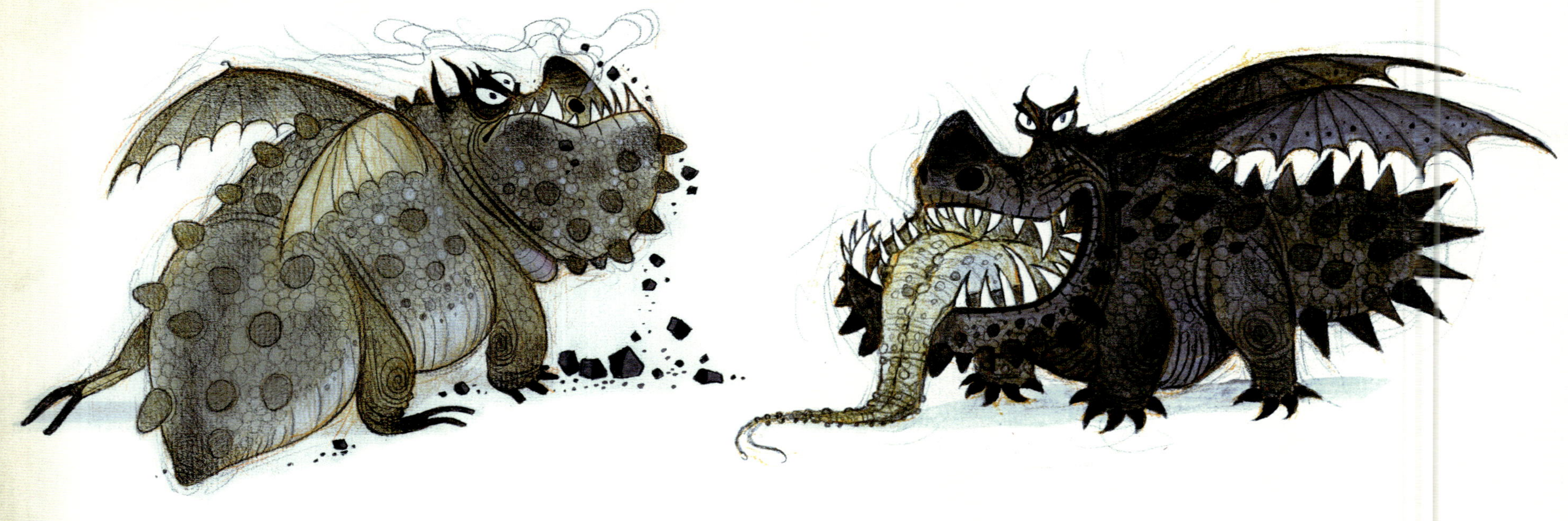

Gronckle

The Gronckle resembles a stack of boulders, wielding a tail that can punch like a battering ram and a mouth that can launch an explosive ball of lava. But this stubborn dragon likes its rest, which makes it the dragon most likely to be described as "sleeping like a rock."

The most atypical-looking dragon in the line-up, the fourteen-foot-long, craggy Gronckle "flies like a cross between a bumblebee and a helicopter, fueled by the roar of a motorcycle," explains Head of Character Animation Simon Otto. The animation team studied the way walruses and rhinoceroses move for inspiration, and then imagined what that creature would do if it had the size and speed of a hummingbird's wings.

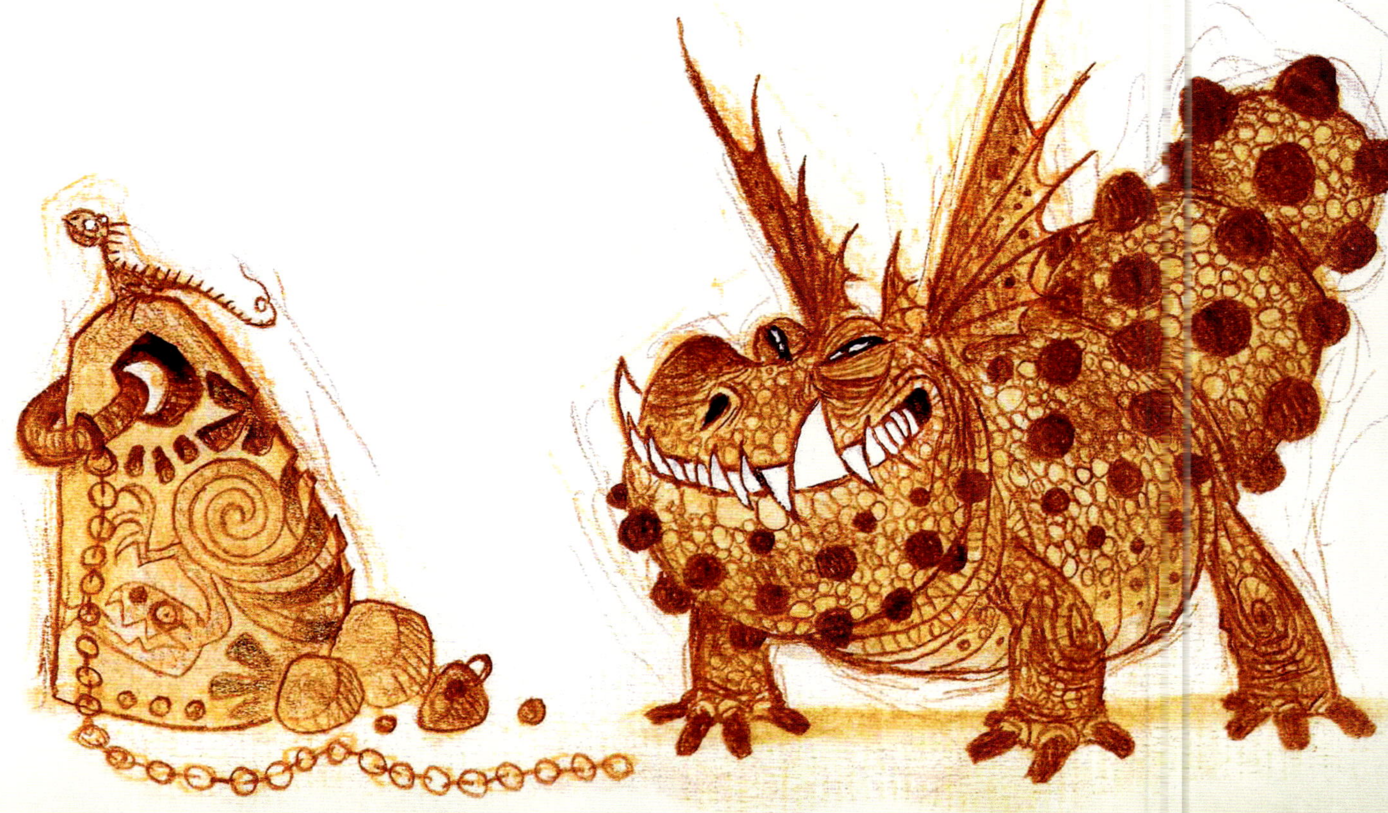

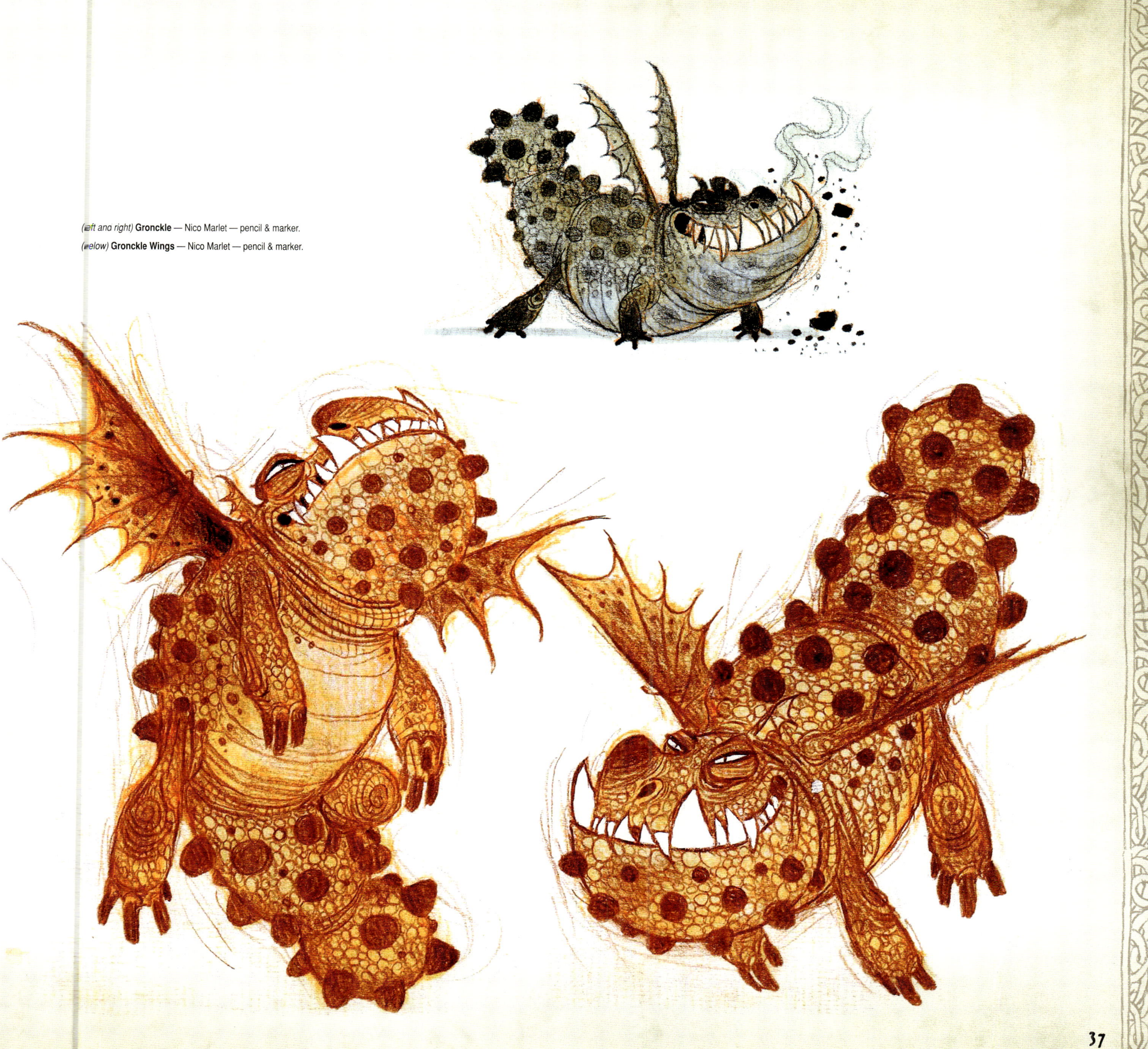

(left and right) **Gronckle** — Nico Marlet — pencil & marker.

(below) **Gronckle Wings** — Nico Marlet — pencil & marker.

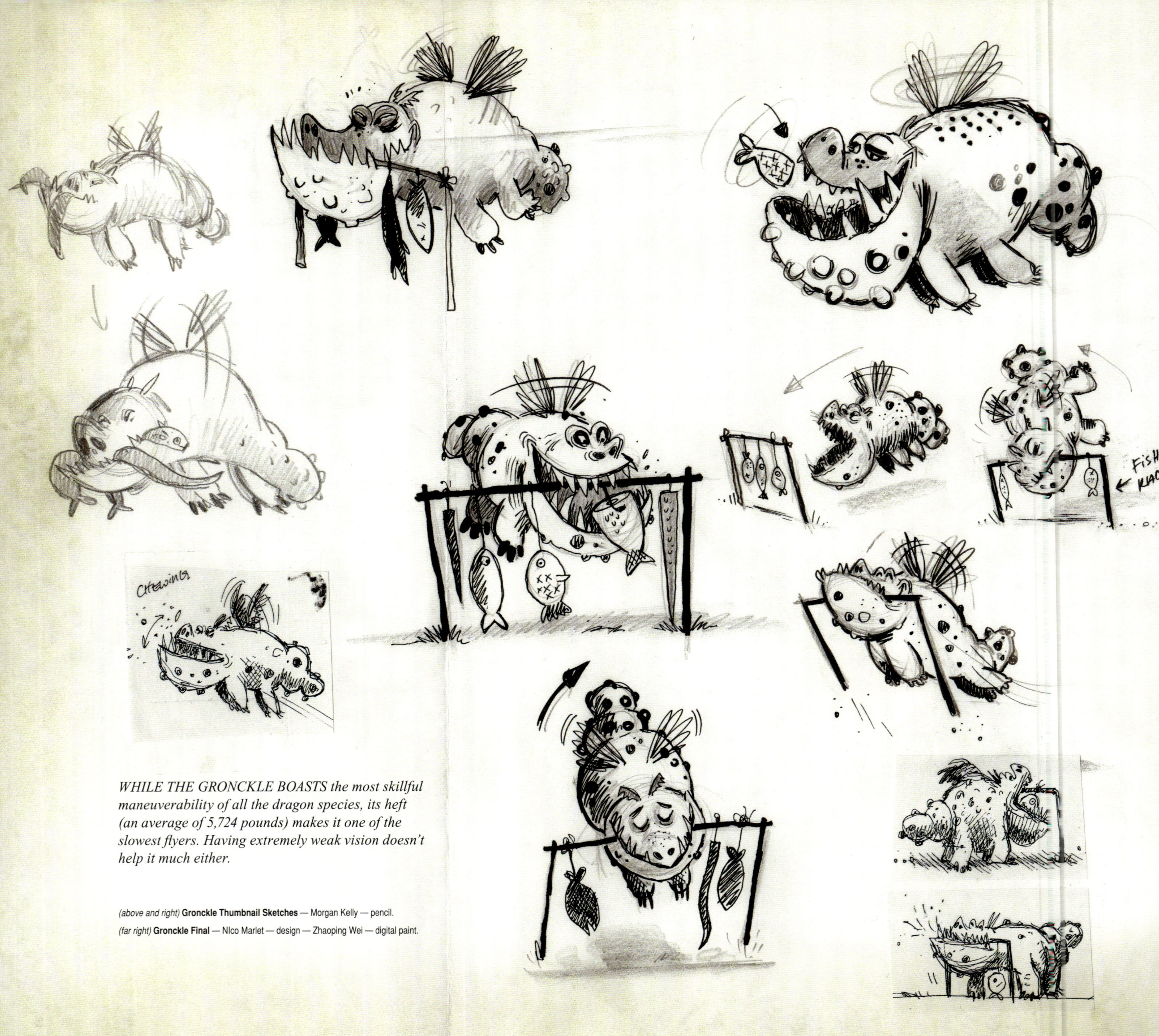

WHILE THE GRONCKLE BOASTS the most skillful maneuverability of all the dragon species, its heft (an average of 5,724 pounds) makes it one of the slowest flyers. Having extremely weak vision doesn't help it much either.

(above and right) **Gronckle Thumbnail Sketches** — Morgan Kelly — pencil.

(far right) **Gronckle Final** — NIco Marlet — design — Zhaoping Wei — digital paint.

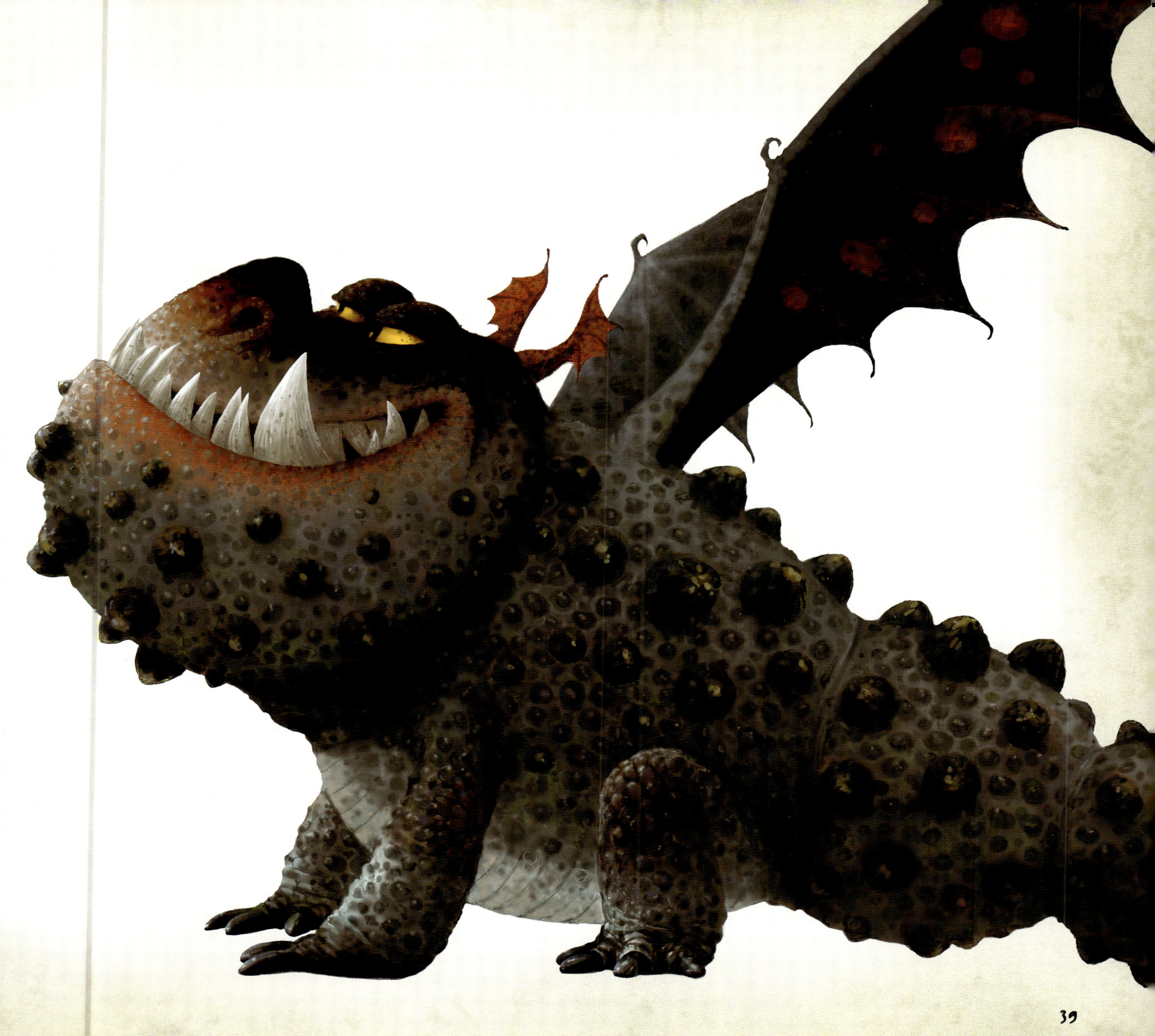

Deadly Nadder

The most colorful and vibrant dragon species, this dragon also projects some of the hottest firepower, "a sparkler type of fire like Asian fireworks, fueled by a magnesium powder that flashes in a white-hot blur with explosive sparks and blow-torchlike flames," explains Visual Effects Supervisor Craig Ring. This skilled flier has an explosive temper that makes it a daunting airborne opponent but if you stand right in front of its nose you'll be in its blind spot and it won't be able to see you.

Character Designer Nicolas Marlet imagined that this dragon was an ancestor of a bird. This idea inspired the animation of the Deadly Nadder, which "moves like a parrot, with a bit of an emu's walk and the posture of a tyrannosaurus rex tossed into our blend of behaviors," says Head of Character Animation Simon Otto.

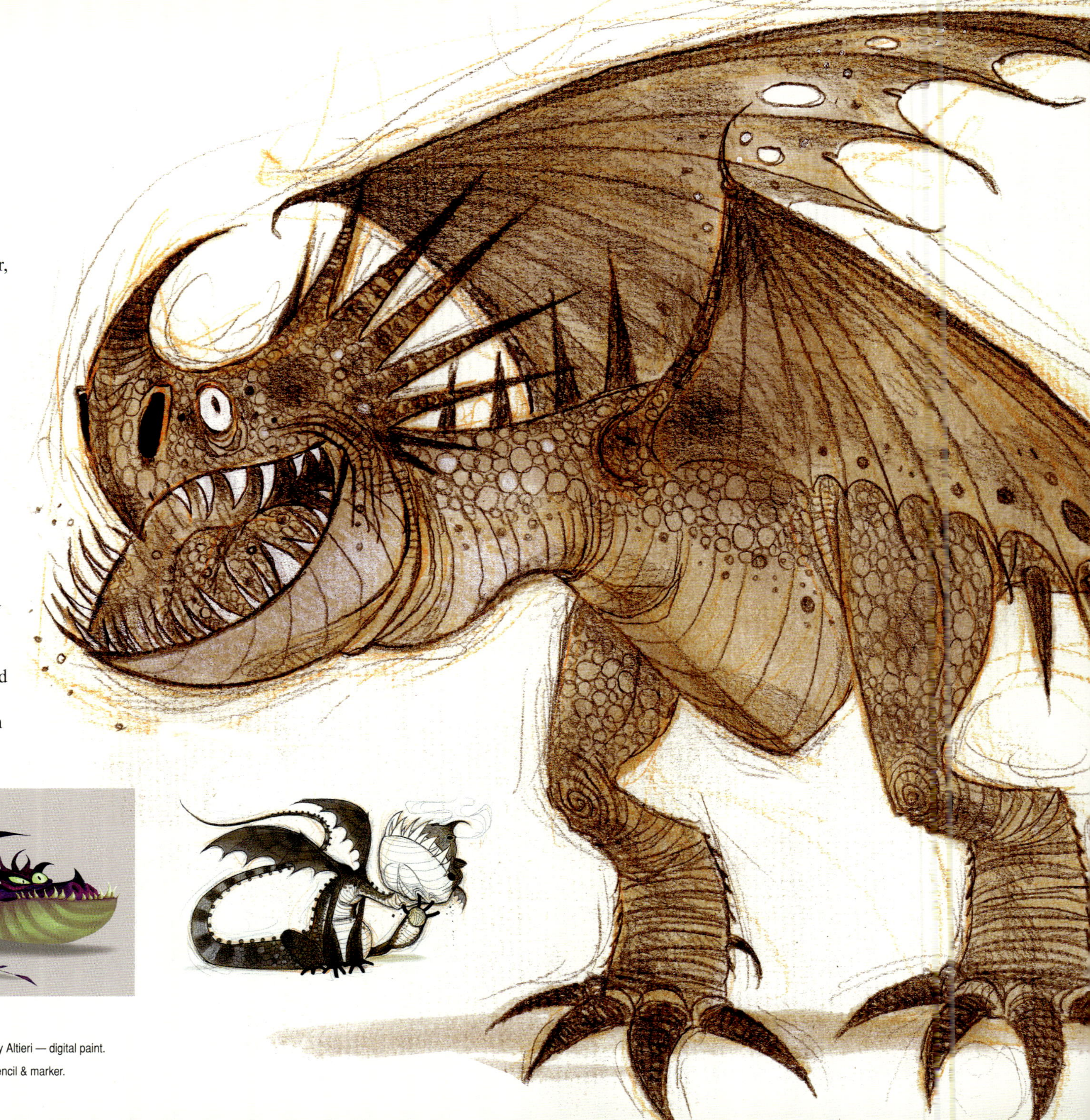

(above) **Nadder** — Nico Marlet — character design — Kathy Altieri — digital paint.
(above center and above right) **Nadder** — Nico Marlet — pencil & marker.
(far right) **Nadder** — Tony Siruno — pencil & marker.

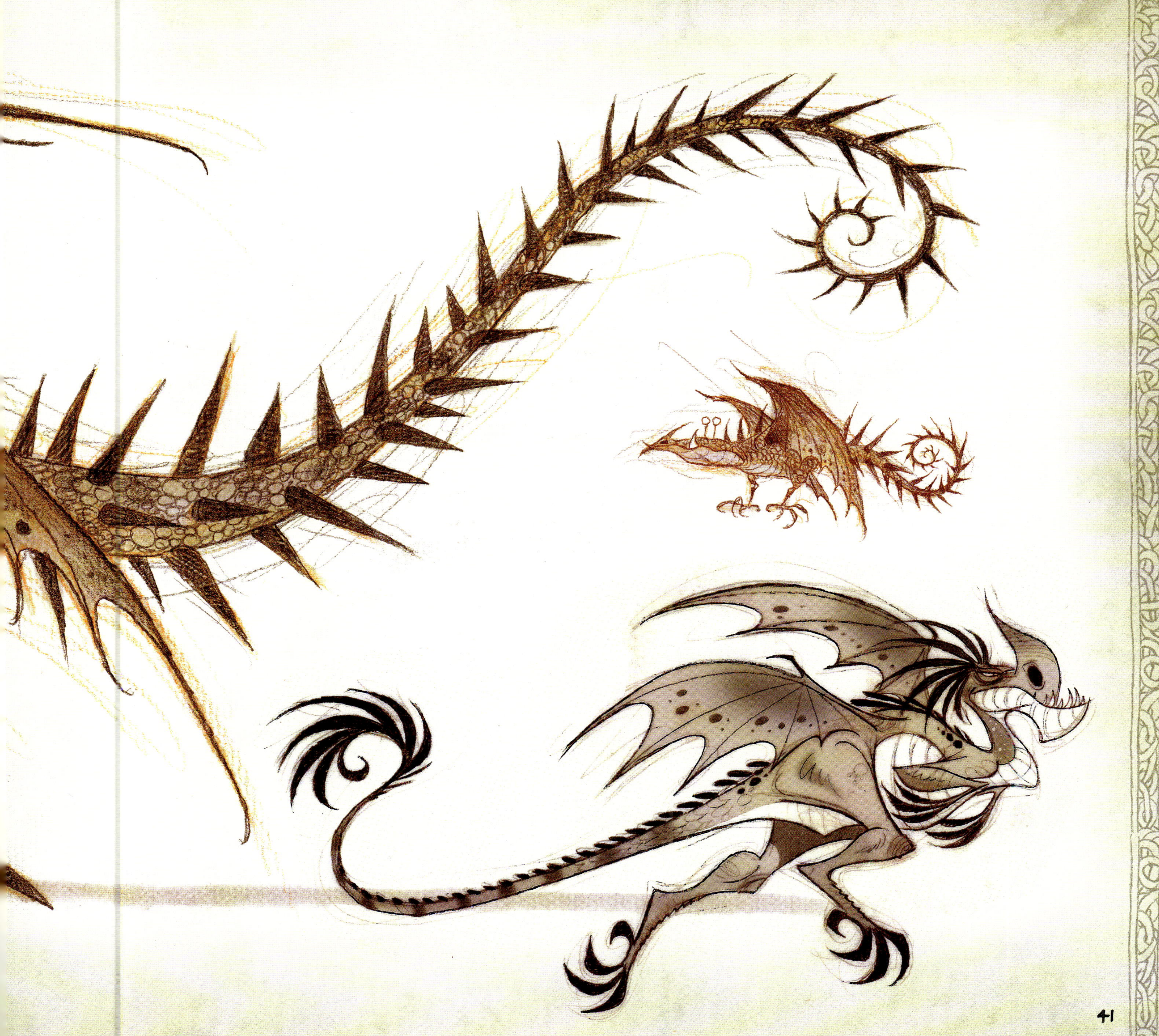

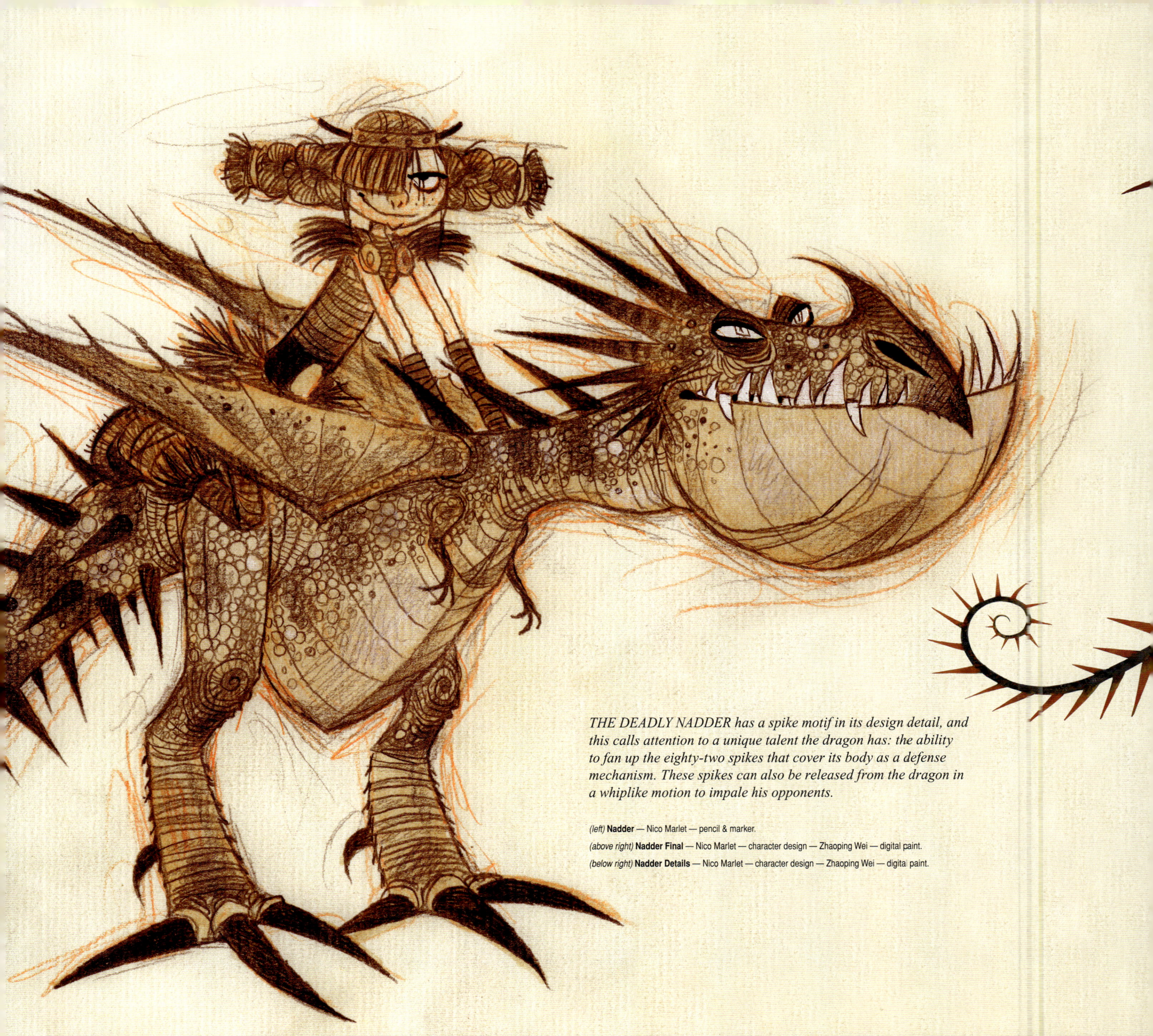

THE DEADLY NADDER has a spike motif in its design detail, and this calls attention to a unique talent the dragon has: the ability to fan up the eighty-two spikes that cover its body as a defense mechanism. These spikes can also be released from the dragon in a whiplike motion to impale his opponents.

(left) **Nadder** — Nico Marlet — pencil & marker.

(above right) **Nadder Final** — Nico Marlet — character design — Zhaoping Wei — digital paint.

(below right) **Nadder Details** — Nico Marlet — character design — Zhaoping Wei — digital paint.

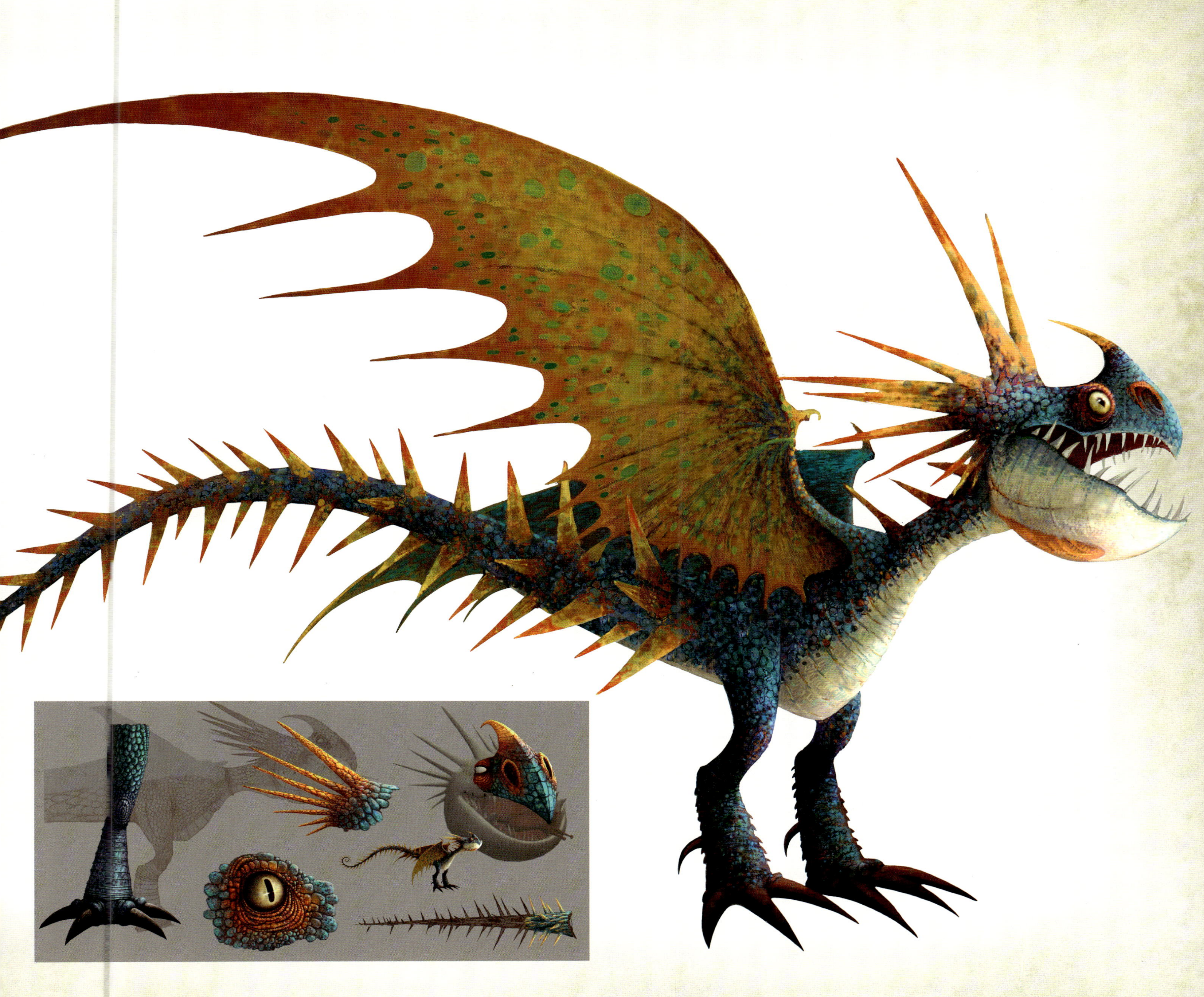

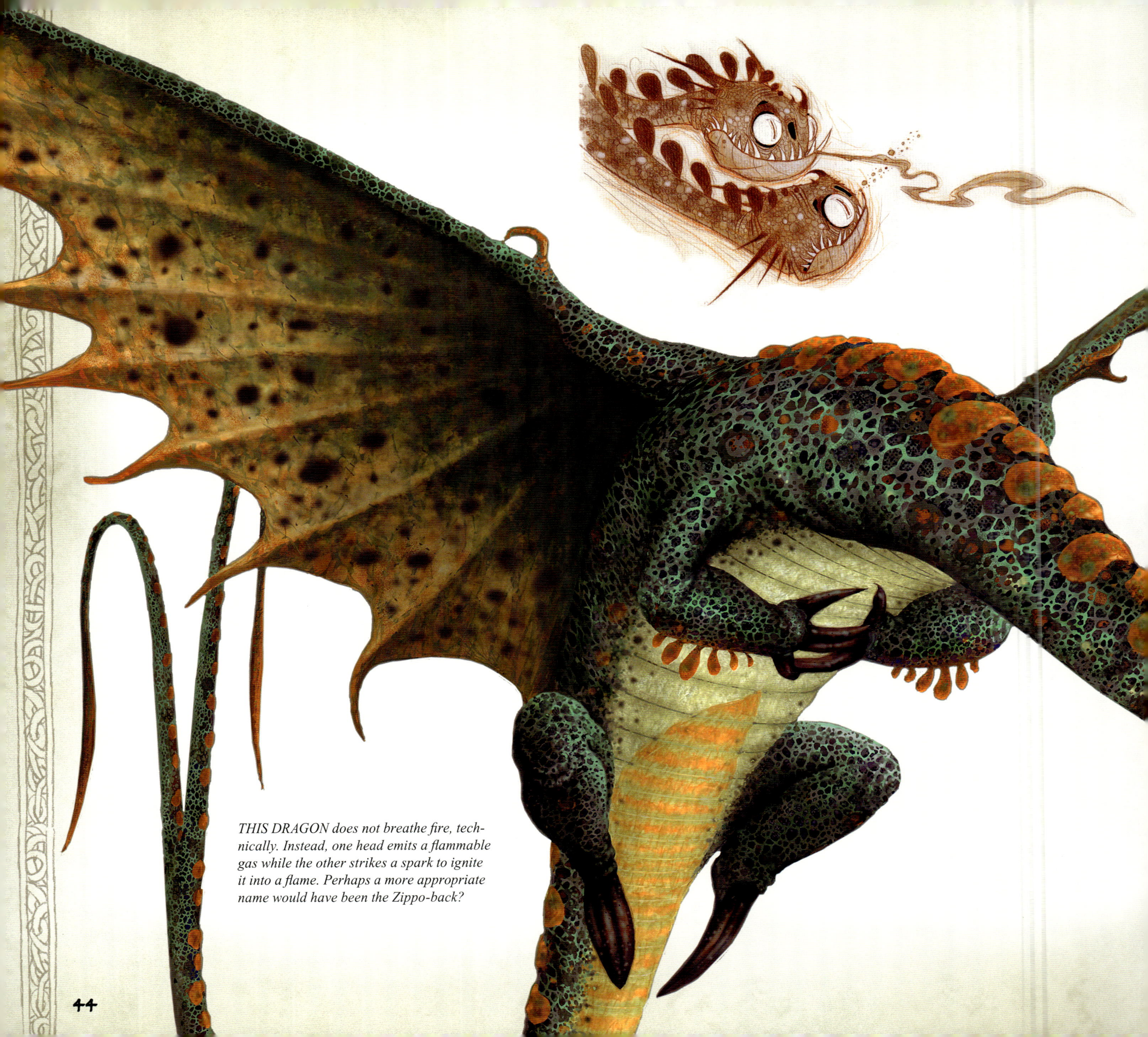

THIS DRAGON does not breathe fire, technically. Instead, one head emits a flammable gas while the other strikes a spark to ignite it into a flame. Perhaps a more appropriate name would have been the Zippo-back?

Hideous Zippleback

While the Hideous Zippleback has the best vision and ground-attack ability amongst the dragon species, it has the least favorable flight proportions, measuring ninety-one feet in length but only seventy-five feet in wingspan. It also has the disadvantage of two brains that think independently, lending some vulnerability to this evasive, devious dragon.

The modeling and rigging teams had more than twice the fun working on the build of this dragon: imagine what they thought when they were told this design "would have two heads and two long necks that should be able to zip together. And they'll need to wind around each other as well," recalls Head of Rigging Jeff Light. This technically complicated dragon contains 4,769 keyable animation controls, as contrasted to the average human character, which contains approximately 1,100 controls.

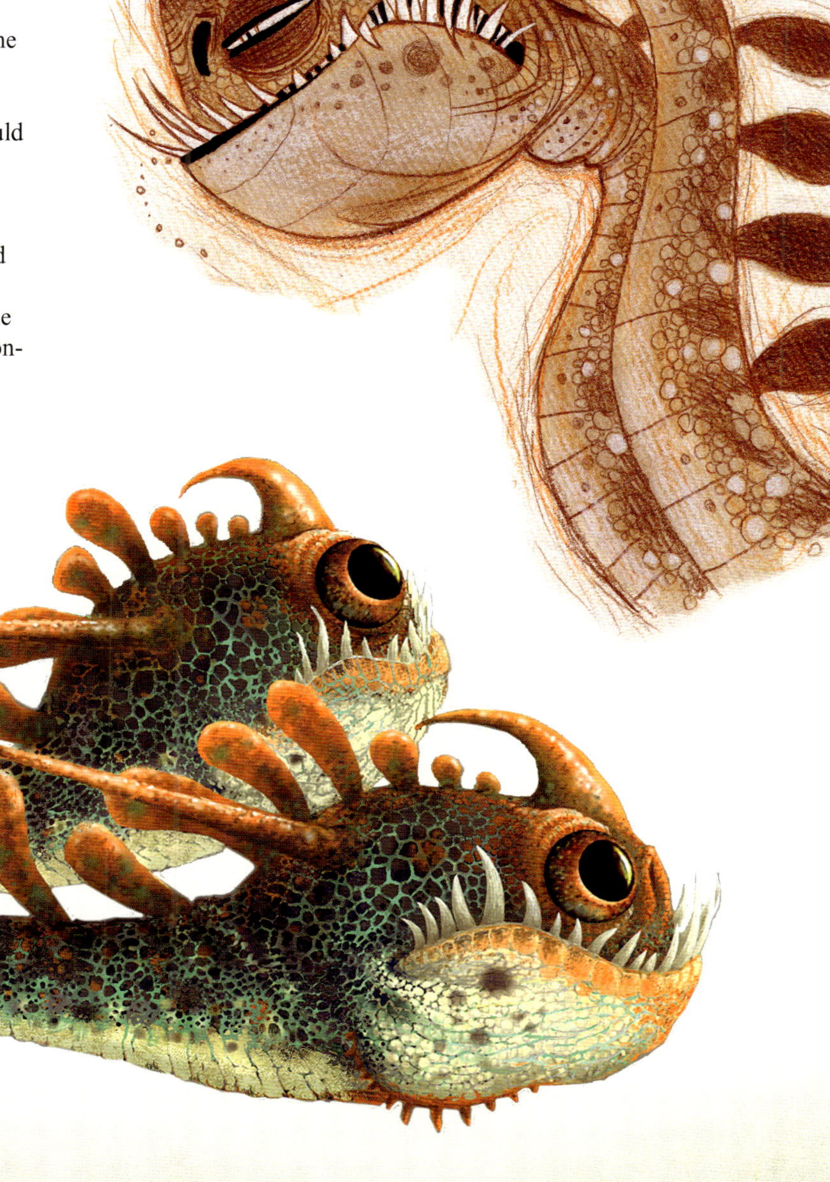

(above left and right) **Two Headed** — Nico Marlet — pencil & marker.

(below) **2headed Final** — Nico Marlet — character design — Zhaoping Wei — digital paint.

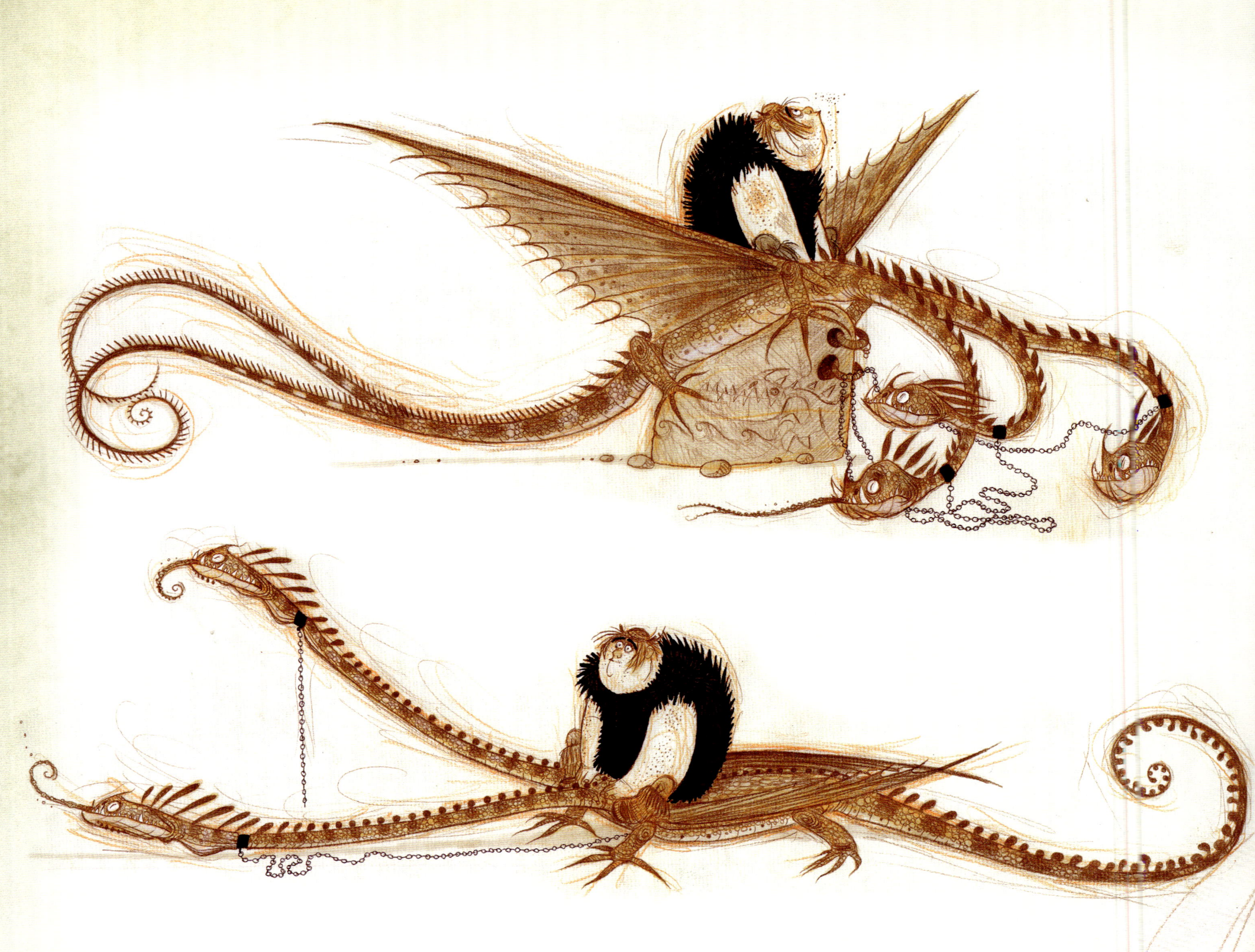

(above and above right) **Two Headed** — Nico Marlet — pencil & marker. *(below right)* **2headed Keys** — Nico Marlet — character design — Zhaoping Wei — digital paint.

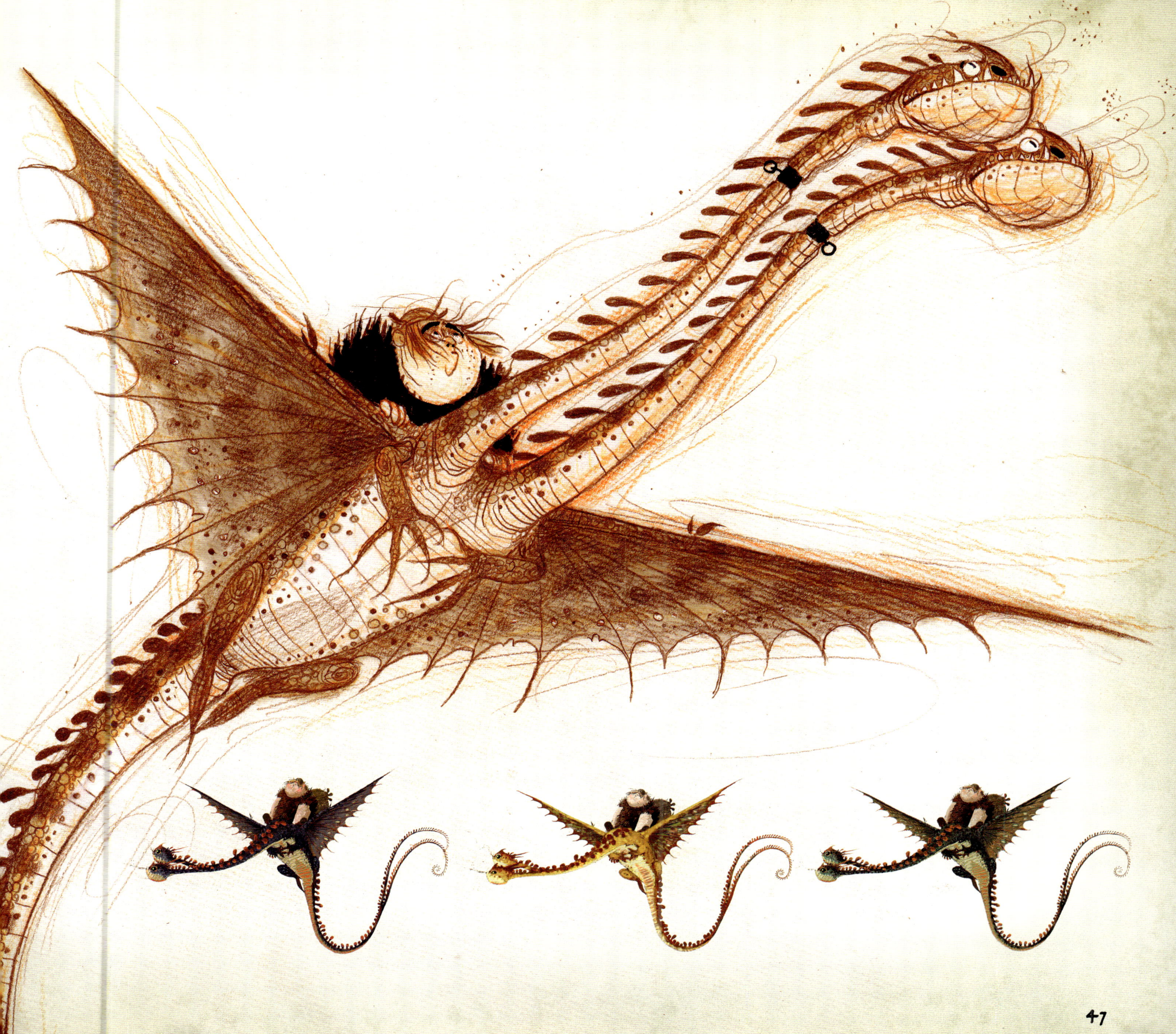

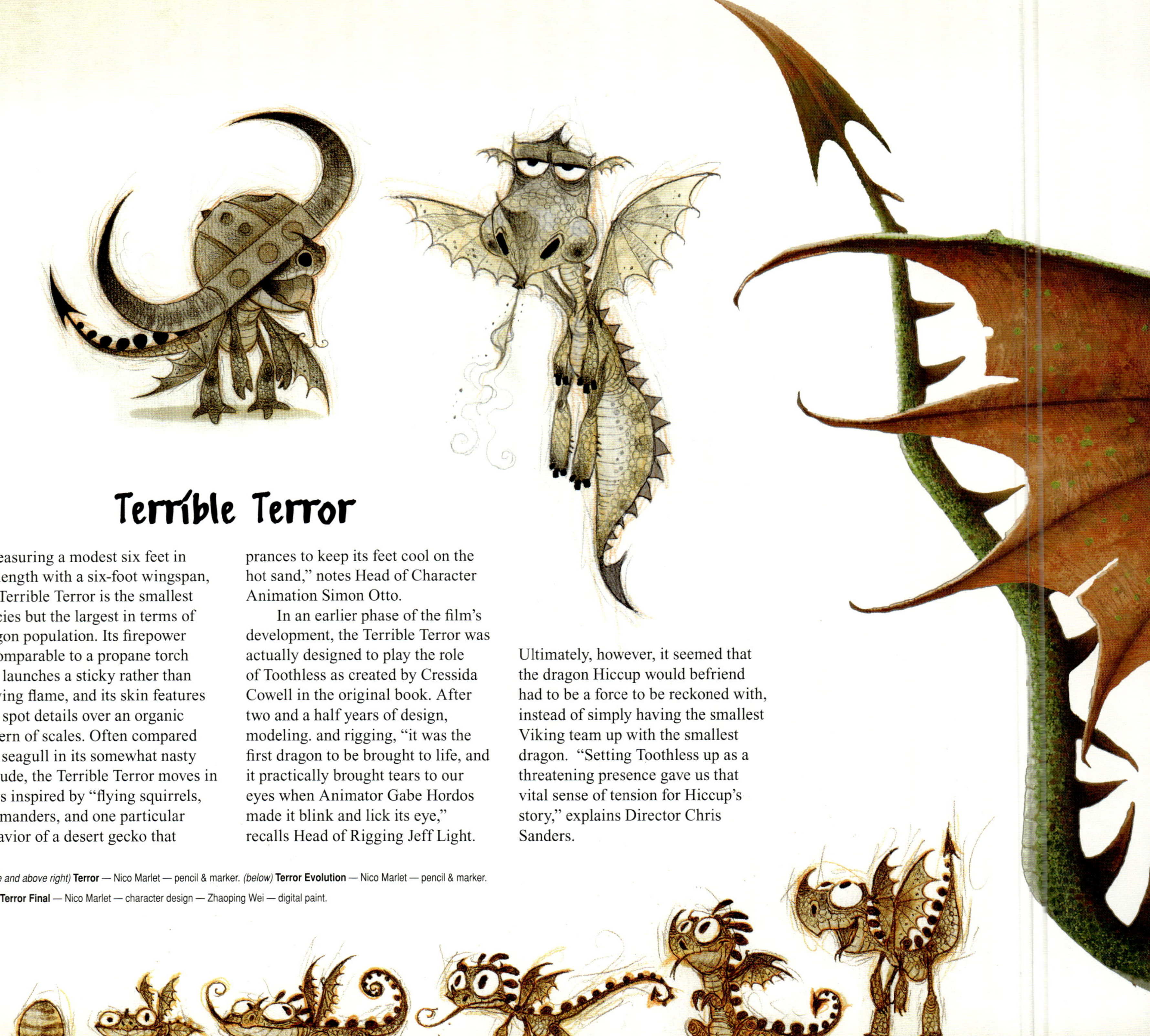

Terrible Terror

Measuring a modest six feet in length with a six-foot wingspan, the Terrible Terror is the smallest species but the largest in terms of dragon population. Its firepower is comparable to a propane torch that launches a sticky rather than flowing flame, and its skin features fine spot details over an organic pattern of scales. Often compared to a seagull in its somewhat nasty attitude, the Terrible Terror moves in ways inspired by "flying squirrels, salamanders, and one particular behavior of a desert gecko that prances to keep its feet cool on the hot sand," notes Head of Character Animation Simon Otto.

In an earlier phase of the film's development, the Terrible Terror was actually designed to play the role of Toothless as created by Cressida Cowell in the original book. After two and a half years of design, modeling. and rigging, "it was the first dragon to be brought to life, and it practically brought tears to our eyes when Animator Gabe Hordos made it blink and lick its eye," recalls Head of Rigging Jeff Light. Ultimately, however, it seemed that the dragon Hiccup would befriend had to be a force to be reckoned with, instead of simply having the smallest Viking team up with the smallest dragon. "Setting Toothless up as a threatening presence gave us that vital sense of tension for Hiccup's story," explains Director Chris Sanders.

(above and above right) **Terror** — Nico Marlet — pencil & marker. *(below)* **Terror Evolution** — Nico Marlet — pencil & marker. *(right)* **Terror Final** — Nico Marlet — character design — Zhaoping Wei — digital paint.

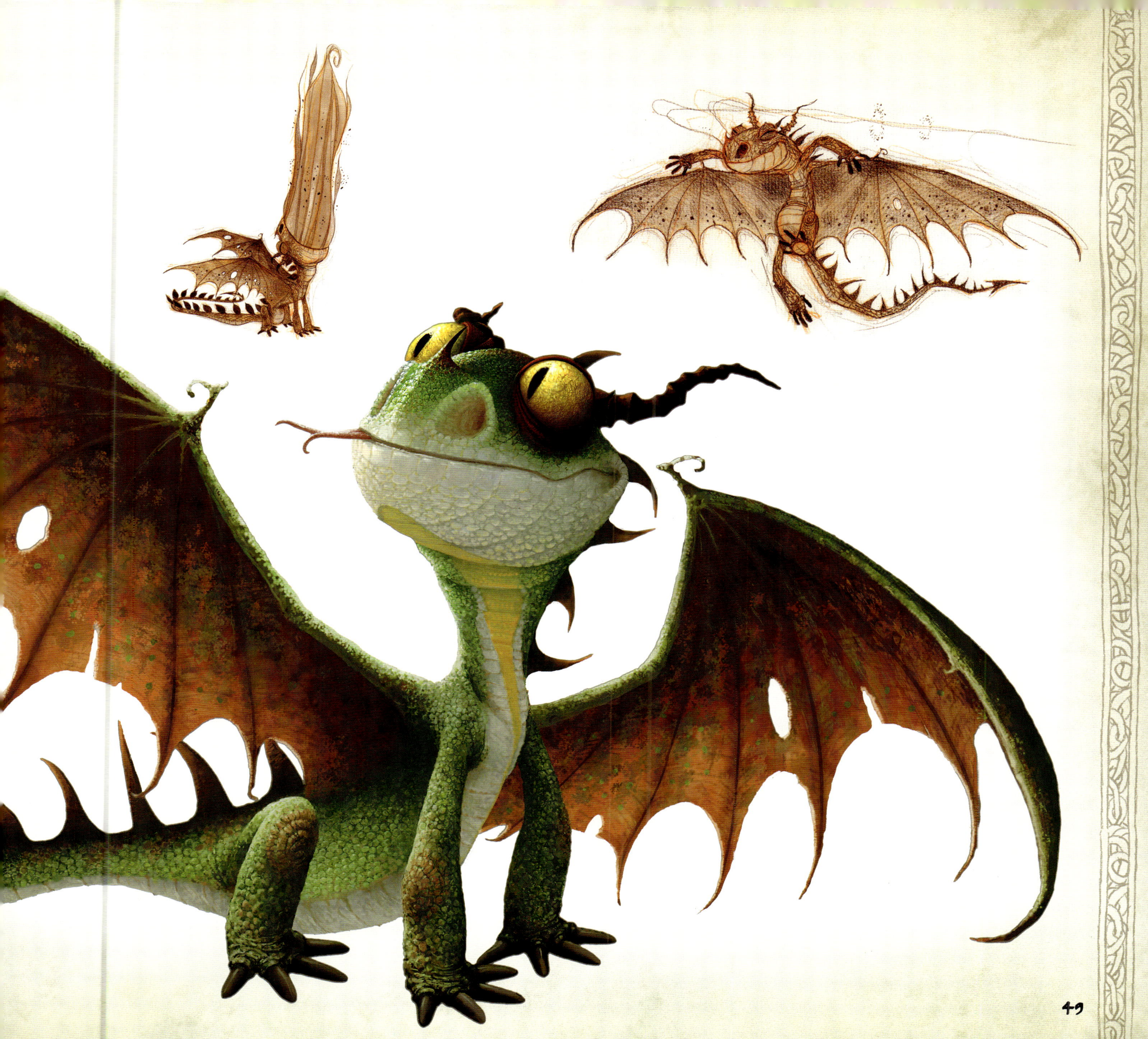

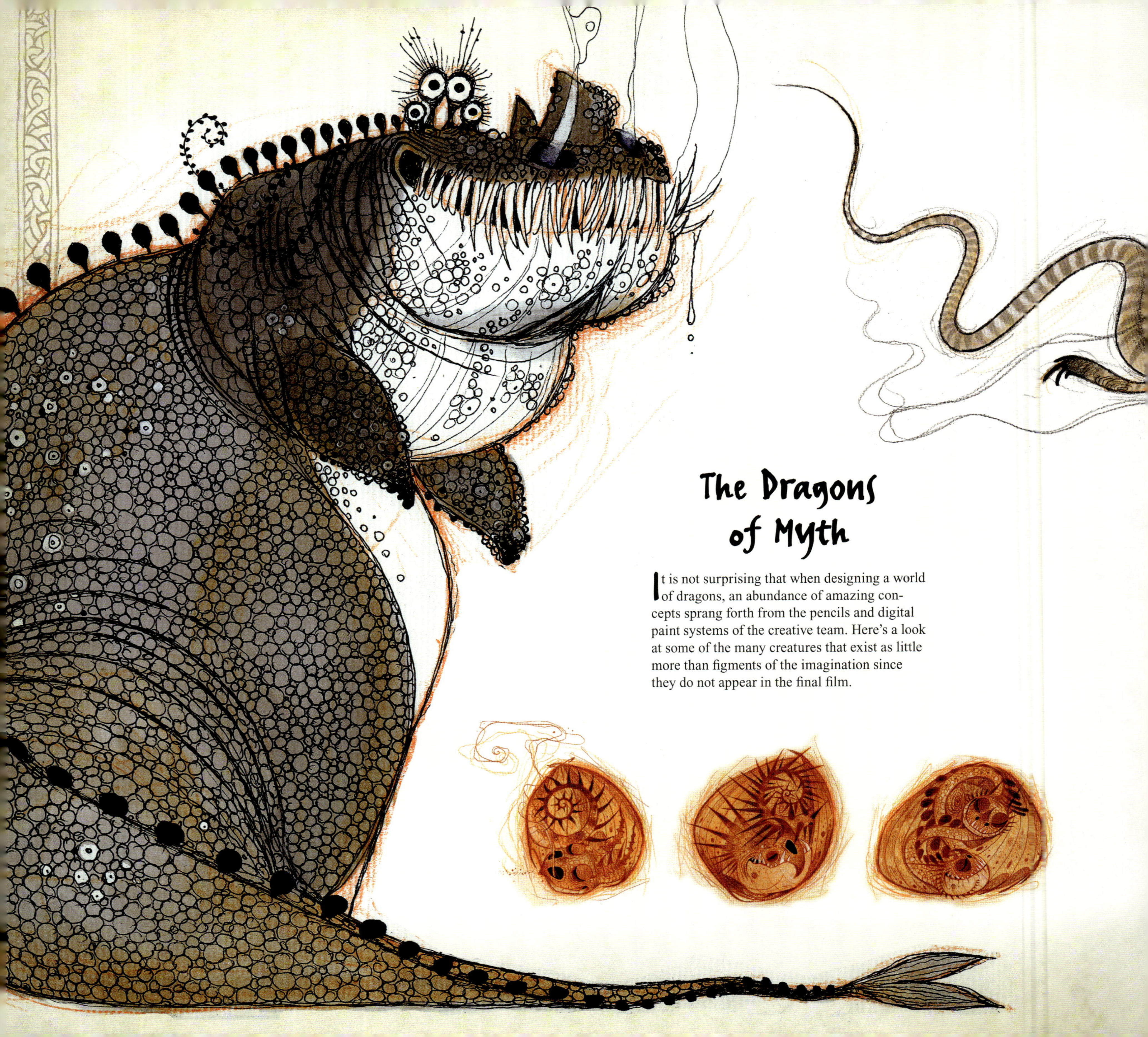

The Dragons of Myth

It is not surprising that when designing a world of dragons, an abundance of amazing concepts sprang forth from the pencils and digital paint systems of the creative team. Here's a look at some of the many creatures that exist as little more than figments of the imagination since they do not appear in the final film.

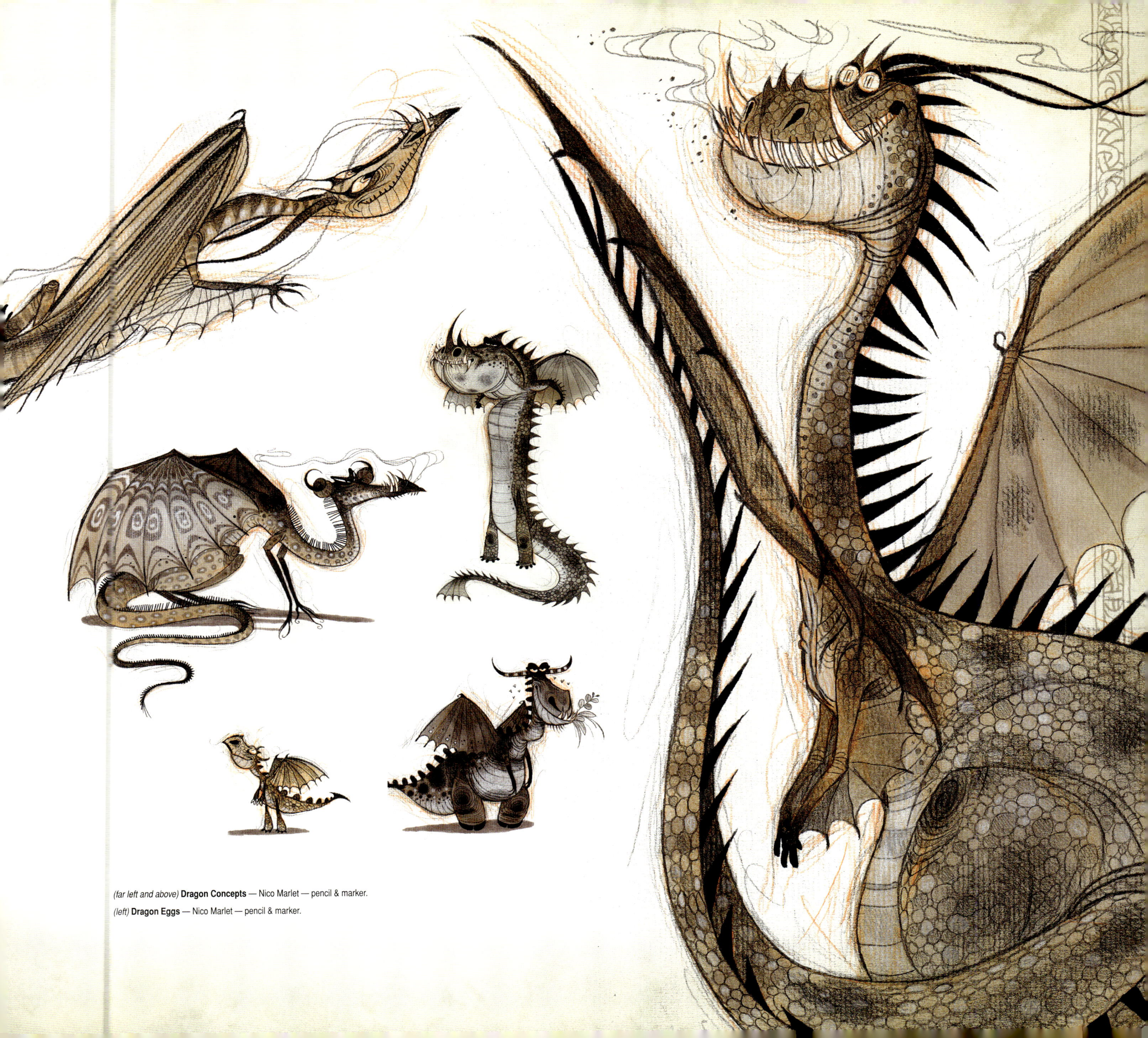

(far left and above) **Dragon Concepts** — Nico Marlet — pencil & marker.

(left) **Dragon Eggs** — Nico Marlet — pencil & marker.

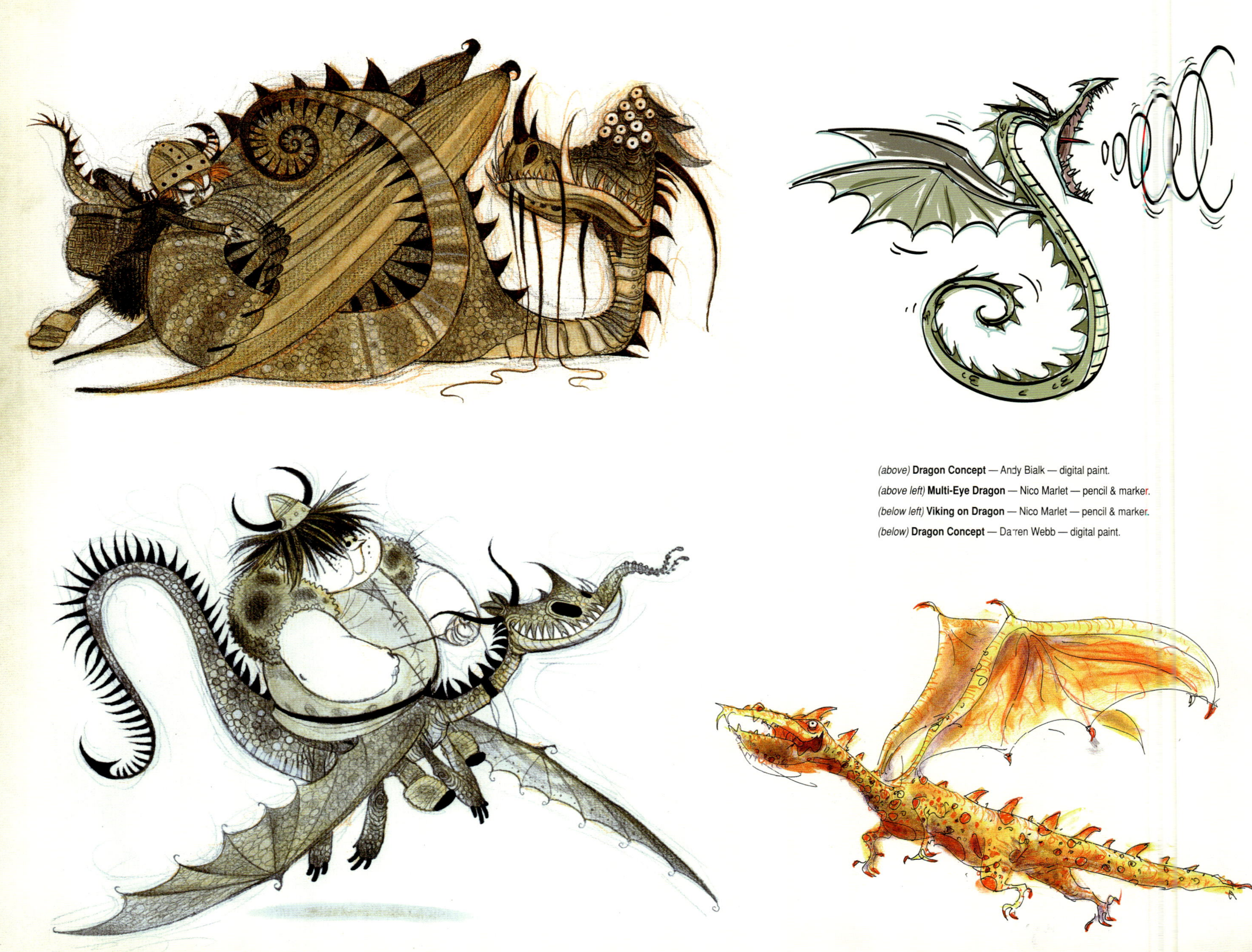

(above) **Dragon Concept** — Andy Bialk — digital paint.

(above left) **Multi-Eye Dragon** — Nico Marlet — pencil & marker.

(below left) **Viking on Dragon** — Nico Marlet — pencil & marker.

(below) **Dragon Concept** — Darren Webb — digital paint.

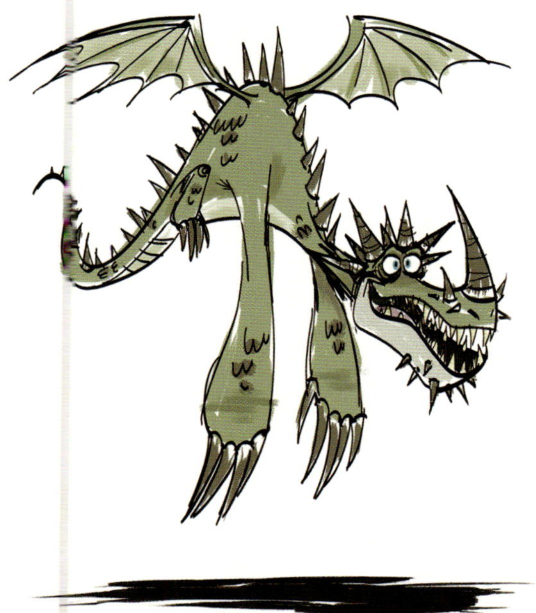

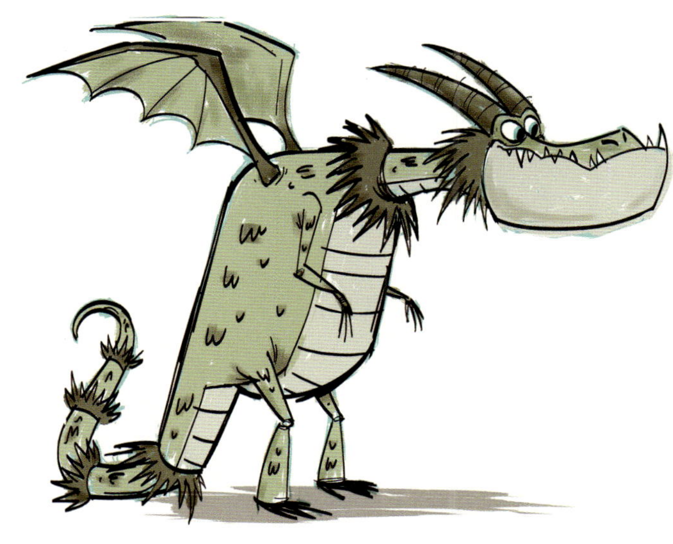

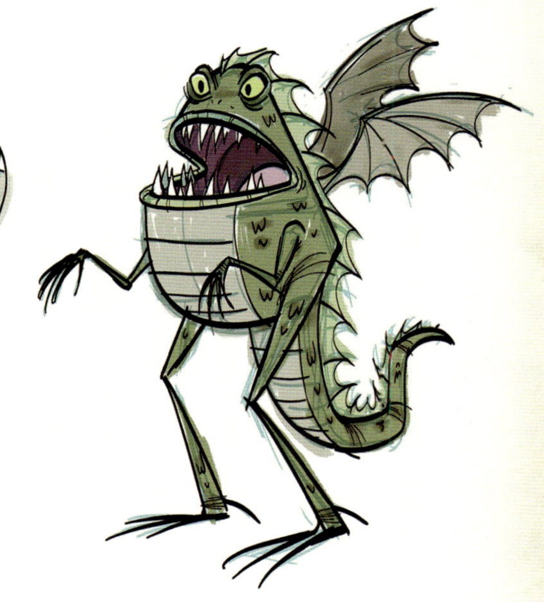

(above) **Dragon Concepts** — Andy Bialk — digital paint.

(below) **Dragon Exploration** — J.J. Villard — digital paint.

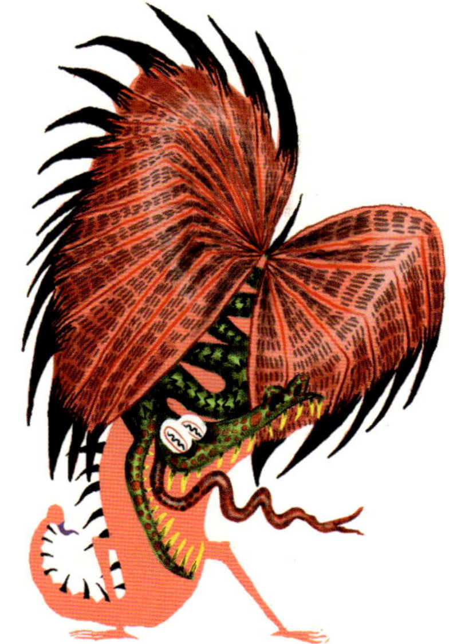

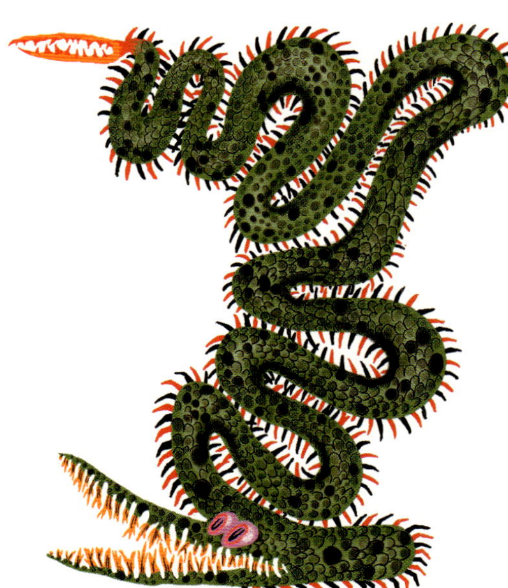

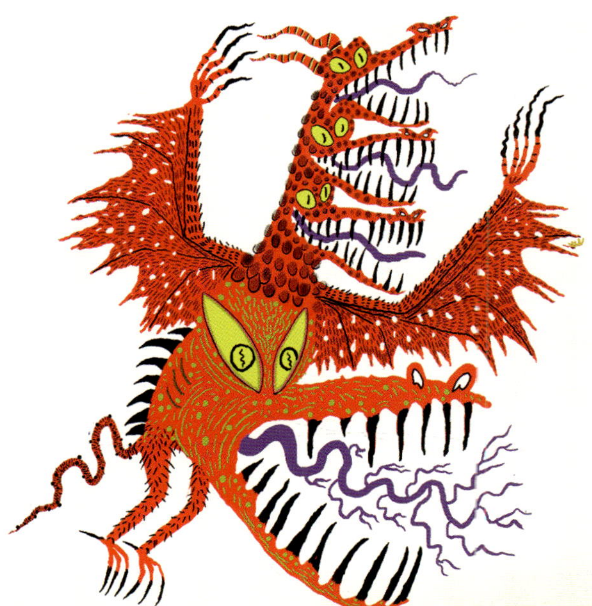

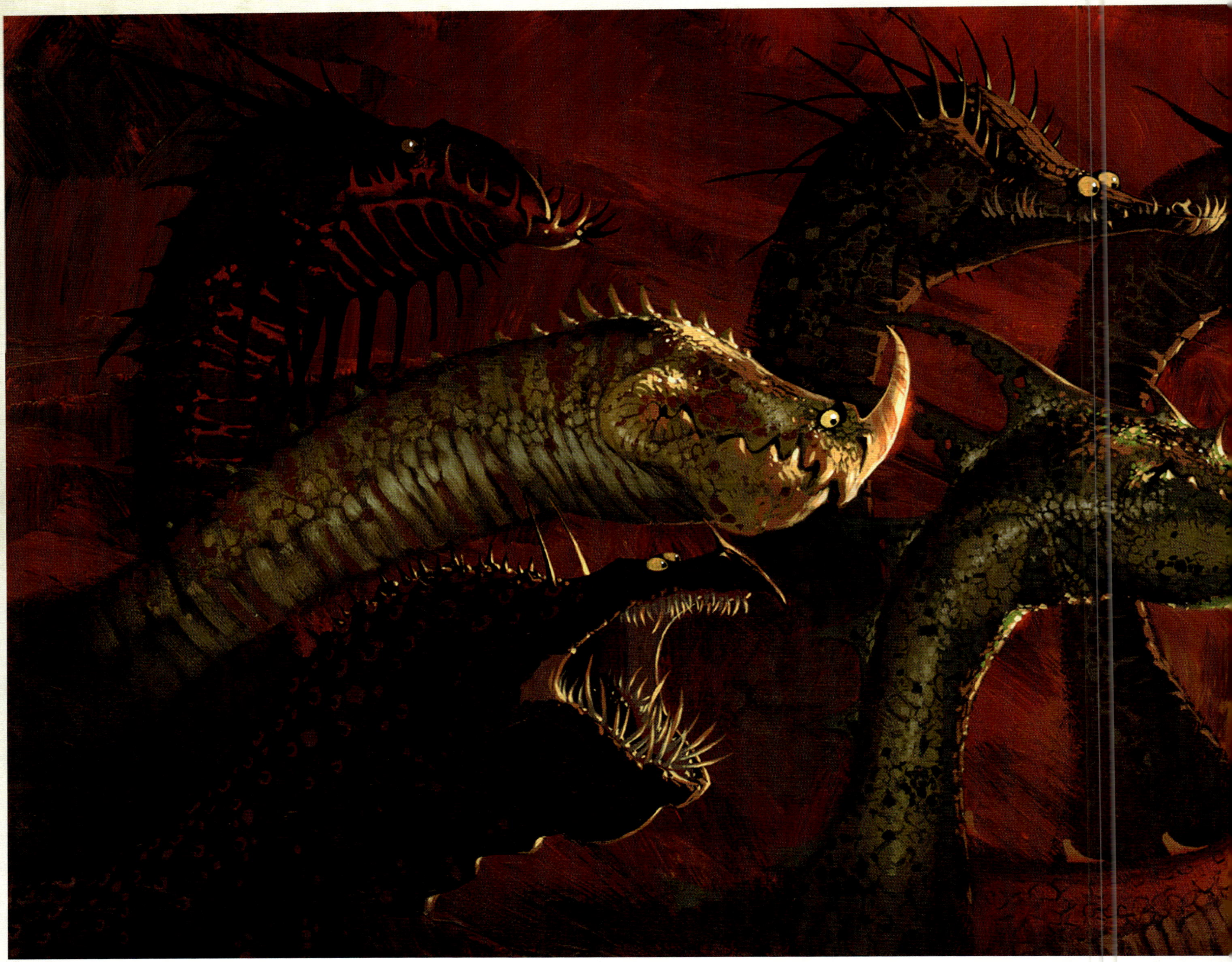

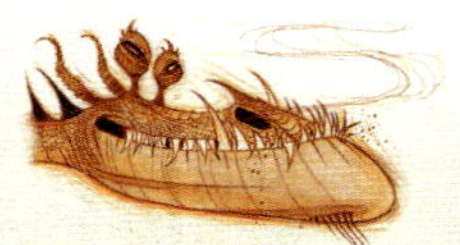
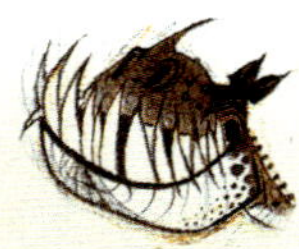
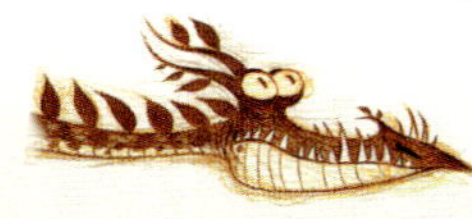
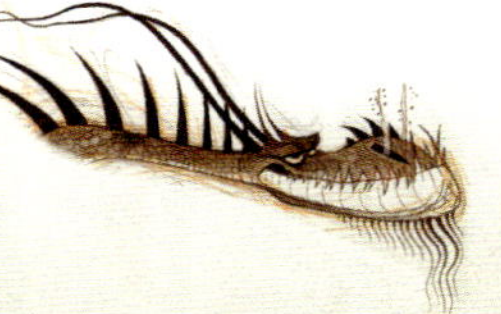
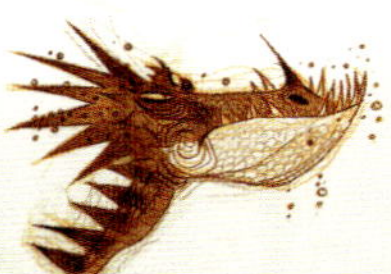
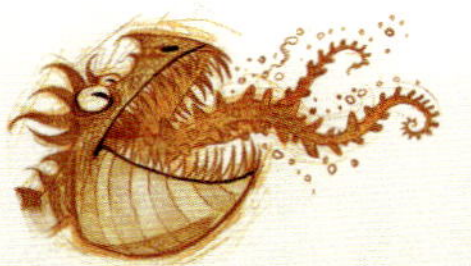
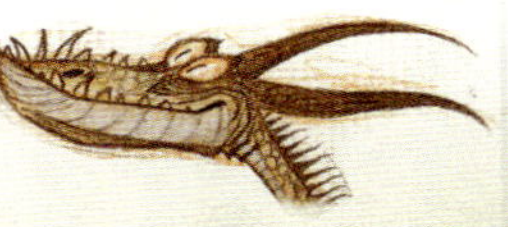
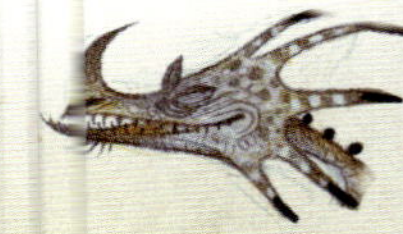

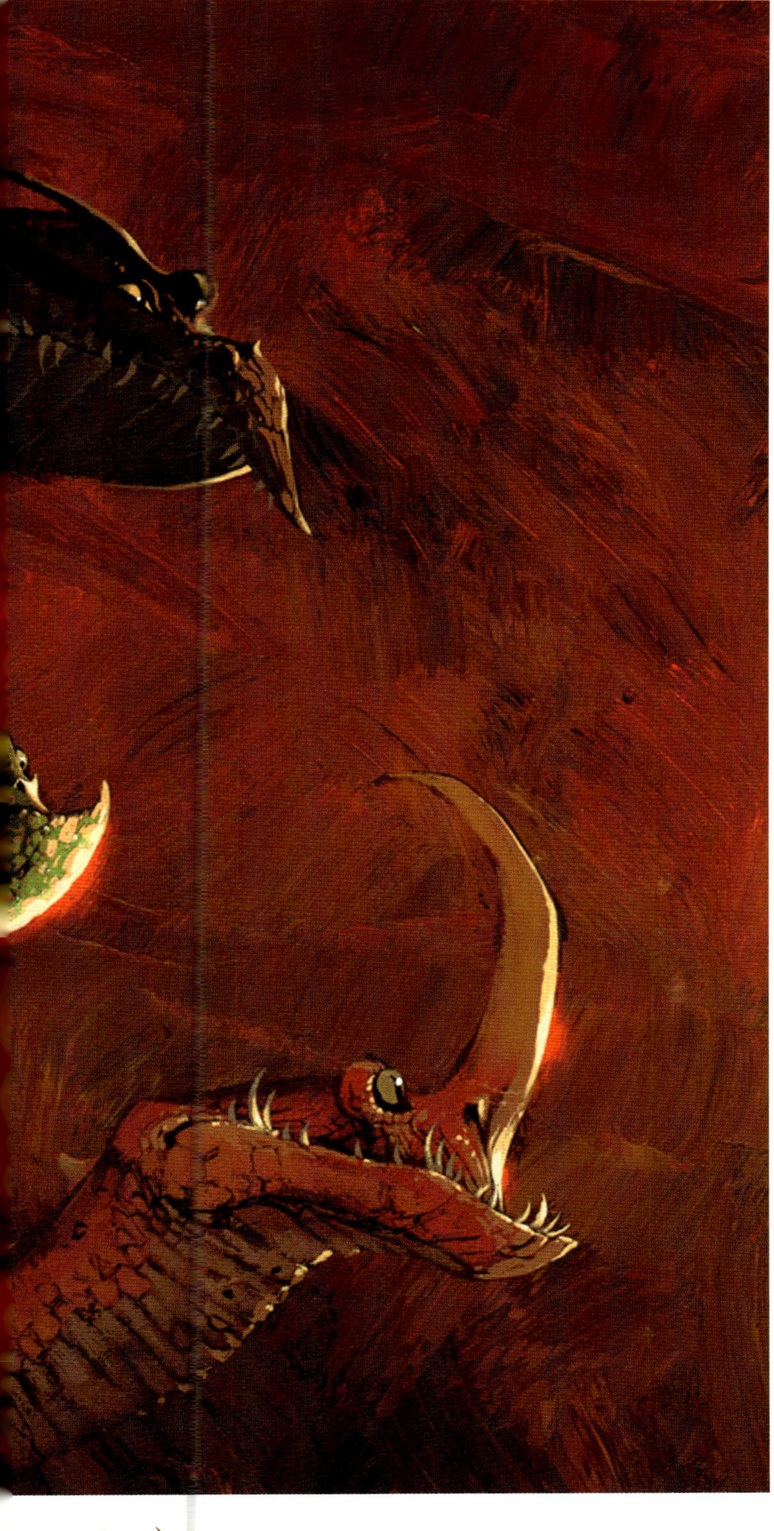

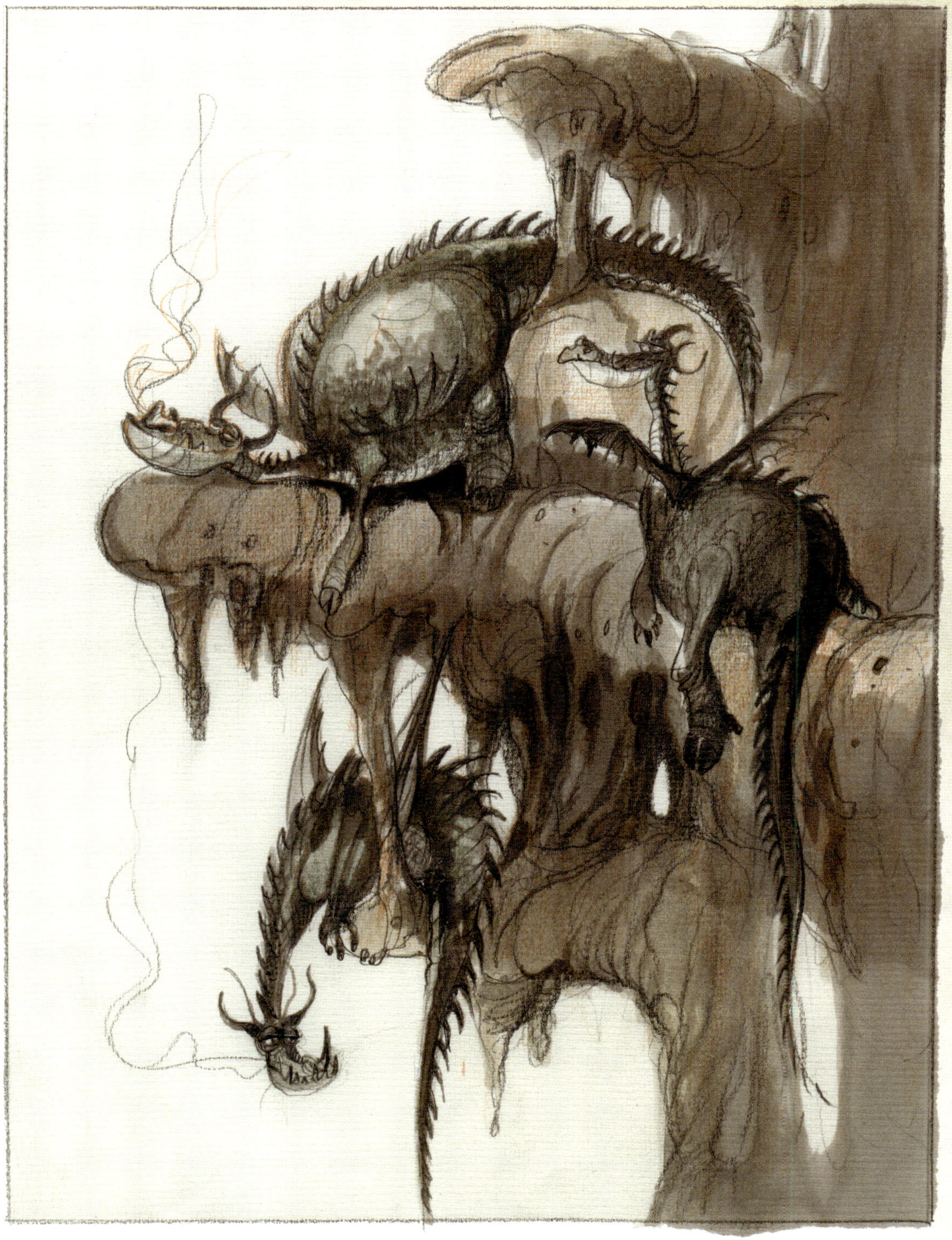

(left) **Dragons Staring** — Jean Francois-Rey — acrylic. *(above)* **Dragon Nursery** — Emil Mitev — digital paint. *(below)* **Dragon Heads** — Nico Marlet — pencil & marker.

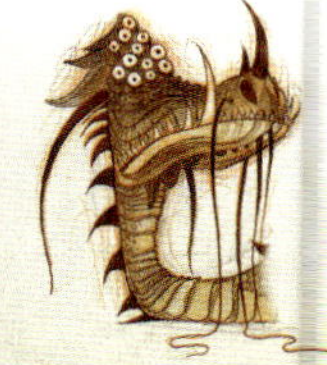
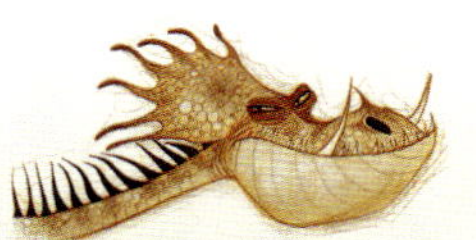
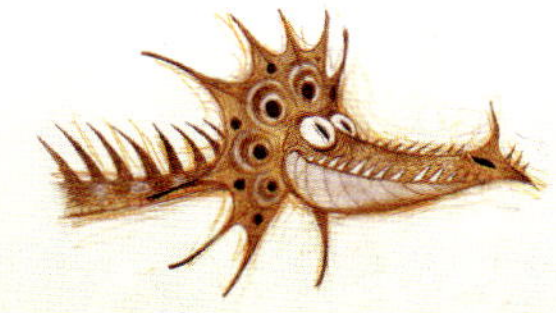
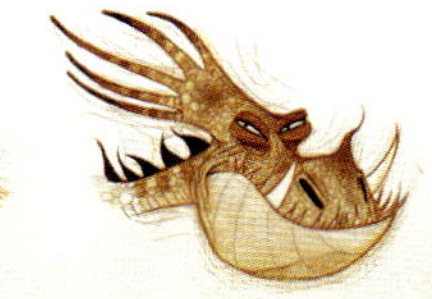
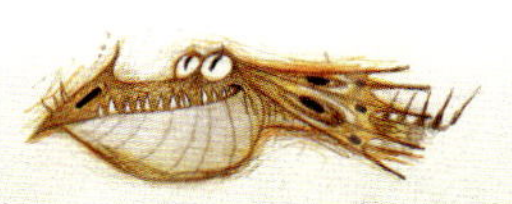
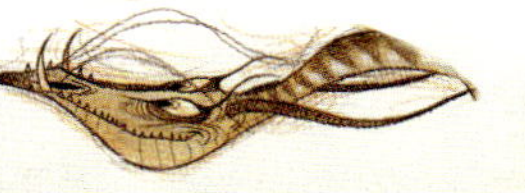
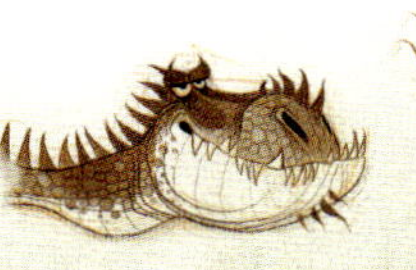
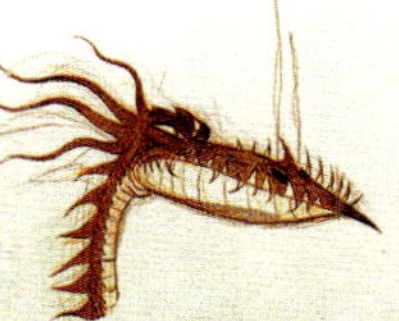

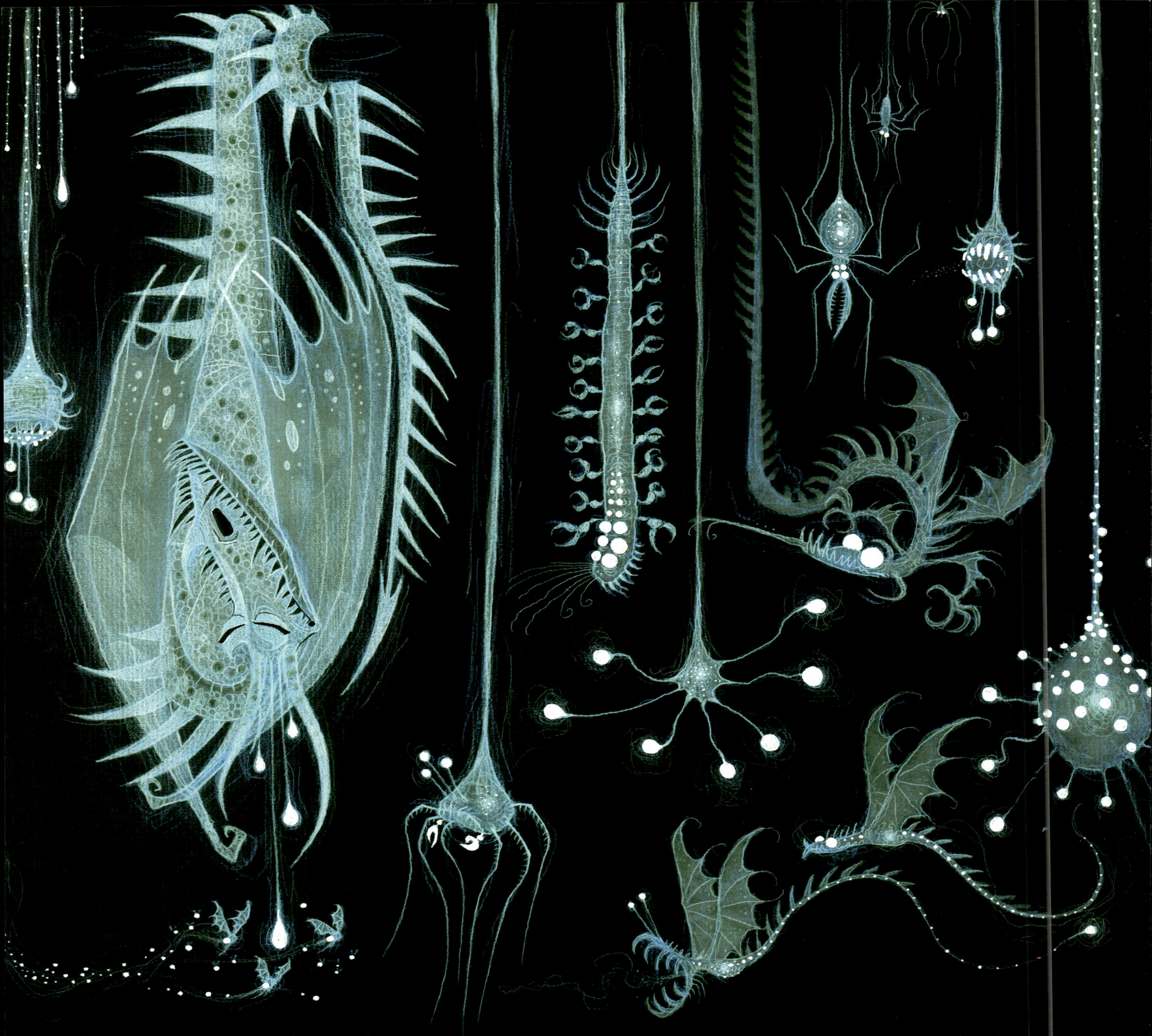

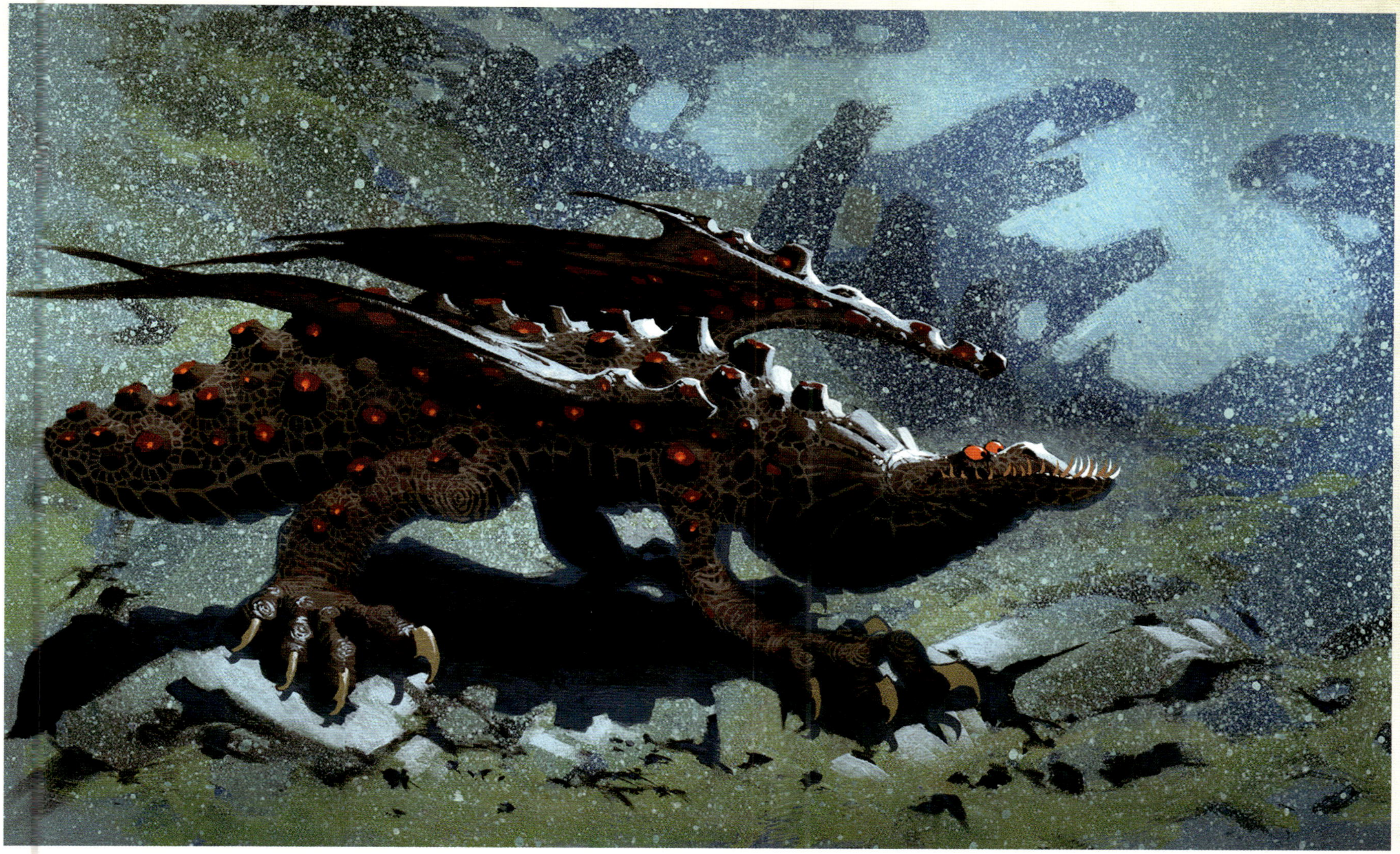

(left) **Cave Creatures** — Nico Marlet — pencil & marker. *(above)* **Dragon Concept** — Jean Francois-Rey — acrylic. *(below)* **Dragon LIneup** — Nico Marlet — pencil & marker.

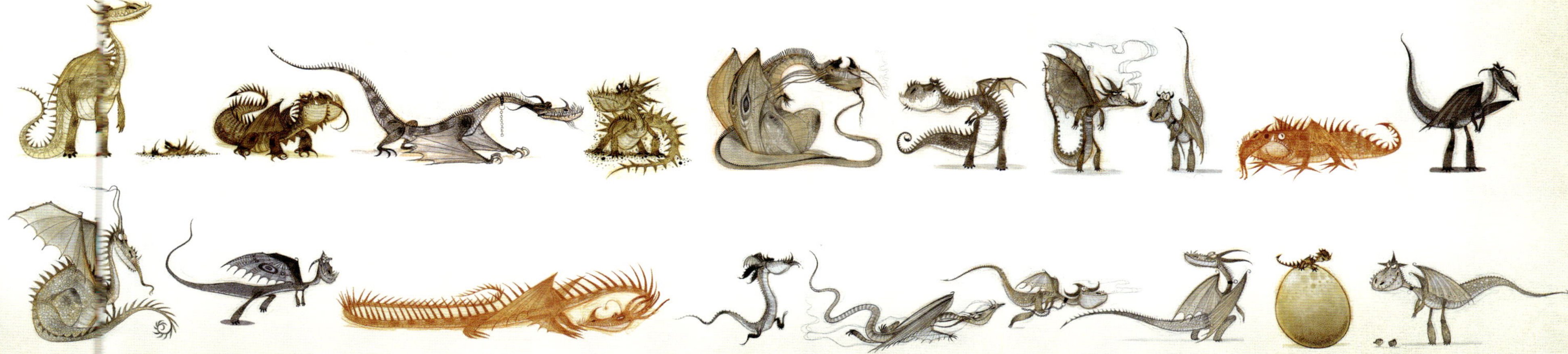

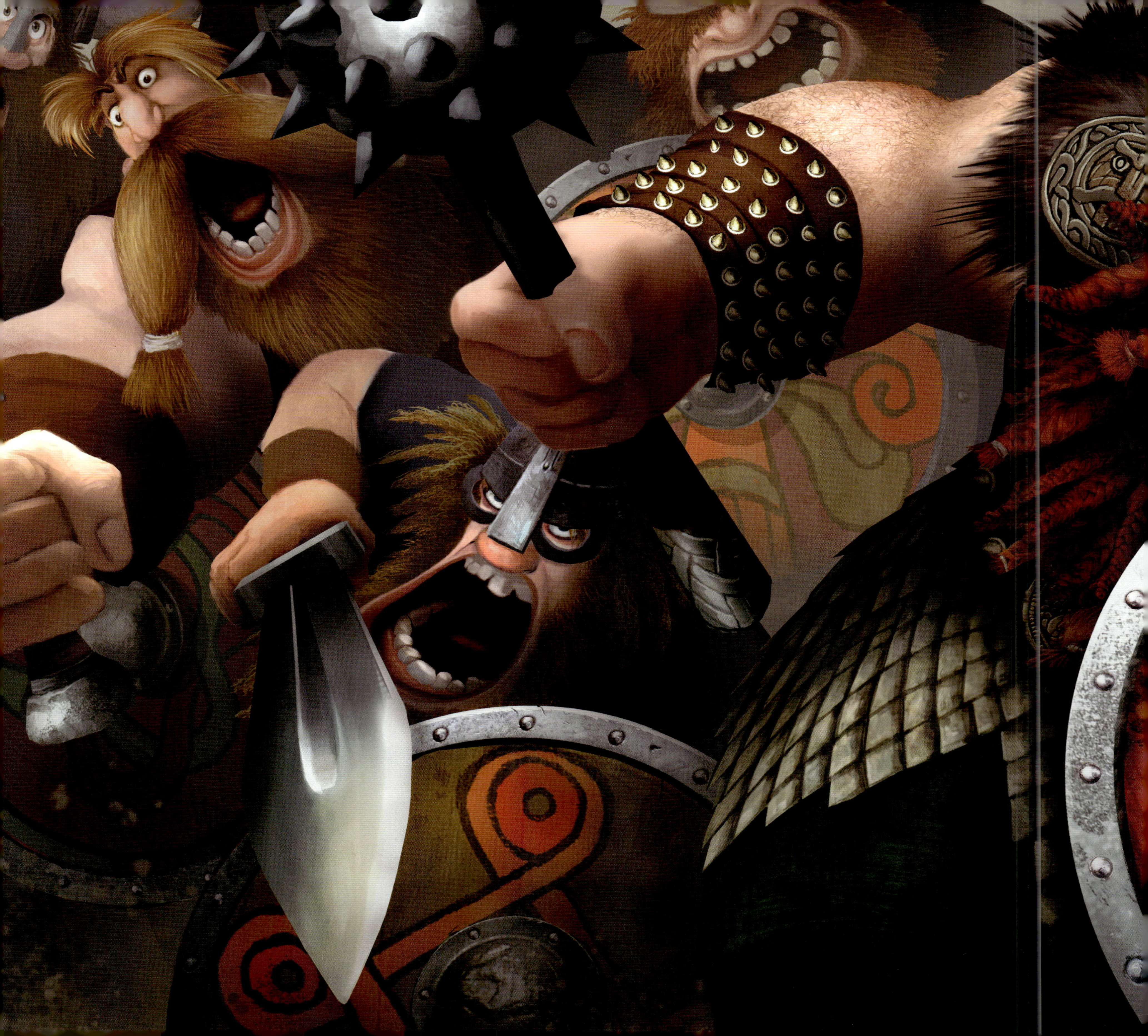

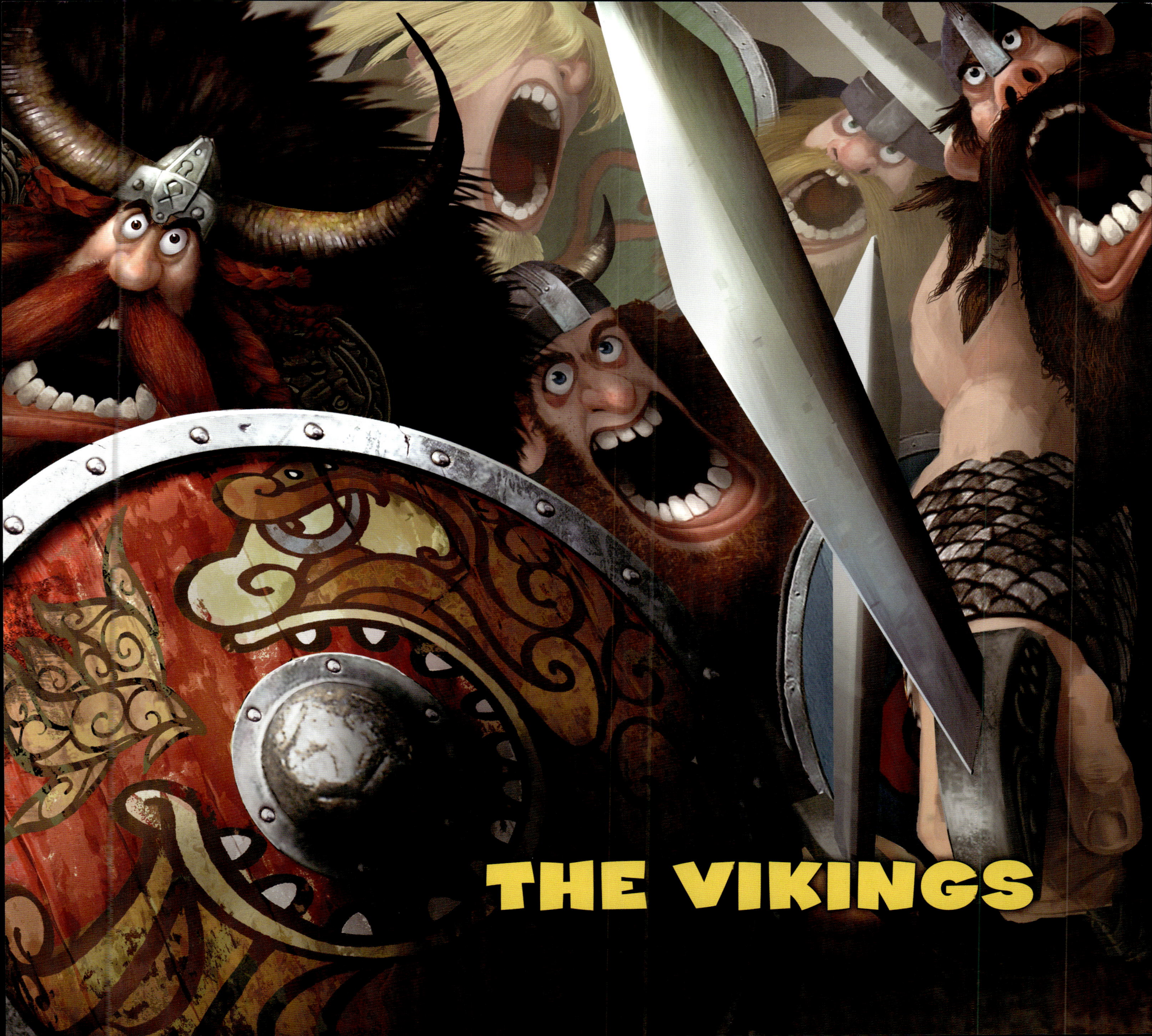

THE VIKINGS

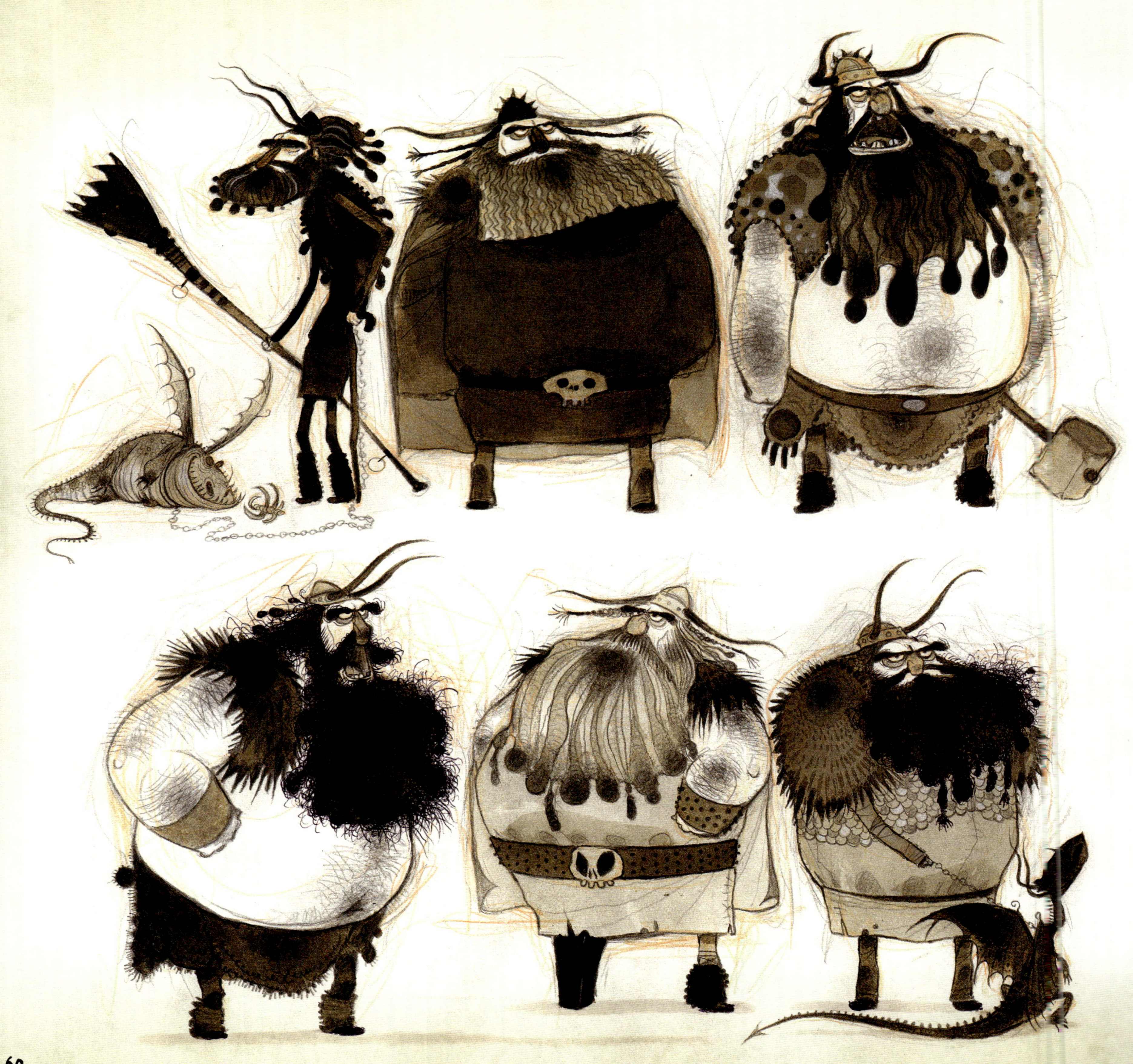

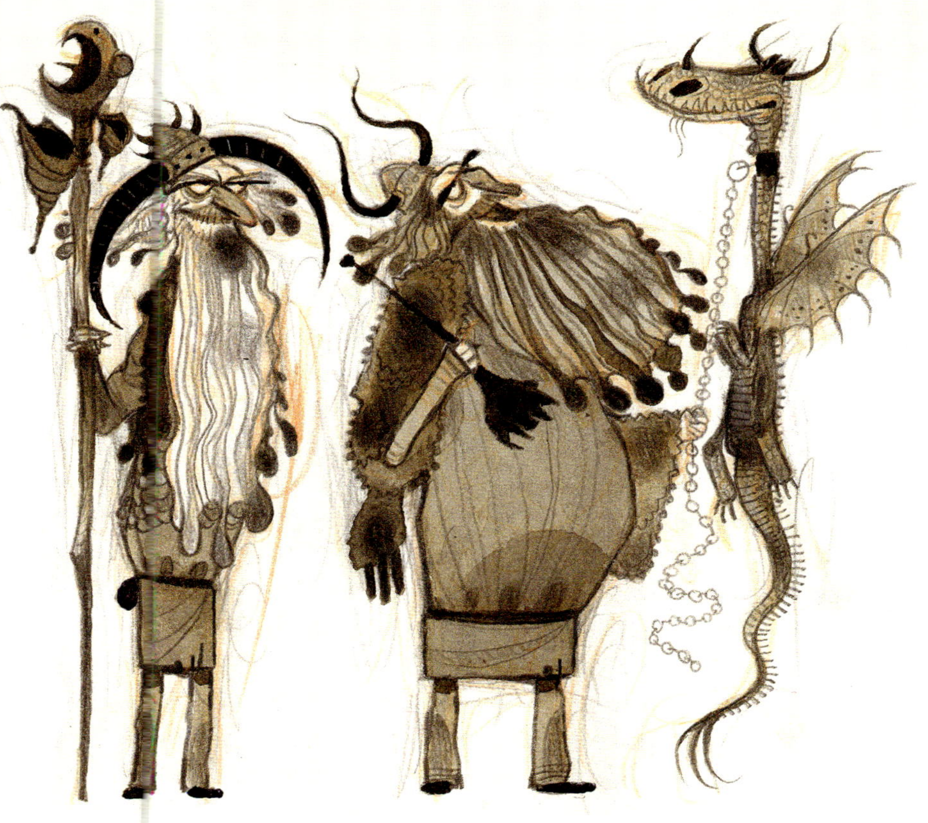

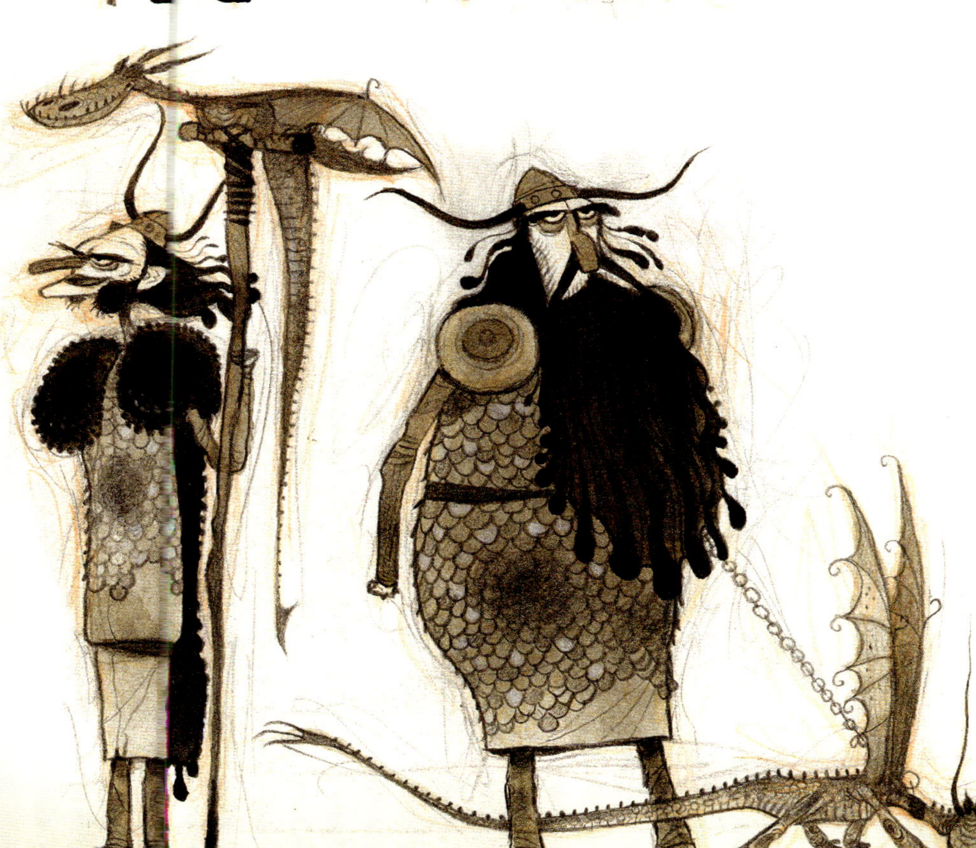

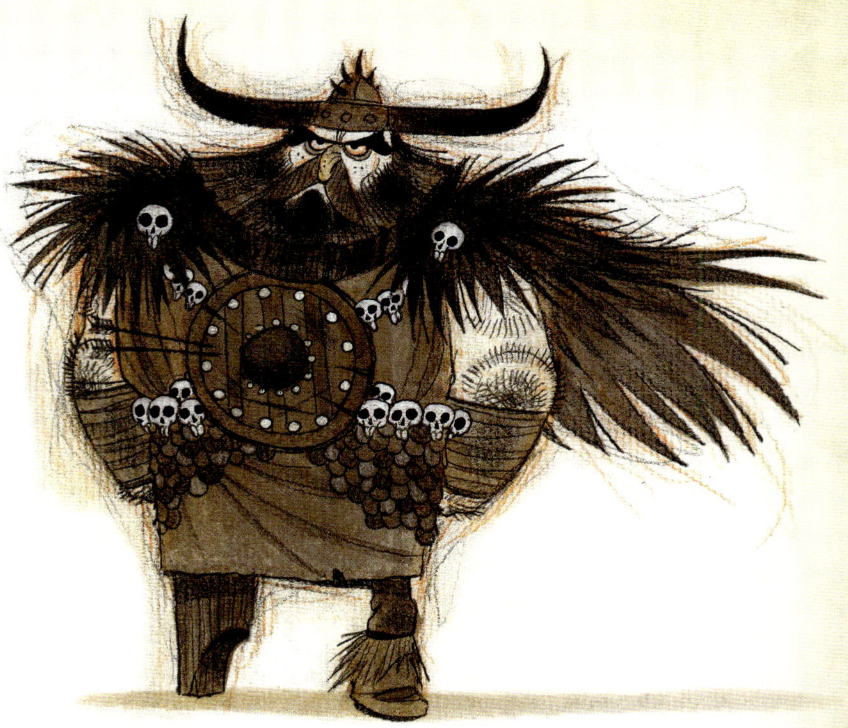

A Sturdy Cast of Characters

The Viking people possess their own energy and style, an intriguing mix of barbarianism, brute force and bullheaded loyalty to one another. It was important to the artistic crew of this film to channel that unique spirit into their cast. Character Designer Nicolas Marlet developed a shape language that conveyed a sense of physical strength using solid bases of squares and rectangles and then created a very diverse lineup of characters from there.

Models for the human characters were built with great enough detail to appear naked, all the way down to each of their toes. "We do that just in case they end up losing their shirts or other accessories somewhere in the story, plus it helps make clothing contact more realistic," explains Modeling Supervisor Matt Paulson. Speaking of wardrobe issues, the Viking costumes present a number of rigging and animation challenges due to their richly furred and/or chain-laden features. While the production did not want to make the cast look underdressed to account for technical concerns, "fur vests were used sparingly due to hair interactions and fur-topped boots were a problem because they kept penetrating the characters' legs when animated. So we simply rationalized that shorter, matted fur made sense on these items for both story and practical reasons," recalls Visual Effects Supervisor Craig Ring. While all costumes were rigged to move with the skin underneath them, some required special attention in order to portray a realistic motion, and the character effects department was quick to smooth out such issues.

(previous pages) **Viking Charge** — Pierre-Olivier Vincent — digital paint.

(left and above) **Sturdy Vikings** — Nico Marlet — pencil & marker.

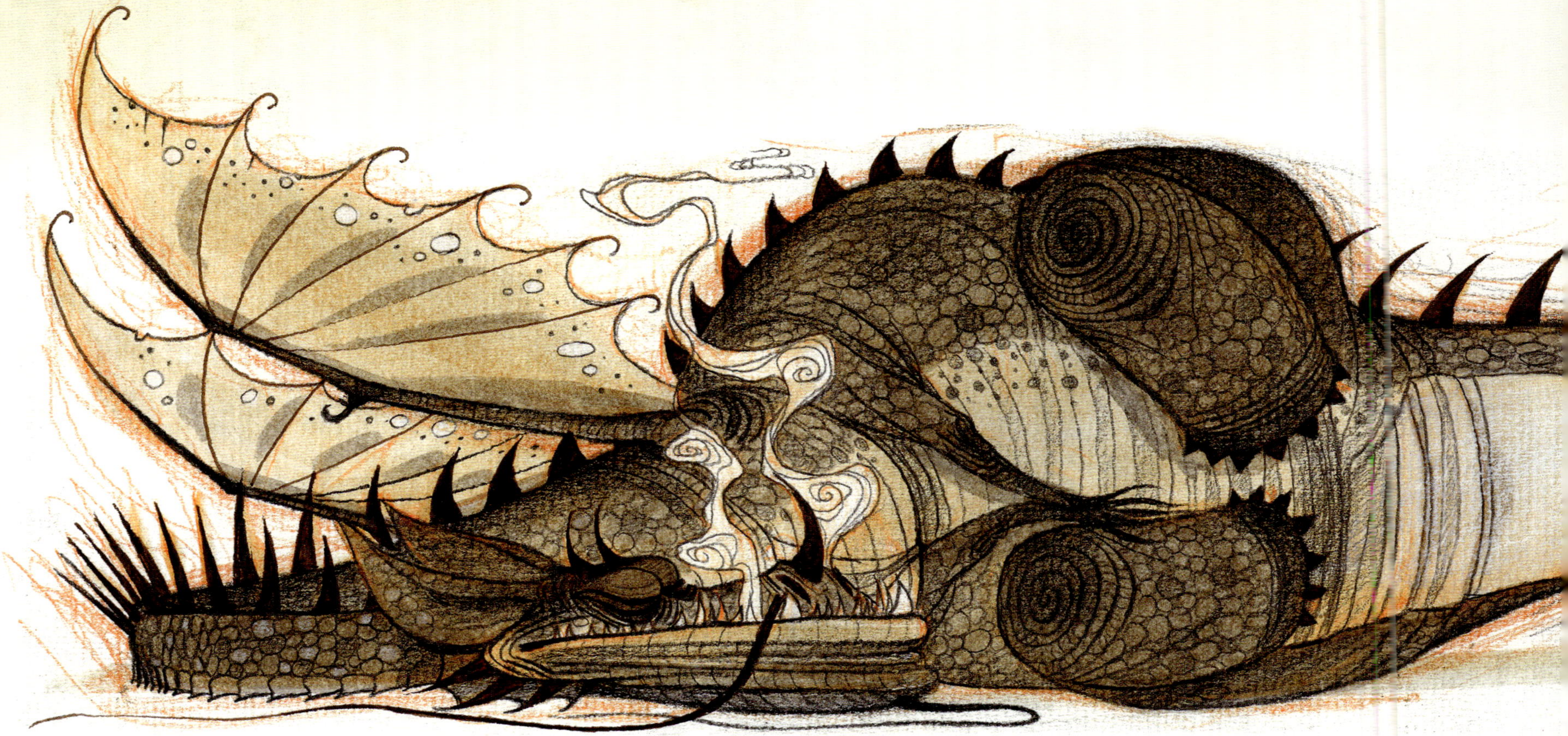

Hiccup

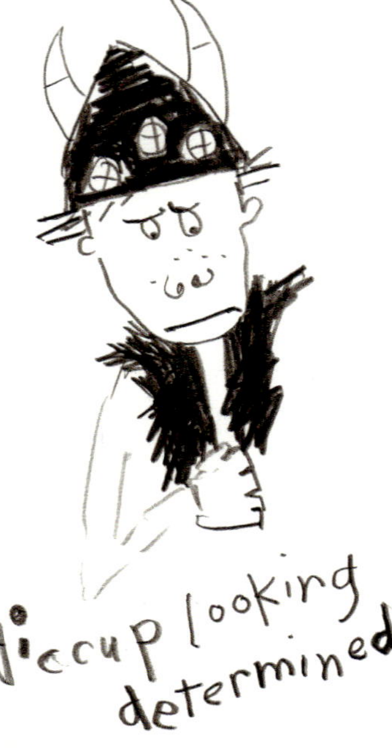

Developing Hiccup was a balancing act. He had to be appealing, but he also had to be enough of an individual to frustrate his father at the same time," explains Director Chris Sanders. As a teenager Hiccup still wants to be a true Viking but he has come to realize his intellect and physical stature are not typical Viking material. As such, "he feels he hasn't gotten his father's approval and respect," notes Director Dean DeBlois.

Hiccup grew up a lot over the course of this production, both in social maturity and physical design. In the earliest days of development, his character was much younger, pegged in the range of six or seven years of age and more aligned with the character in the original book. His final build and look is not as stylized as the other young characters in the film, which was a means to help the audience connect with him.

"It was important to make Hiccup a normal kid who would not stand out in our modern world—he's a smart, charming, and mild-mannered guy. It's when he's placed in the Viking world occupied by outrageous characters that he doesn't quite fit in, and the audience can empathize with this awkwardness," explains Head of Character Animation Simon Otto.

Our biggest challenge was taking the young Hiccup that Cressida Cowell had envisioned and turning him into a teenager. That he would maintain the appeal and charm Cowell had given him was important to the story.

—Bonnie Arnold, Producer

(above) **Hiccup** — Nico Marlet — pencil & marker. *(above left)* **Hiccup Determined** — Cressida Cowell — pencil.

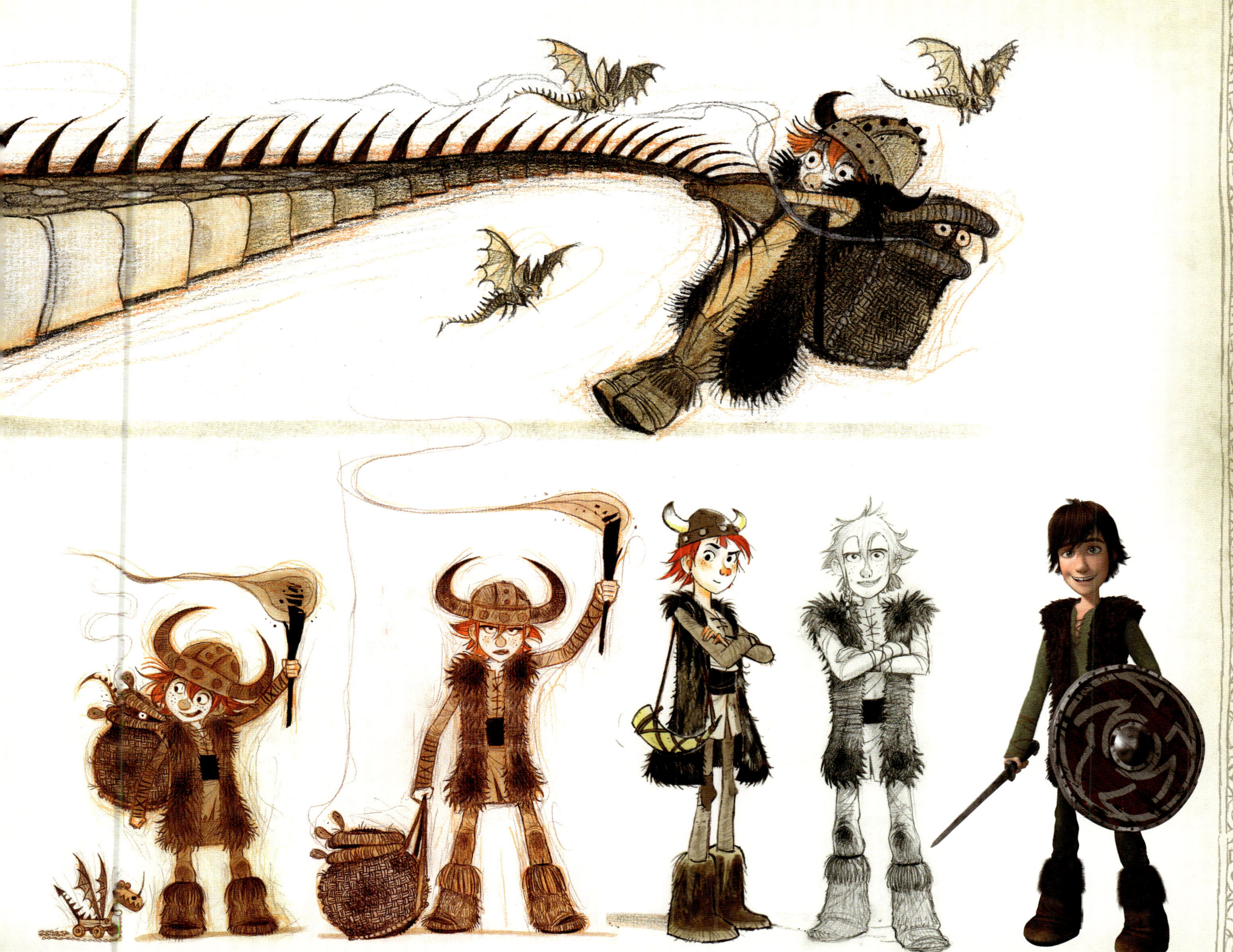

(above from left) **Hiccup 1** and **Hiccup 2** — Nico Marlet — pencil & marker; **Hiccup 3** — Carlos Grangel — pencil & marker; **Hiccup 4** — Simon Otto — pencil; **Hiccup Final** — Takao Noguchi — CG rough model.

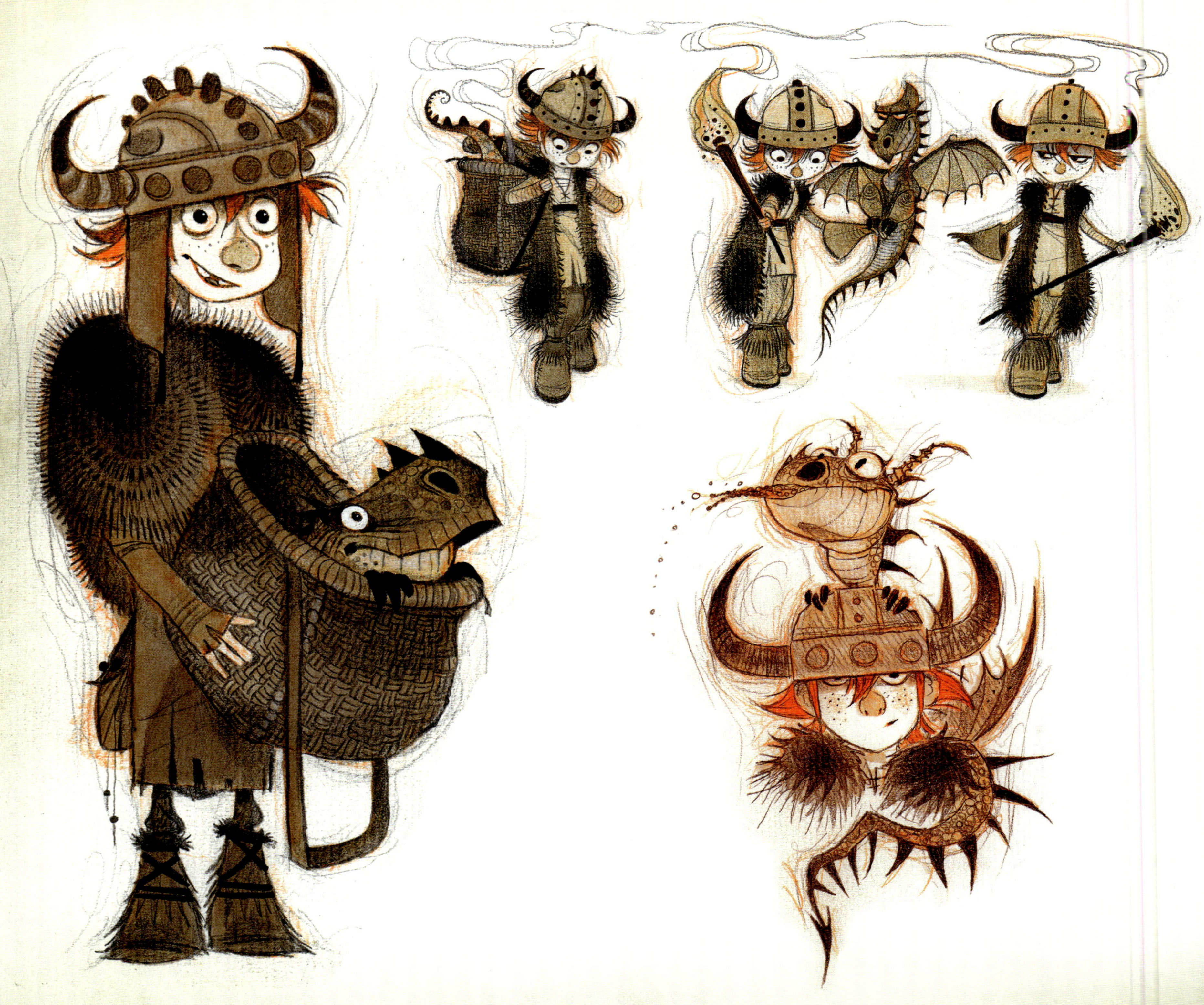

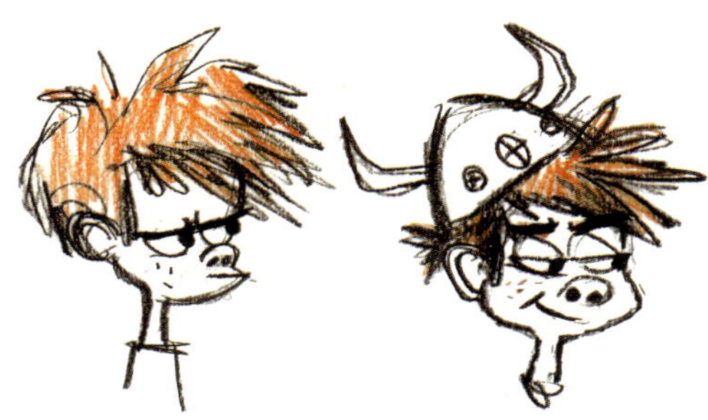

This classic archetypal protagonist tends to go either the arrogant way: "You are all wrong and you'll see," or the self-deprecating one: "I am lame, I wish I could be like all of you." We went with the latter; we wanted a more empathetic character, a humble protagonist that learns the value of himself and is accepted for who he is.

—Alessandro Carloni, Head of Story

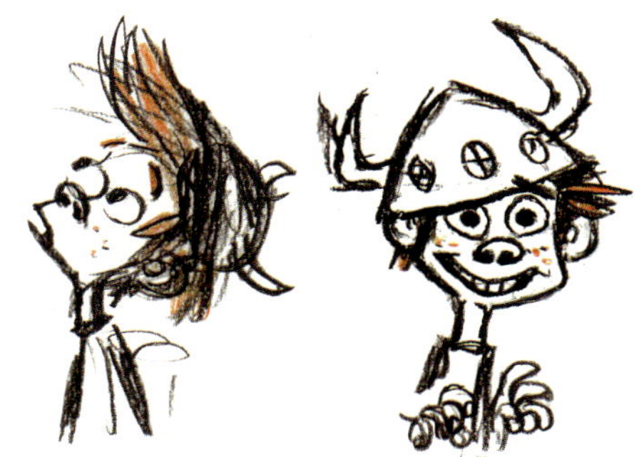

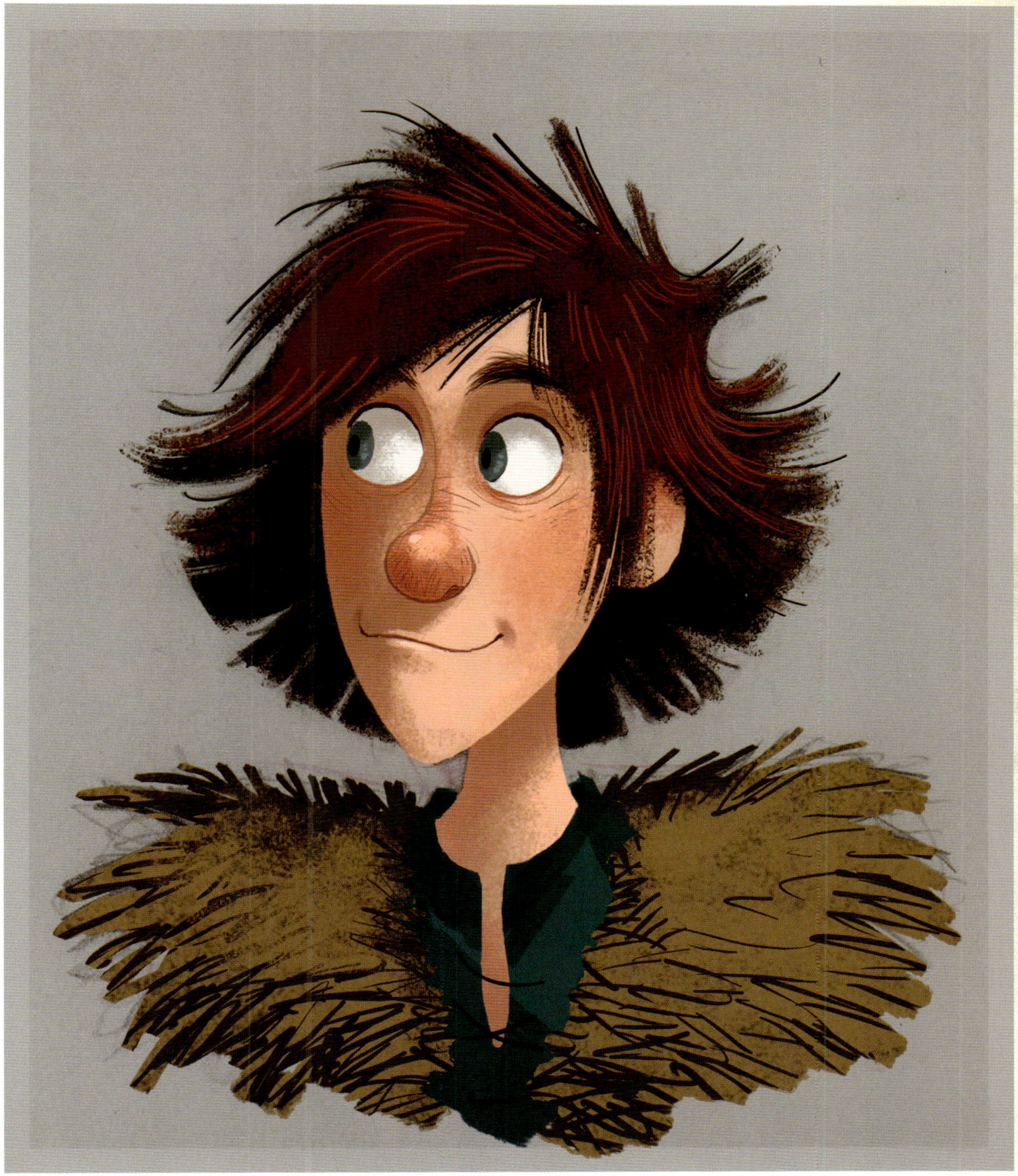

(far left and above) **Hiccup** — Nico Marlet — pencil & marker. *(left)* **Hiccup** — David Soren — pencil. *(above)* **Hiccup** — Nico Marlet — pencil & marker. *(above right)* **Hiccup** — Shane Prigmore — digital paint.

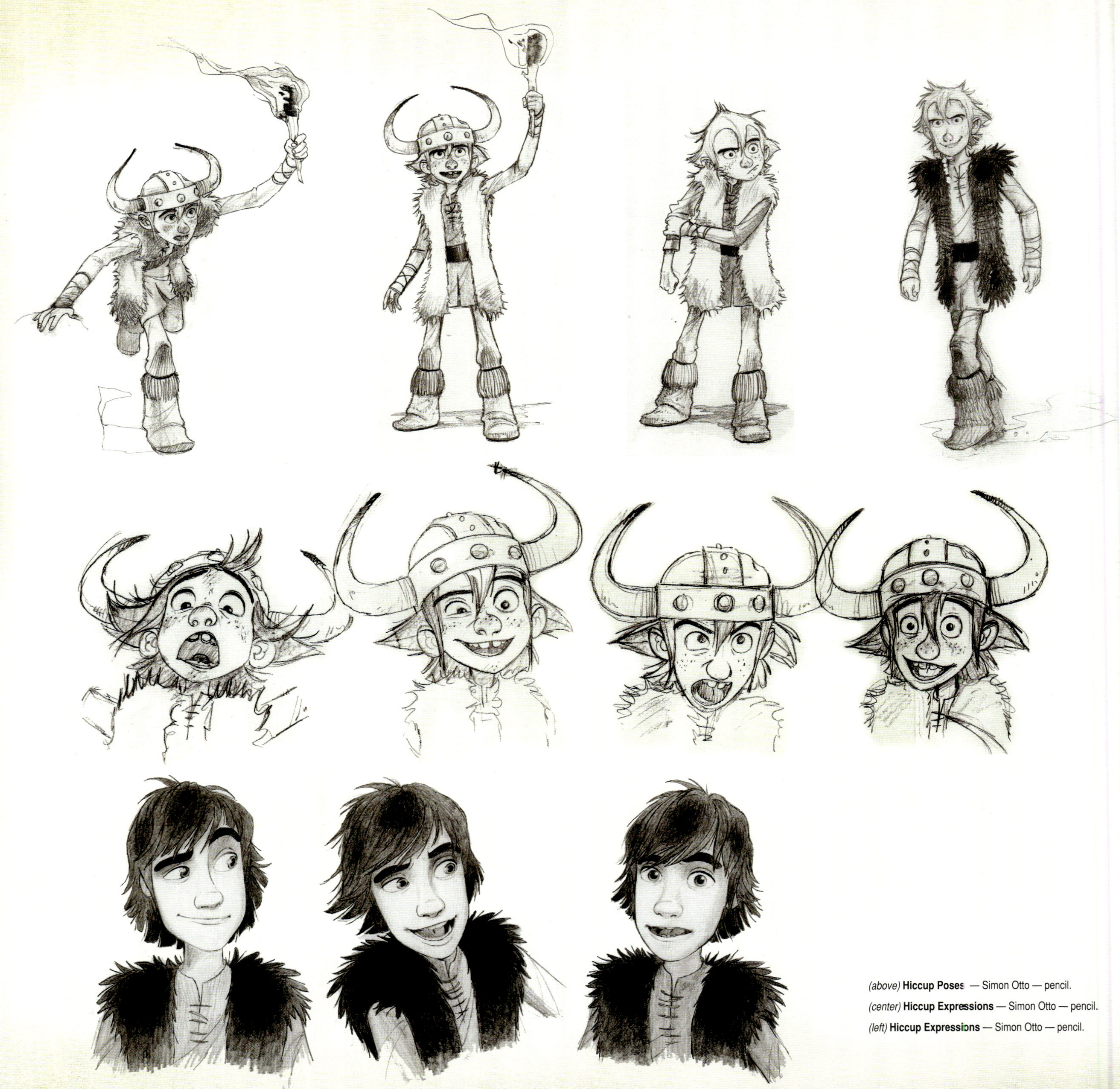

(above) **Hiccup Poses** — Simon Otto — pencil.

(center) **Hiccup Expressions** — Simon Otto — pencil.

(left) **Hiccup Expressions** — Simon Otto — pencil.

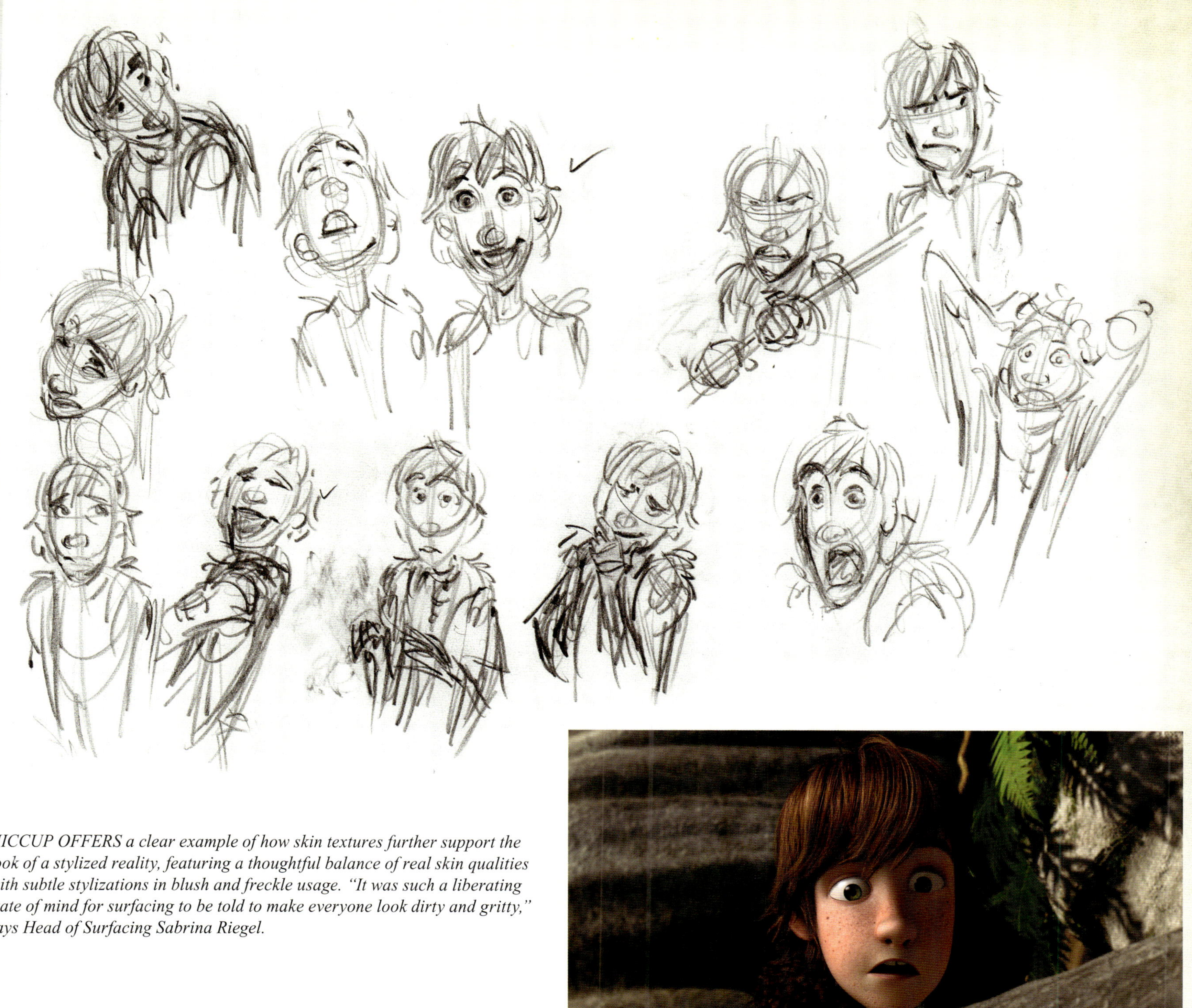

HICCUP OFFERS a clear example of how skin textures further support the look of a stylized reality, featuring a thoughtful balance of real skin qualities with subtle stylizations in blush and freckle usage. "It was such a liberating state of mind for surfacing to be told to make everyone look dirty and gritty," says Head of Surfacing Sabrina Riegel.

(above) **Hiccup Expressions** — Gabe Hordos — pencil. *(right)* **CG Still.**

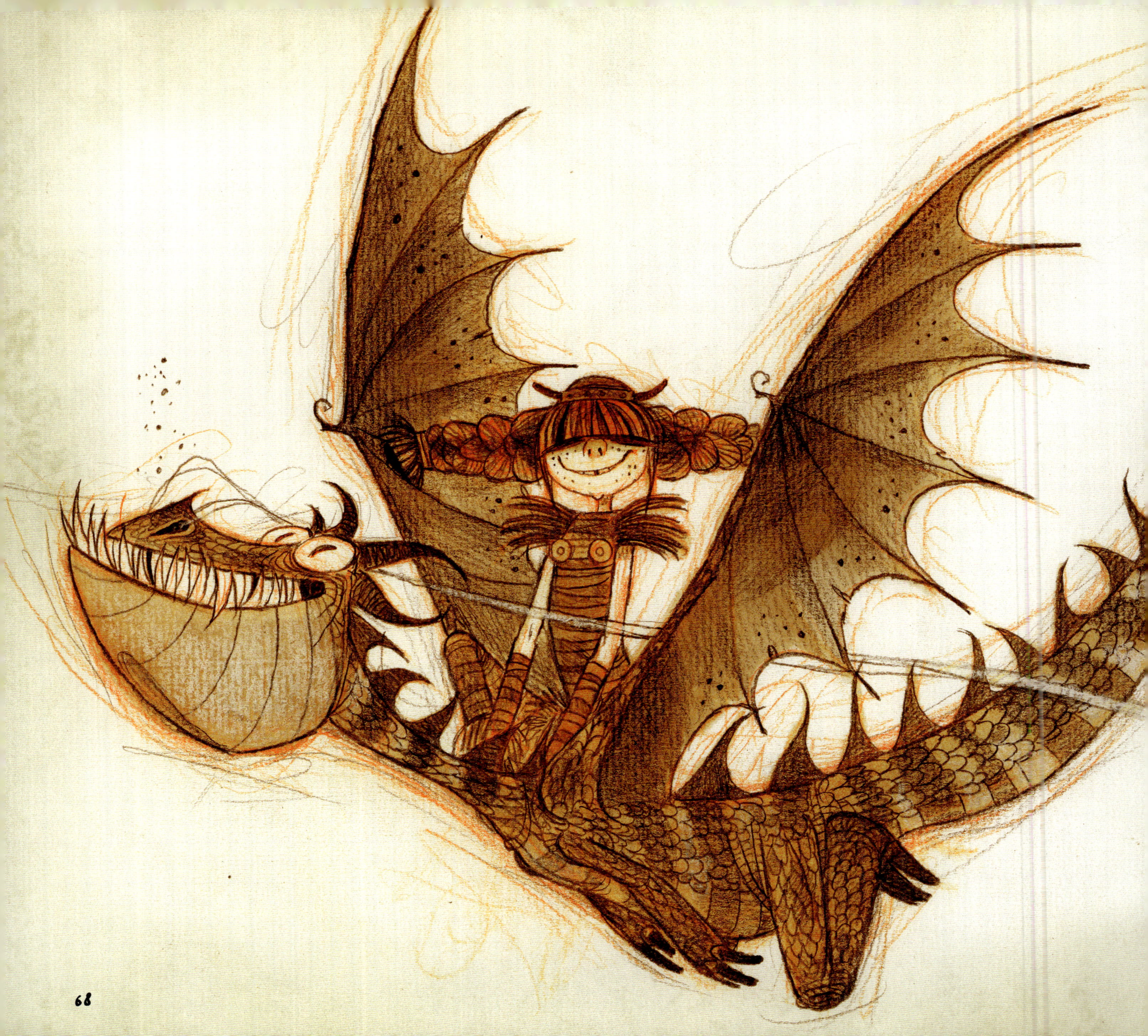

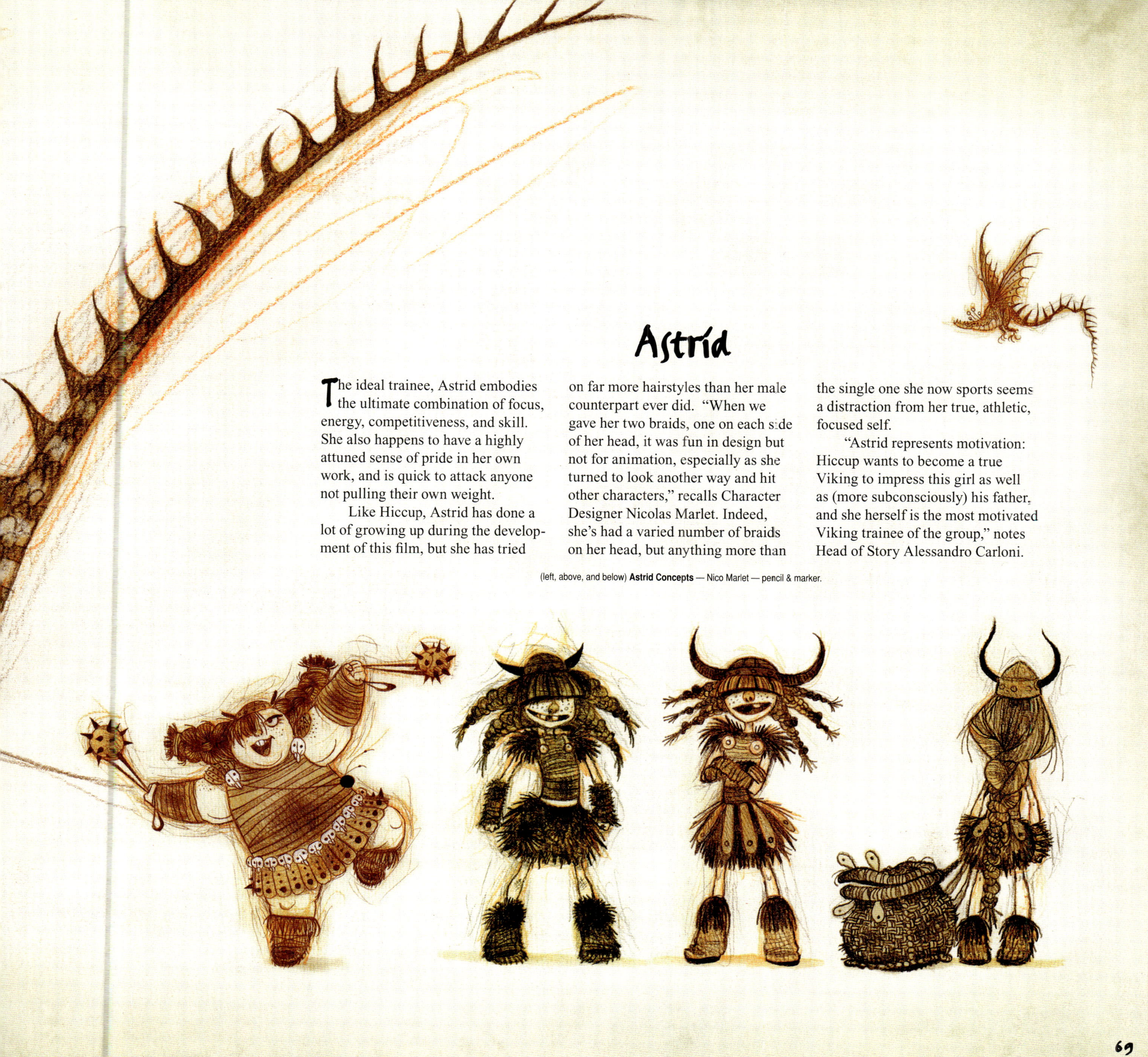

Astrid

The ideal trainee, Astrid embodies the ultimate combination of focus, energy, competitiveness, and skill. She also happens to have a highly attuned sense of pride in her own work, and is quick to attack anyone not pulling their own weight.

Like Hiccup, Astrid has done a lot of growing up during the development of this film, but she has tried on far more hairstyles than her male counterpart ever did. "When we gave her two braids, one on each side of her head, it was fun in design but not for animation, especially as she turned to look another way and hit other characters," recalls Character Designer Nicolas Marlet. Indeed, she's had a varied number of braids on her head, but anything more than the single one she now sports seems a distraction from her true, athletic, focused self.

"Astrid represents motivation: Hiccup wants to become a true Viking to impress this girl as well as (more subconsciously) his father, and she herself is the most motivated Viking trainee of the group," notes Head of Story Alessandro Carloni.

(left, above, and below) **Astrid Concepts** — Nico Marlet — pencil & marker.

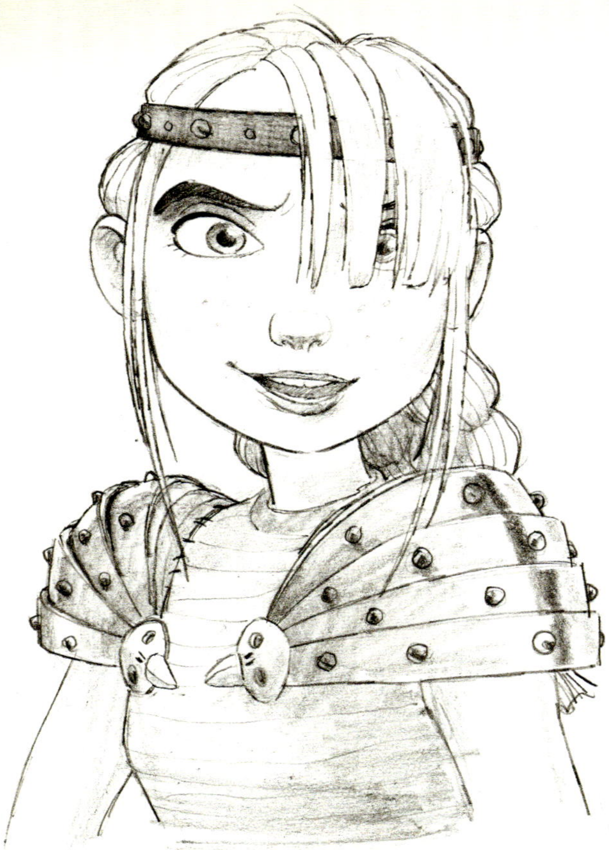

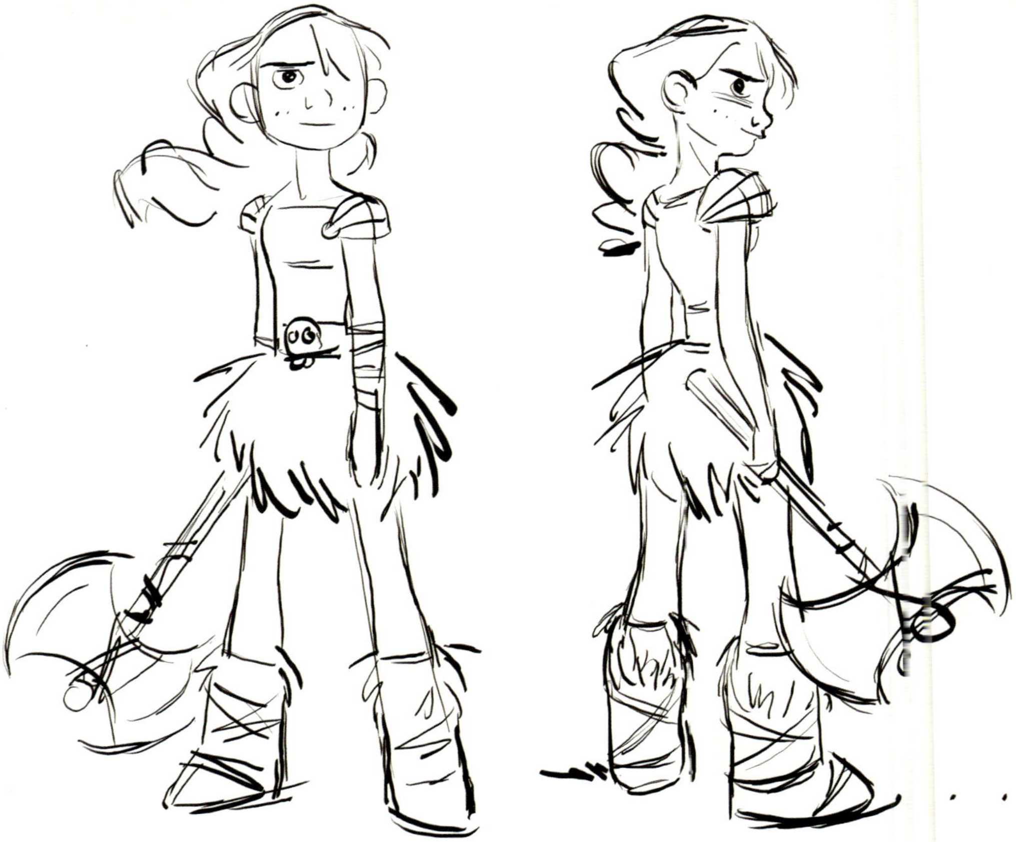

We love that she is more of a lean, athletic beach volleyball player as opposed to the bulky, shot-putting type of Viking woman.

—Simon Otto, Head of Character Animation

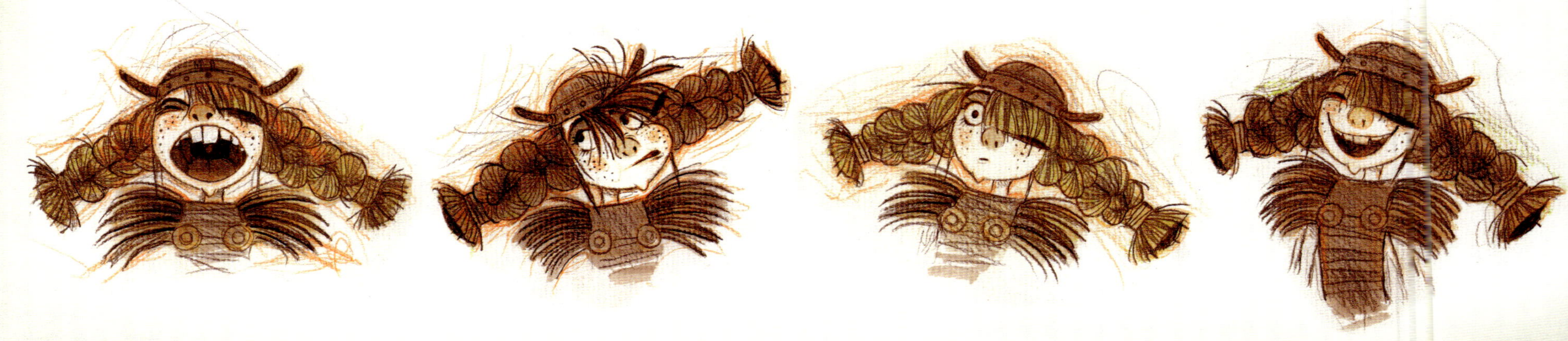

(top left) **Astrid Expression** — Simon Otto — pencil. *(top right)* **Astrid Story Sketch** — Tron Mai — digital paint. *(above)* **Astrid** — Nico Marlet — pencil & marker.

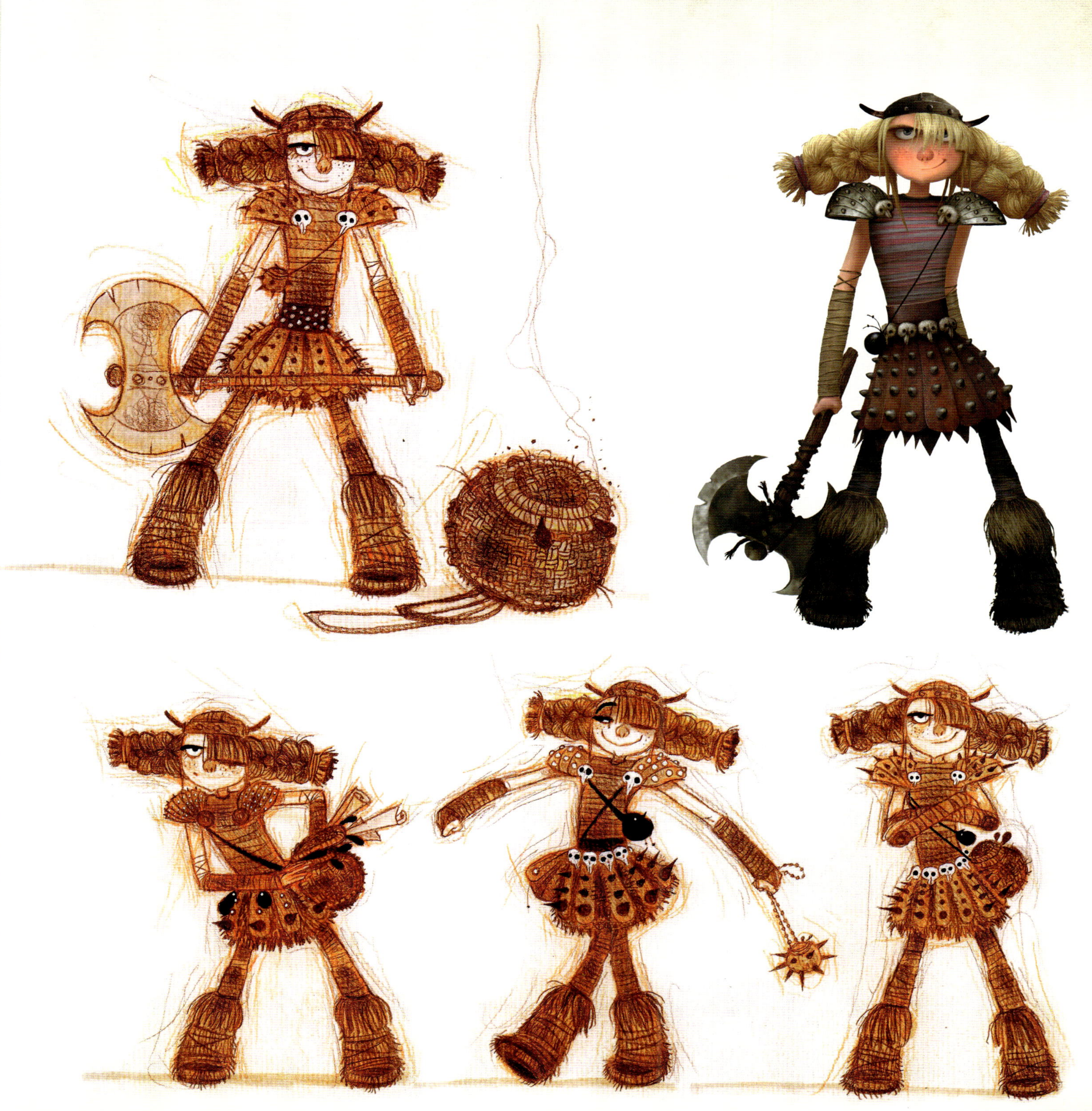

(top left and bottom) **Astrid** — Nico Marlet — pencil & marker. *(top right)* **Astrid Final** — Nico Marlet — character desigr — Zhaoping Wei — digital paint.

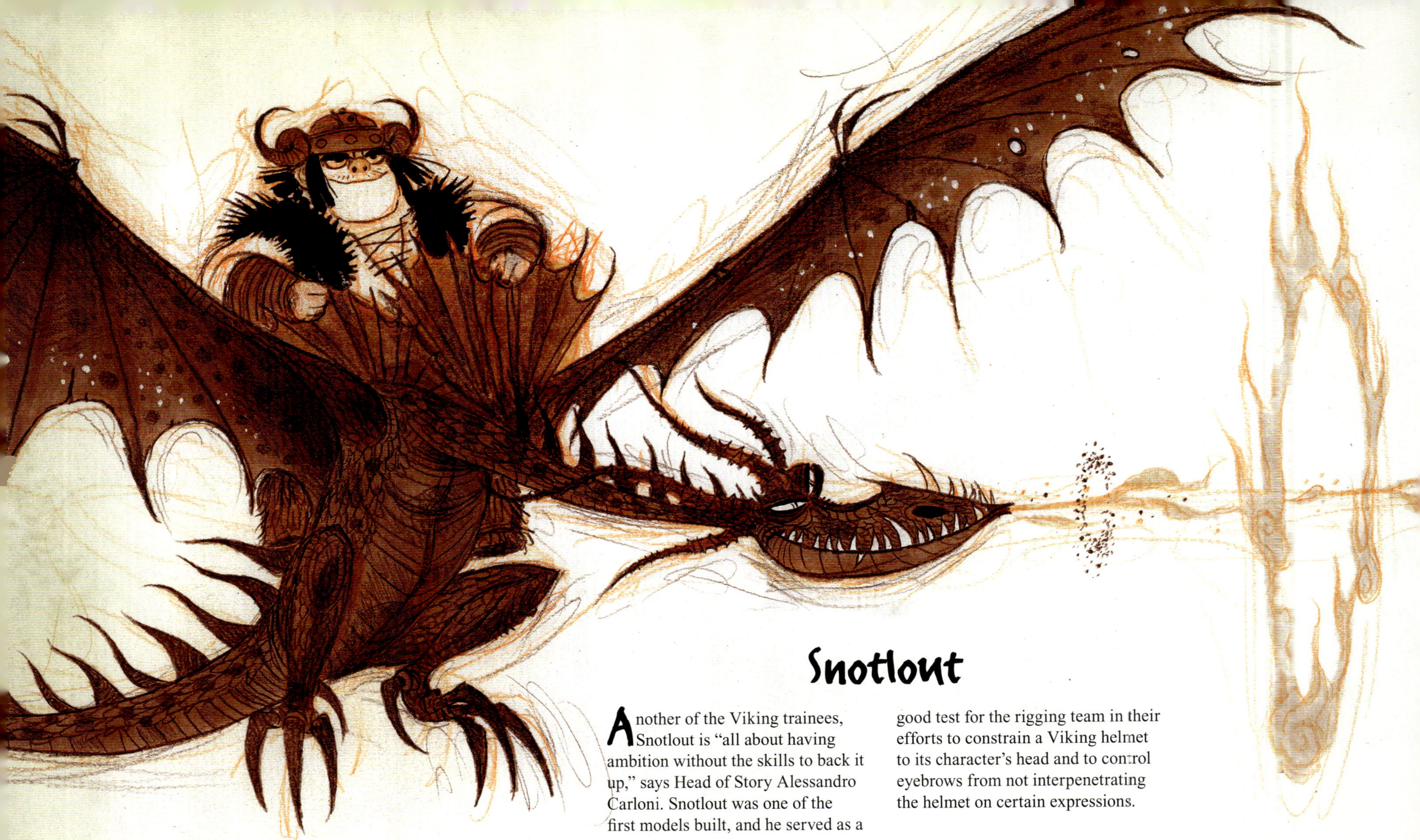

Snotlout

Another of the Viking trainees, Snotlout is "all about having ambition without the skills to back it up," says Head of Story Alessandro Carloni. Snotlout was one of the first models built, and he served as a good test for the rigging team in their efforts to constrain a Viking helmet to its character's head and to control eyebrows from not interpenetrating the helmet on certain expressions.

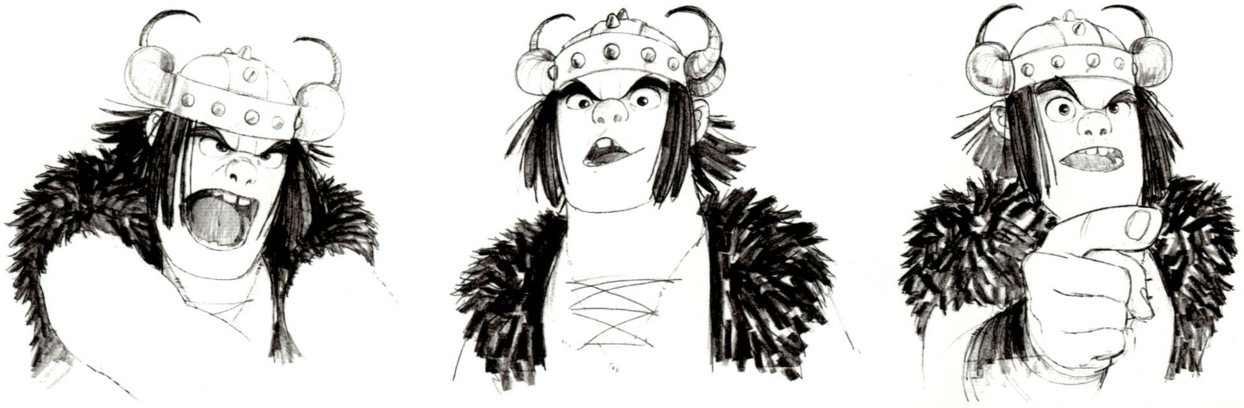

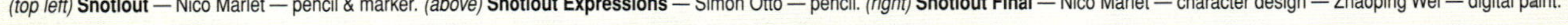

(top left) **Snotlout** — Nico Marlet — pencil & marker. *(above)* **Snotlout Expressions** — Simon Otto — pencil. *(right)* **Snotlout Final** — Nico Marlet — character design — Zhaoping Wei — digital paint.

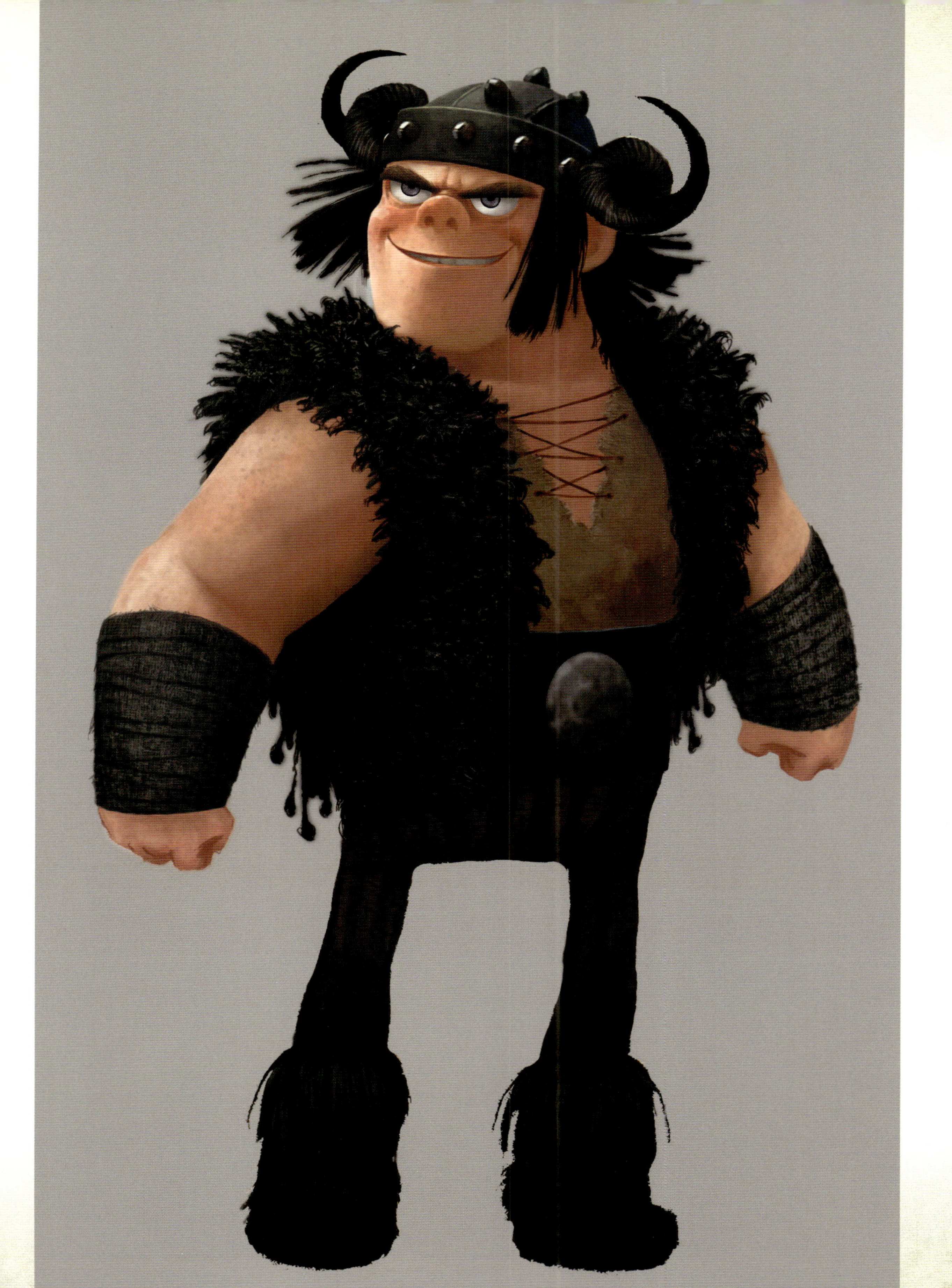

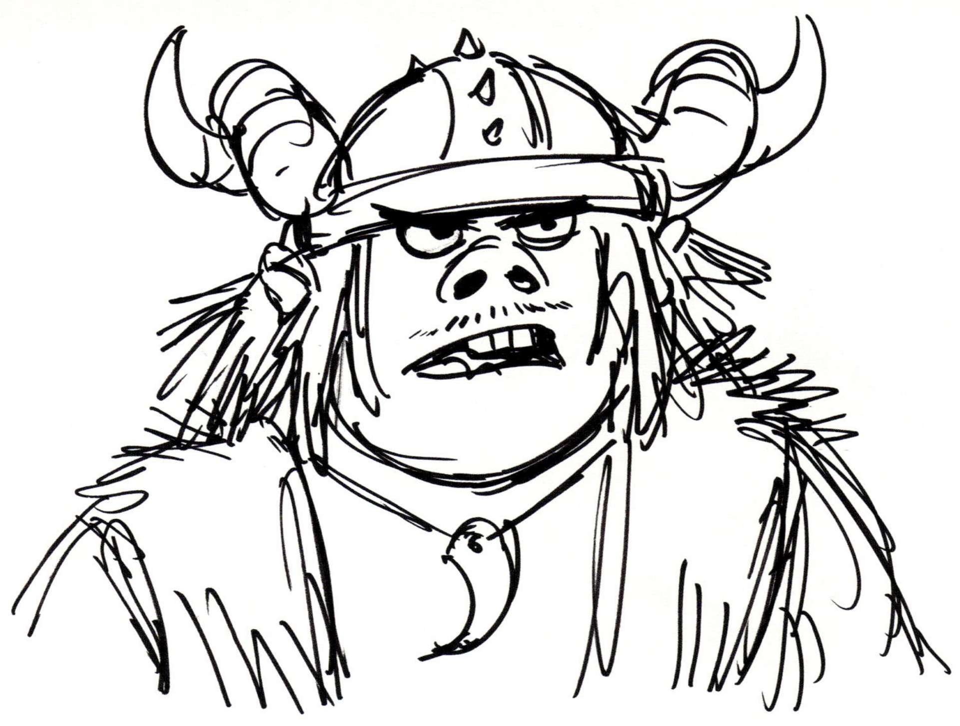

(above) **Snotlout** — Lorna Cook — marker. *(below)* **Snotlout Expressions** — Nico Marlet — pencil & marker.

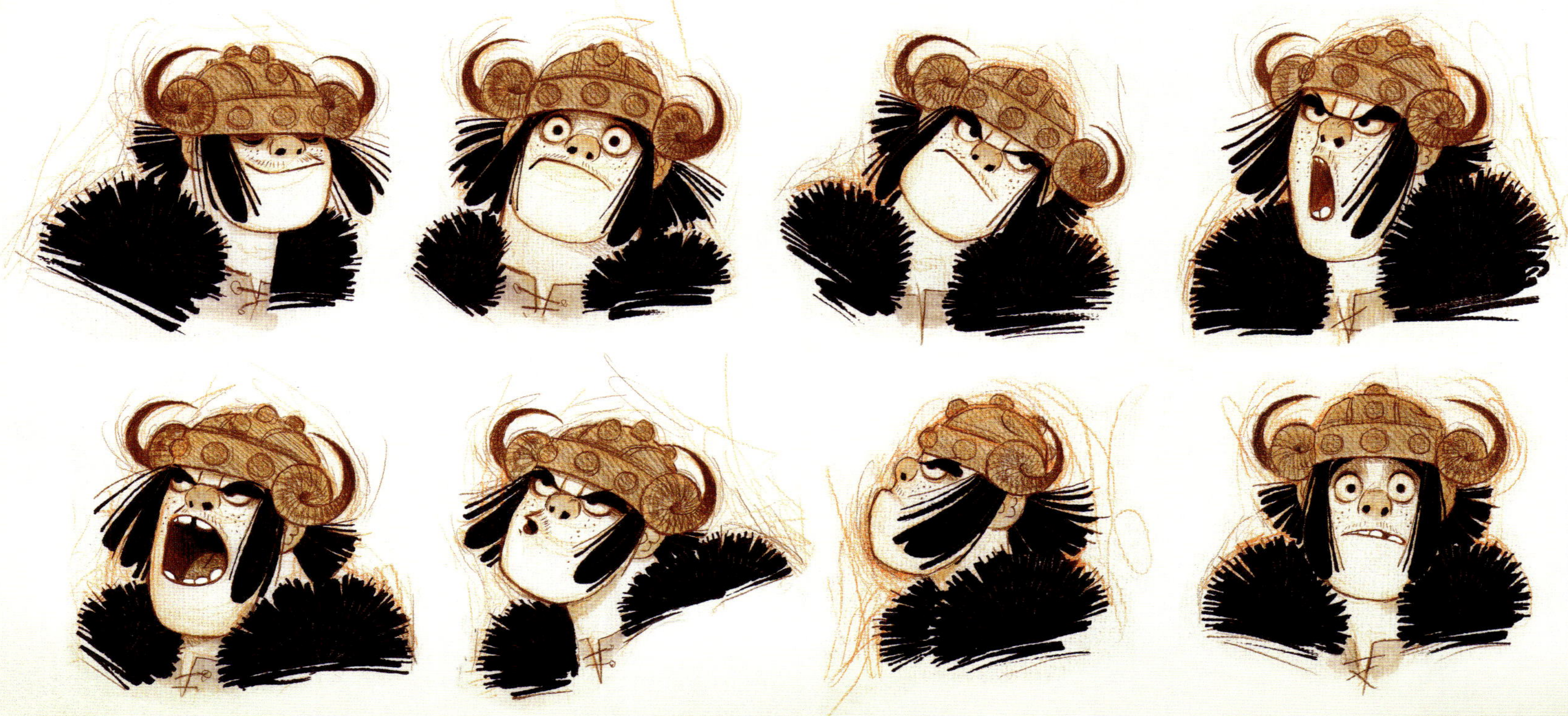

AT ONE POINT in character development, there was a consideration of making Snotlout a female, and a tough one at that. But it's probably not wise to mock this kid for wearing a dress now.

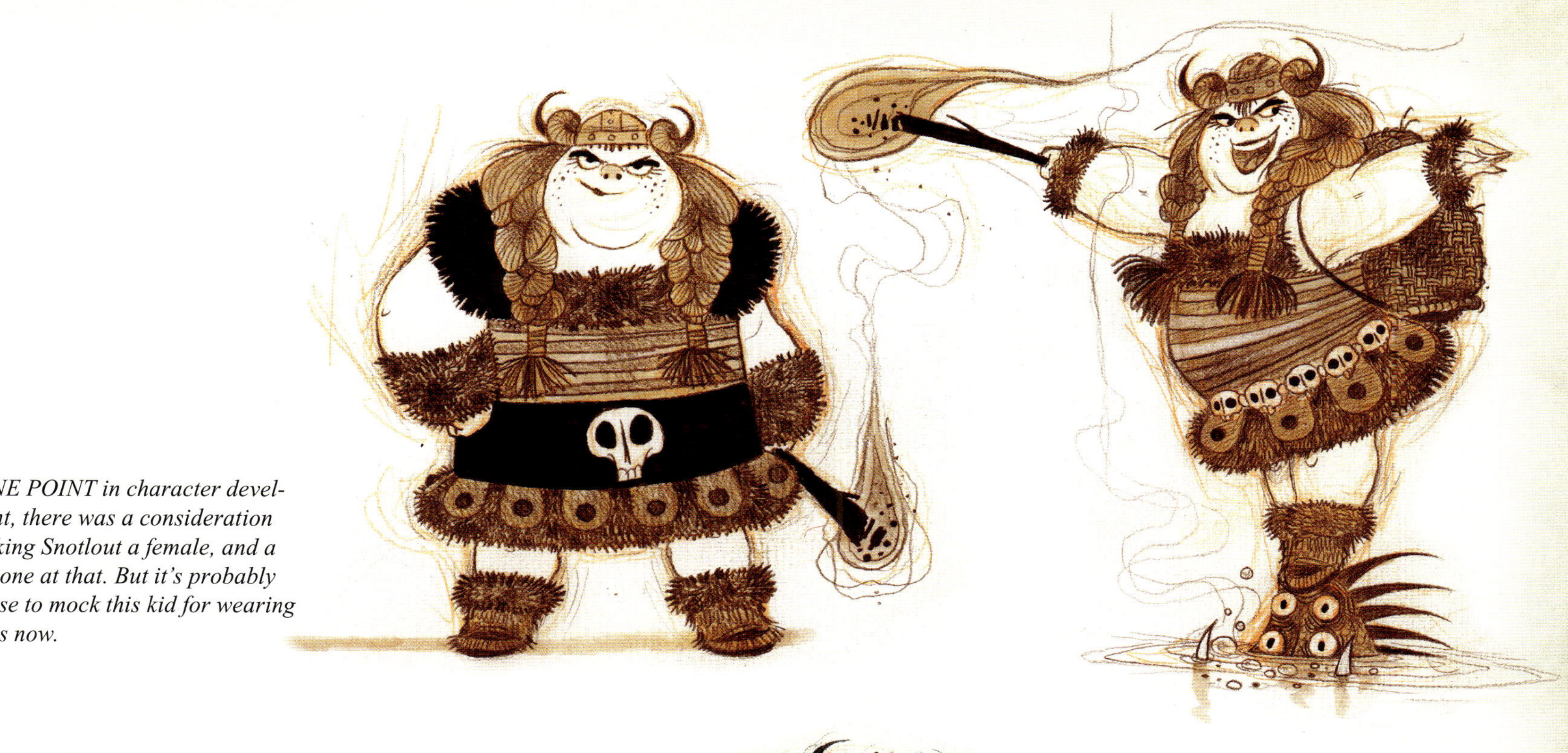

(above) **Snotlout Girl** — Nico Marlet — pencil & marker.

(below) **Snotlout** — Nico Marlet — pencil & marker.

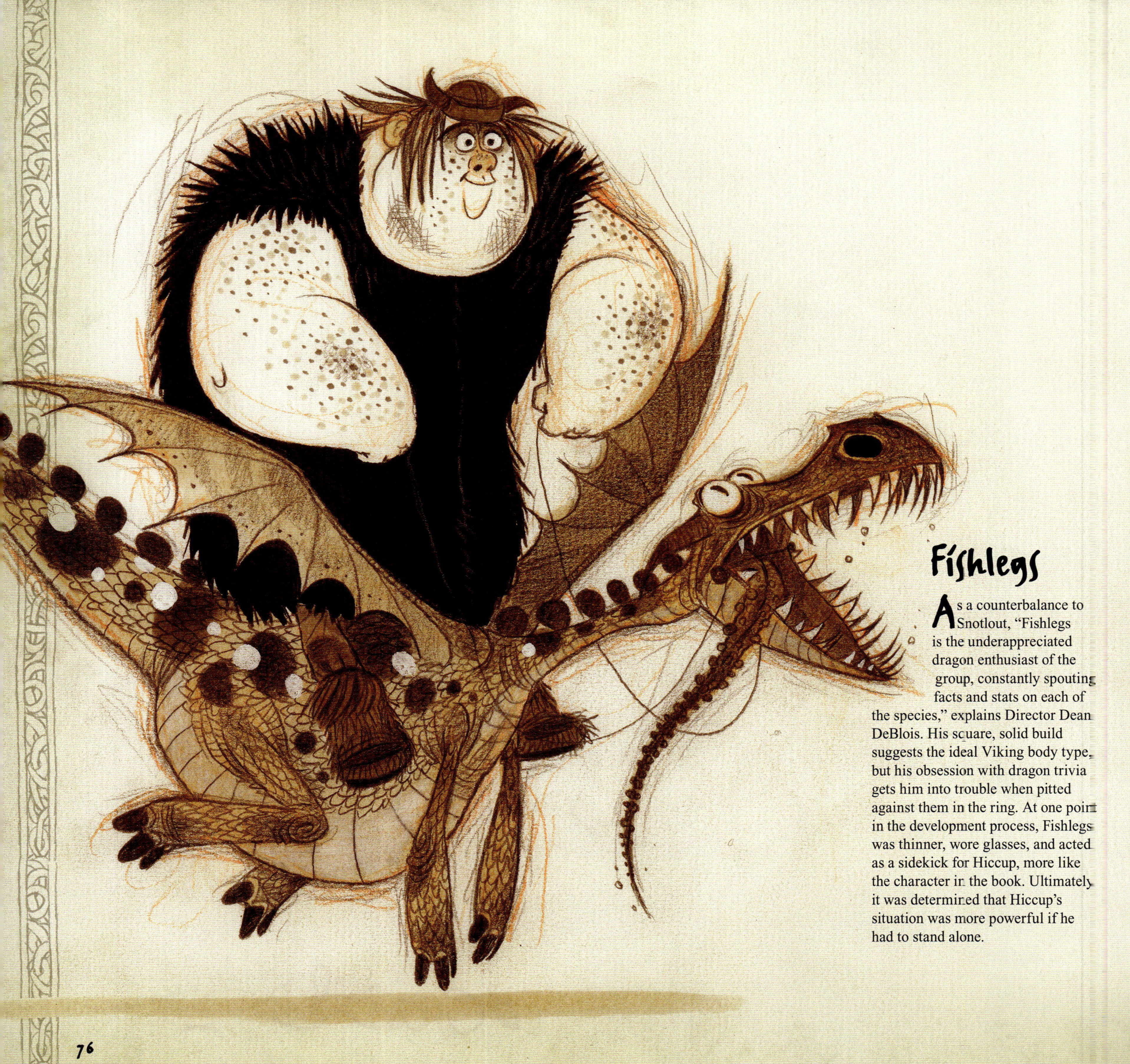

Fishlegs

As a counterbalance to Snotlout, "Fishlegs is the underappreciated dragon enthusiast of the group, constantly spouting facts and stats on each of the species," explains Director Dean DeBlois. His square, solid build suggests the ideal Viking body type, but his obsession with dragon trivia gets him into trouble when pitted against them in the ring. At one point in the development process, Fishlegs was thinner, wore glasses, and acted as a sidekick for Hiccup, more like the character in the book. Ultimately, it was determined that Hiccup's situation was more powerful if he had to stand alone.

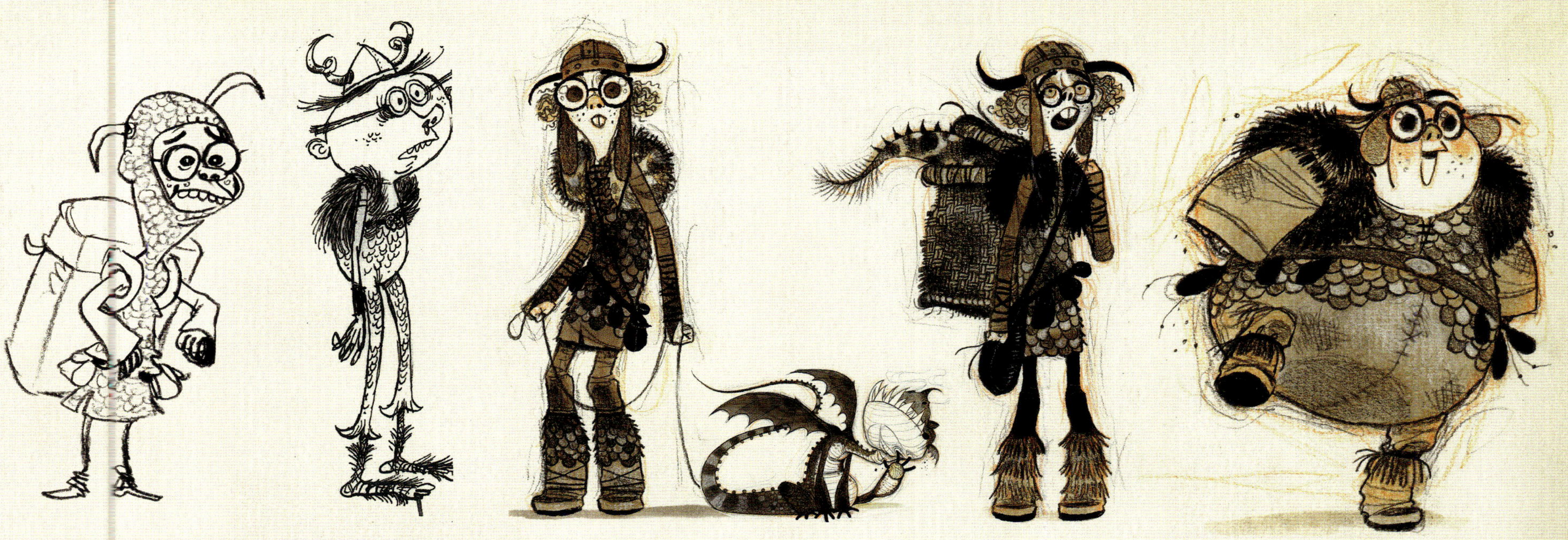

(far left) **Fishlegs** — Nico Marlet — pencil & marker. *(above, left to right)* **Fishlegs 1** — David Soren — marker; **Fishlegs 2** — Dan Krall — marker; **Fishlegs 3, 4, 5** — Nico Marlet — pencil & marker. *(below)* **Fishlegs Expressions** — Simon Otto — pencil & marker. *(bottom)* **Fishlegs Expressions** — Nico Marlet — pencil & marker. *(right)* **Fishlegs Final** — Nico Marlet — character Design — Zhaoping Wei — digital paint.

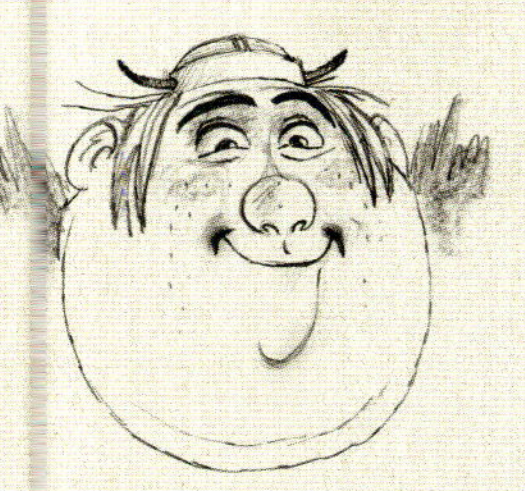

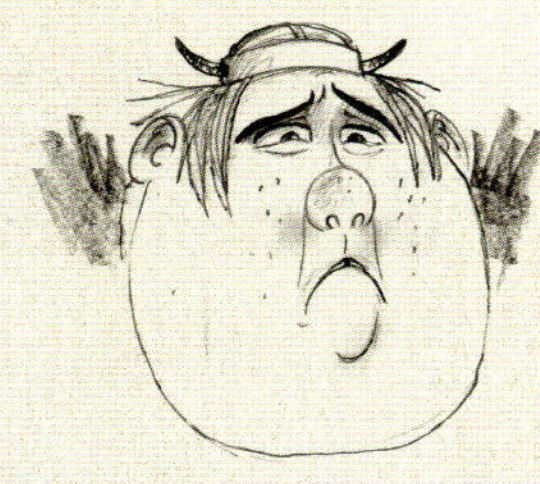

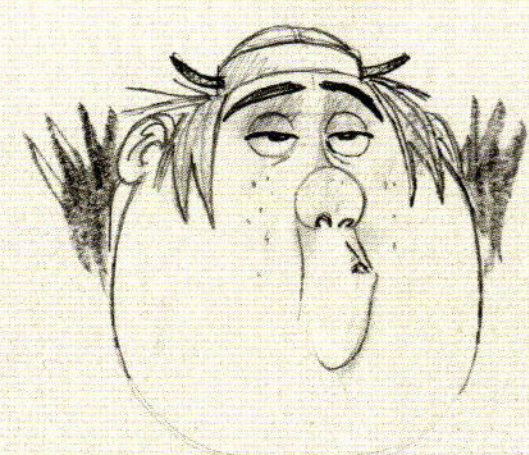

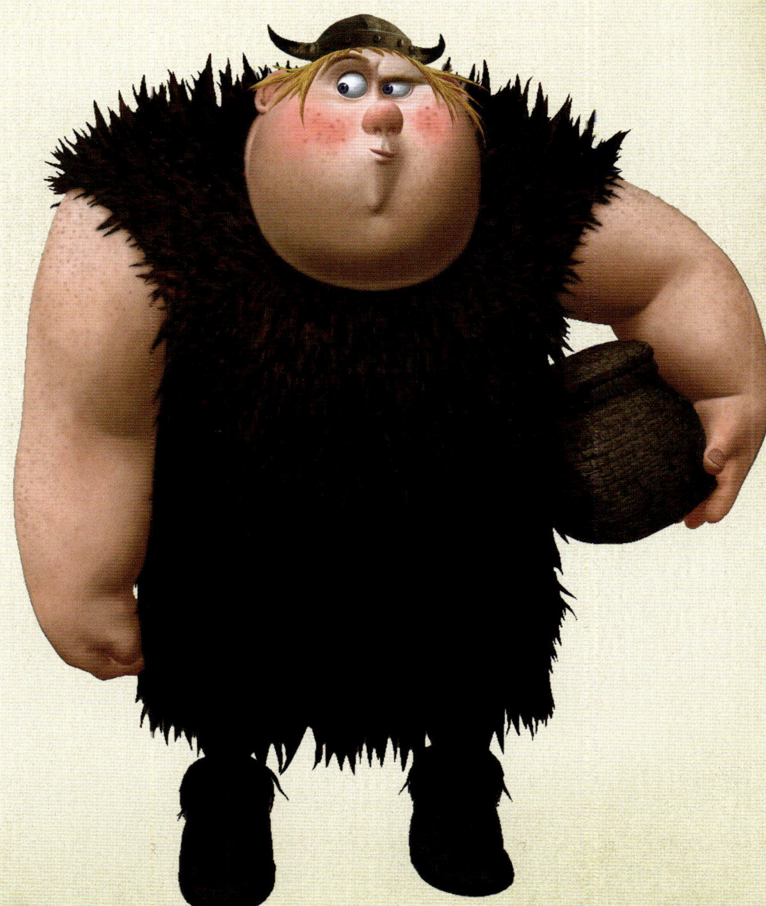

FISHLEGS IS AN EXCELLENT EXAMPLE of talented character modeling. "This model shows a true understanding of anatomy that is necessary when you're building off of a design that's as graphic as Nico's," says Production Designer Kathy Altieri. Without such structural knowledge, the flat shapes of the drawings could translate into an under-shaped mass of skin, but here the believable way the chin sets into the jaw and the cheekbones lay on the face provides an authentic interpretation of Marlet's strength of style.

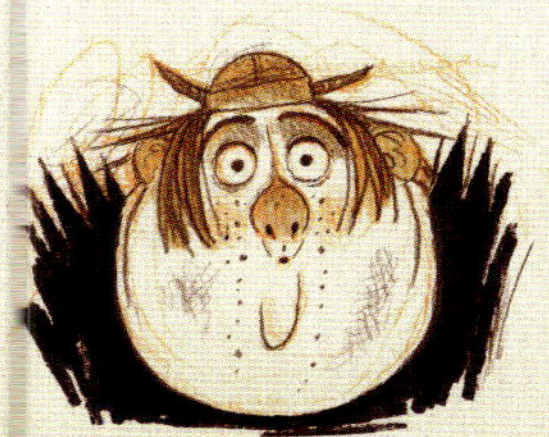

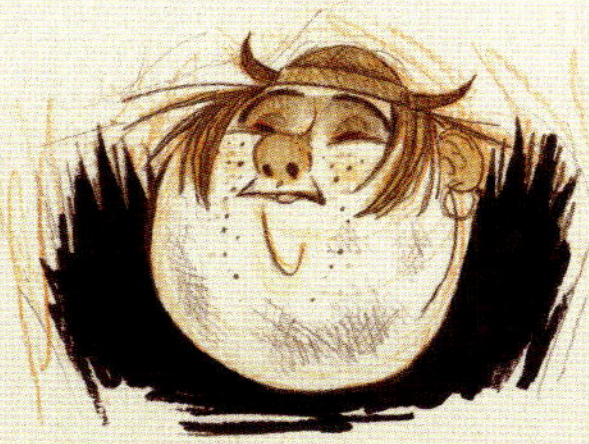

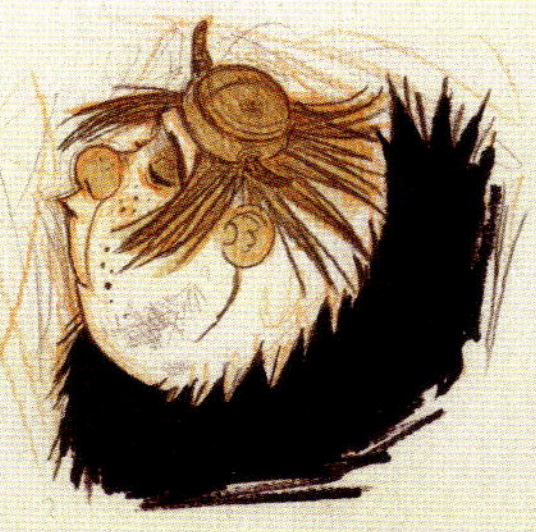

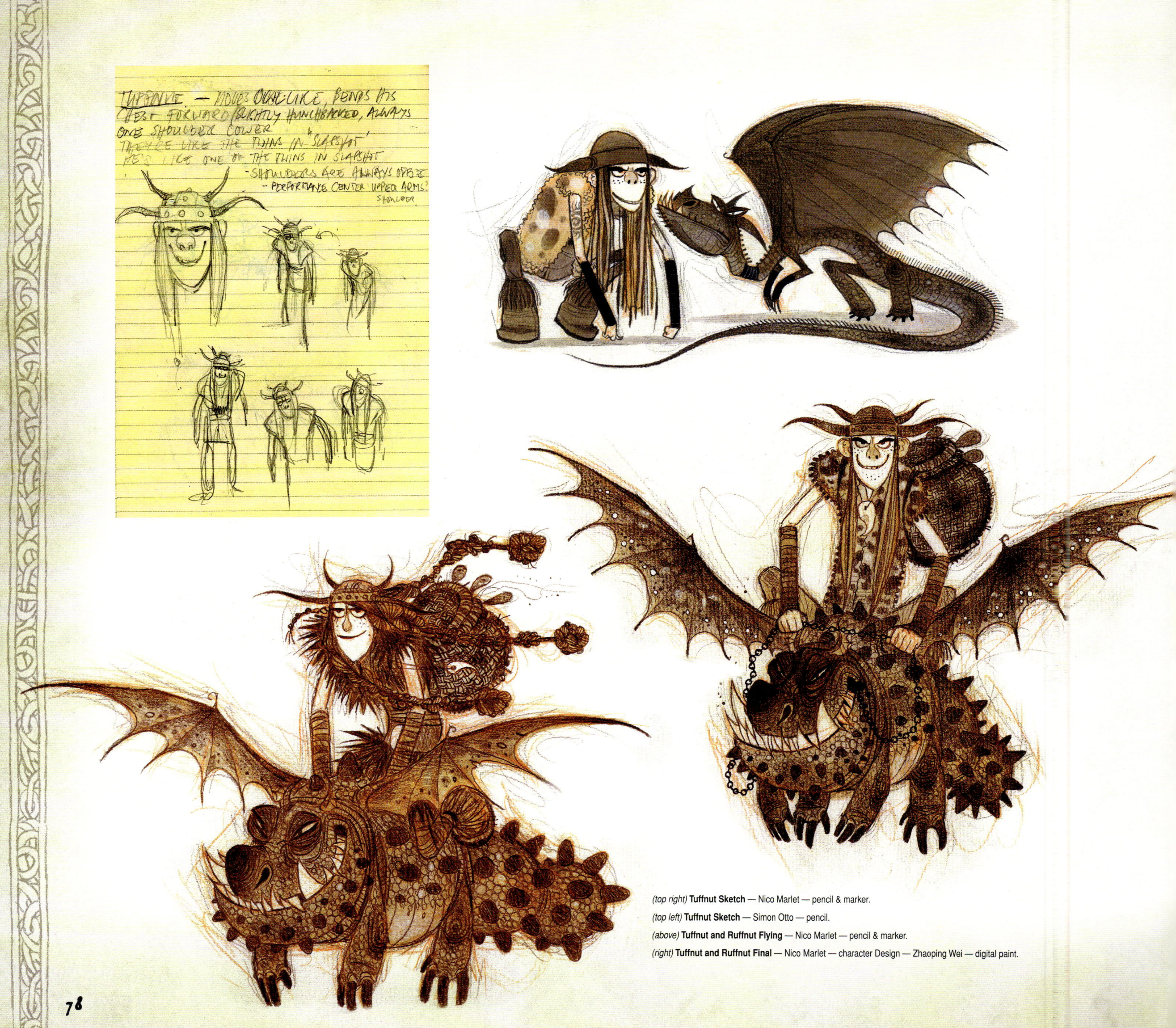

(top right) **Tuffnut Sketch** — Nico Marlet — pencil & marker.

(top left) **Tuffnut Sketch** — Simon Otto — pencil.

(above) **Tuffnut and Ruffnut Flying** — Nico Marlet — pencil & marker.

(right) **Tuffnut and Ruffnut Final** — Nico Marlet — character Design — Zhaoping Wei — digital paint.

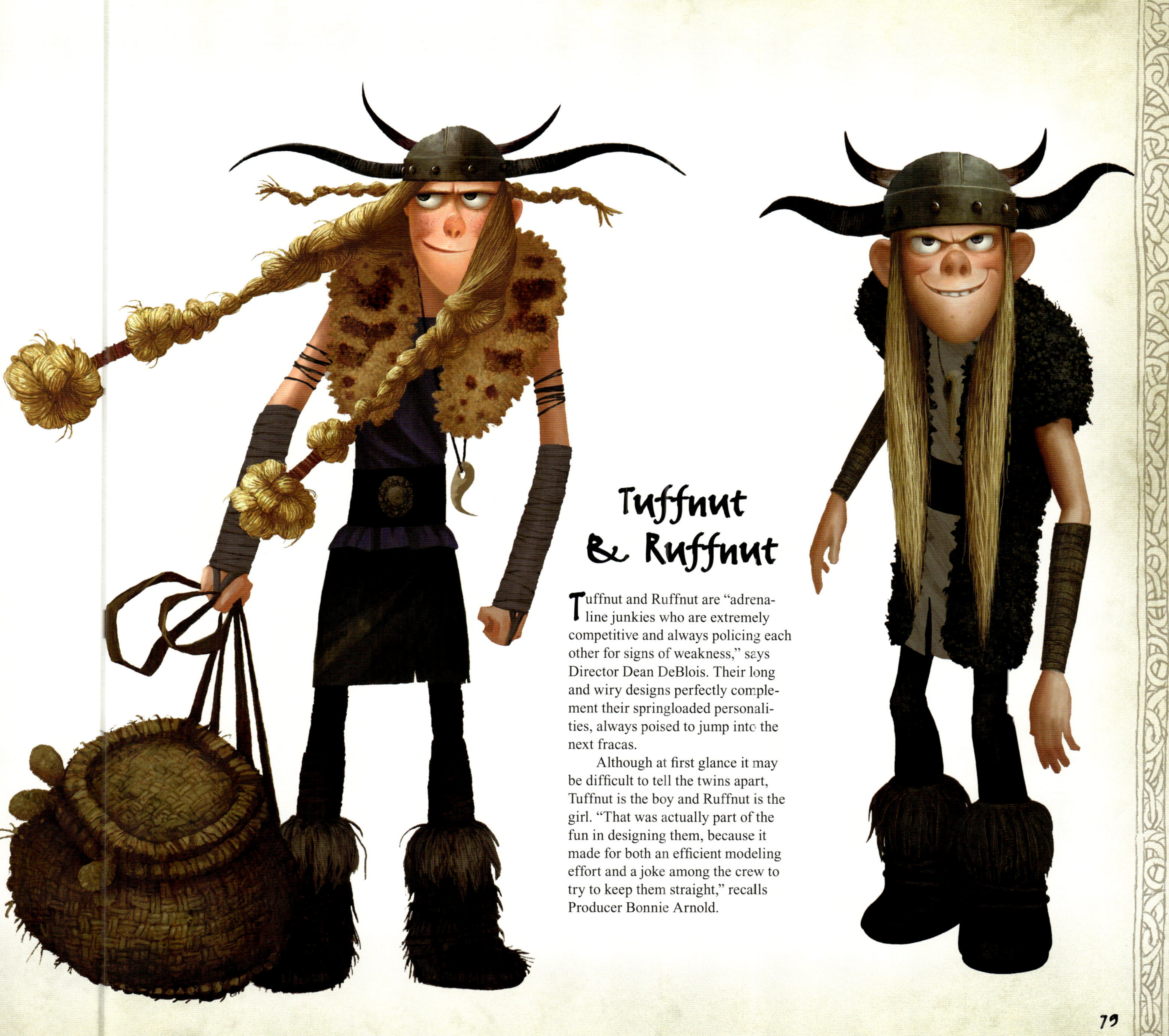

Tuffnut & Ruffnut

Tuffnut and Ruffnut are "adrenaline junkies who are extremely competitive and always policing each other for signs of weakness," says Director Dean DeBlois. Their long and wiry designs perfectly complement their springloaded personalities, always poised to jump into the next fracas.

Although at first glance it may be difficult to tell the twins apart, Tuffnut is the boy and Ruffnut is the girl. "That was actually part of the fun in designing them, because it made for both an efficient modeling effort and a joke among the crew to try to keep them straight," recalls Producer Bonnie Arnold.

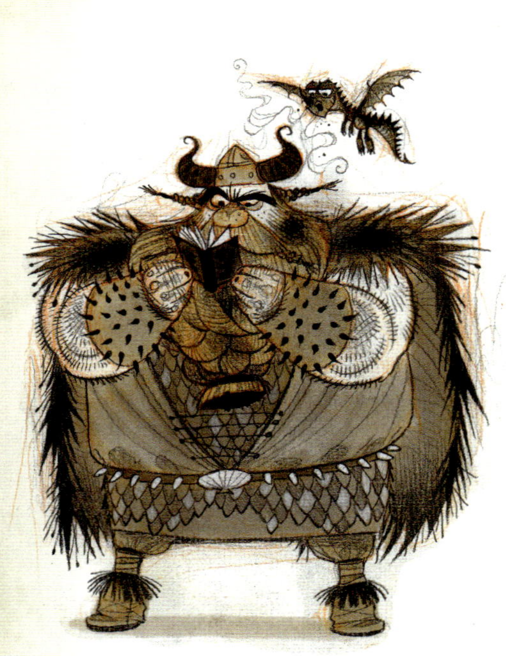

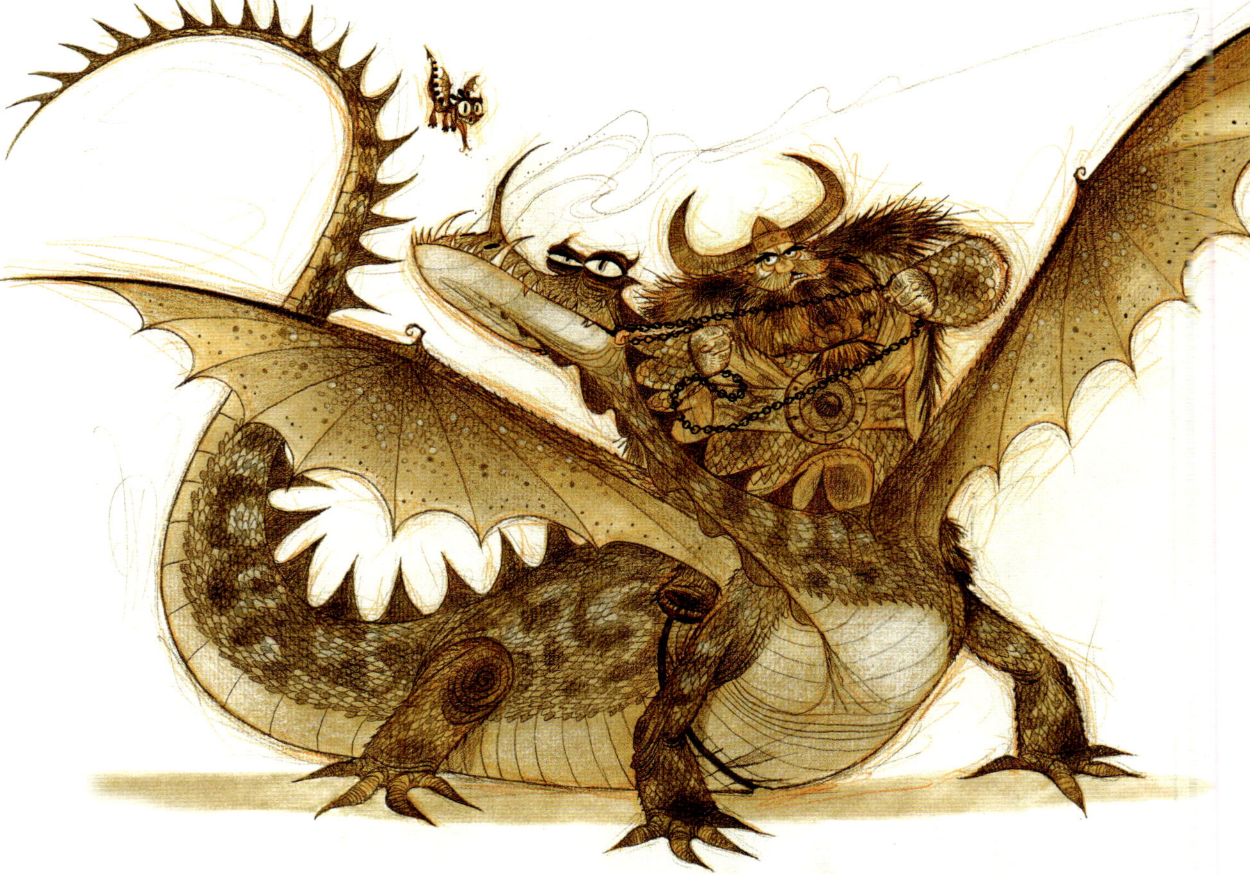

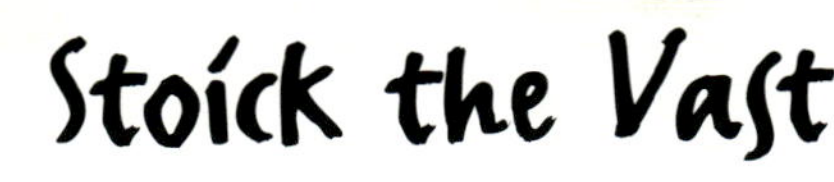

Stoick the Vast

For all the confidence that Stoick the Vast projects when leading the Vikings, he exhibits the total absence of such assurance when parenting his son, Hiccup. While his heart is in the right place performing both roles, his emotional capacity is not nearly as strong as his brawny muscles.

As the chief of his Viking tribe, Stoick must stand tall and carry an air of strength and authority above and beyond all other human characters in the film. Character Designer Nicolas Marlet conveys this by establishing Stoick's very foundation as a large, hulking square shape. His cape further accentuates this stature, and even his beard helps portray his true personality because it limits his movement, suggesting a steadfast, unwavering fortitude.

In terms of character development, "we wanted the father-and-son relationship to be first and foremost in our story, so that's what we used as the building block of the film," recalls Director Dean DeBlois. In its essence, it is a story about a father who is frustrated with his son and the son being resigned to this fact. The two are intellectual and physical opposites, a tenet highlighted by their contrasting character designs. While this dynamic seems very dramatic, it actually provides humor in moments when the communication is unbelievably awkward between these two. Stoick is a father who genuinely cares about his son and actually fears for his safety more than anything. He is very hard on Hiccup in the opening of the film, which is the ideal

(above left) **Stoick Pose** — Nico Marlet — pencil & marker. *(above)* **Stoick on Dragon** — Nico Marlet — pencil & marker. *(left)* **Stoick Pose** — Carlos Grangel — pencil & marker.

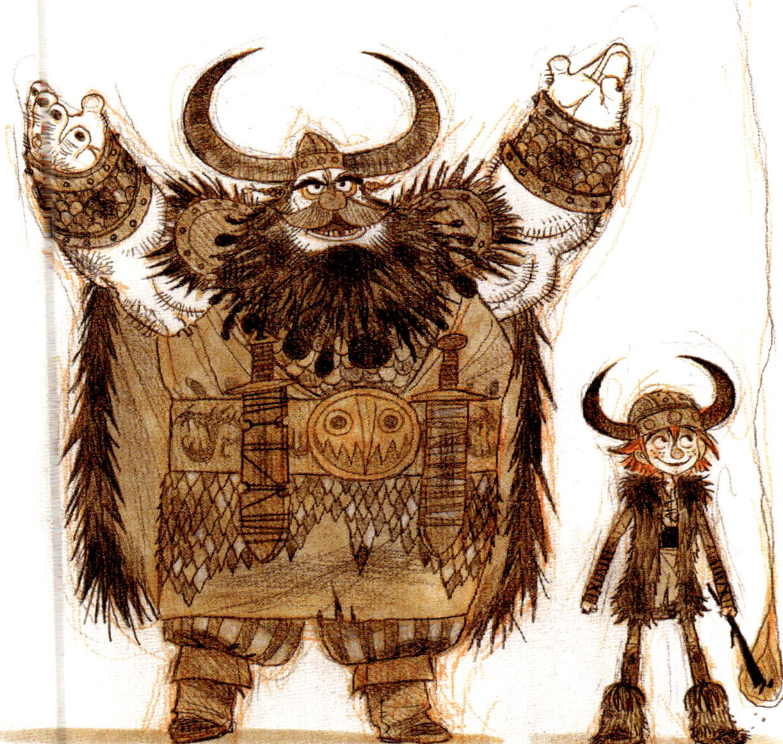

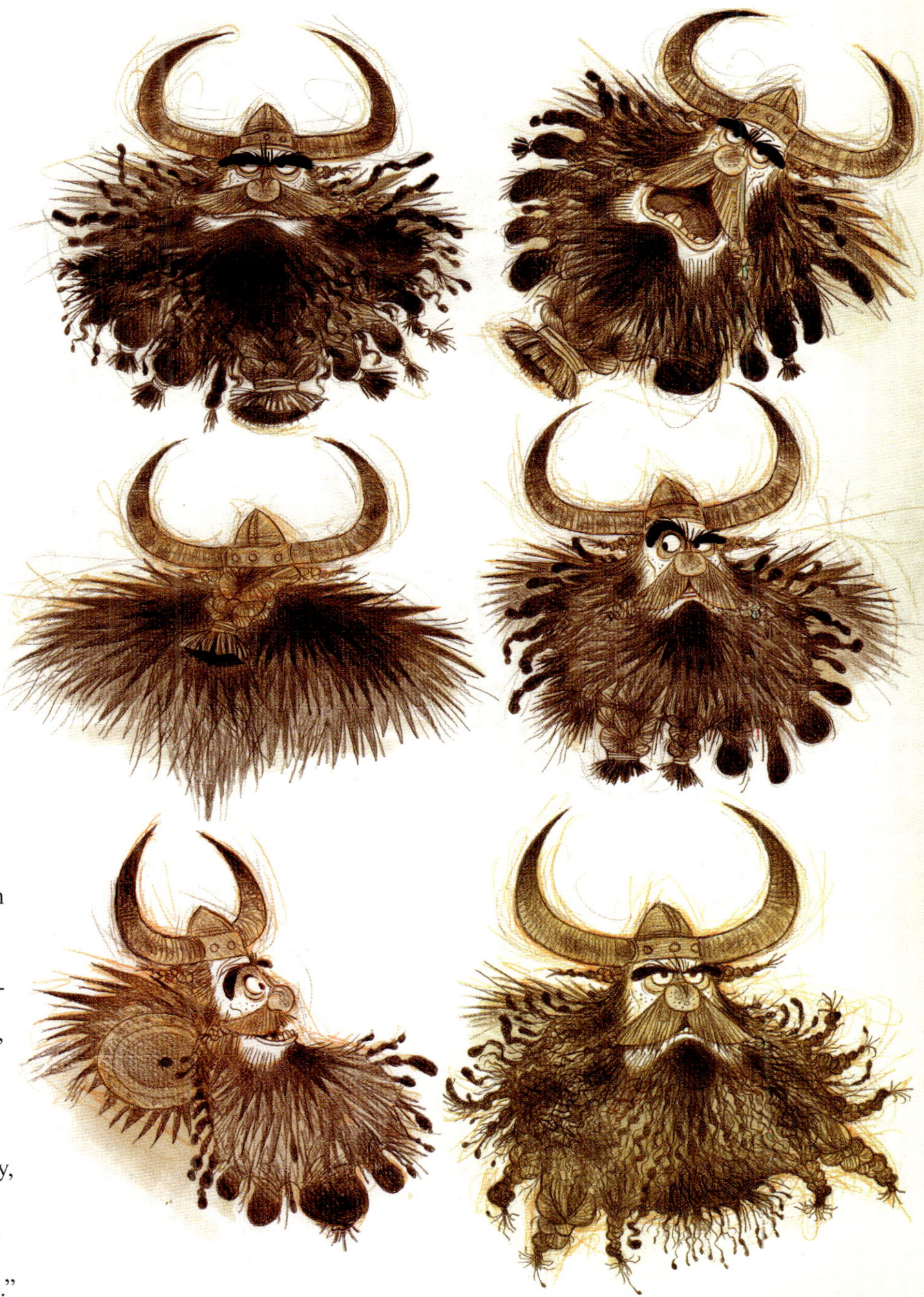

starting place for his character arc: if Stoick seems really irrational in the beginning, then when he finally opens up and shows some vulnerability in the end, it is a much more satisfying progression.

Stoick's design demonstrates one of the most ambitious undertakings on this cast of characters with his abundance of facial hair, most notably his beard. Once an initial design was established, beard grooming became a lengthy cross-departmental challenge, "where modeling would produce span lines; rigging would provide animation controls and simulation parameters; and then animation would run motion tests. Meanwhile, surfacing would add color, texture, and small-scale variation and finally, lighting would pull it all together to render test images," explains Visual Effects Supervisor Craig Ring. What made this effort even more involved was the final goal of 3D stereoscopic film delivery, "which meant that even the inside layers of the beard would be visible, so it had to move correctly all the way through, not just on the surface."

(above left) **Hiccup & Stoick** — Nico Marlet — pencil & marker. *(above)* **Stoick Expressions** — Nico Marlet — pencil & marker.

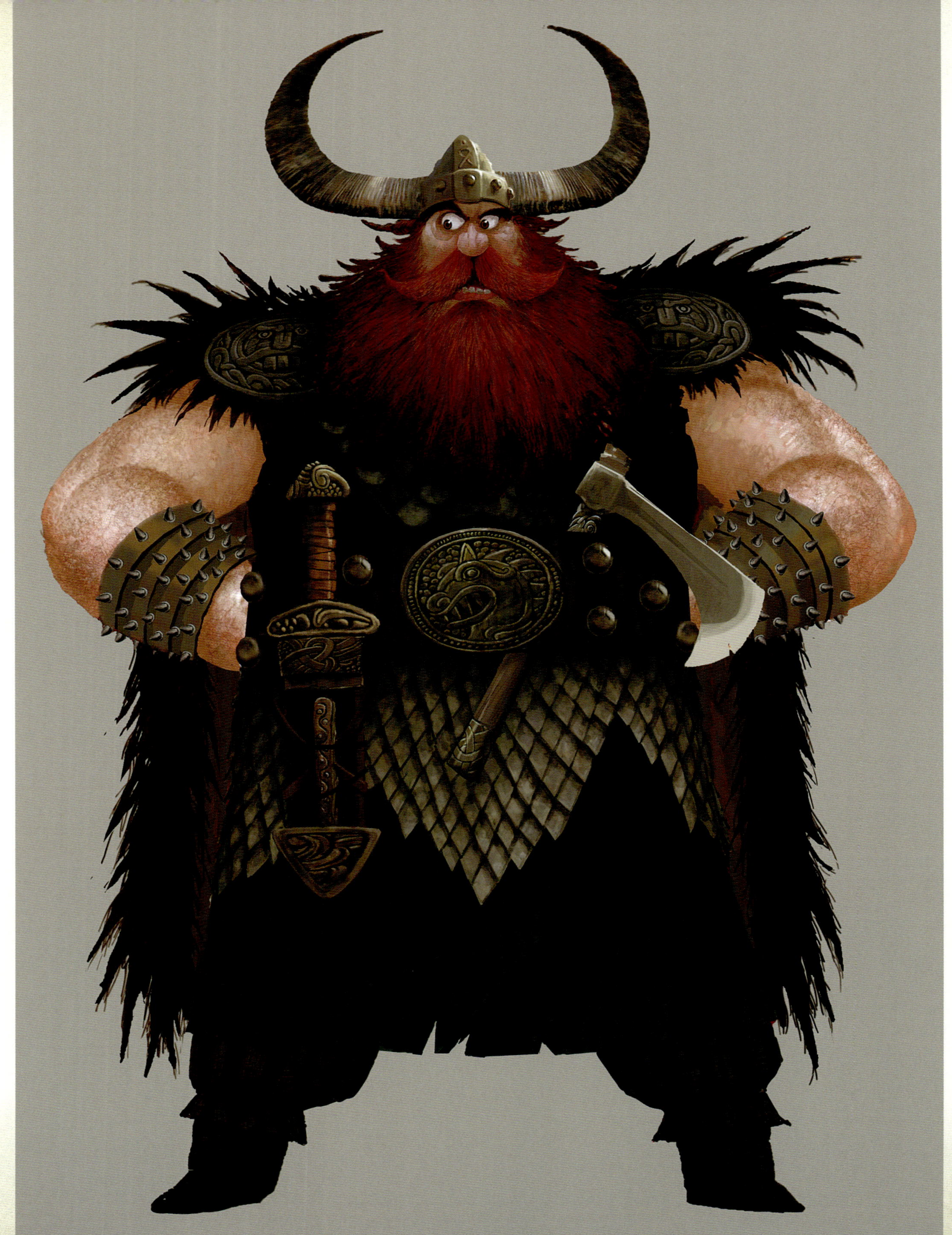

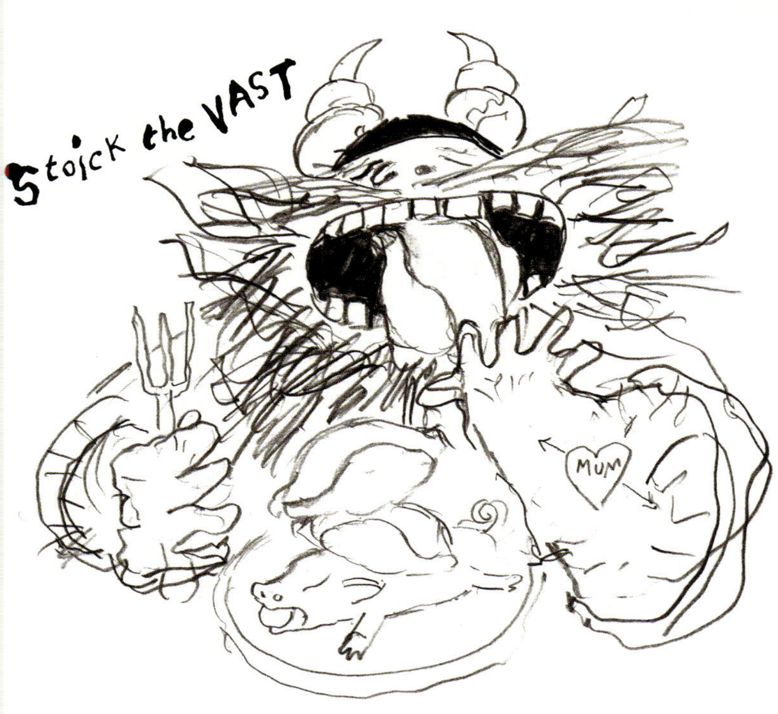

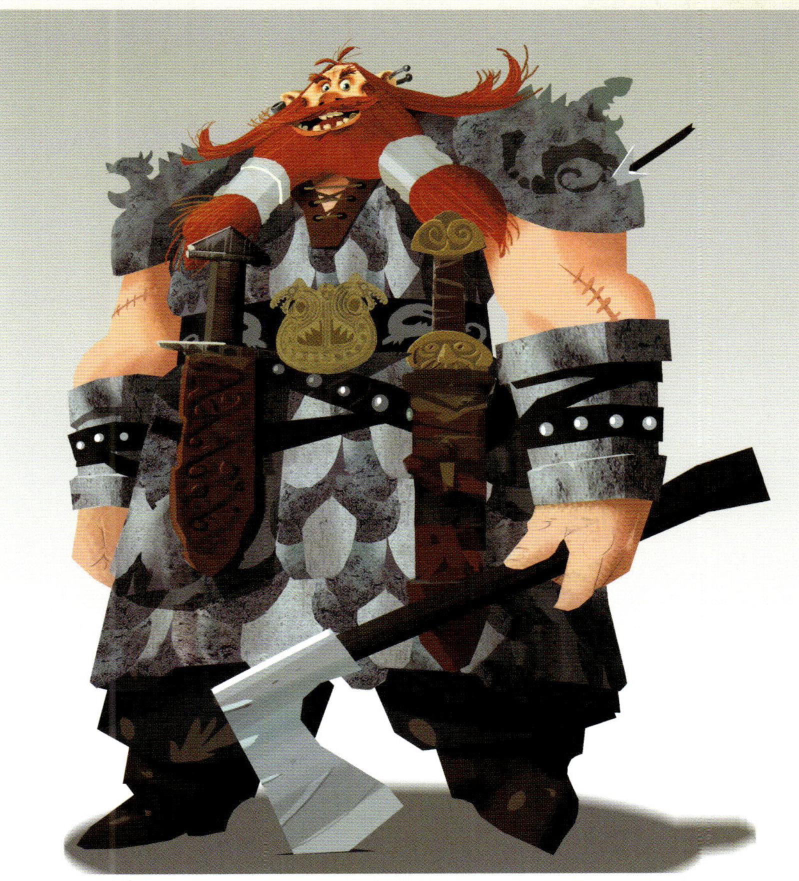

(left) **Stoick Final** — Nico Marlet — character design — Zhaoping Wei — digital paint.

(above) **Stoick the Vast** — Cressida Cowell — pencil. *(right)* **Stoick 2** — Pierre-Olivier Vincent — digital paint

(below) **Stoick Fire** — Dominique Louis — digital paint.

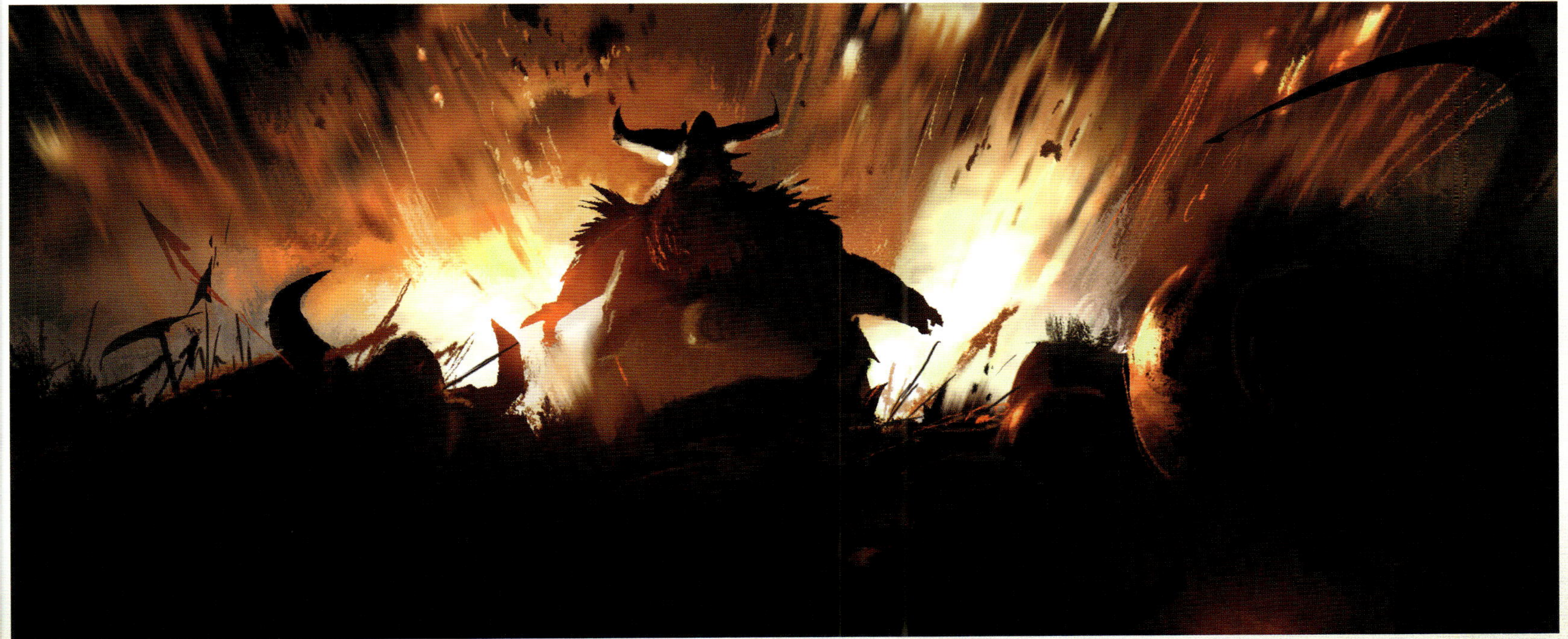

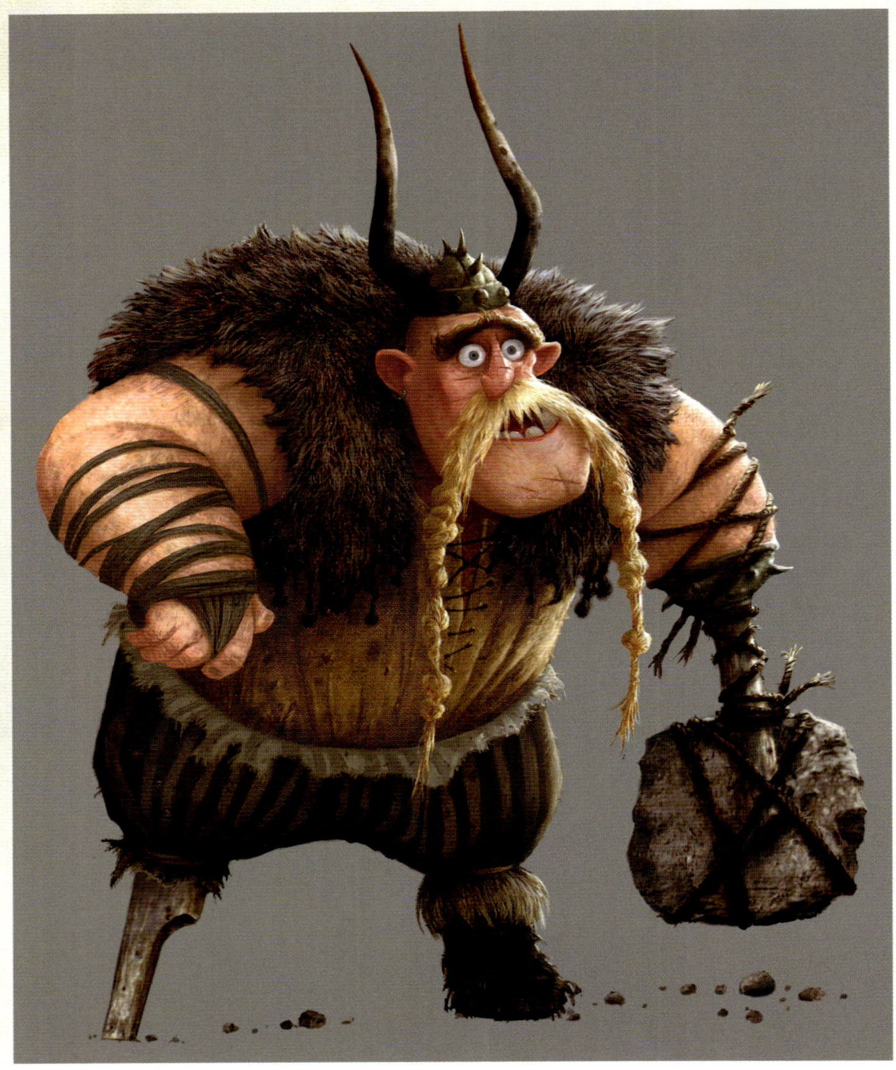

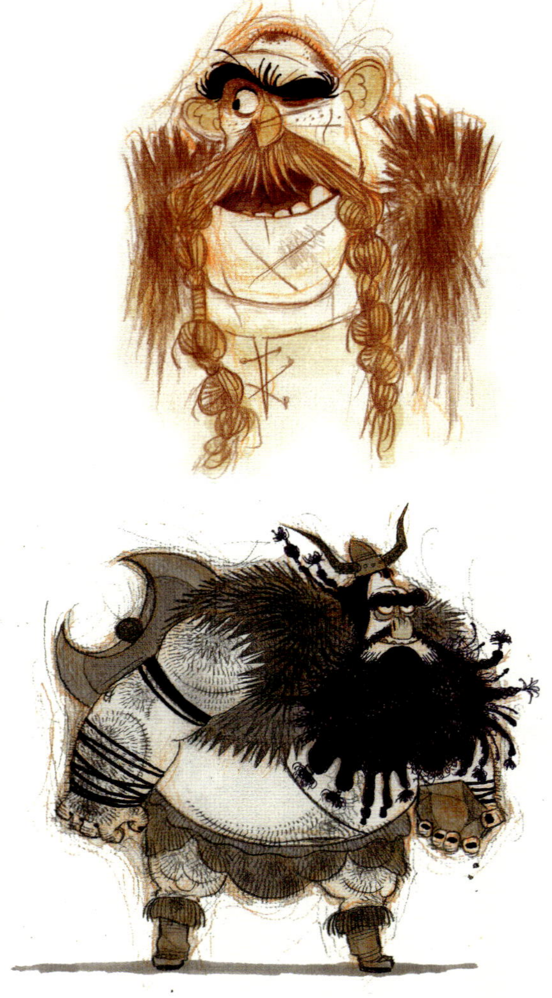

Gobber

Clearly the most battle-worn of all the characters in the lineup, Gobber has the physical markings to show that he has gathered years of firsthand experience with dragons and is the ideal candidate to serve as the trainer of the recruits. He is also the blacksmith for the village, but more importantly, Gobber is the necessary intermediary between Hiccup and Stoick. "He's like a family counselor by nature of his relationship with them—as the best friend of one and mentor to the other—and he serves that role even if he's not equipped to do so," say Director Dean DeBlois. With a colorful personality and a humorously varied selection of prosthetic appendages, Gobber is the most incomplete character physically, but he is emotionally more complete.

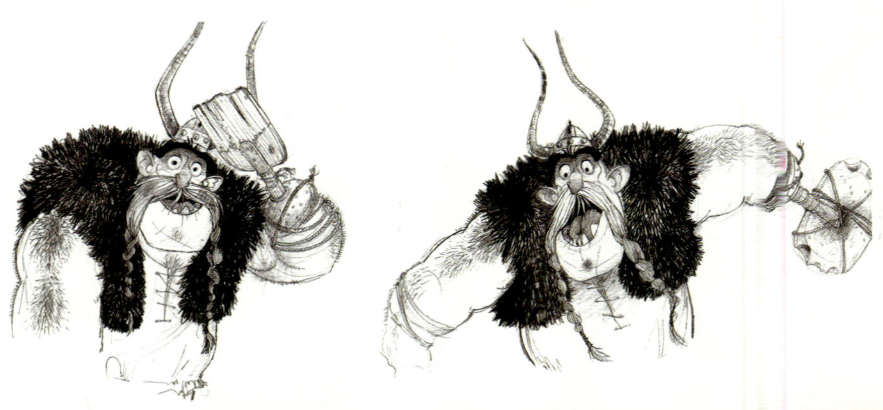

(above) **Gobber Final** — Nico Marlet — character design — Zhaoping Wei — digital paint. *(top right and center)* **Gobber** — Nico Marlet — pencil & marker.

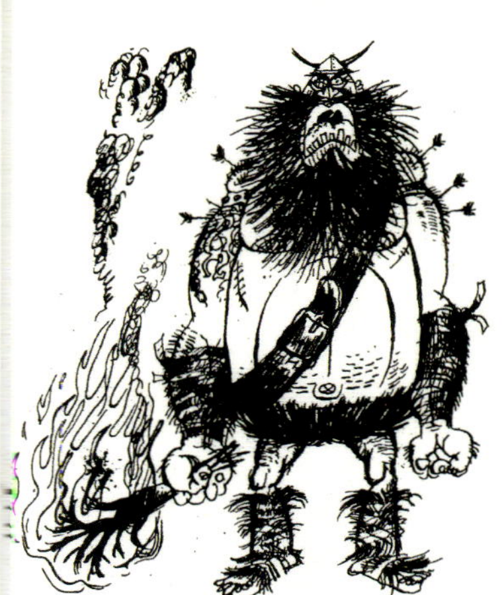

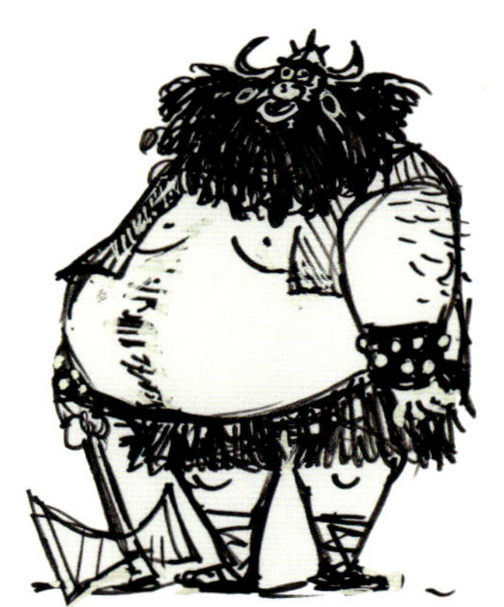

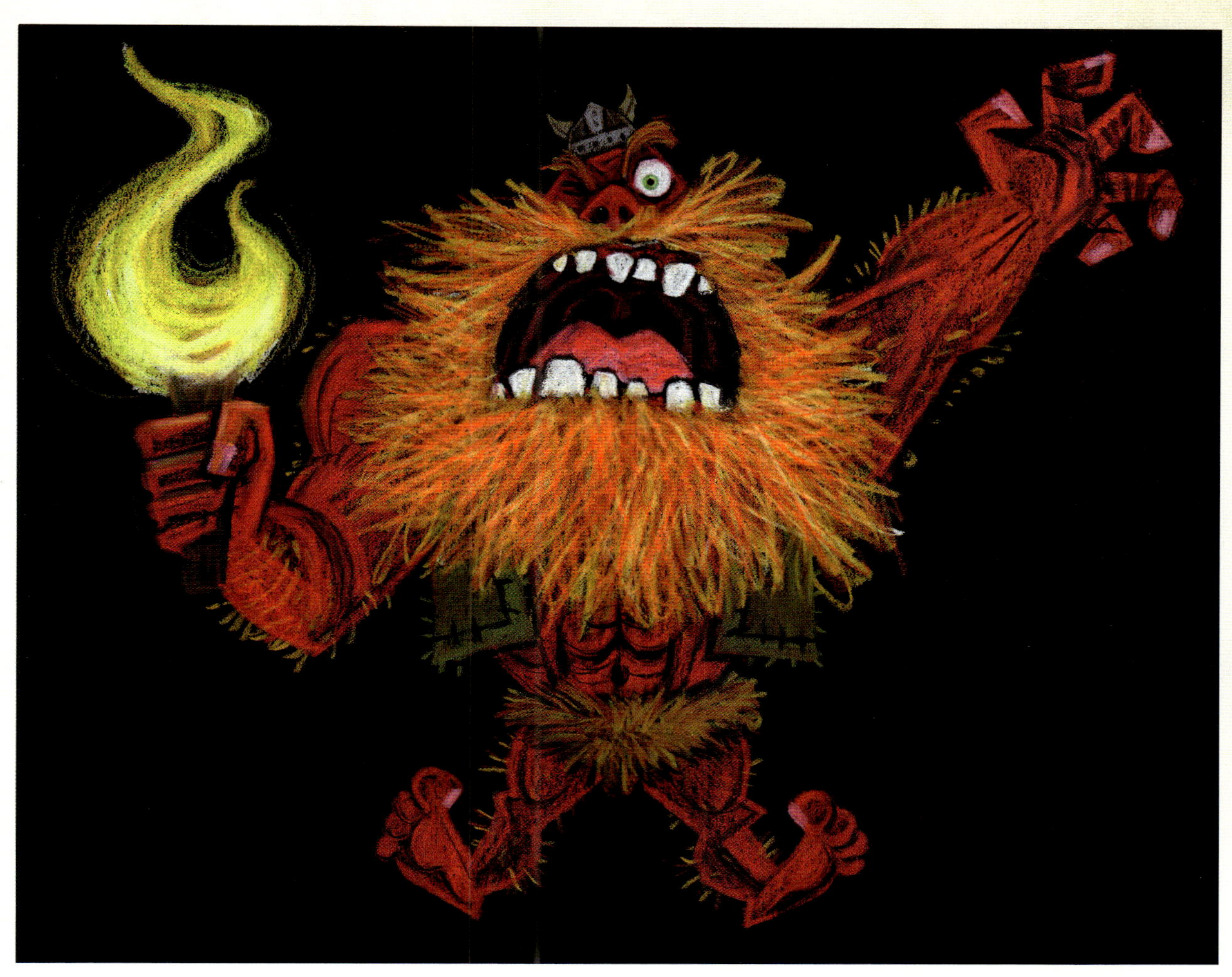

Gobber is the best friend of Stoick, the only person in the world who knows that Stoick almost cried once.

—Chris Sanders, Director

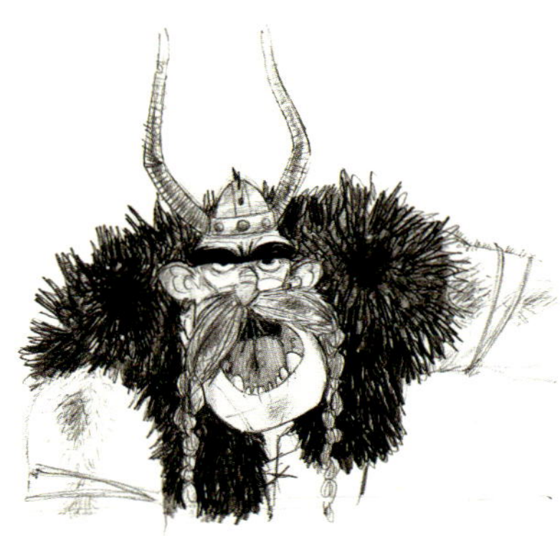

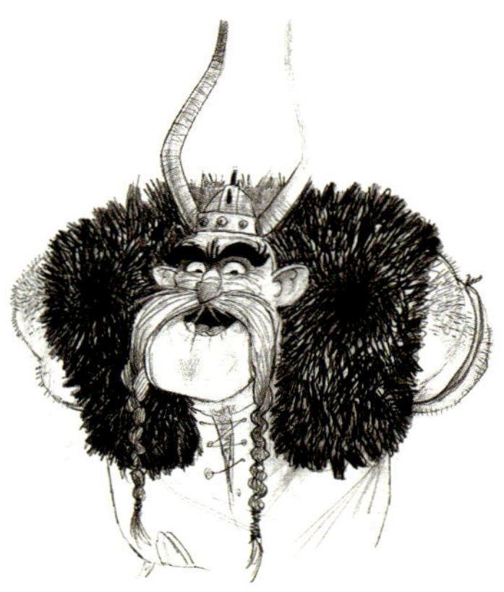

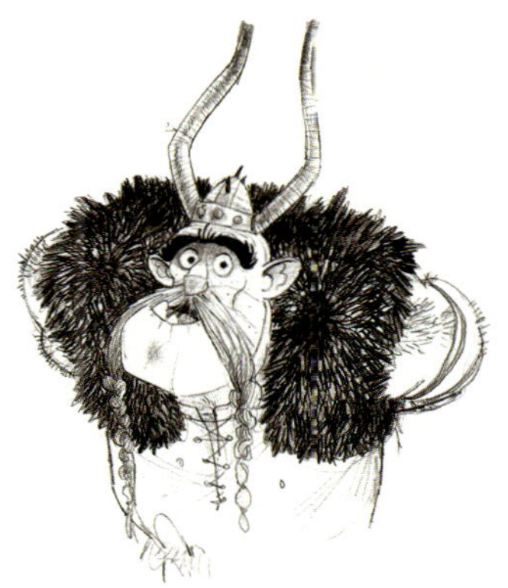

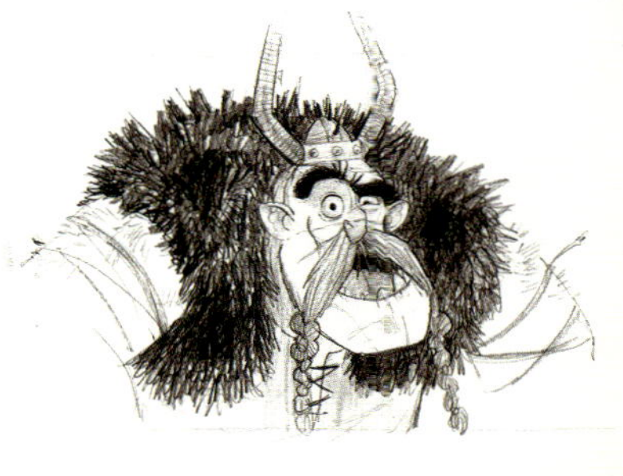

(top left) **Gobber** — Dan Krall — marker. *(top right)* **Gobber** — Geefwee Boedoe — pastel. *(Above)* **Gobber Expressions** — Simon Otto — pencil.

Old Wrinkly & Gothi

Based on the grandfather character in the original book, the now out-of-picture Old Wrinkly once served the Viking community as its "wise old man." His character was a predecessor to Gothi, a soothsayer who fulfilled a number of different duties over the course of her time in the film. Her role varied from shaman of the village when a mythic element had to be explained to an empathetic confidant for Hiccup when he needed to talk to her current role as village elder.

(below center) **Gothi 1** — Darren Webb — pencil & marker. *(left)* **Gothi 2** — David Soren — pencil & marker.
(below right) **Gothi 3** — Nico Marlet — pencil & marker.

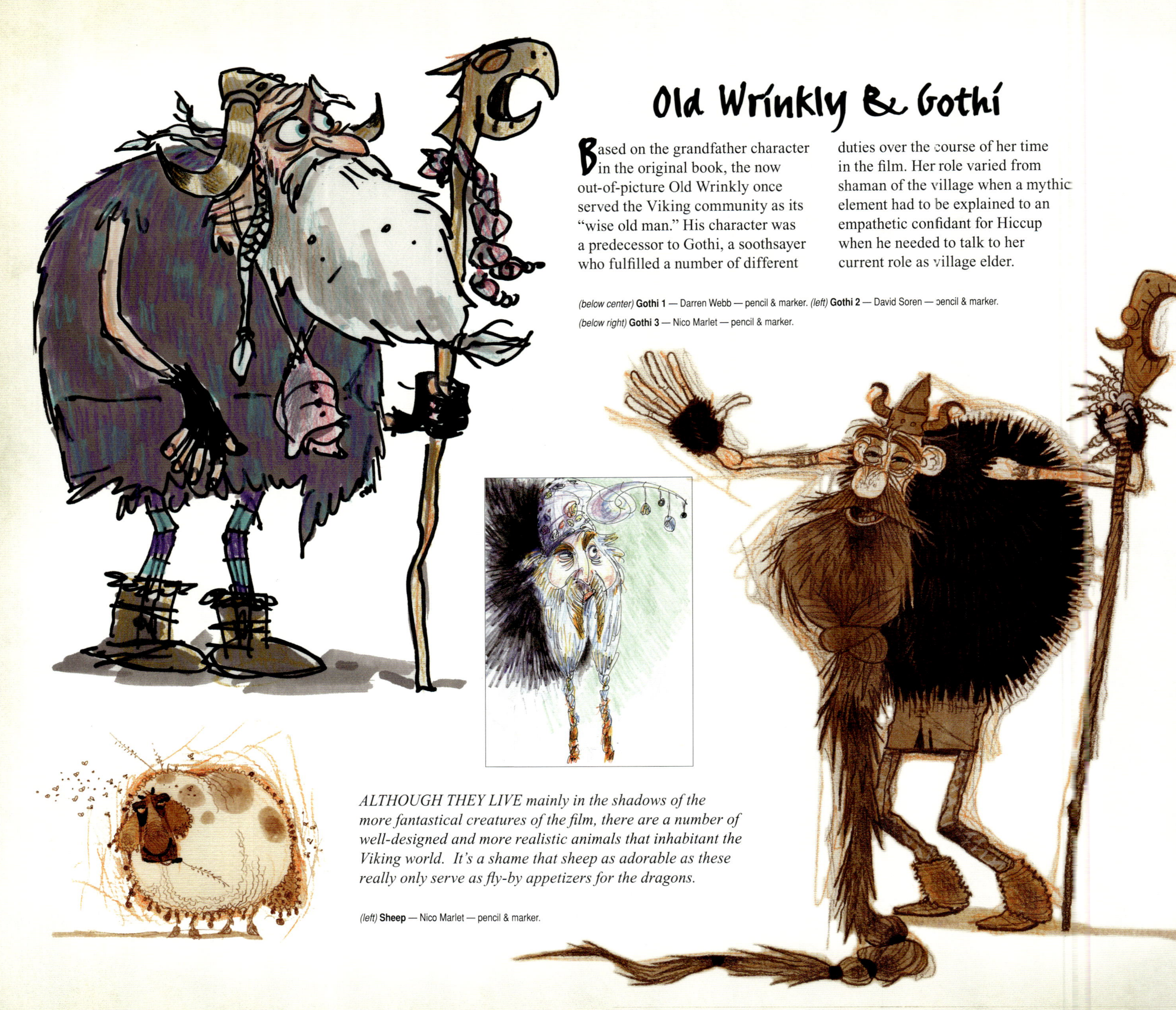

ALTHOUGH THEY LIVE mainly in the shadows of the more fantastical creatures of the film, there are a number of well-designed and more realistic animals that inhabitant the Viking world. It's a shame that sheep as adorable as these really only serve as fly-by appetizers for the dragons.

(left) **Sheep** — Nico Marlet — pencil & marker.

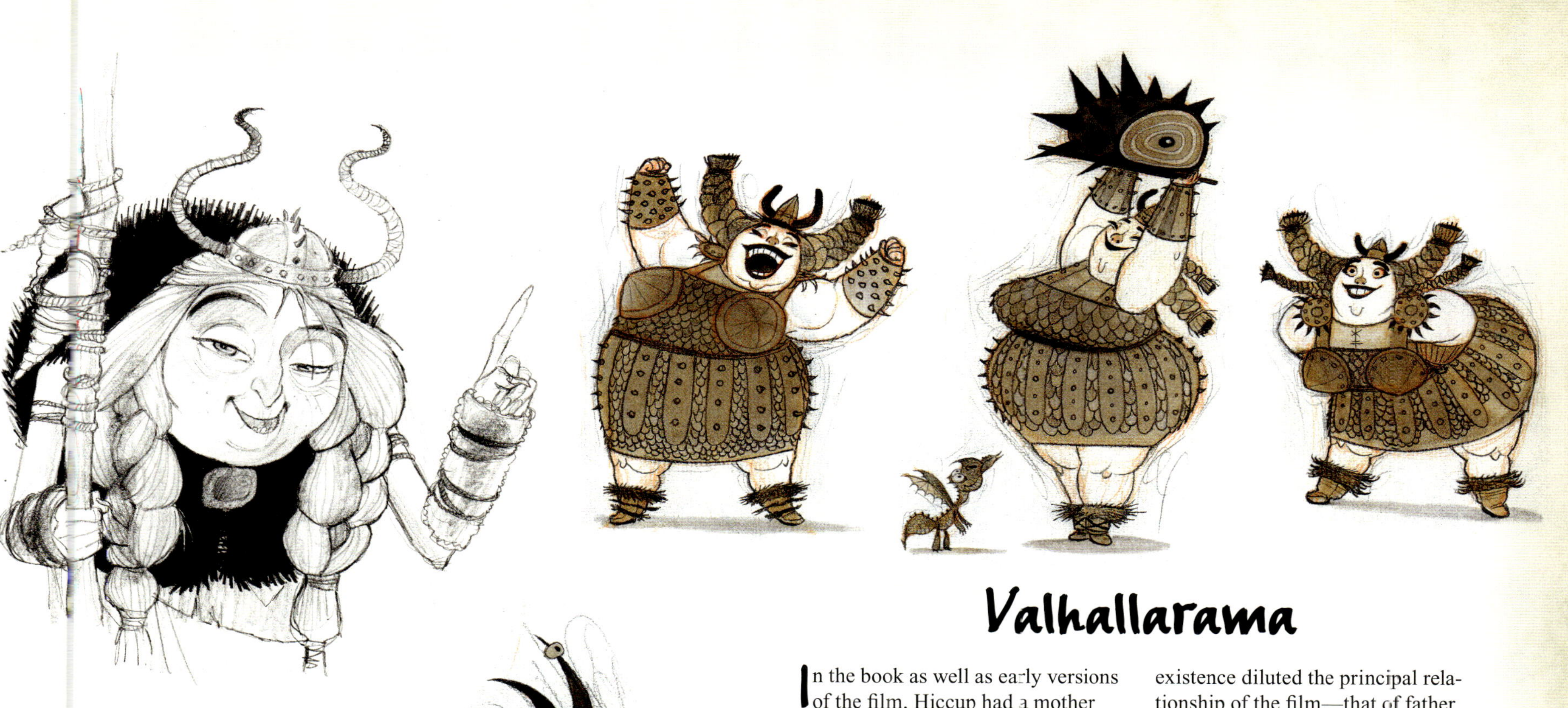

Gothi was a challenge because she was the oldest character to surface, and her skin qualities were quite different from the other Vikings. "We gave her more dull and desaturated skin, and even an old lady beard," recalls Head of Surfacing Sabrina Riegel. Gothi makes a brief cameo appearance along with the young Hiccup and young Astrid models when the Vikings set sail in search of Dragon Island.

Valhallarama

In the book as well as early versions of the film, Hiccup had a mother named Valhallarama. "But due to time constraints and the fact that her existence diluted the principal relationship of the film—that of father and son—she had to go," explains Producer Bonnie Arnold.

(above left) **Gothi** — Simon Otto — pencil.

(above and below) **Valhallarama** — Nico Marlet — pencil & marker.

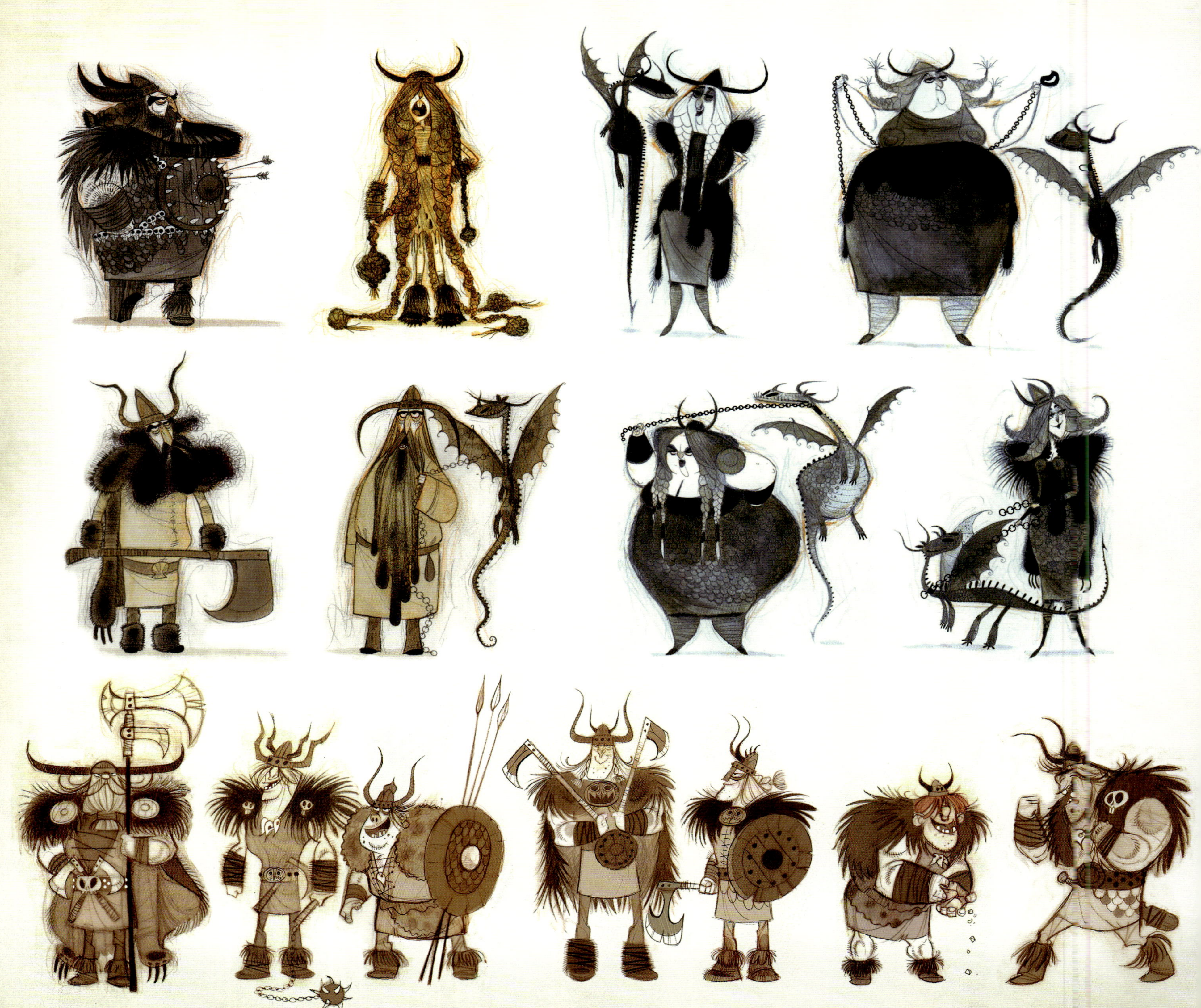

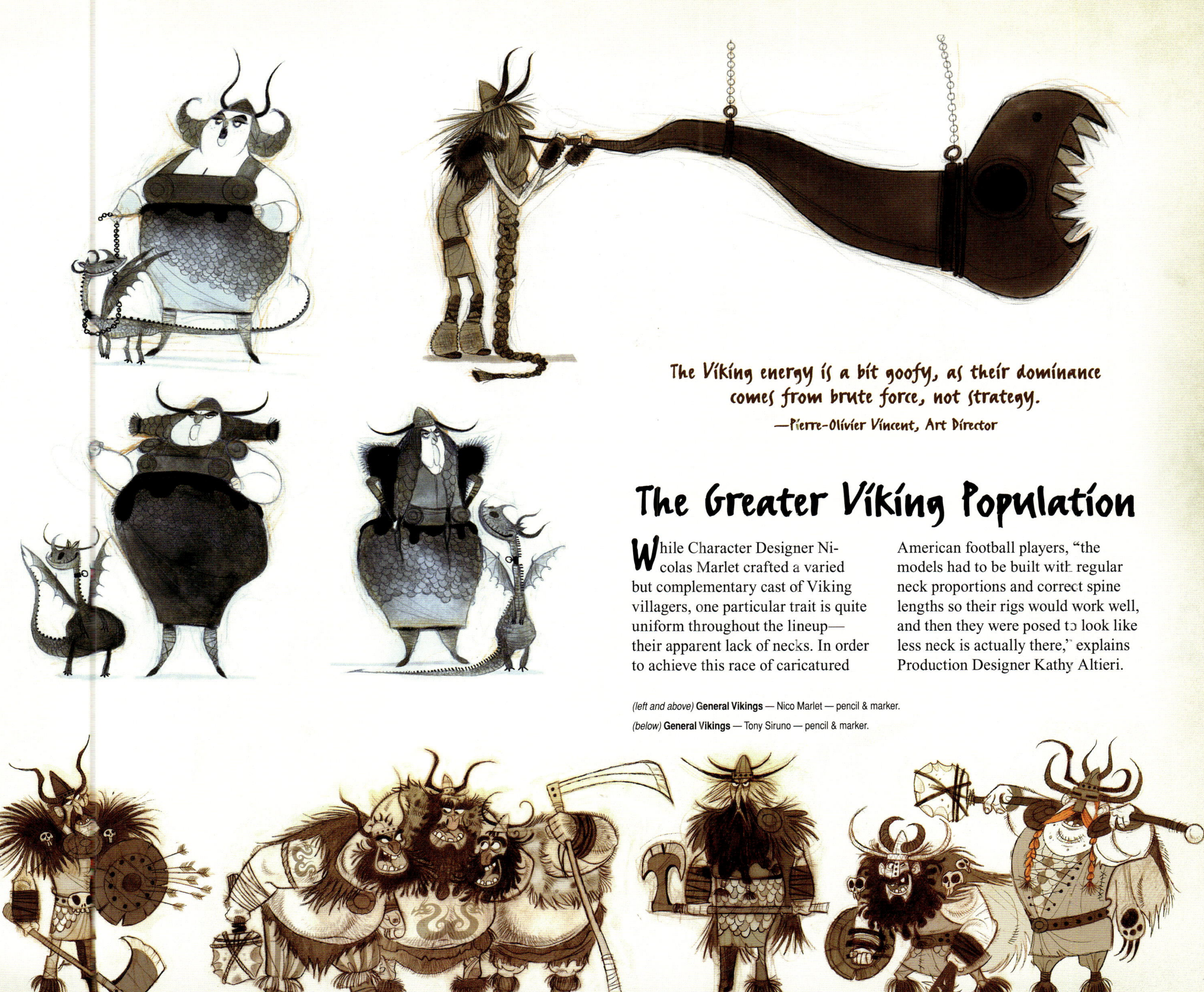

The Viking energy is a bit goofy, as their dominance comes from brute force, not strategy.

—Pierre-Olivier Vincent, Art Director

The Greater Viking Population

While Character Designer Nicolas Marlet crafted a varied but complementary cast of Viking villagers, one particular trait is quite uniform throughout the lineup—their apparent lack of necks. In order to achieve this race of caricatured American football players, "the models had to be built with regular neck proportions and correct spine lengths so their rigs would work well, and then they were posed to look like less neck is actually there," explains Production Designer Kathy Altieri.

(left and above) **General Vikings** — Nico Marlet — pencil & marker.

(below) **General Vikings** — Tony Siruno — pencil & marker.

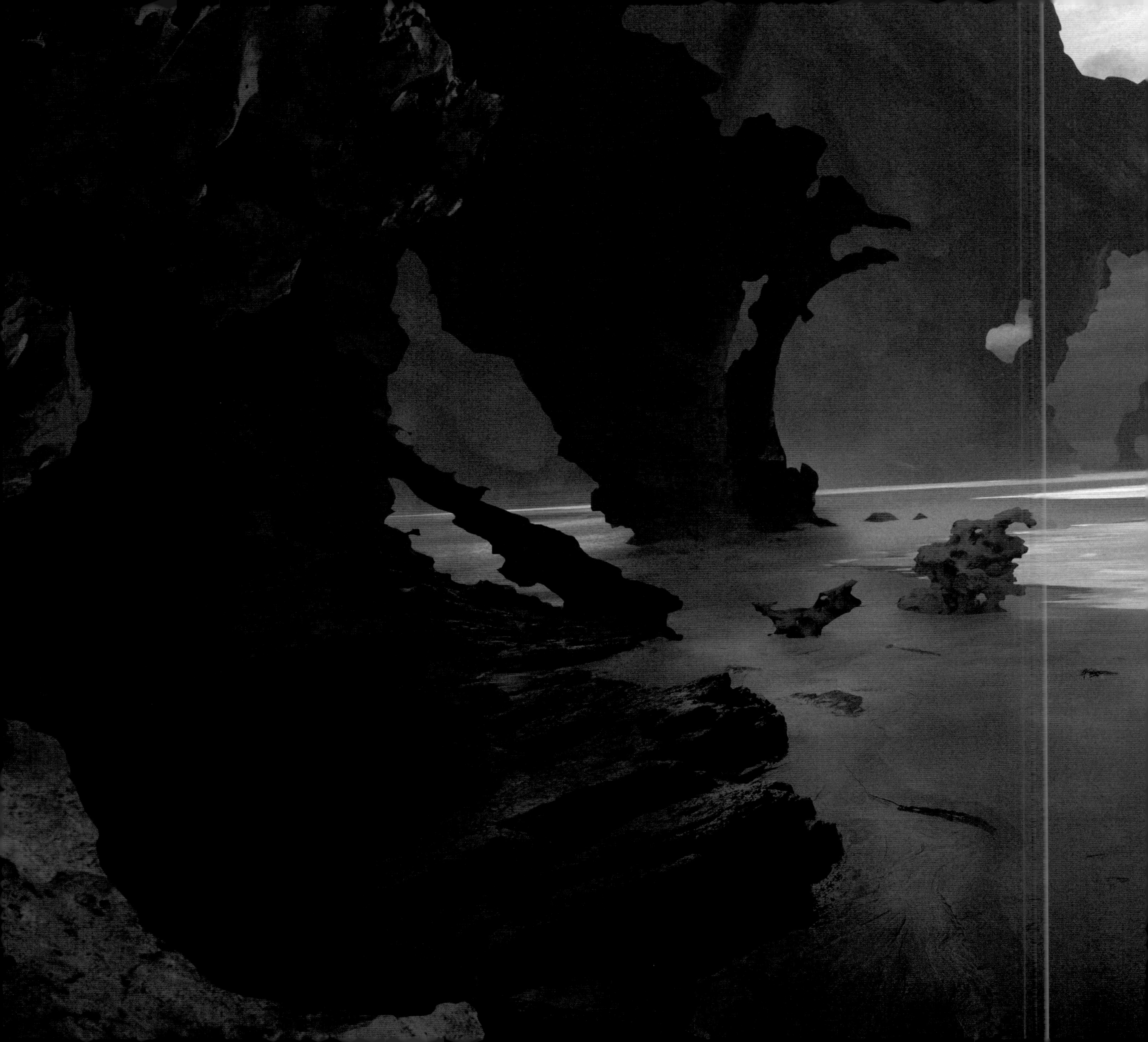

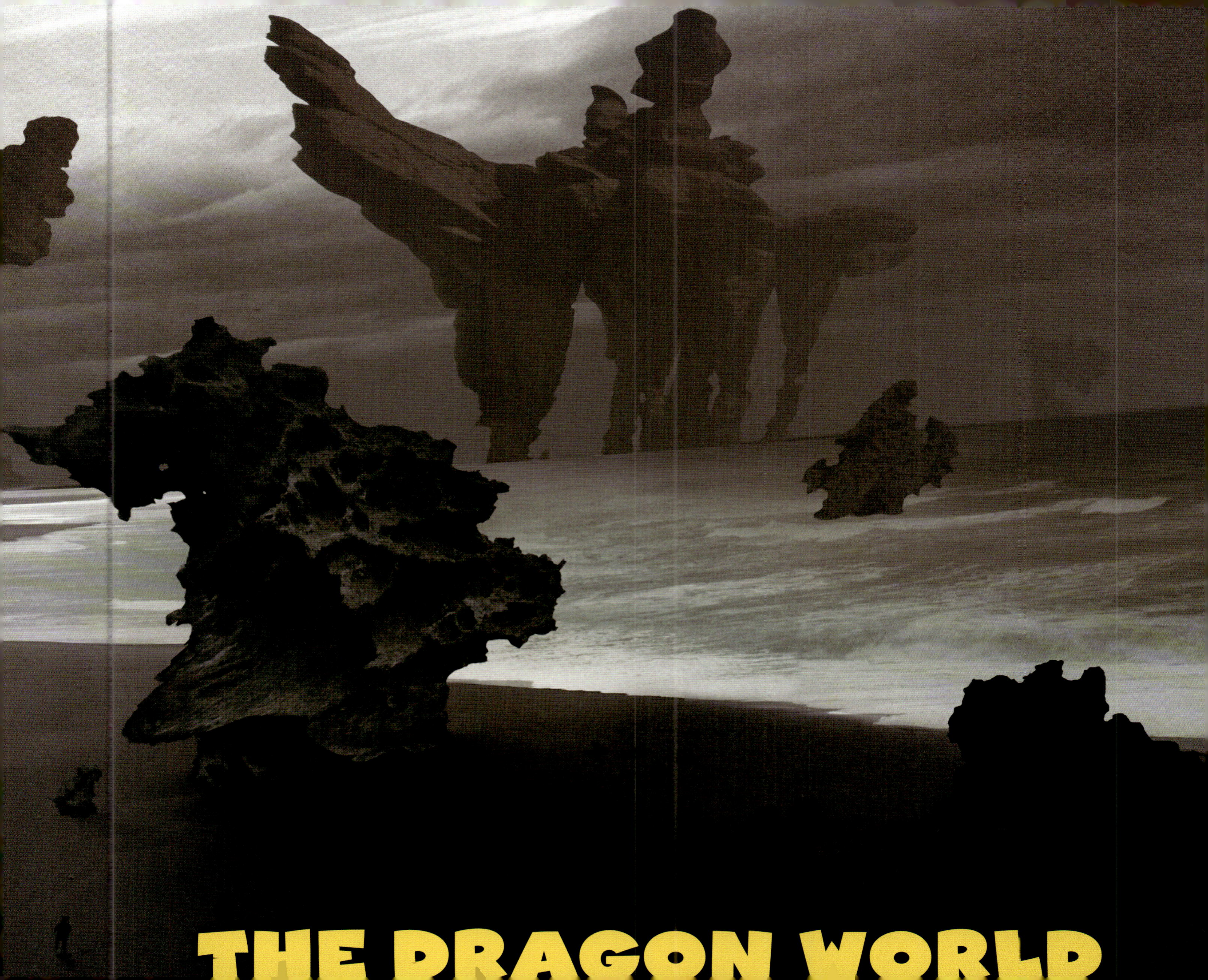
THE DRAGON WORLD

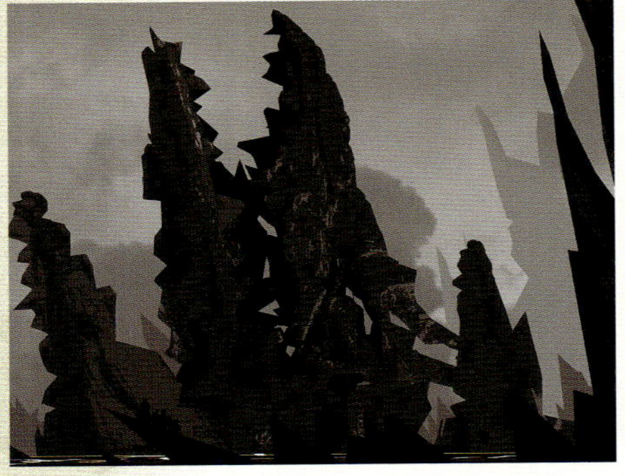
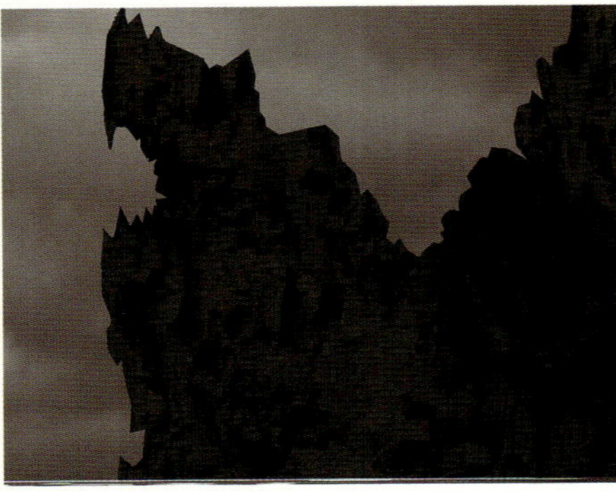

Dragon Island

Home base for the dragons is a location undiscovered by the Vikings. Around the island, "there is heavy fog which blocks out the view of the stars and other cues of navigation, the sky is choked with dragons, and the coastal landscape is populated with creepy towers of rock that are disorienting. Thus, the Viking ships would generally get lost, get devoured by dragons, or crash into these rocks," explains Director Chris Sanders.

Dragon Island is composed of jagged, black, lava-formed structures that blend into its dark skies to create an eerily imposing and mysterious environment. Its volcanic presence has an infernal atmosphere "due to the common association between dragons and demons," explains Art Director Pierre-Olivier Vincent. Earlier designs featured rock structures that suggested dragon shapes, but the production went away from these less realistic images in favor of a more intimidating and dramatic set for the dragons' lair.

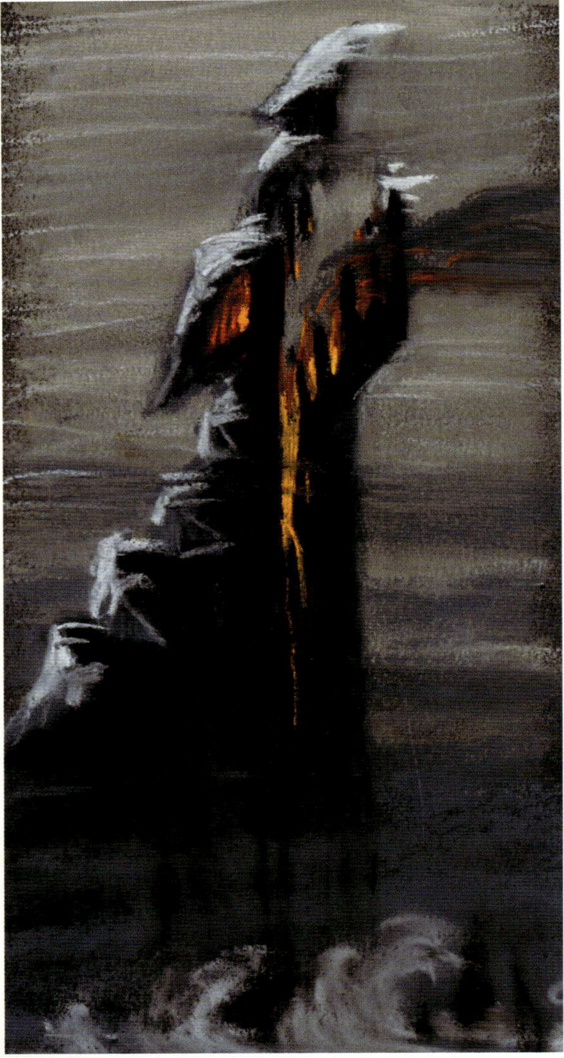
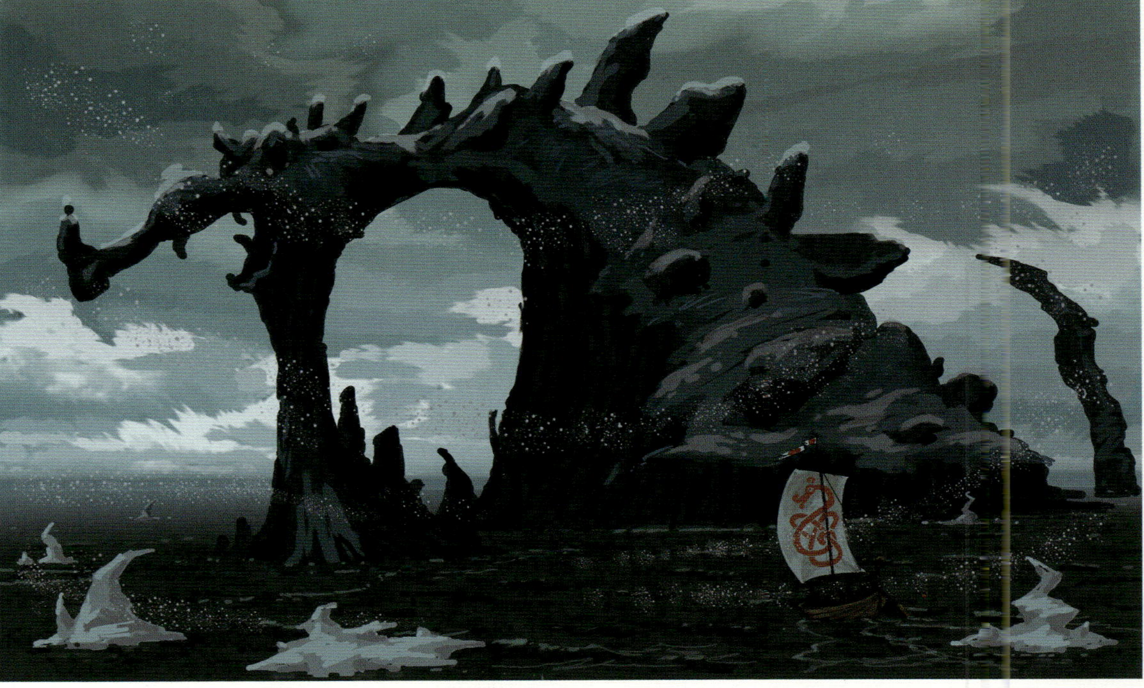

IN EARLIER DEVELOPMENT concepts, there was one shared island, with dragons living on one side and Vikings on the other. "That's what inspired the Fire and Ice image," explains Art Director Pierre-Oliver Vincent, who took the traditional associations of an icy arctic Viking environment and a fiery dragon den and blended them into one intriguing land mass.

(previous pages) **Dragon Island Beach** — Pierre-Olivier Vincent — digital paint. *(top left)* **Dragon Island Concepts** — Pierre-Olivier Vincent — digital paint. *(above left)* **Dragon Island Concept** — Geefwee Boedoe — digital paint. *(above right)* **Dragon Island Concept** — Paul Shardlow — digital paint. *(right)* **Dragon Island** — Pierre-Olivier Vincent — digital paint.

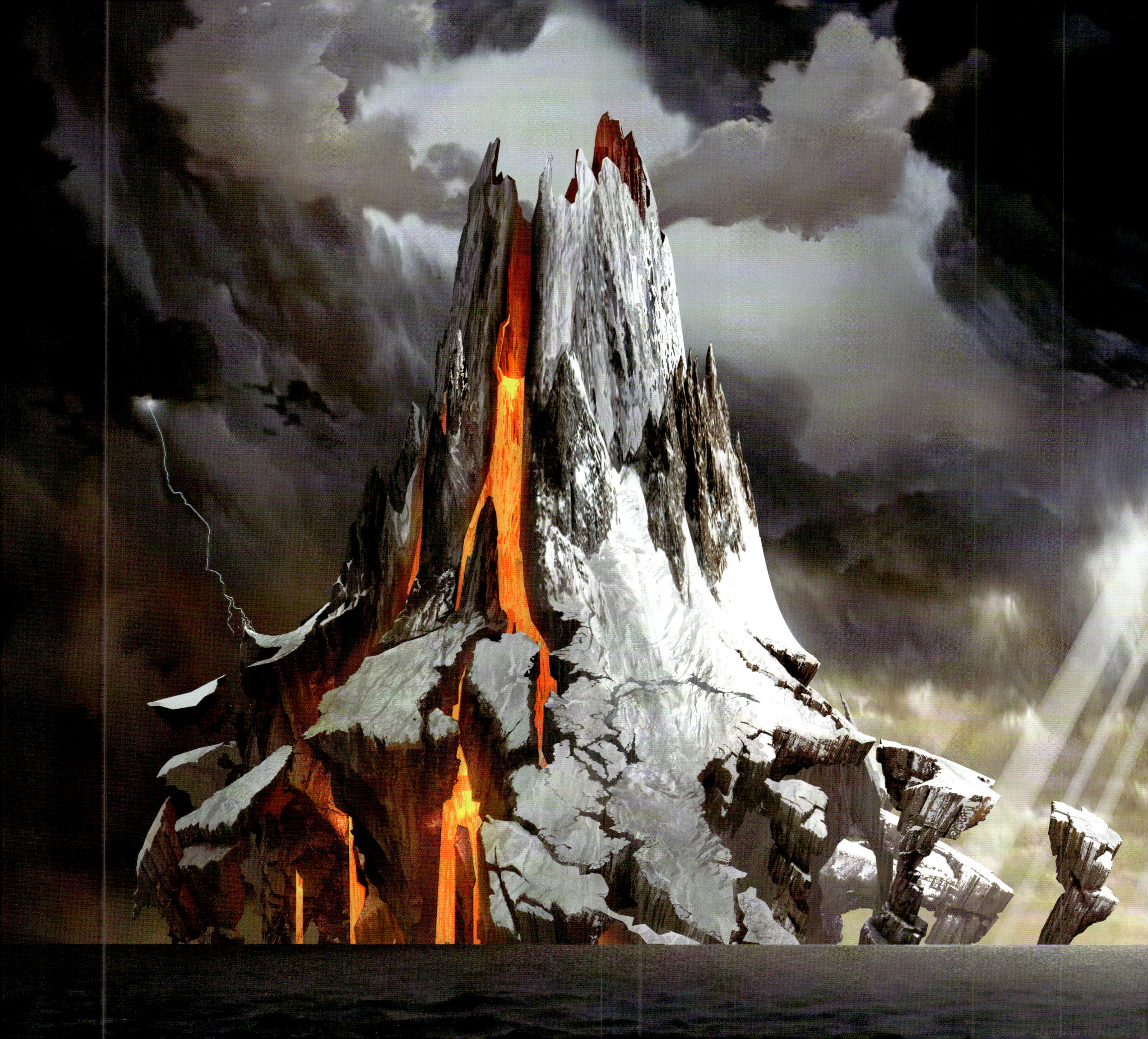

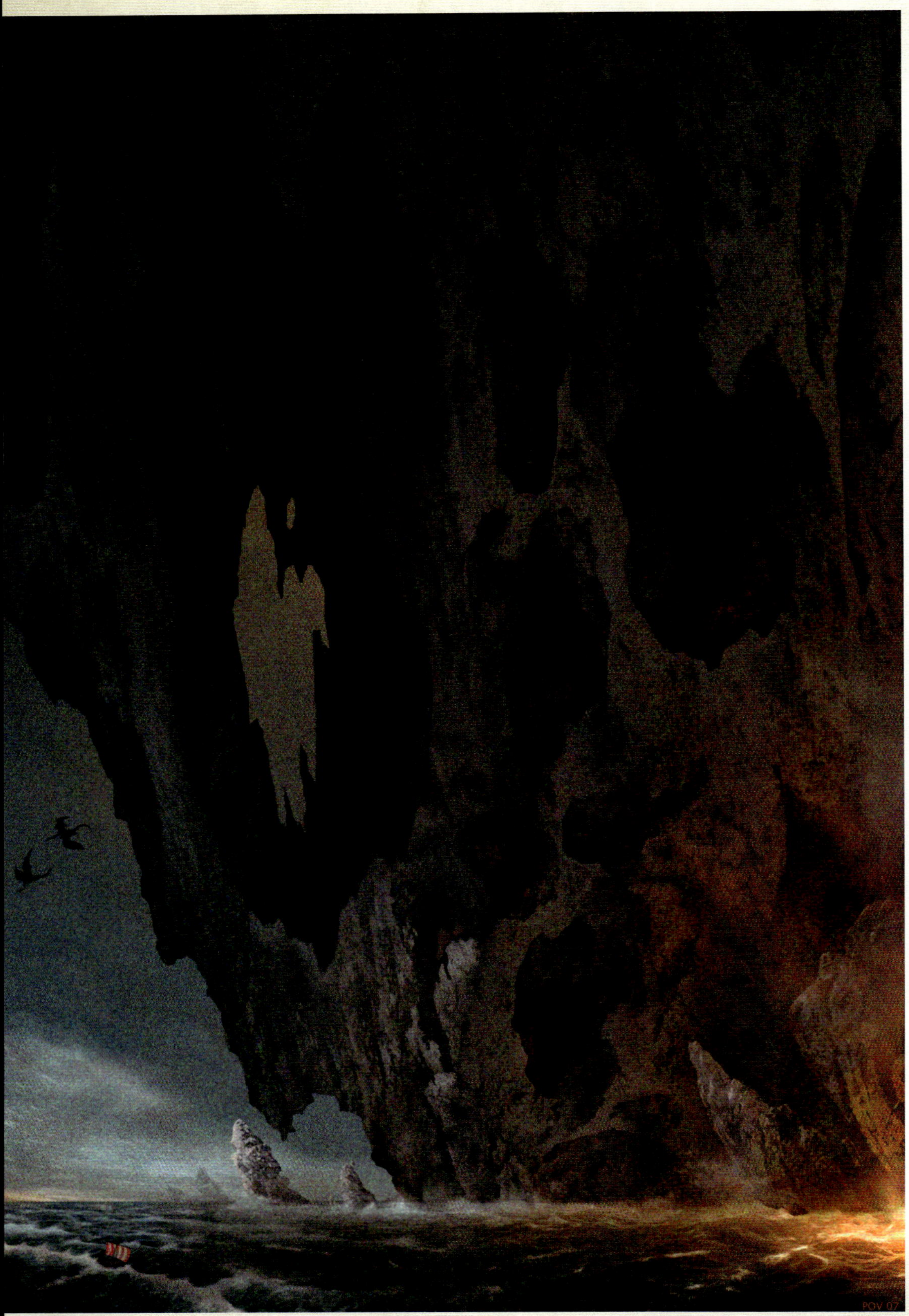

Dragon Island is the most twisted, off-kilter, abstract, unwelcoming, pointy and volcanic environment imaginable. It's no wonder the Vikings lost all their ships whenever they went to look for it.

—Kathy Altieri, Production Designer

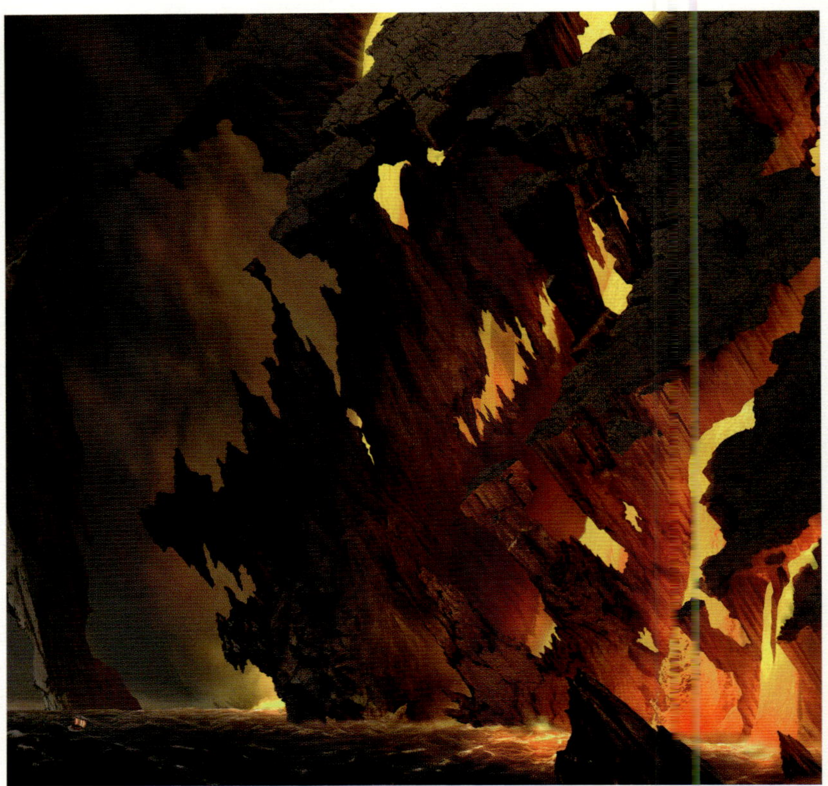

(left) **Dragon Cliff** — Pierre-Olivier Vincent — digital paint.

(above) **Dragon Cliff Lava** — Pierre-Olivier Vincent — digital paint.

(right) **Dragon Island Final** — Pierre-Olivier Vincent — digital paint.

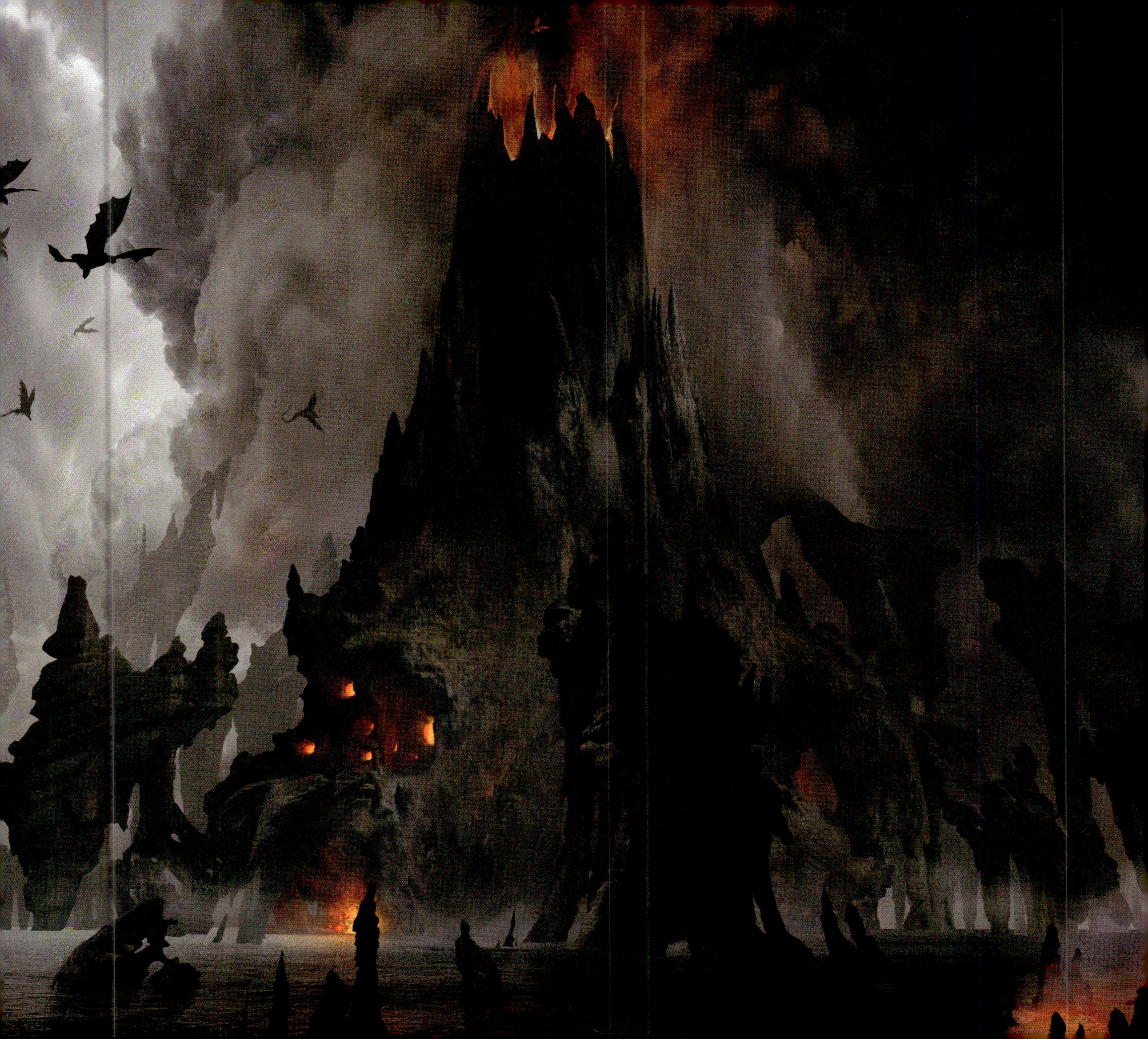

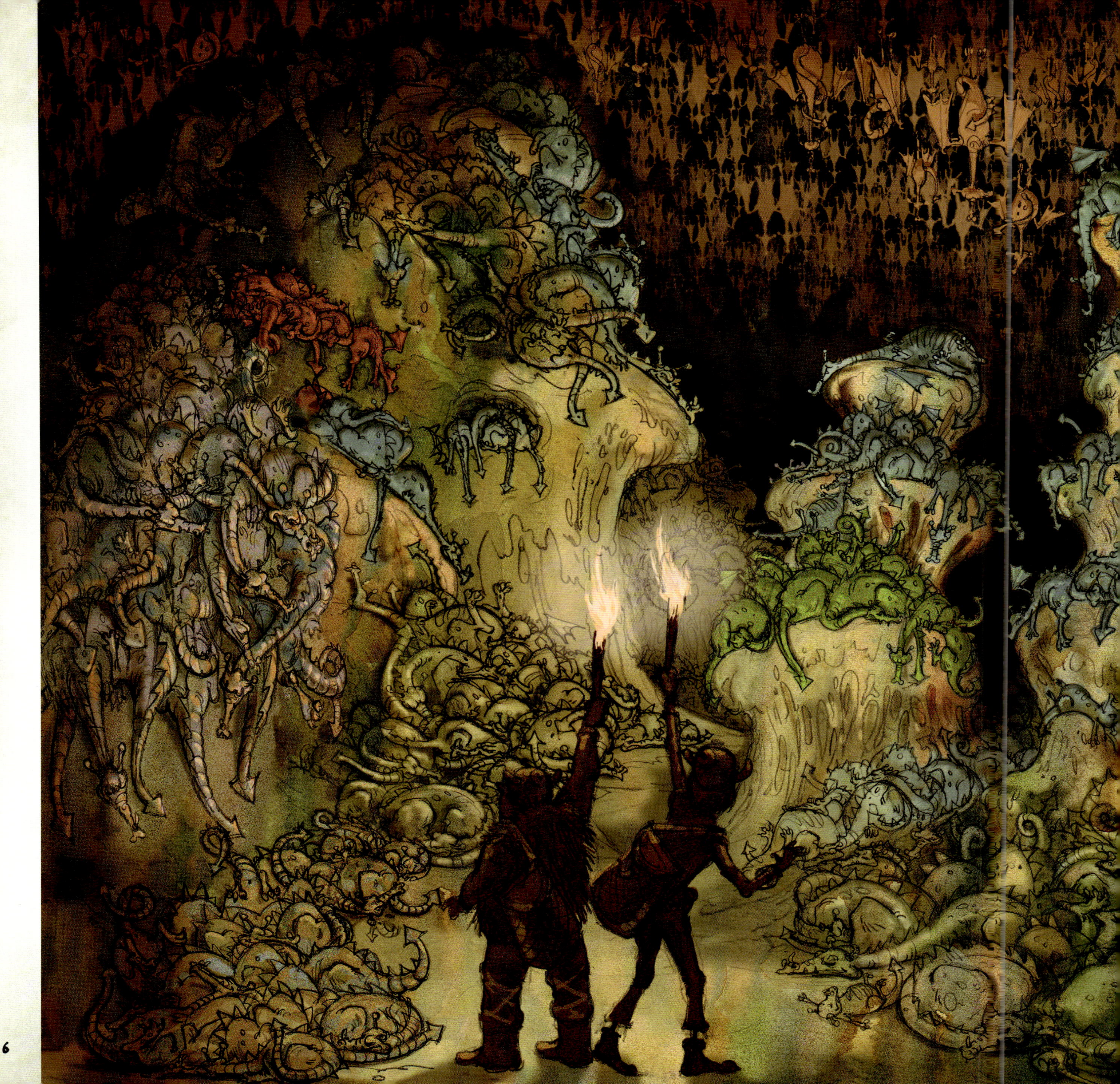

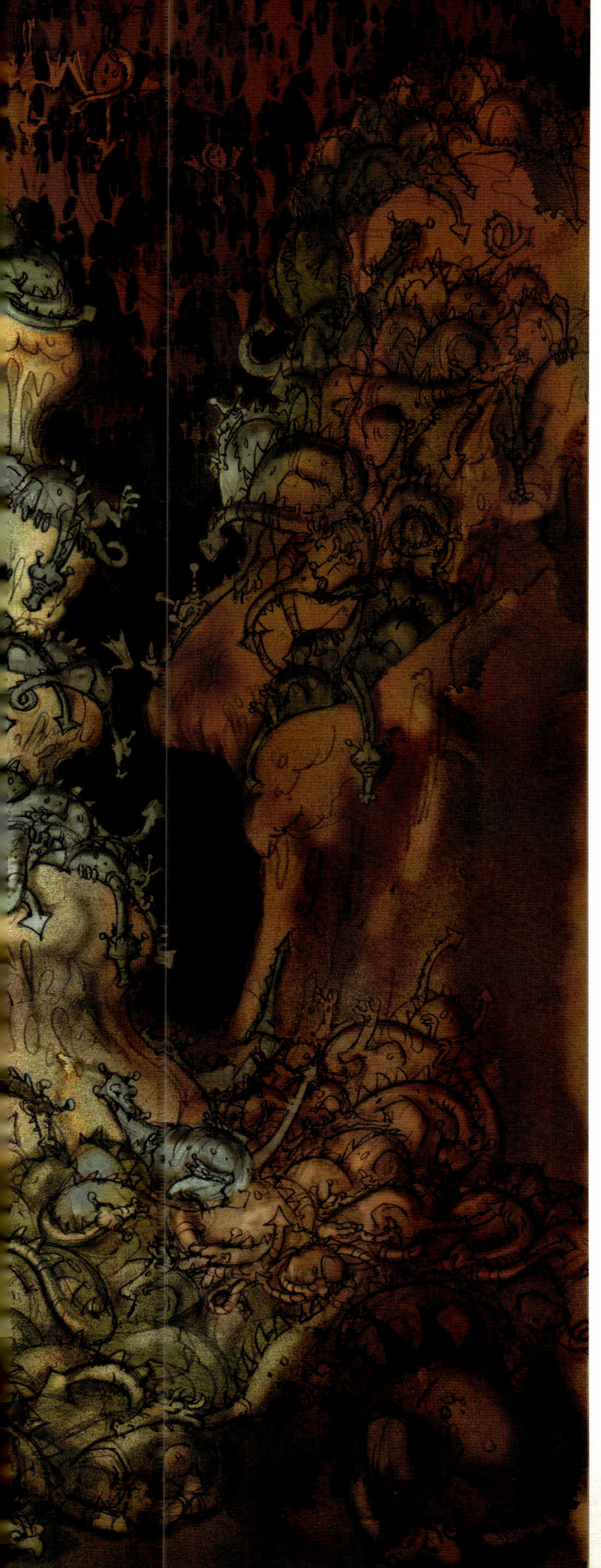

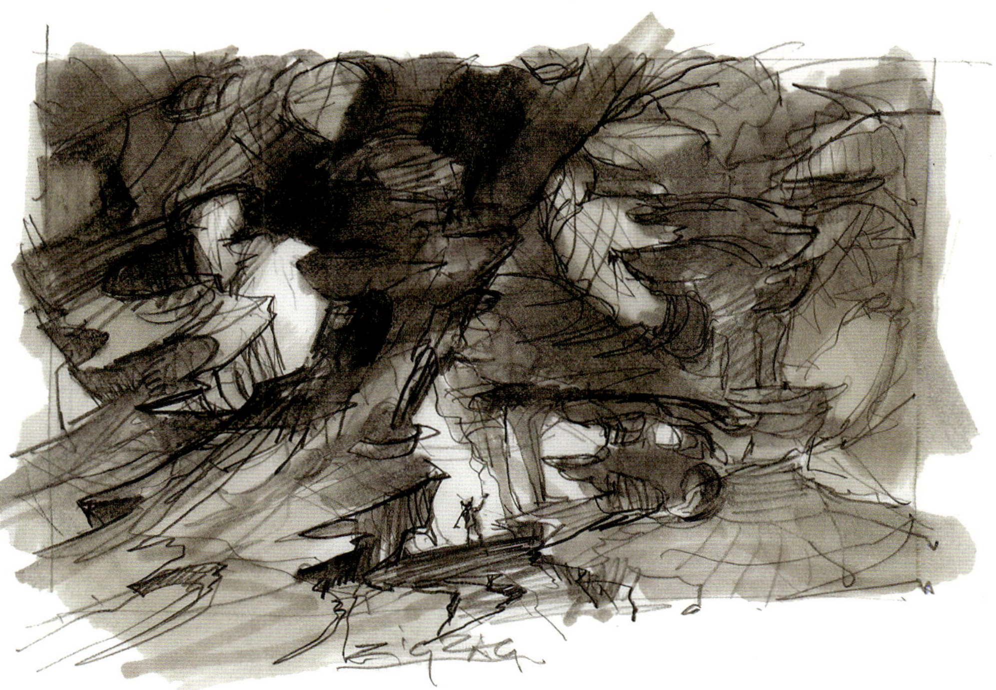

Dragon Cave

The interior of the island is essentially a caldera—a cavernous basin created in the collapsed center of a volcano. It is rife with stalactites and stalagmites, for which the modeling department sculpted a series of columns to convey the desired shape language, and then placed and scaled them throughout the cavern to create a sense of chaotic, maze-like depth.

The inner sanctum of the caves houses the nest of the Red Death, and the entrance to this location was fondly called the "Swiss Cheese set" by the modeling department. "It's our term of endearment for the space in which we were asked to build many holes, a task which is as difficult to model in CG as it is in physical sculpting," notes Modeling Supervisor Matt Paulson. This set was originally intended to serve as the dragon rookery, a protected colony where countless baby dragons awaited their moments to fly in an earlier version of the story.

(left) **Nursery** — Paul Shardlow — digital paint. *(above)* **Dragon Cave Sketch** — Emil Mitev — pencil.

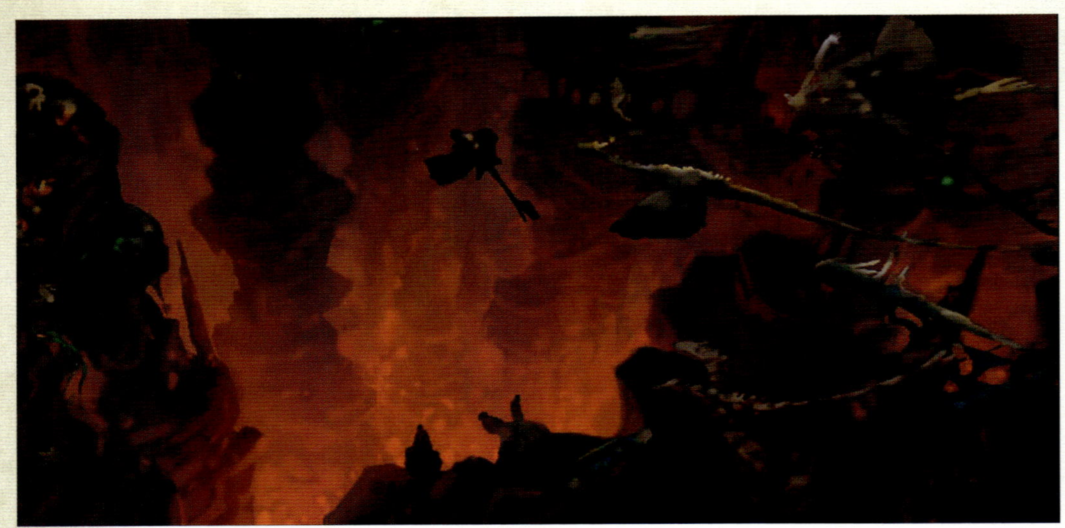

(above) **Cave Lighting Key** — Zhaoping Wei — digital paint. *(below)* **Dragon Cave** — Pierre-Olivier Vincent — digital paint.
(right) **Cave Platform** — Pierre-Olivier Vincent — digital paint.

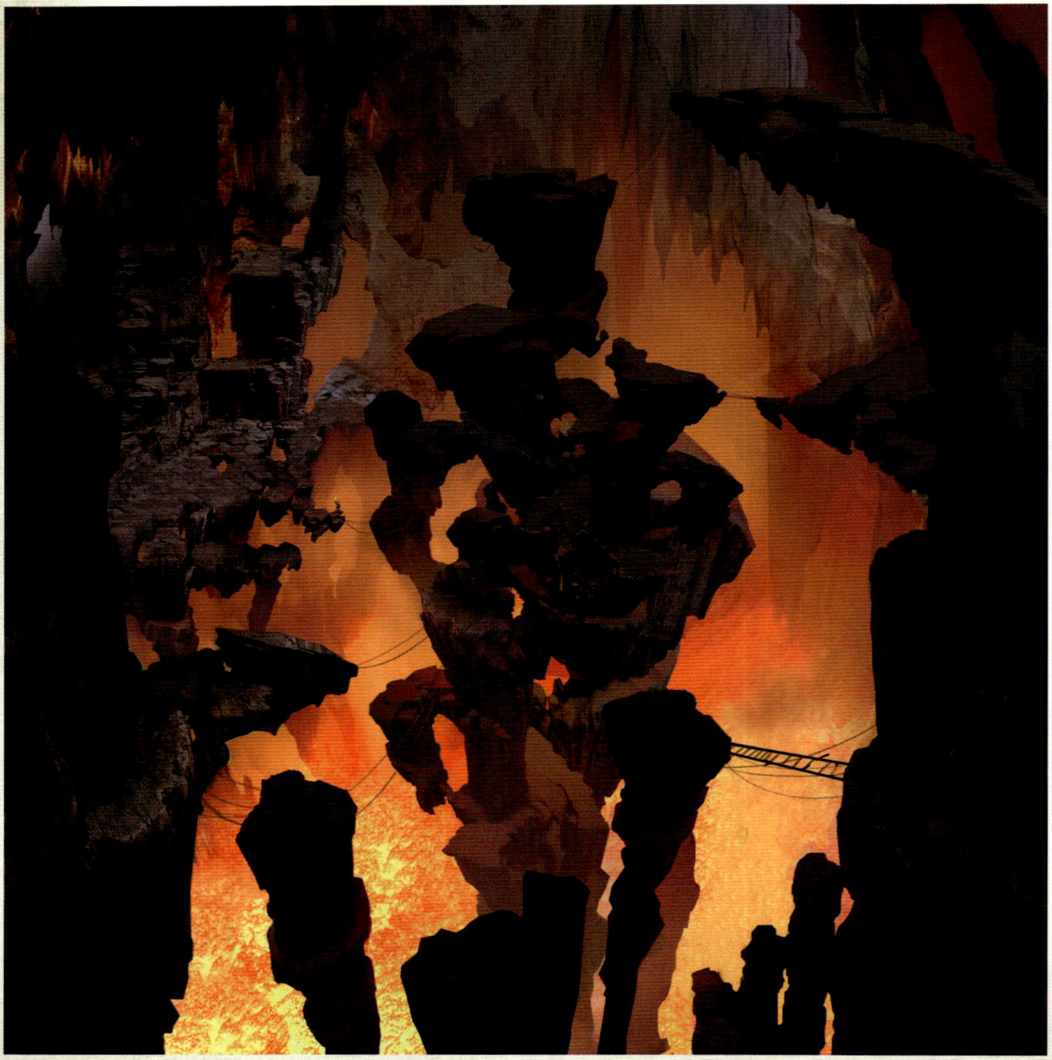

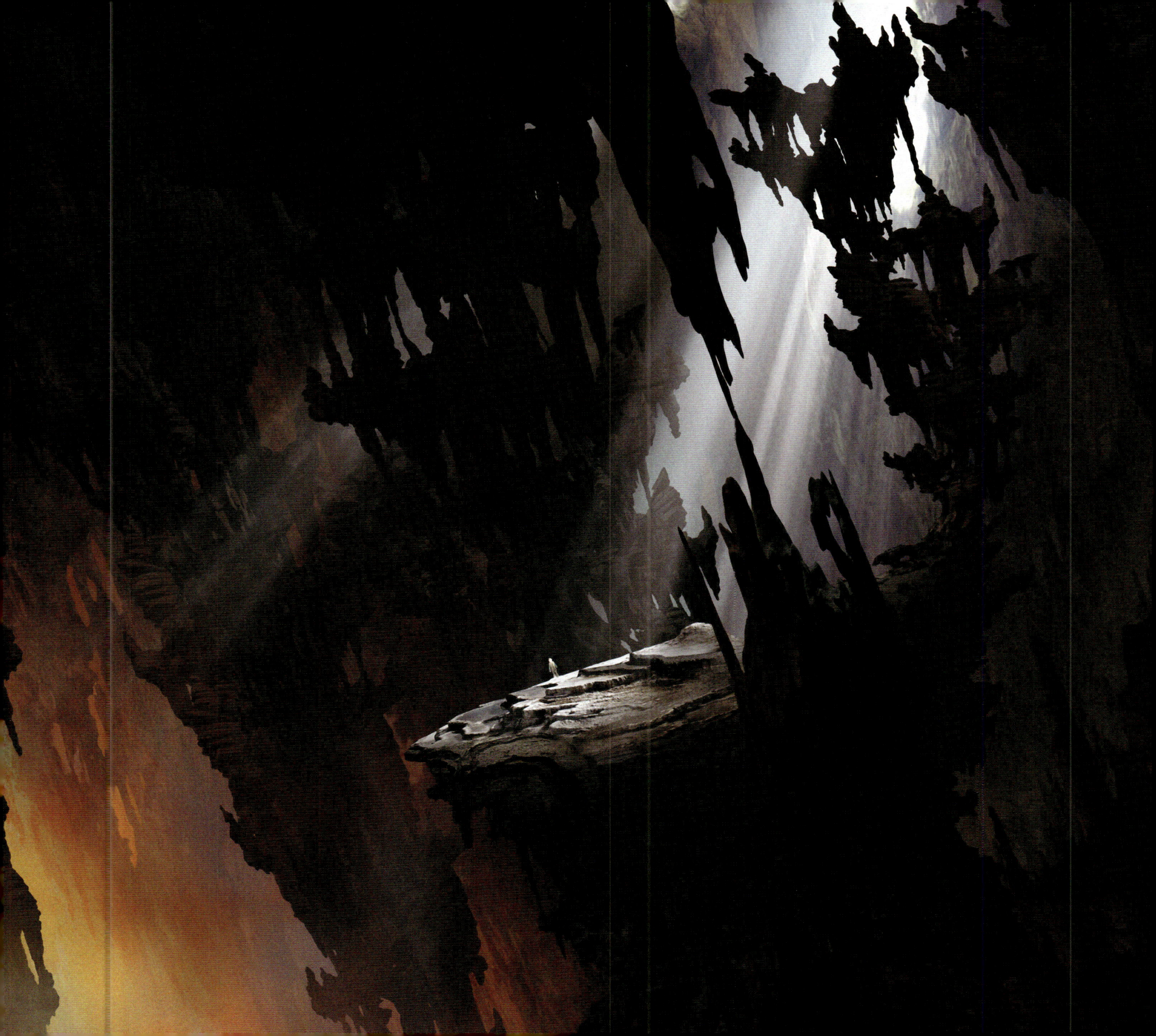

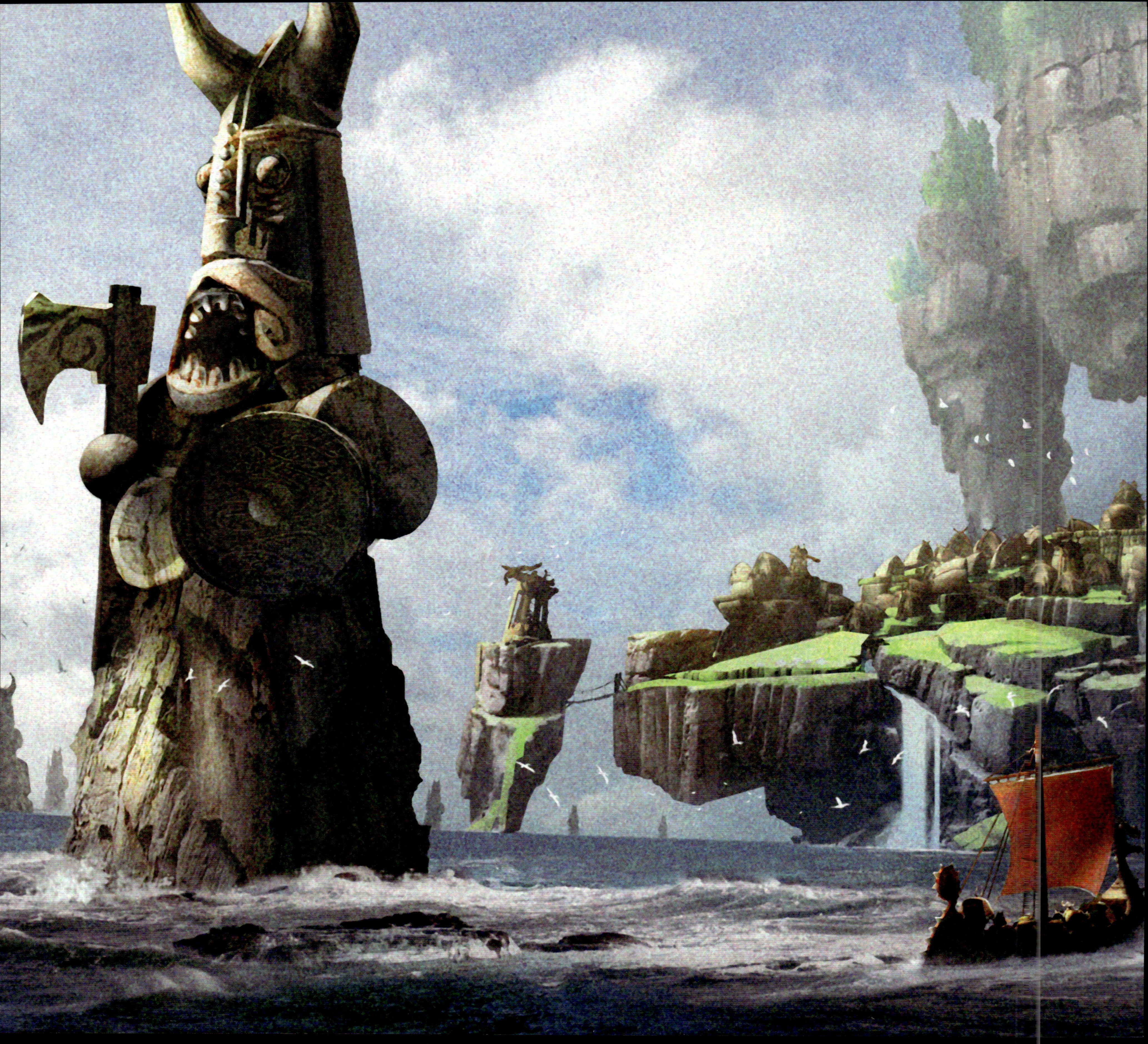

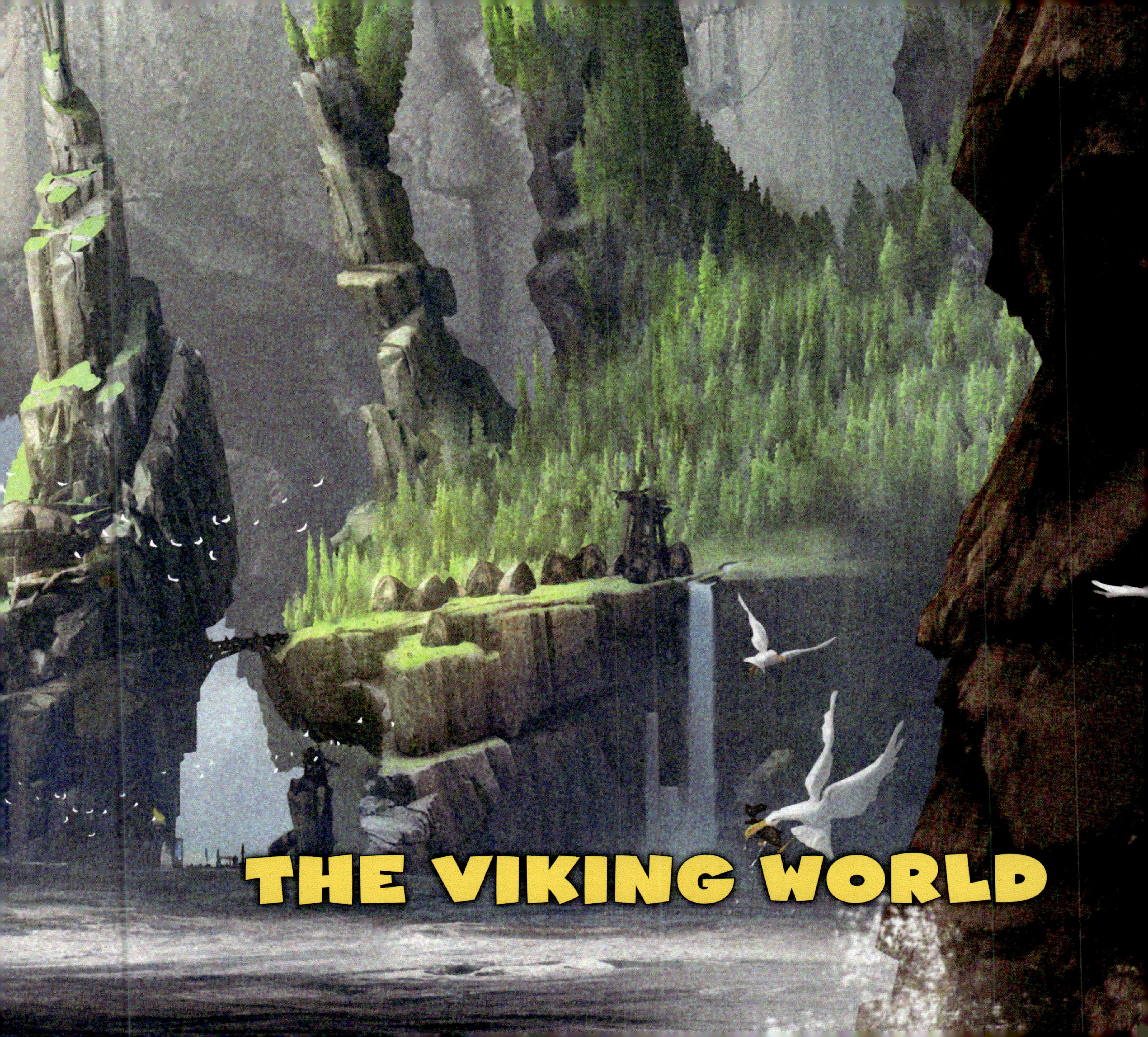

THE VIKING WORLD

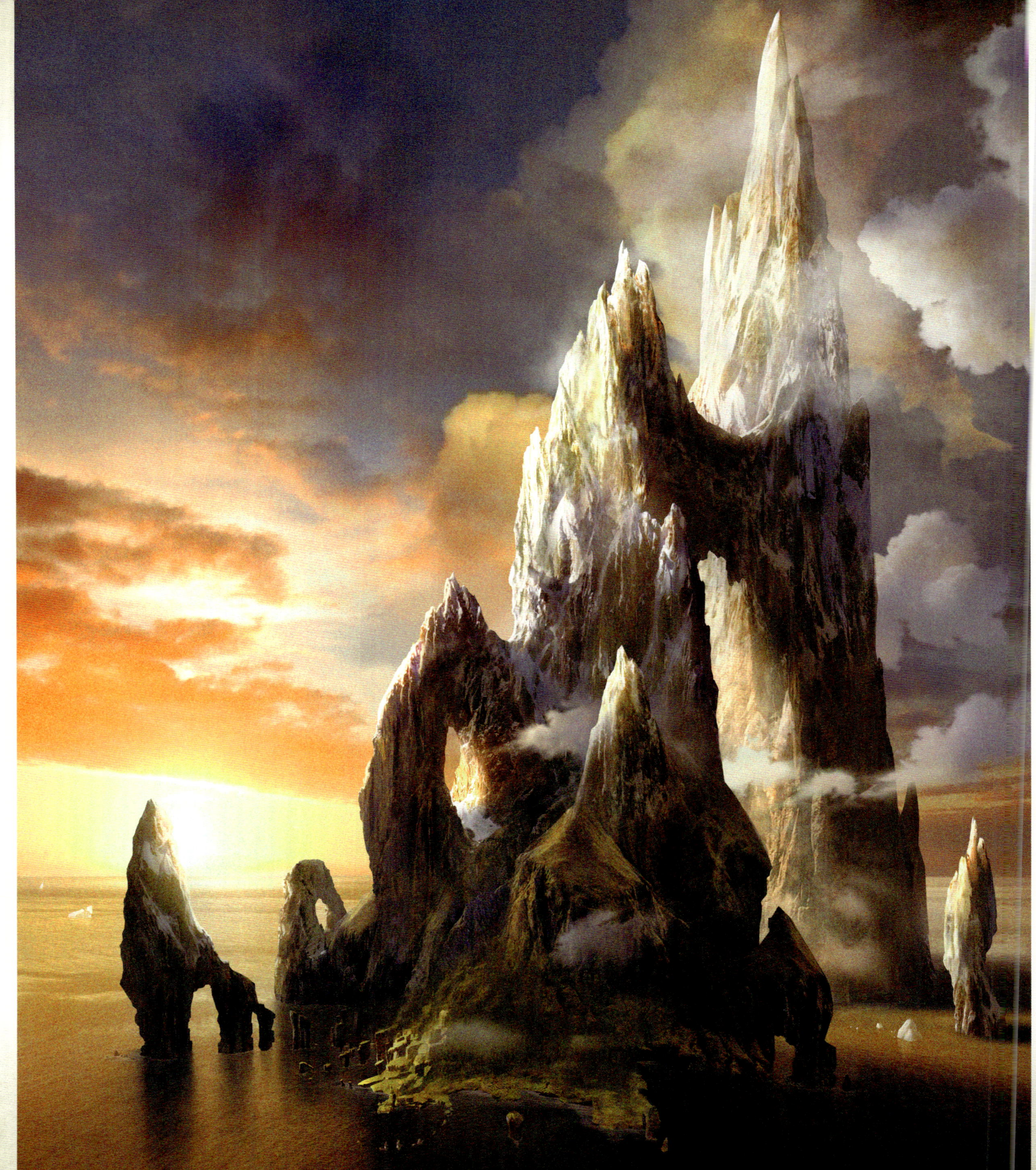

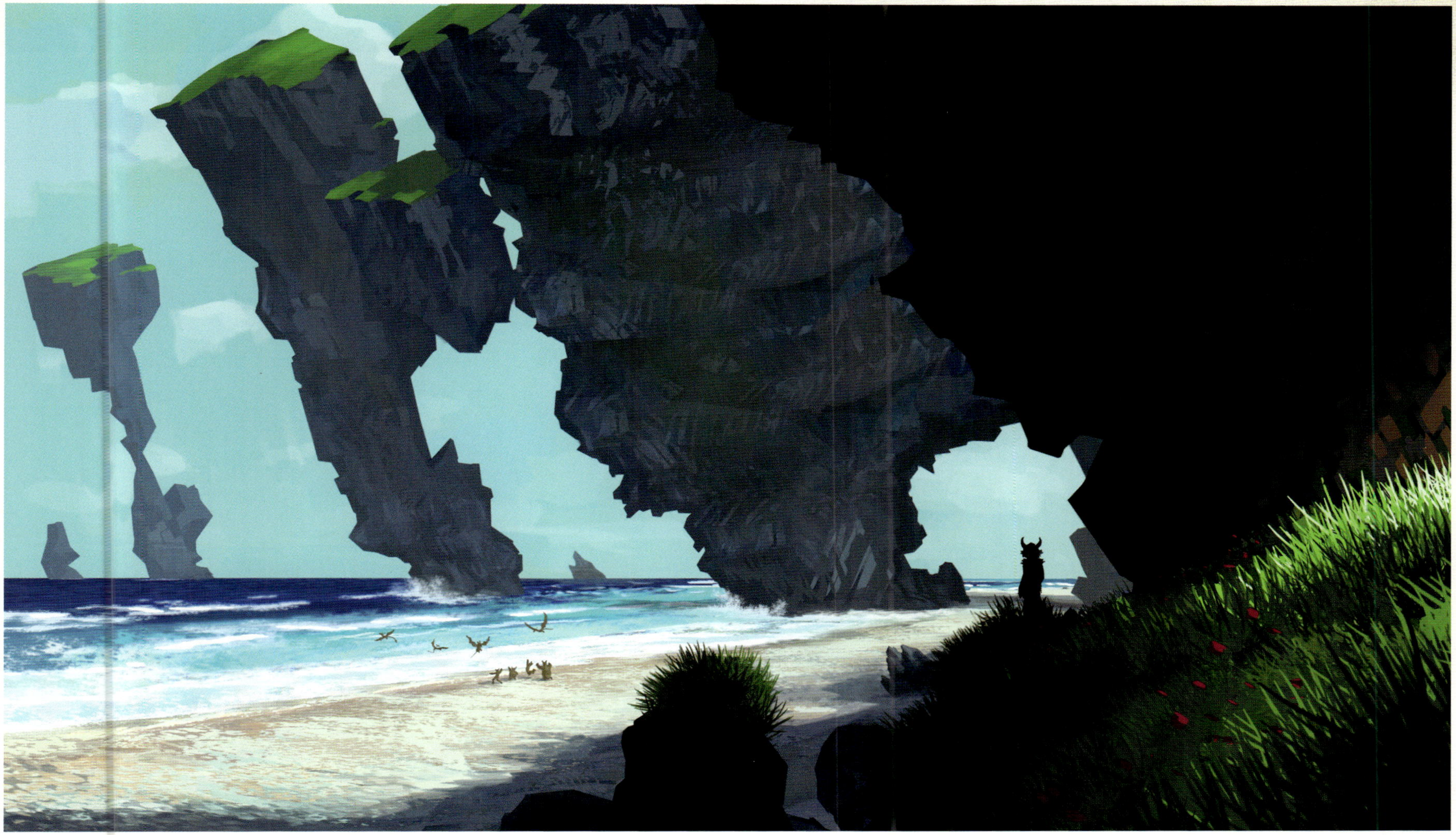

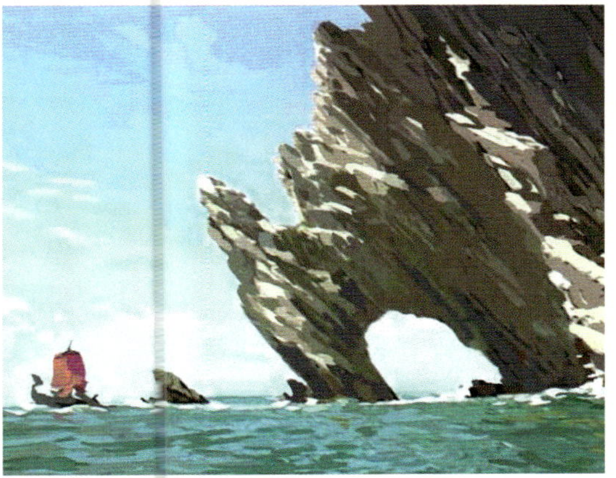

The Isle of Berk

To come upon the Isle of Berk is like discovering a mountainous forest in the middle of the ocean. Huge rocky peaks jut out from the sea and reach into the rich blue of the sky, with a lush, green oasis nestled between the precipices. At its conception, Art Director Pierre-Olivier Vincent envisioned a mountain so high as to triple the height of Hawaii's Mauna Kea, and although scale is not pushed to quite that level in the final version, the island still makes an impressive statement. "It features landscapes that are made of stylized shapes to bring whimsy to the environment, but are treated with realistic lighting and surfacing to give a sense of tangible space. We all felt that Berk should be a place you would want to visit," says Production Designer Kathy Altieri.

The crescent-shaped tip of the island is actually the only portion of Berk that has been fully modeled. "Every time you see Berk outside of the village, it's done by matte painting. They've created trees, rocks, distant snow, grass, and other amazing touches that do a great job giving scale and detail to the island," notes Visual Effects Supervisor Craig Ring.

(previous pages) **Village Sea Statues** — Pierre-Olivier Vincent — digital paint. *(left)* **Berk Final** — Pierre-Olivier Vincent — digital paint. *(above)* **Berk Color** — Zhaoping Wei — digital paint. *(above right)* **Berk Coast Beach** — Pierre-Olivier Vincent — digital paint

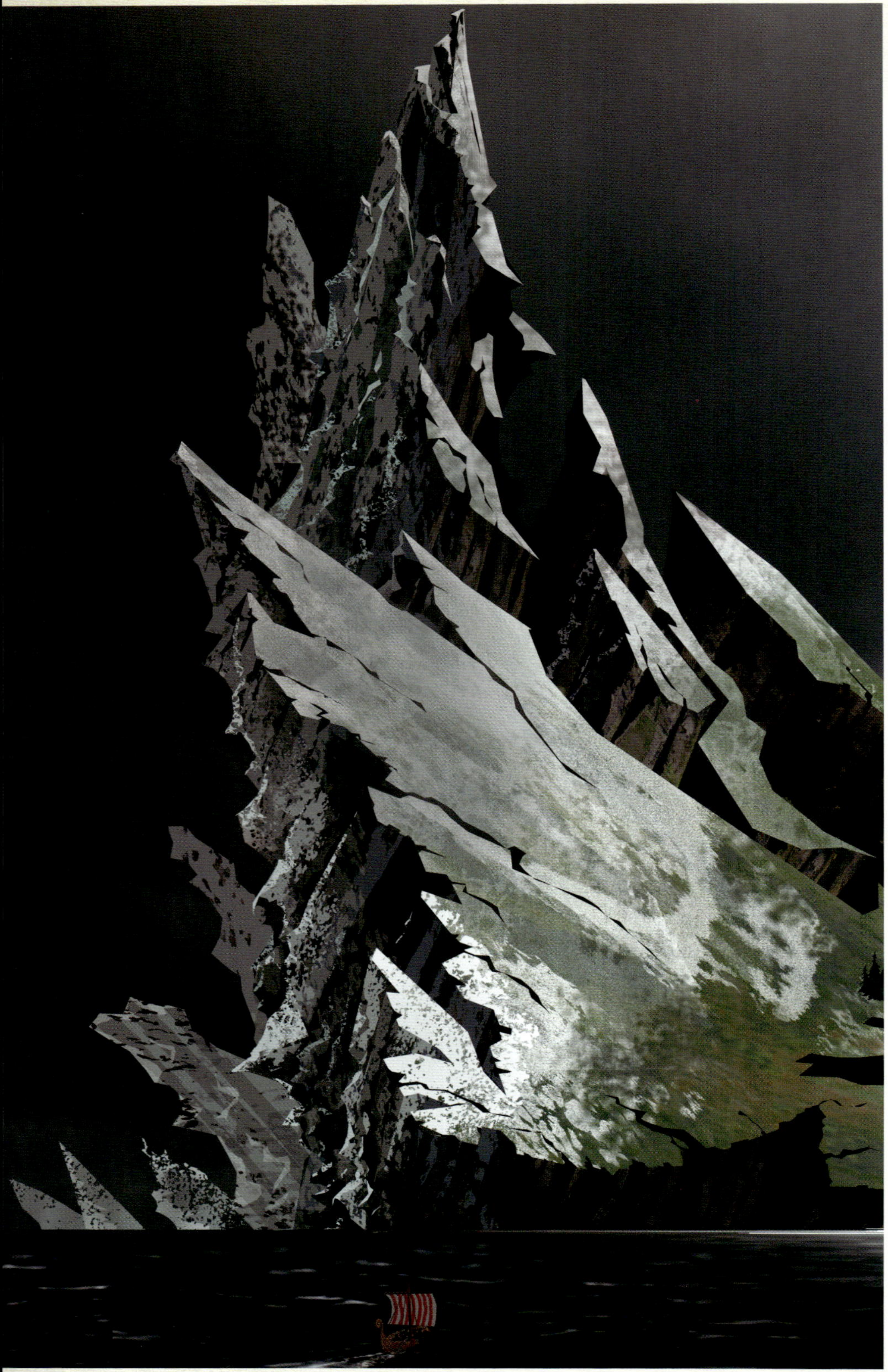

It's a balancing act to create an environment that is as bleak and tough as only Vikings would brave, yet believable and appealing enough to make it a place you would want to visit.

—Bonnie Arnold, Producer

The ocean is also an integral part of the island of Berk. To bring energy and life to this vast body of water, the effects and lighting departments "used depth, texture, and cloud patch reflections to create visual interest," says Visual Effects Supervisor Craig Ring. In general, the ocean has an all-encompassing displacement effect that incorporates well-choreographed foam and splash effects. "One of our effects team members wrote a tool to figure out where the ocean touches rocks, then used a paint package to apply foam into a 2D image, which he then projected back into the set. Another member of the team developed a system that automatically snaps curves around rocks that trigger a variety of pre-simulated splashes," explains Head of Effects Matt Baer.

This world has the weight of reality, only it's super-sized.

—Chris Sanders, Director

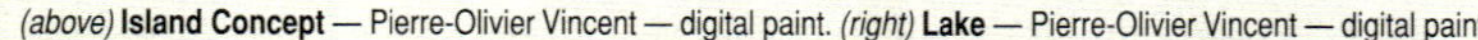

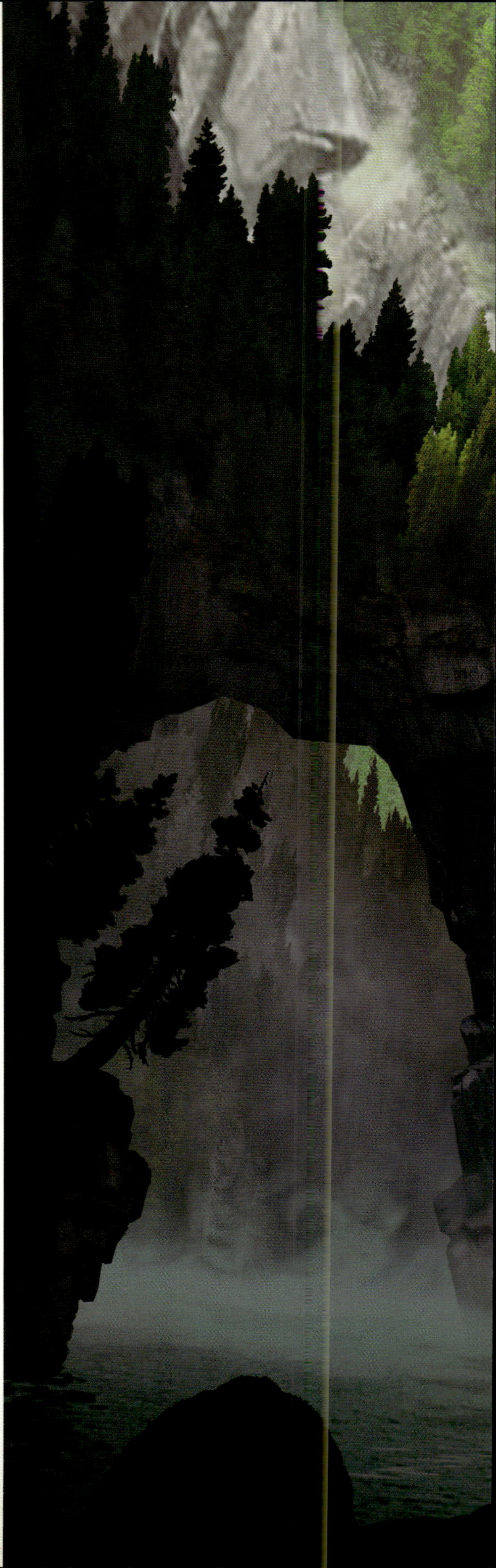

(above) **Island Concept** — Pierre-Olivier Vincent — digital paint. *(right)* **Lake** — Pierre-Olivier Vincent — digital paint.

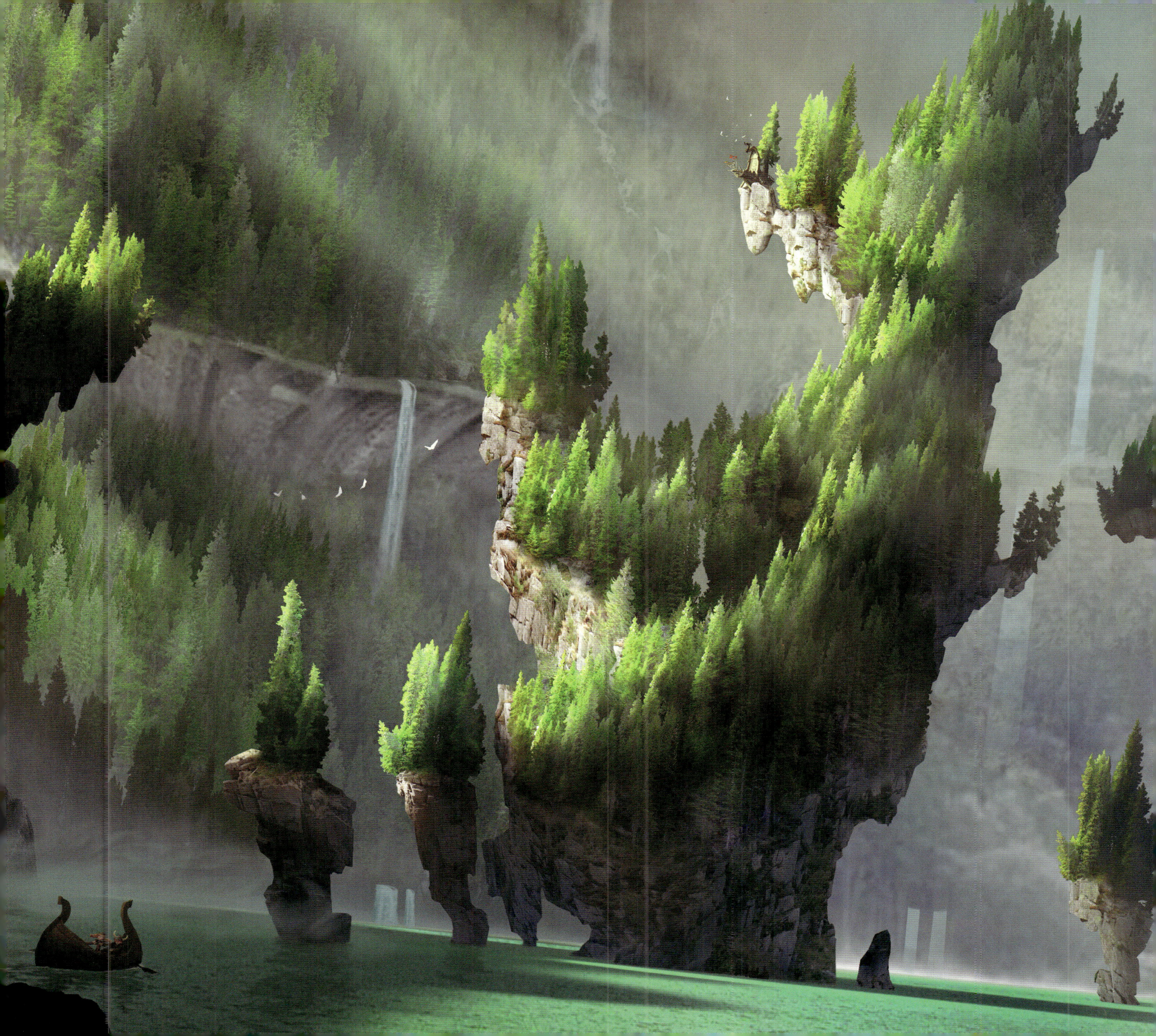

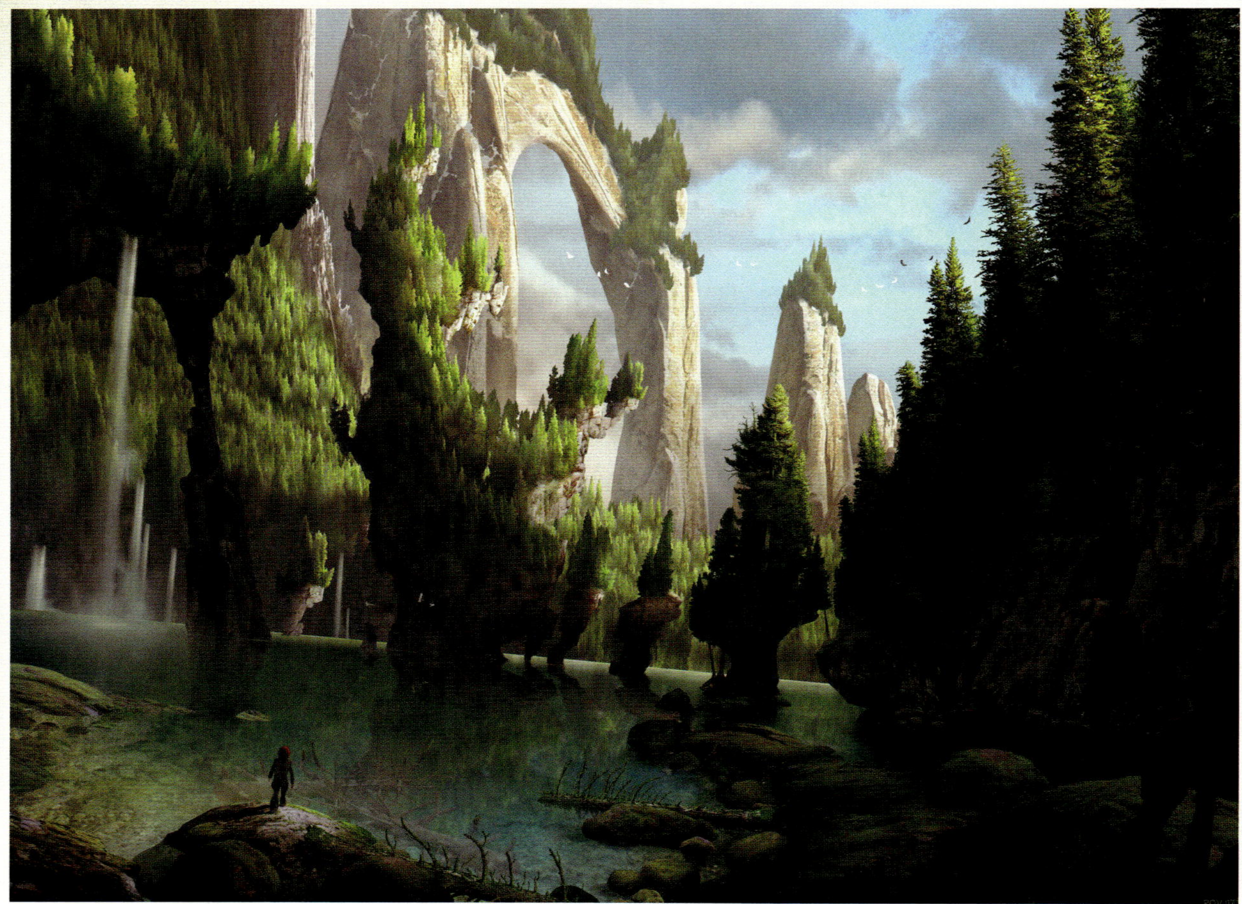

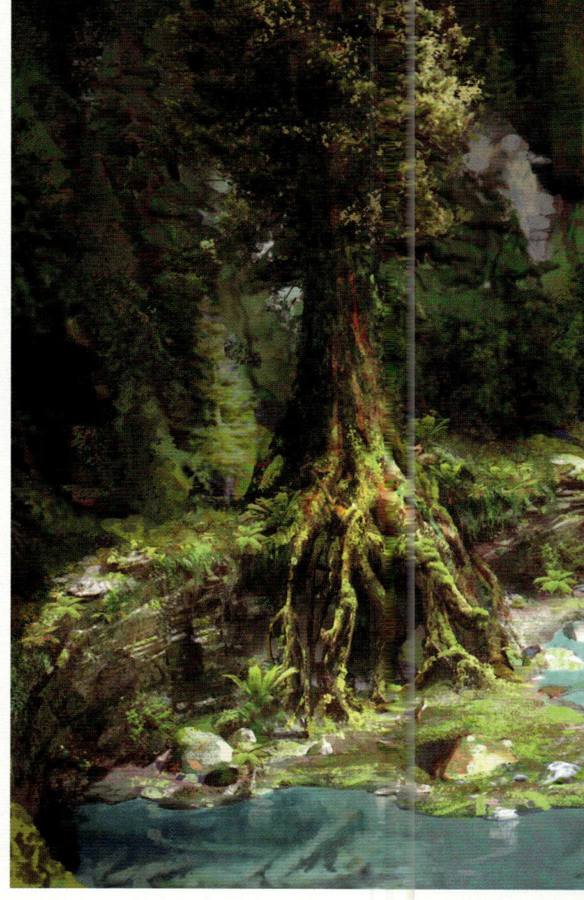

The Cove

The cove is a prominent location in the film, as it is the hidden sanctuary in which Hiccup and Toothless establish their relationship. To give the cove a sense of being a safe-haven for these characters, art direction called for "softer colors, the application of moss along trees, and calm water on the lake," recalls Head of Surfacing Sabrina Riegel. "Even the rocks are softer in style, modeled with softer edges and more rounded shapes like sandstone," adds Modeling Supervisor Matt Paulson, whose department also had the task of set-dressing the massive stone walls with foliage and tree roots in order to provide a more pleasant backdrop.

Although a calm body of water seems like it would be easier to produce than a stormy ocean, the lake in the cove presented its own set of technical challenges. Whereas the cameras over the ocean shots were generally moving, and often at a high speed, the camerawork in the cove is locked off for a majority of the time. The still camera draws more attention to reflections on the water, which are difficult to resolve in a 3D stereoscopic film. "When we tried faster environment map reflections—which is how the cliff walls were initially projected onto the water—weird depth problems would occur, making the lake hard to look at in 3D, so we ended up using ray tracing instead," explains Head of Effects Matt Baer.

Of all the sets in the film, we cheated the lighting the most in the cove. Honestly, it's really just a hole in the ground, very difficult to get light into—so we filtered light through the trees, bounced it off the walls, pushed it and pulled it until our shots told the story we were looking for.

—Kathy Altieri, Production Designer

(above) **Lake Cove** — Pierre-Olivier Vincent — digital paint. *(above right)* **Cove Overview** — Nathan Fowkes — digital paint.

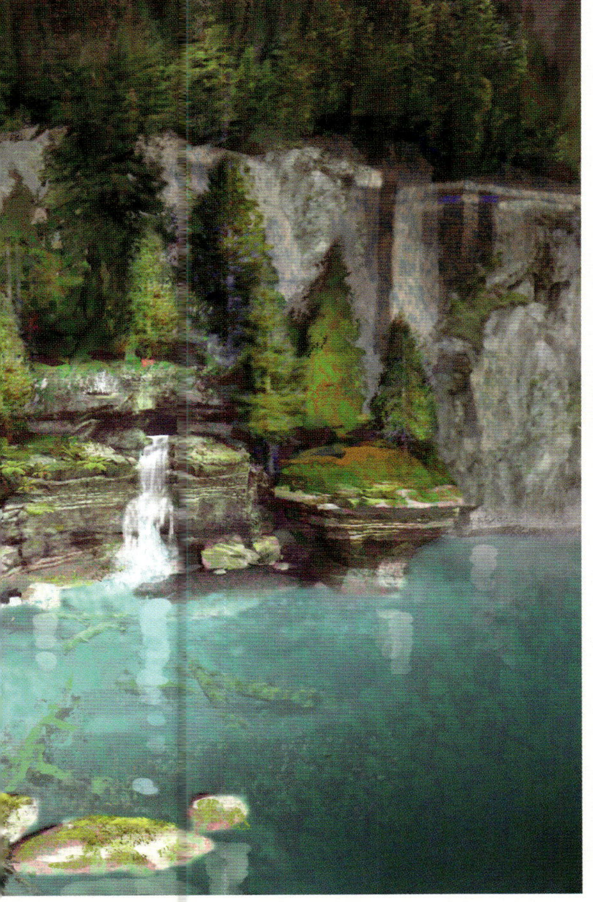

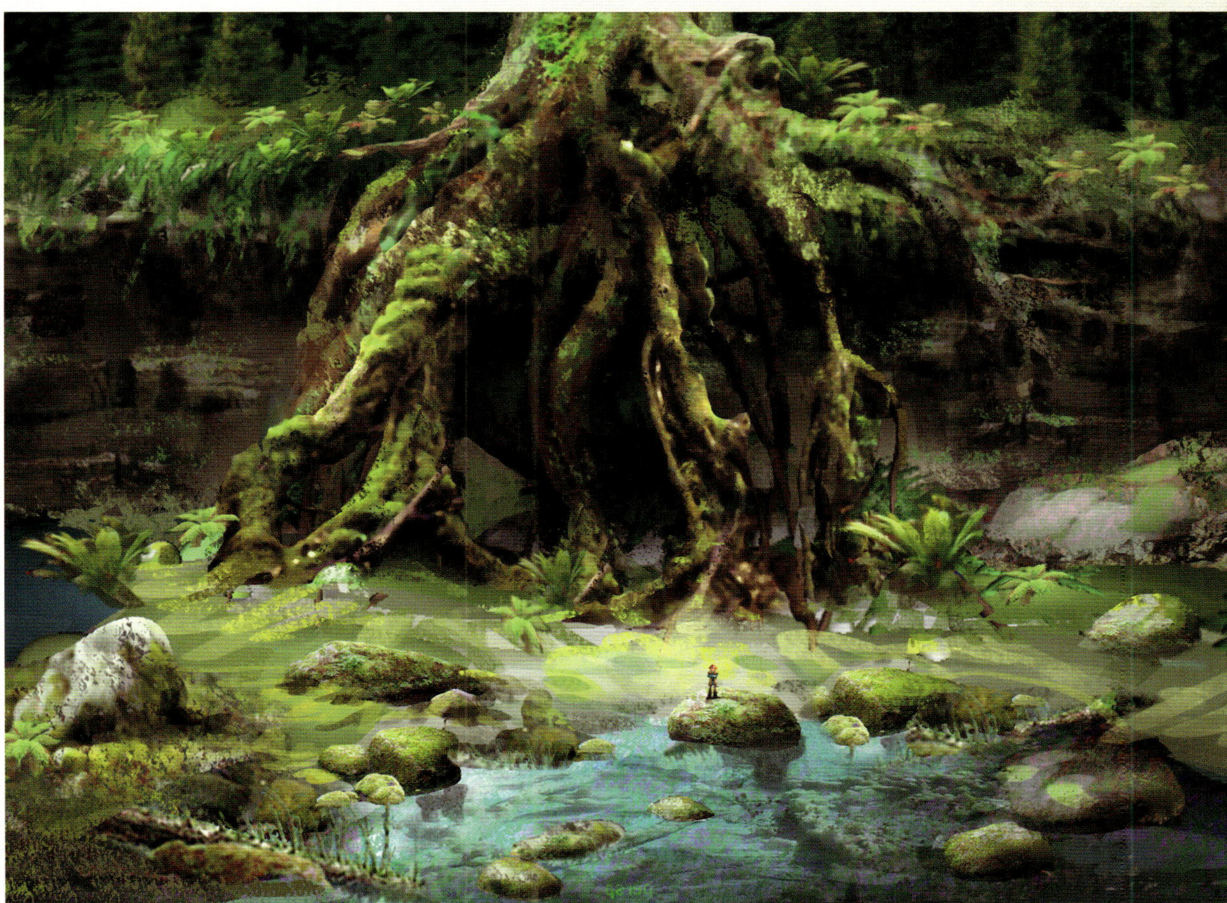

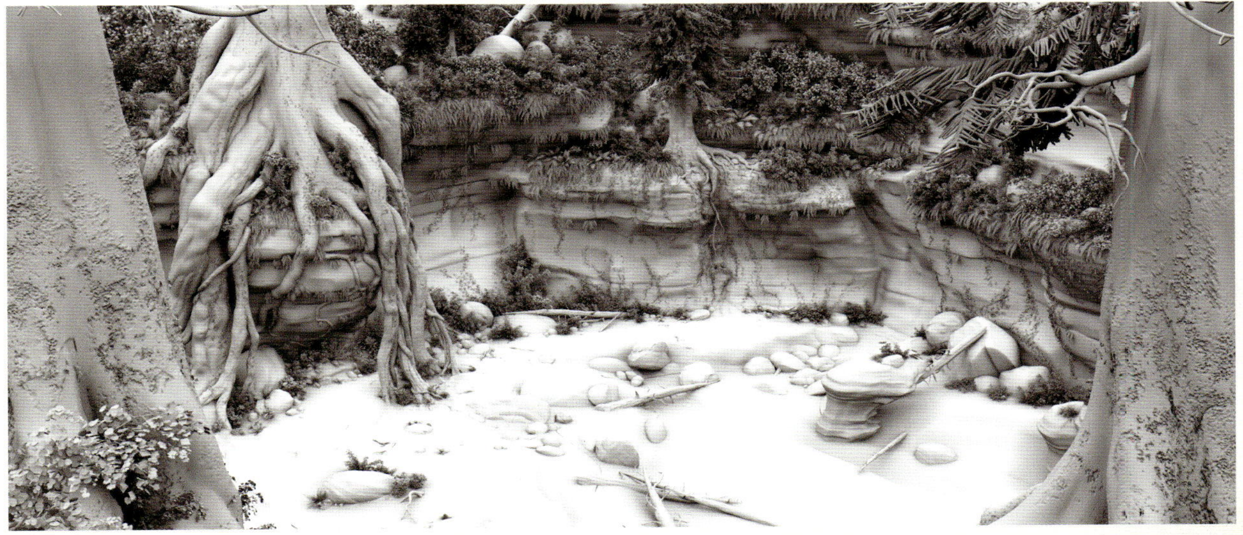

THERE IS ALSO a lovely waterfall in the cove, which was built for another use in the film and then installed in this location. It uses full fluid simulation to make water flow across rocks and down, and it calls for particle-rendering tools that allow it to break in the mist. "Once you get a waterfall going and stay a safe distance from it, it adds a nice complexity in the background," notes Visual Effects Supervisor Craig Ring.

(above right) **Cove Roots** — Nathan Fowkes — digital paint. *(above)* **The Cove** — Jason Turner & Luis Labrador — CG model.

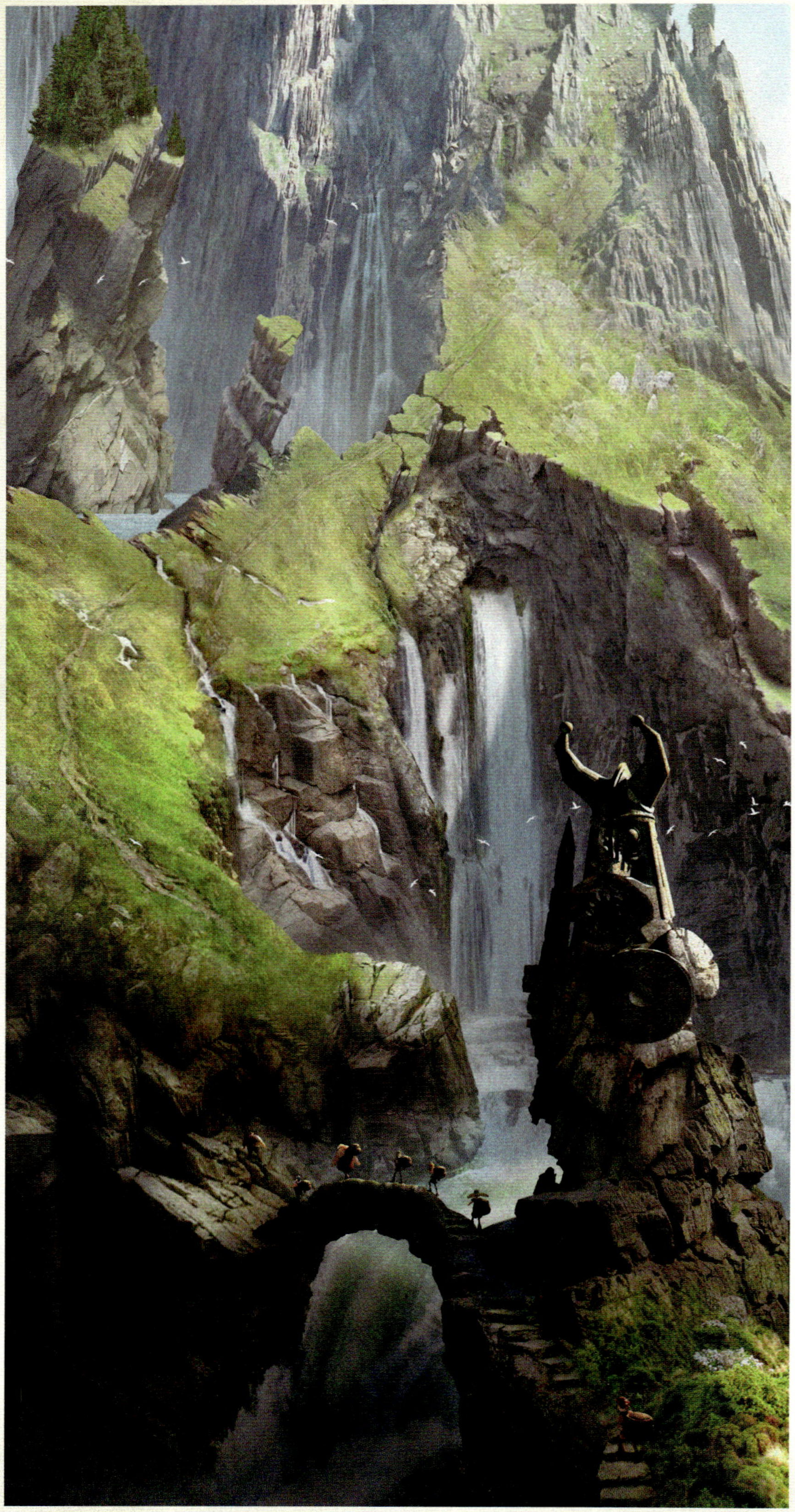

Landscapes Beyond the Adventure

A great deal of visual development artwork was created for other locations on the island of Berk. While these scenic spots did not make it to the final film, they are nonetheless spectacular.

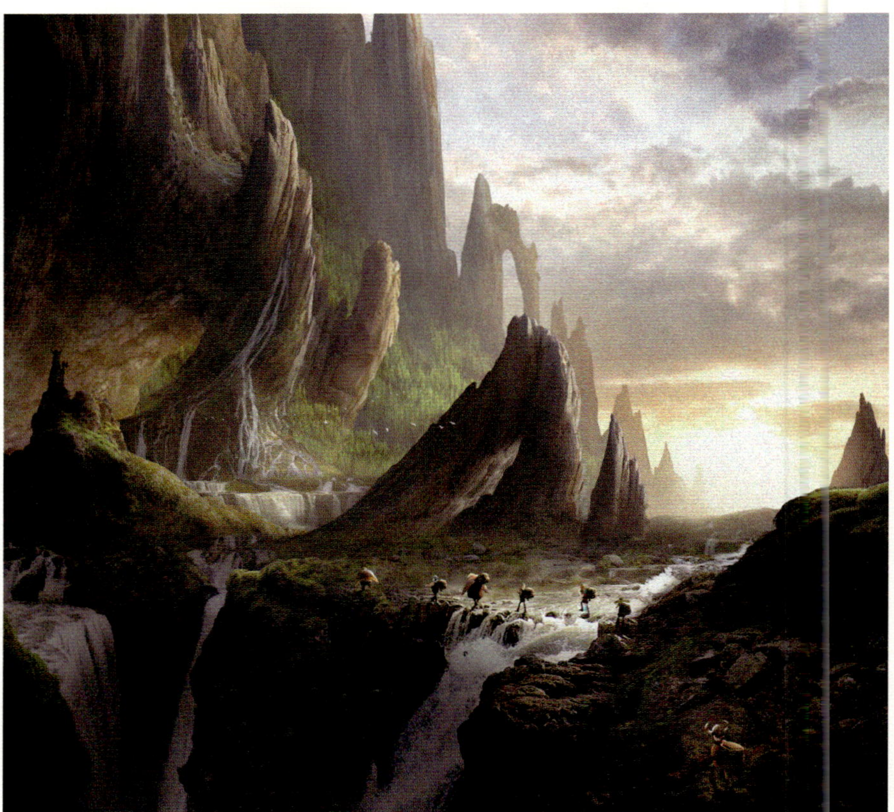

The Trek

In an earlier version of the story, the young Vikings had to trek to find a dragon rookery. Here are a few of the breathtaking locations they would have passed through on this adventure, all capturing the energy and scale of Art Director Pierre-Olivier Vincent's vision for a lush, sweepingly whimsical, and natural wonderland.

(left, above and right) **The Trek** — Pierre-Olivier Vincent — digital paint.

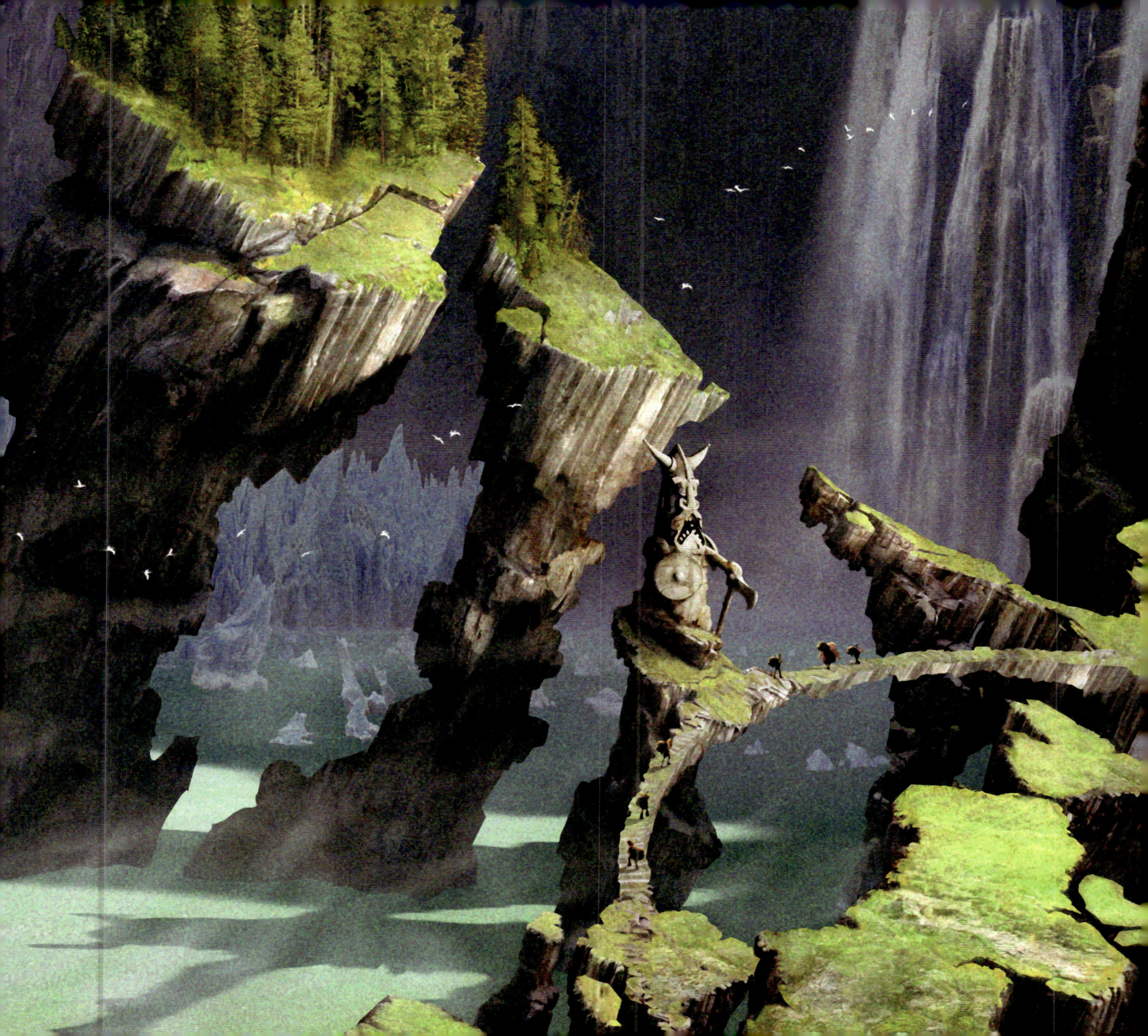

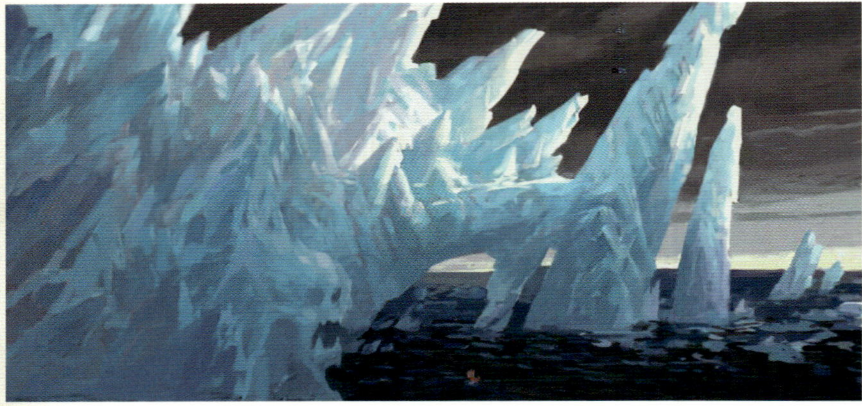

Snowy Island

At one time, the design team envisioned Berk as a more arctic isle, dressed in snow-capped mountains, icy arches, and glaciers. Although the white of the snow provided interesting visual contrast within the images, the production felt that the island should be a more warm and welcoming place.

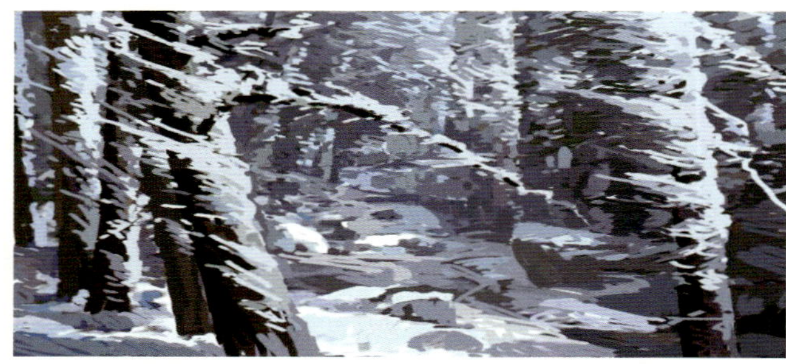

(top) **Berk Color** — Zhaoping Wei — digital paint. *(above)* **Berk Snow** — Zhaoping Wei — digital paint.
(right) **Village Ice Arches** — Pierre-Olivier Vincent — digital paint.

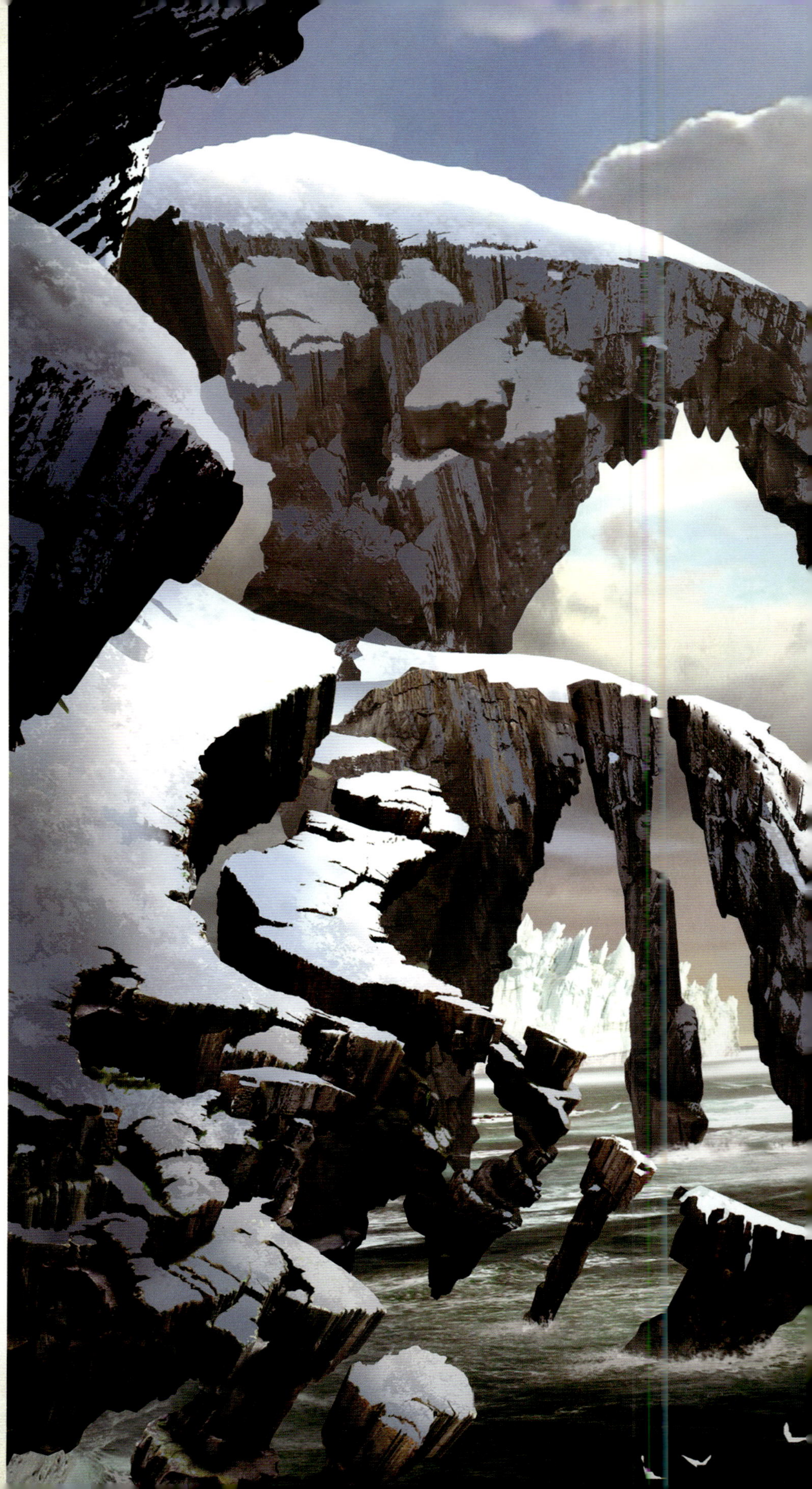

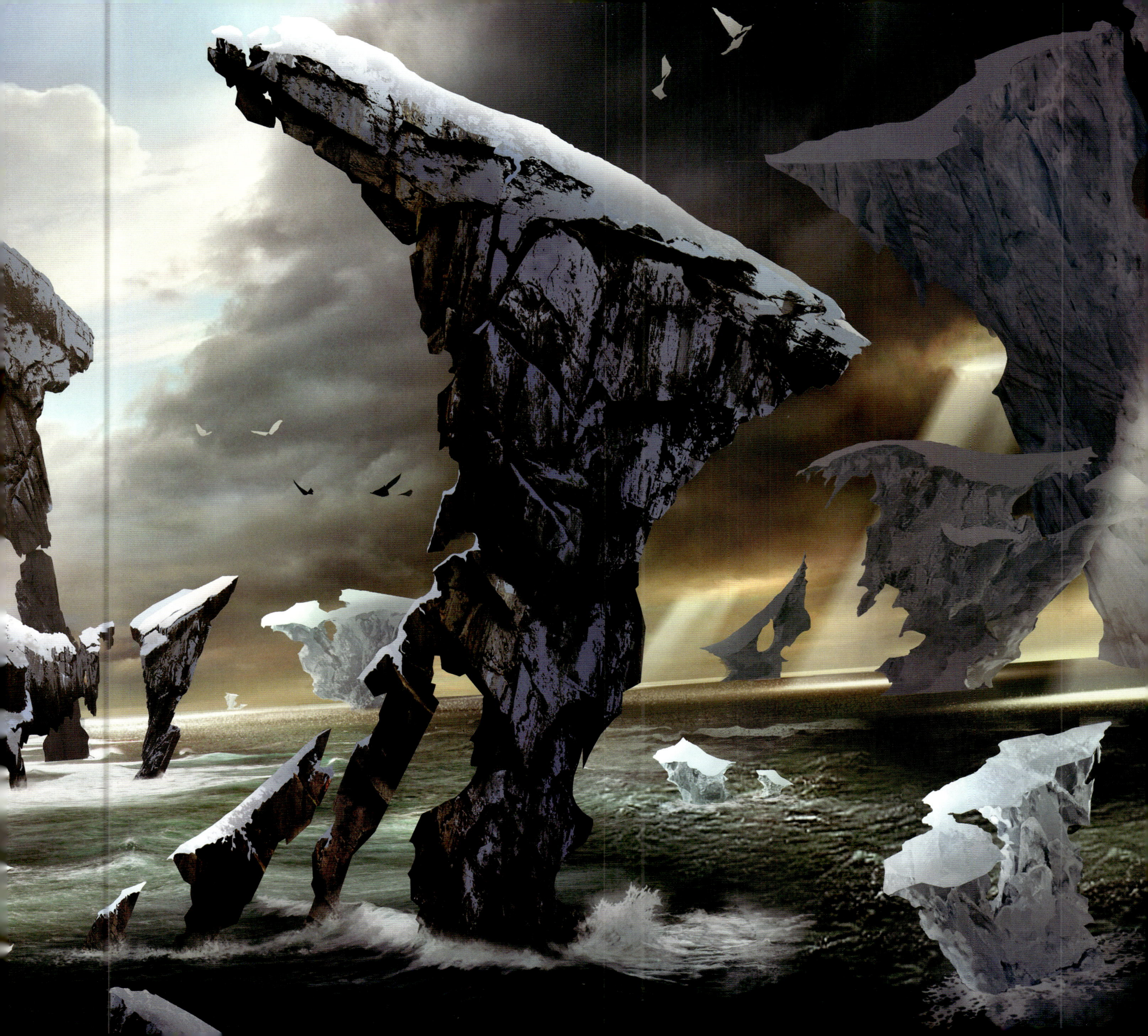

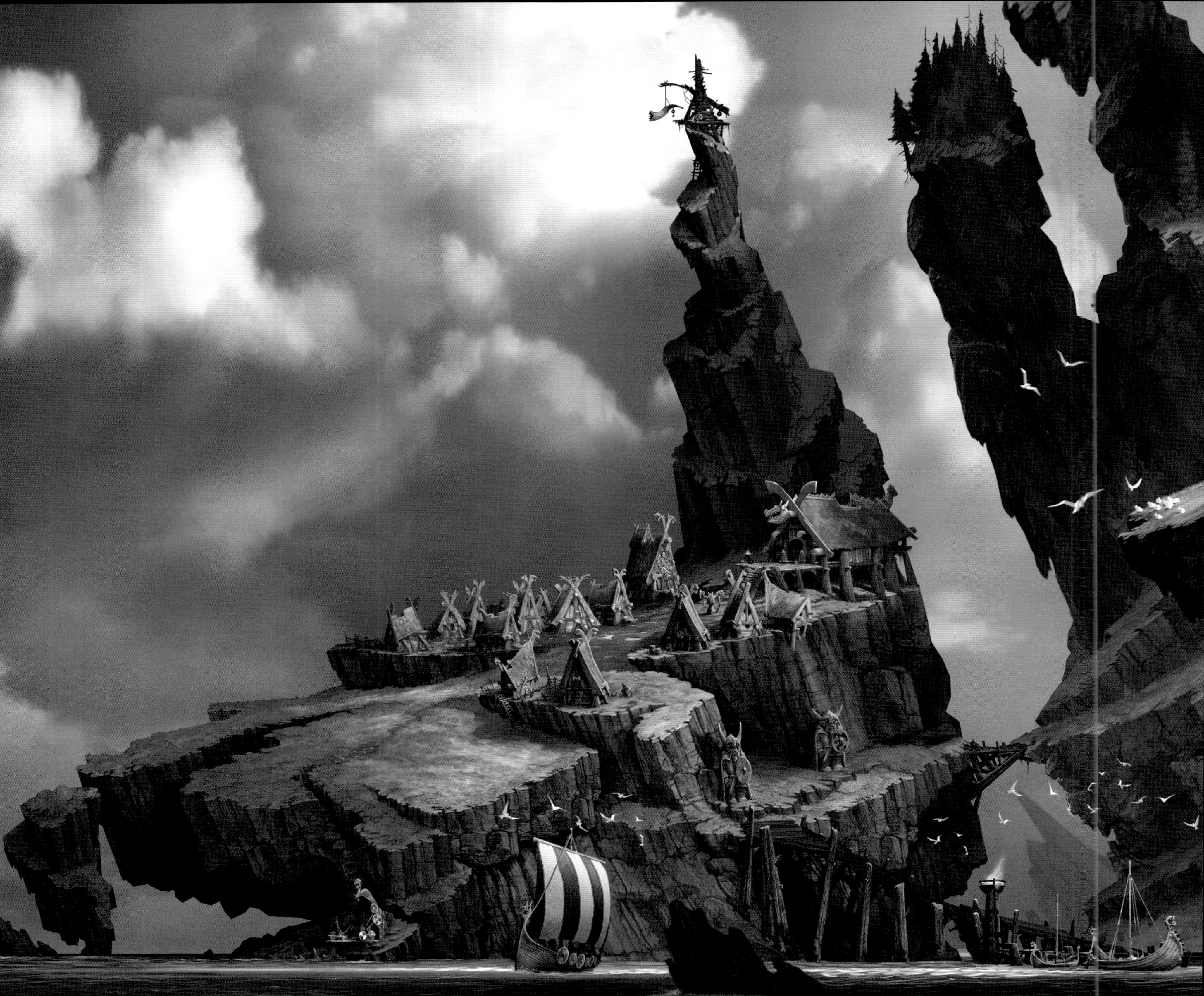

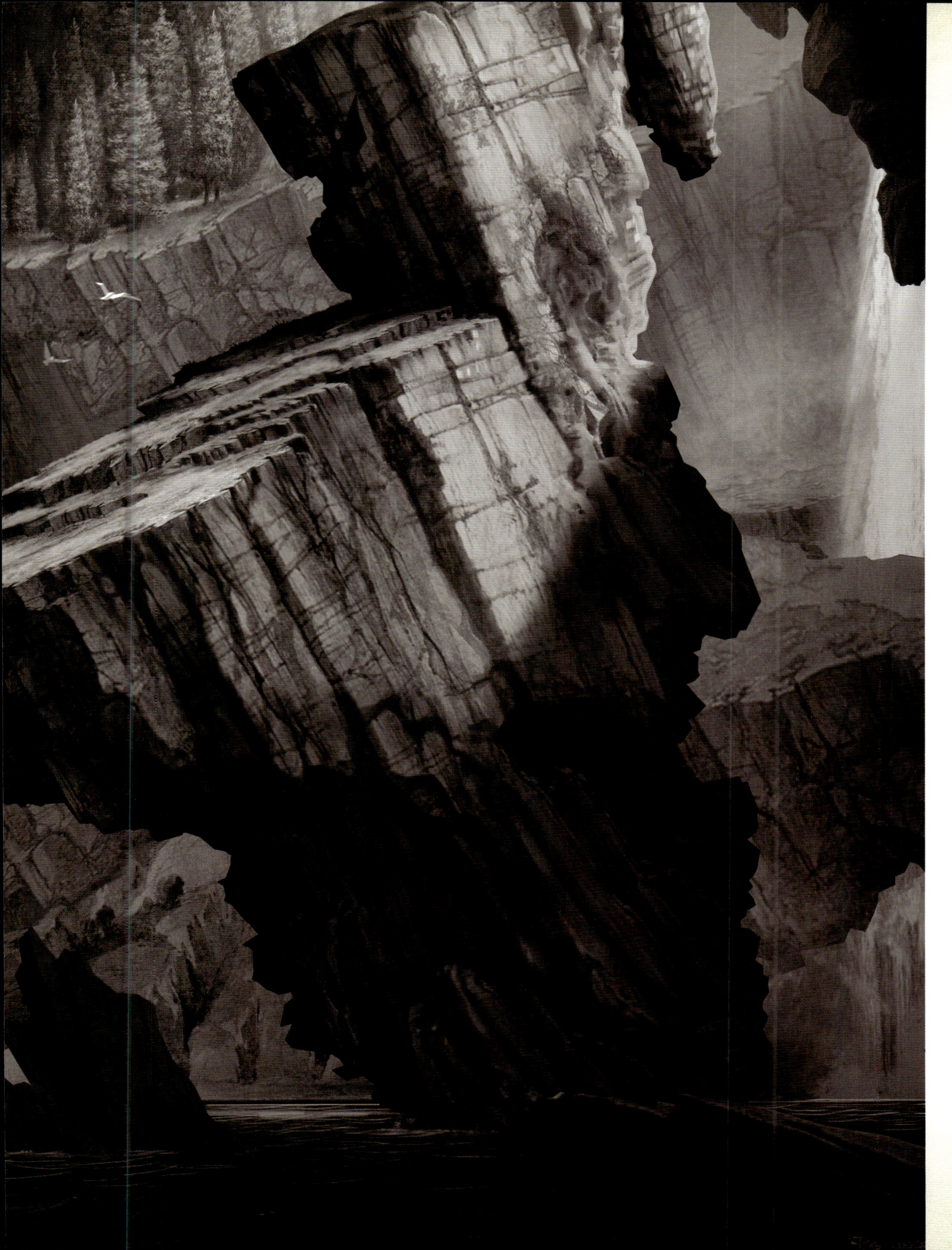

The Village

Although it is picturesque, the village is also a challenging place to occupy, given its slope and proximity to dangerous surf. "It's as if the Vikings thought 'flat fields are stupid, and we are big and strong and don't need that,'" explains Art Director Pierre-Olivier Vincent. The essence of Vincent's vision captured in his original black-and-white concept painting remains intact in the final renders some four years later.

(left) **Village View** — Pierre-Olivier Vincent — digital paint.

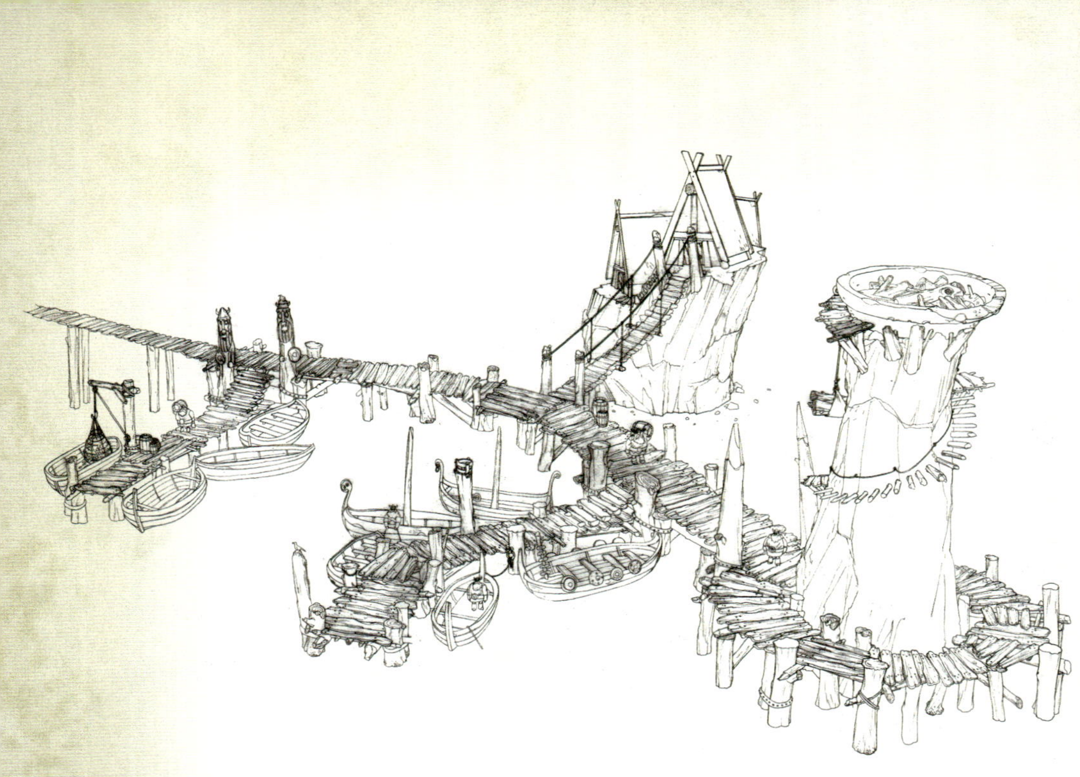

THE VILLAGE was more storybook-like in an earlier version of the story when the main characters of the film were younger. As appealing and fun as these quaint hamlets were, they could never stand up to the firepower of the film's deadly dragons.

(above) **Docks Concept** — Mike Yamada — digital paint. *(below)* **Village Model** — Cundo Rabaudi — mixed media.
(right) **Village from Sea** — Paul Shardlow — digital paint.

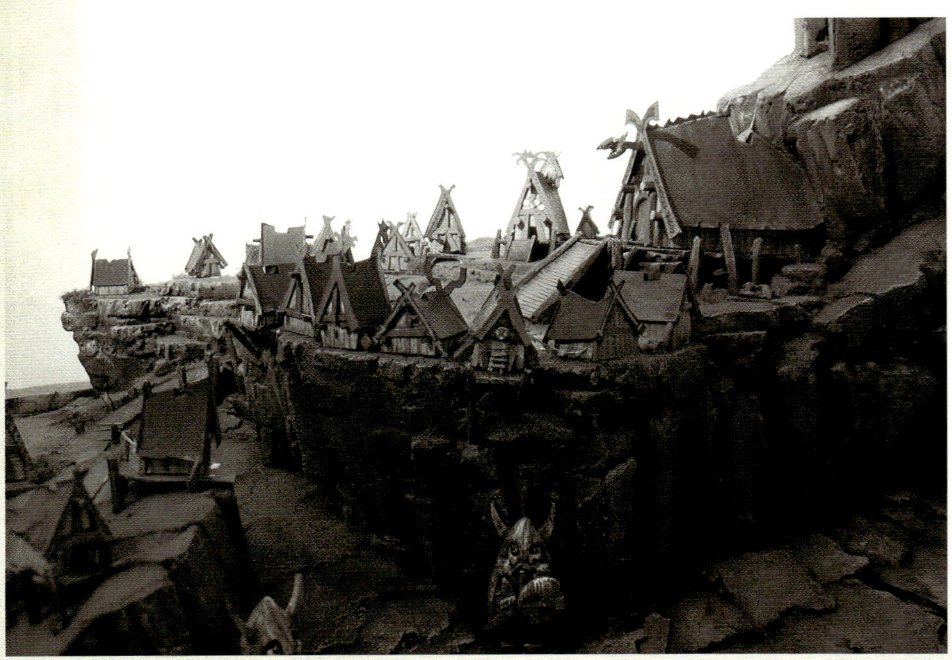

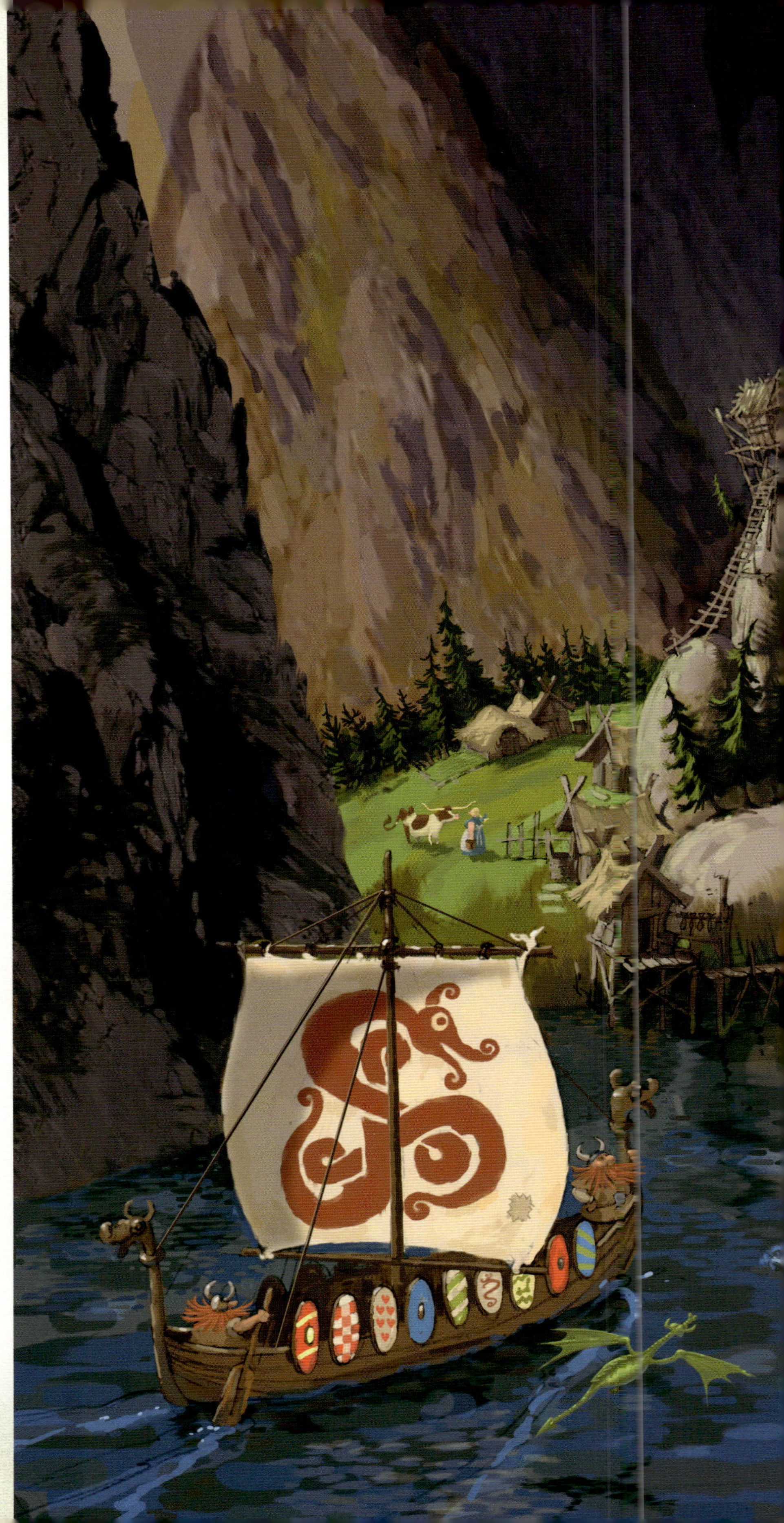

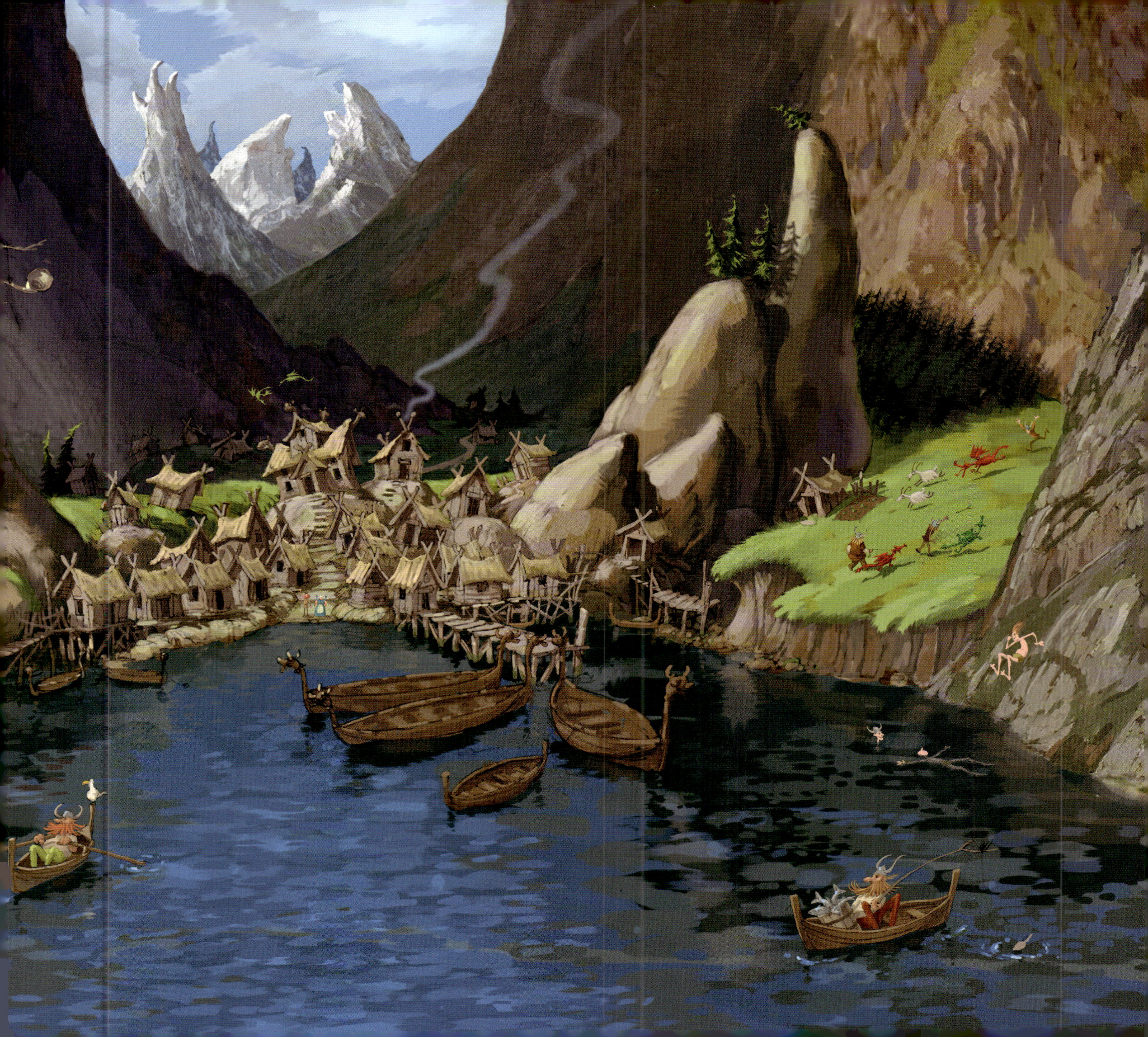

Village Houses

The houses in the village offer a fun dose of color and caricature that one might not expect from a society as gruff as this. "Our Vikings have unlimited passion and energy for the battles between themselves and the dragons. They carved dragon heads on their houses and placed screaming Viking stone statues throughout the village as monuments to their struggles and victories," according to Production Designer Kathy Altieri. The look of the houses is brought back into a more realistic realm "by surfacing with heavily textured details such as moss-covered wood, a natural occurrence in the humid Nordic summers," adds Art Director Pierre-Olivier Vincent.

The dragon motif on a house reflects what type of dragon the homeowner defeated in the past, and these are emblems of what they have conquered.

—Pierre-Olivier Vincent, Art Director

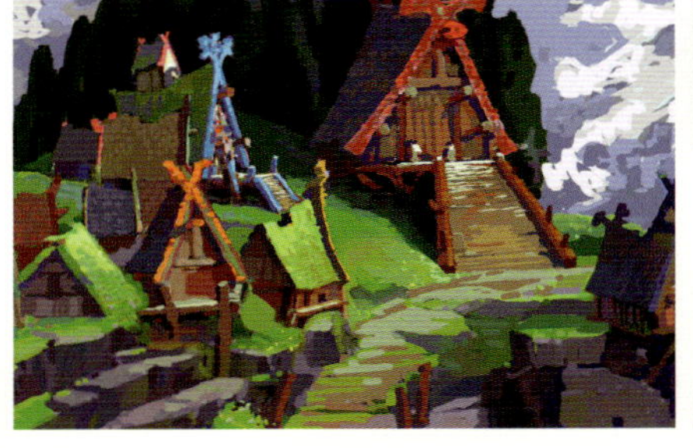

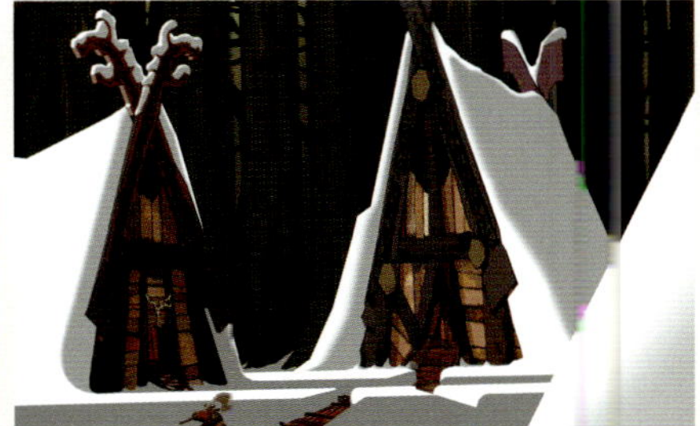

(top) **House Concept** — Pierre-Olivier Vincent — digital paint. *(above left)* **Village Color key** — Zhaoping Wei — digital paint. *(above right)* **Viking Winter Houses** — Pierre-Olivier Vincent — digital paint. *(left)* **Viking Chief House** — Pierre-Olivier Vincent — digital paint. *(below)* **Viking Grass House** — Pierre-Olivier Vincent — digital paint.
(right) **Gothi House** — Pierre-Olivier Vincent — digital paint.

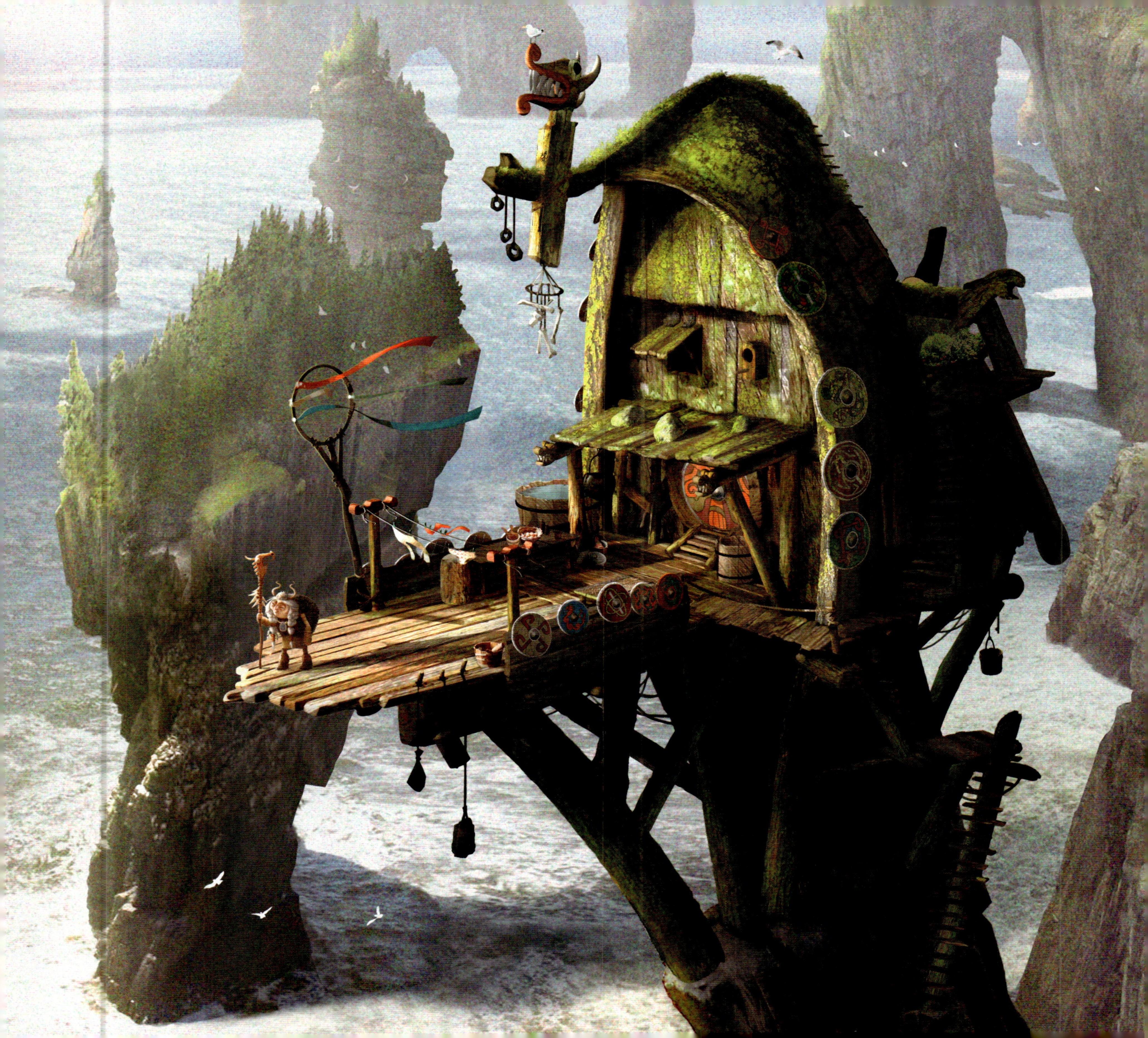

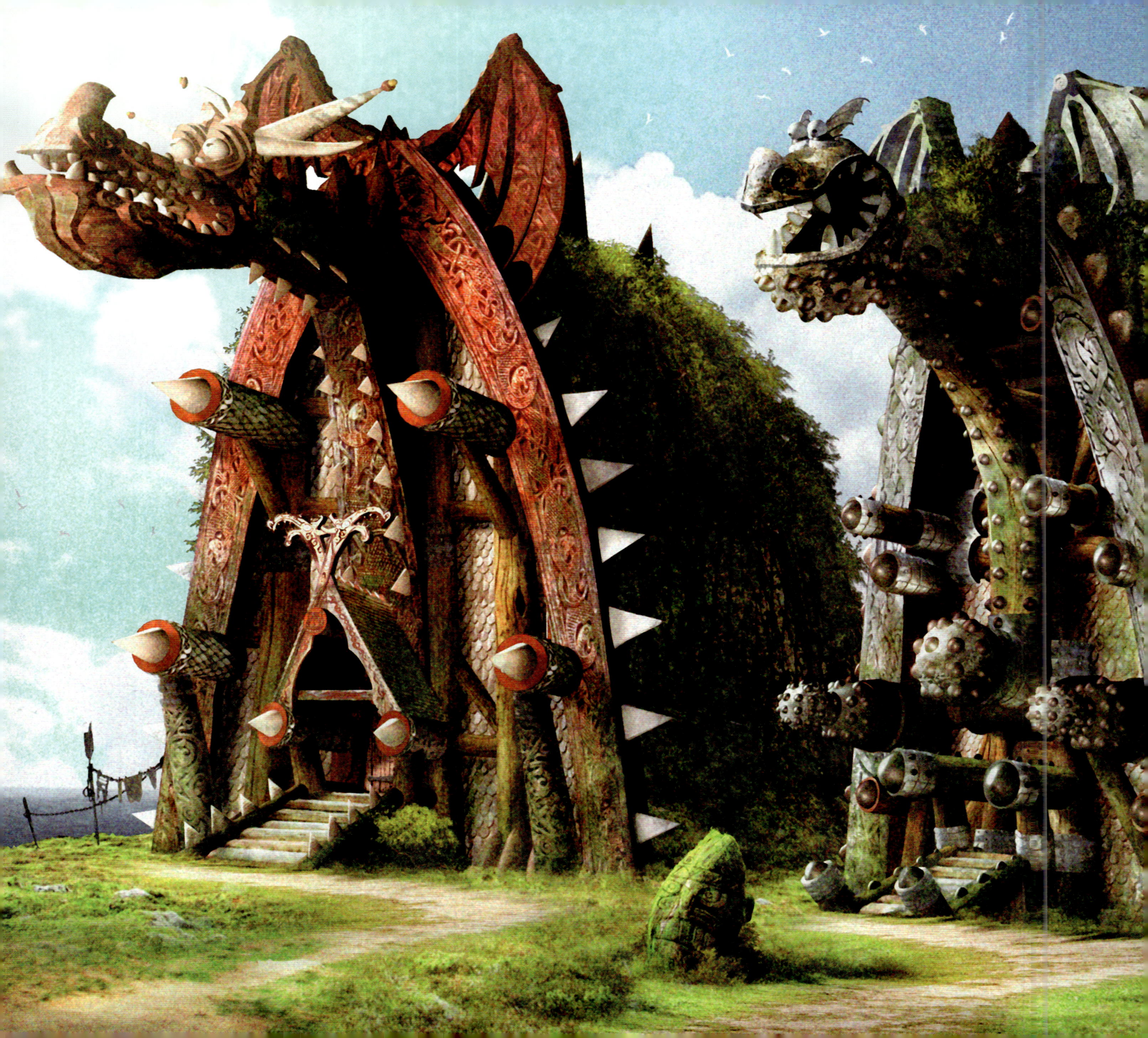

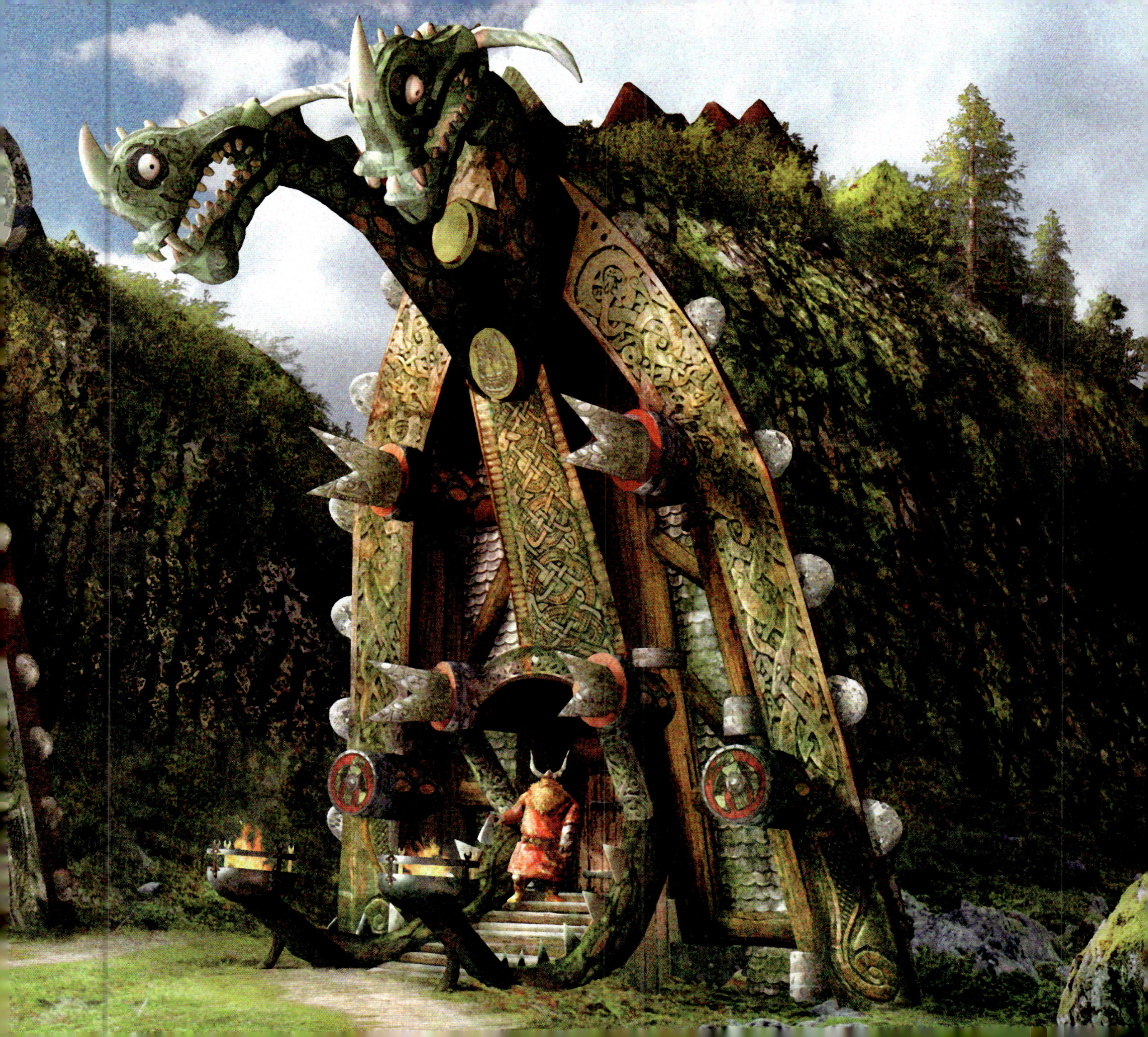

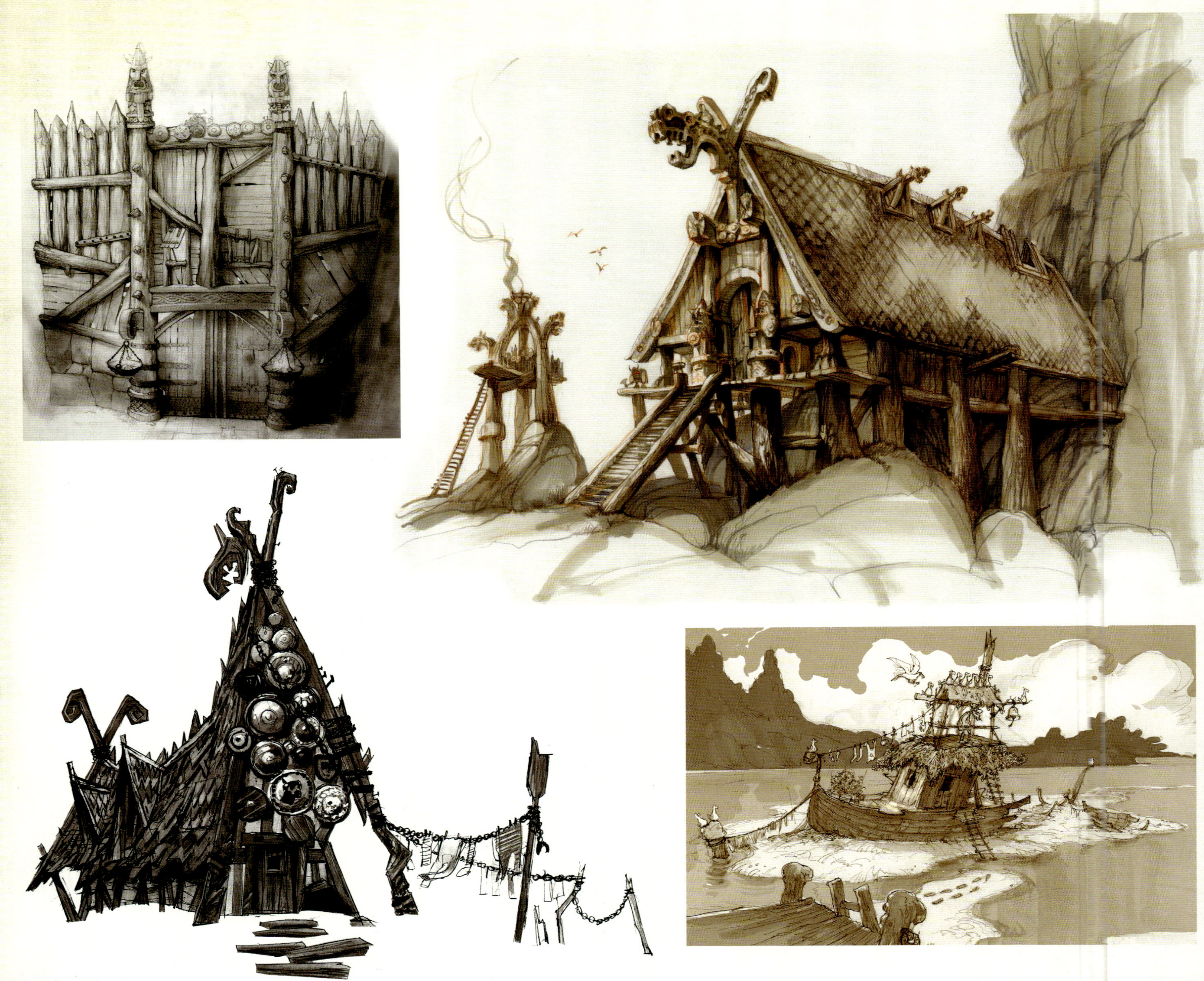

(previous pages) **Houses Main** — Pierre-Olivier Vincent — digital paint. *(top left)* **Village Gate** — Mike Yamada — pencil. *(top right)* **Meade Hall Concept** — Emil Mitev — pencil & marker. *(above left)* **House Concept** — Pierre-Olivier Vincent — digital paint. *(above right)* **Old Wrnkly's House** — Paul Shardlow — digital paint. *(right)* **House Concepts** — Pierre-Olivier Vincent — marker.

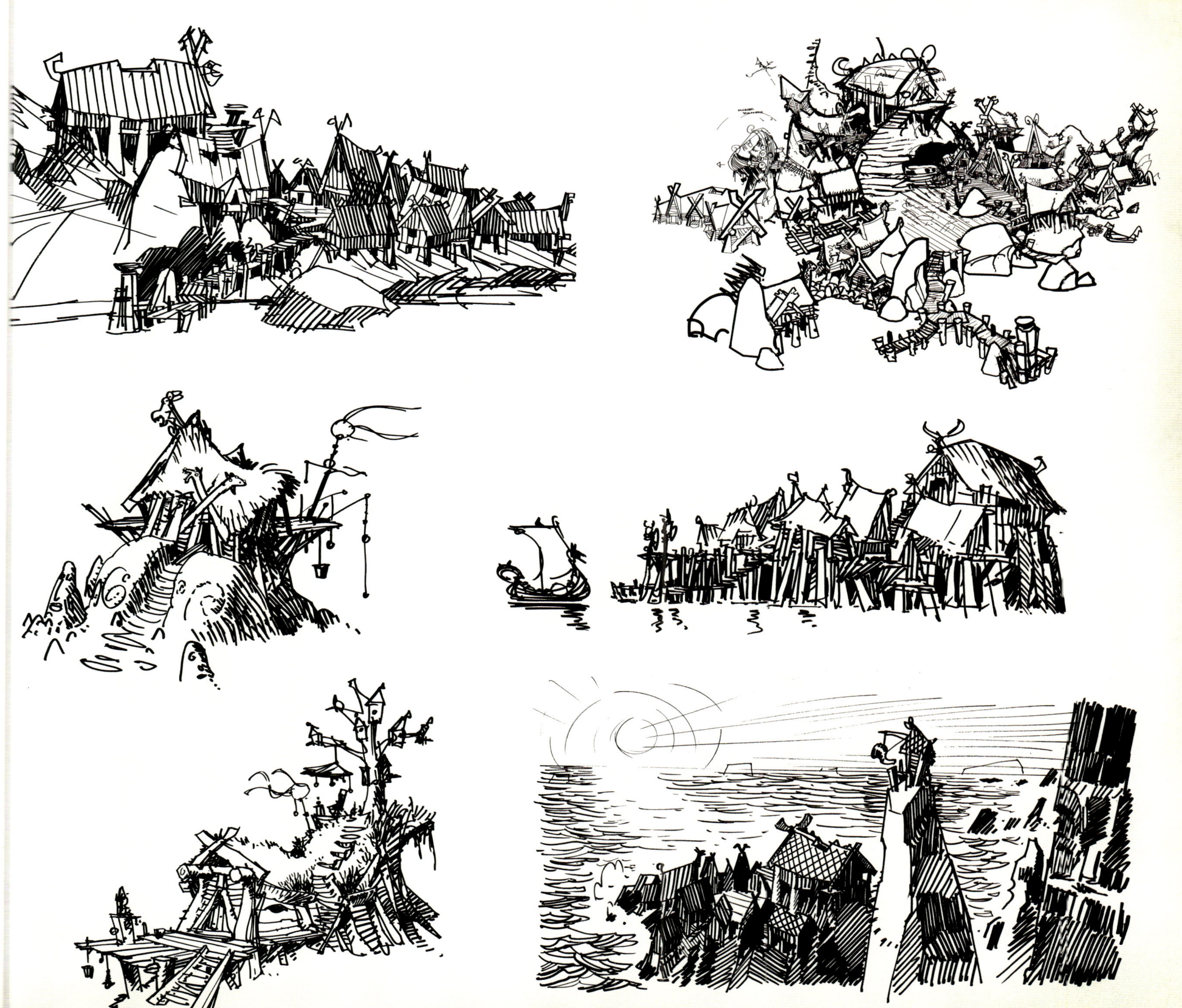

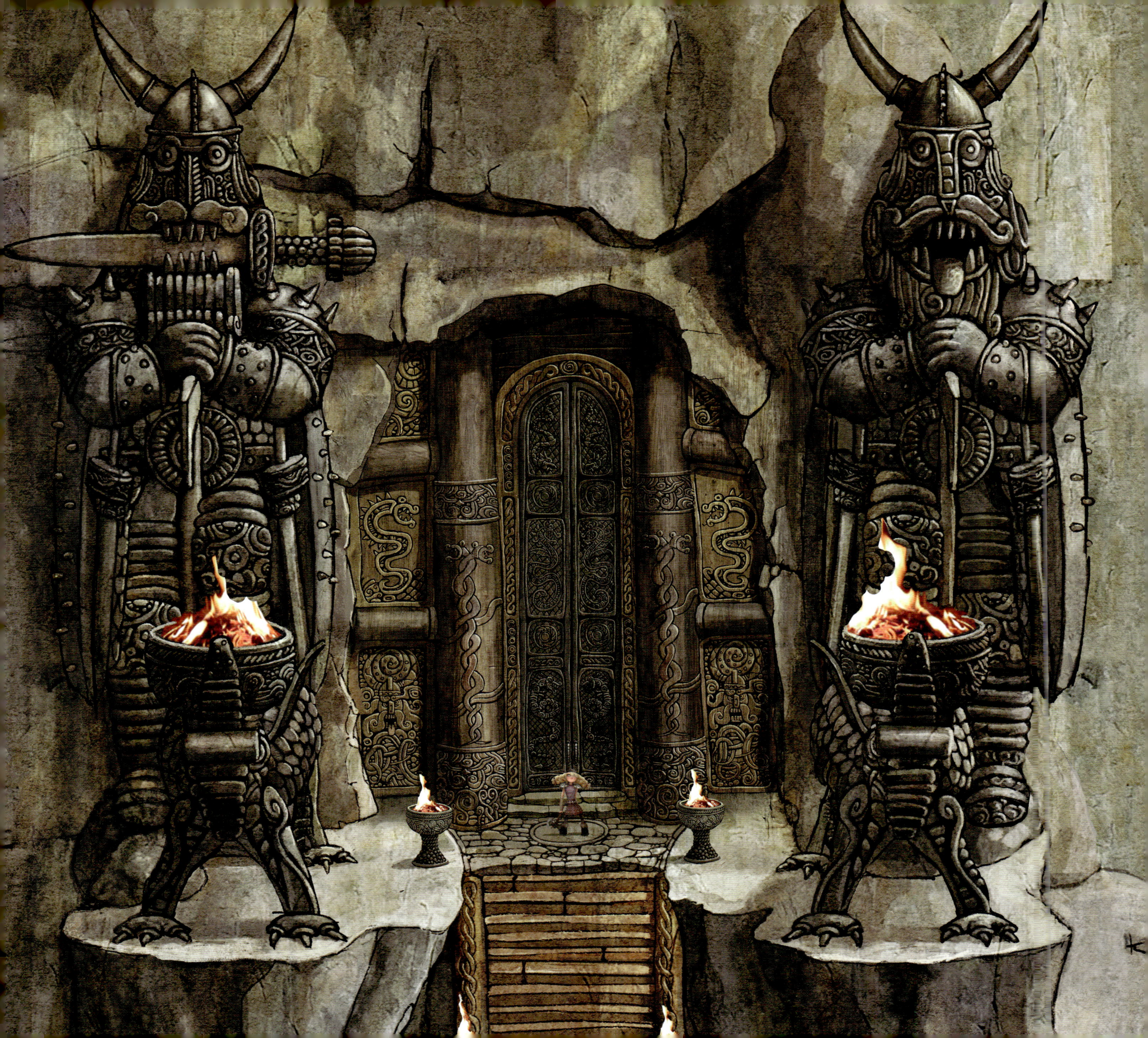

Meade Hall

The Meade Hall, where a number of important Viking societal events take place, is the most impressive, solid structure on the island. The approach to the hall involves 125 very steep stairs, and the main doors stand approximately sixty-eight feet tall, flanked by two imposing Viking sculptures. The sense of grandeur and intimidation continues once the doors open, wherein huge statues of Viking ancestors line the halls, and tapestries depicting historical battles and achievements adorn the walls. "When we built this set, it was meant to be an impressive, big hall, but it's not until we load a character into it that you realize it's a REALLY big hall," explains Modeling Supervisor Matt Paulson. Even larger-than-life Stoick looks quite diminutive in this environment. Built upon huge square stones, this structure enforces the concept that Viking traditions are founded on strong, long-standing, and intimidating standards that will not sway.

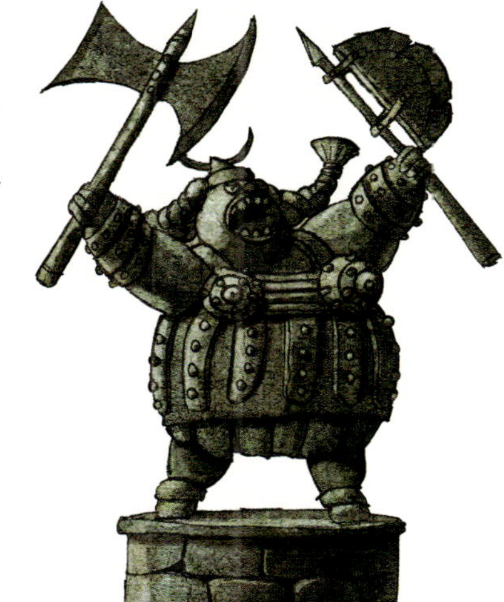

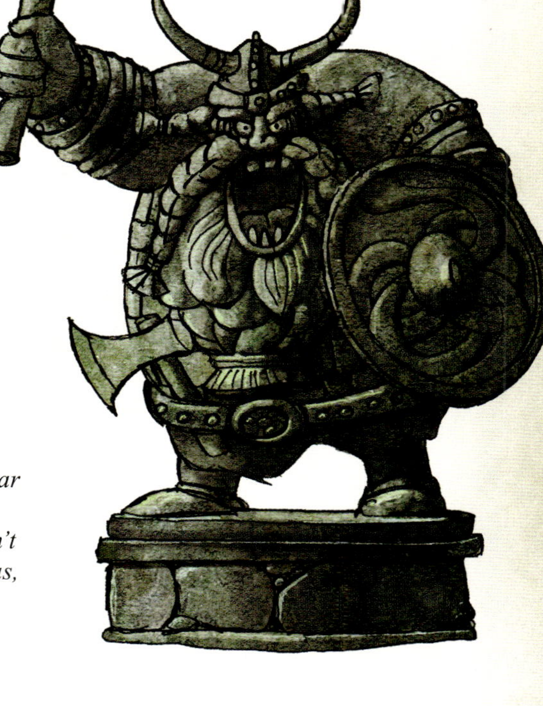

DESPITE commonly held stereotypes, Vikings did not regularly wear helmets with horns. But who today would recognize a Viking if he didn't have such armor on his head? Thus, such icons are in the movie.

(left) **Hall Front Doors** — Kirsten Kawamura — digital paint. *(above)* **Statues** — Kirsten Kawamura — digital paint. *(below left)* **Meade Hall View** — Pierre-Olivier Vincent — digital paint. *(below right)* **Meade Hall Beat** — Jeff Snow — story sketch — Pierre-Olivier Vincent — digital paint.

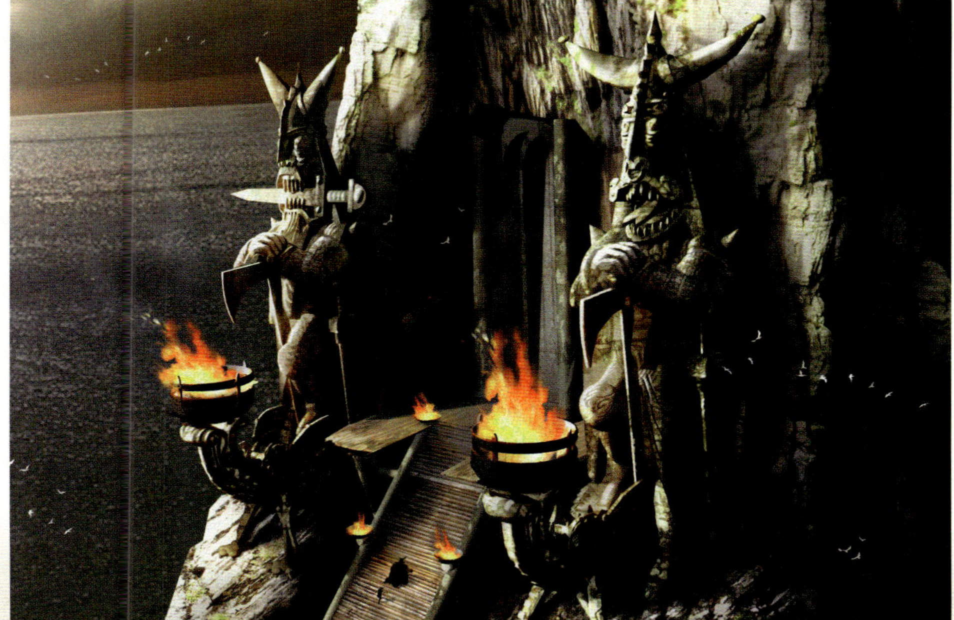

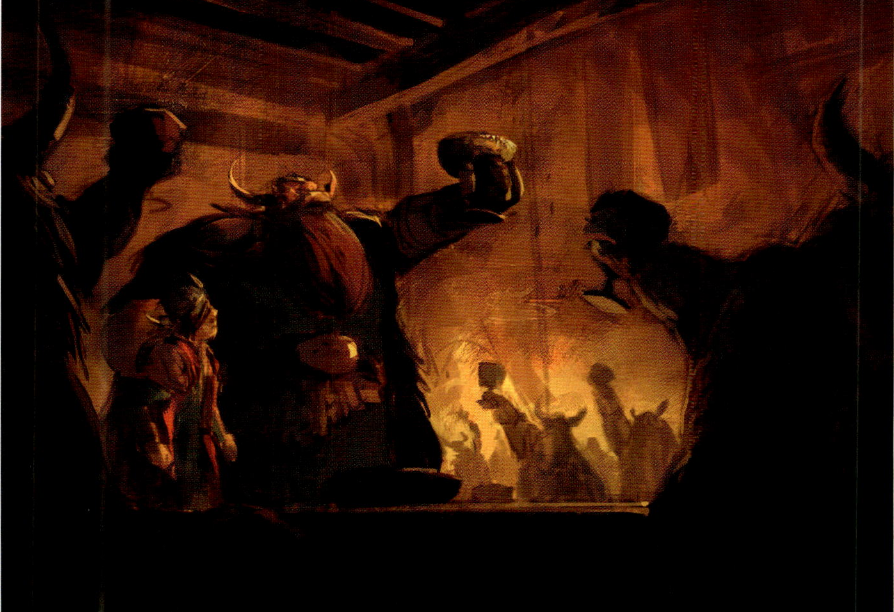

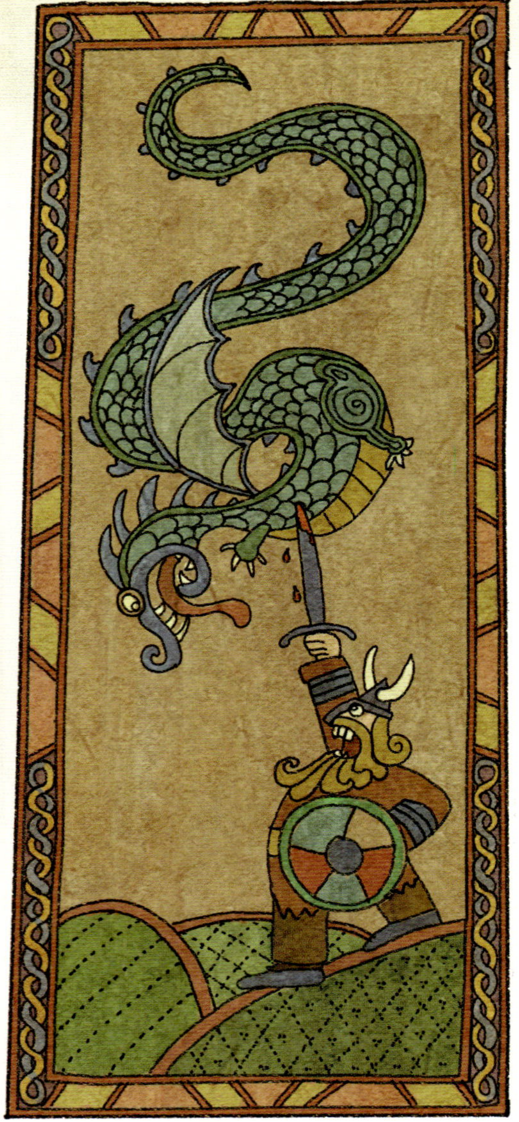
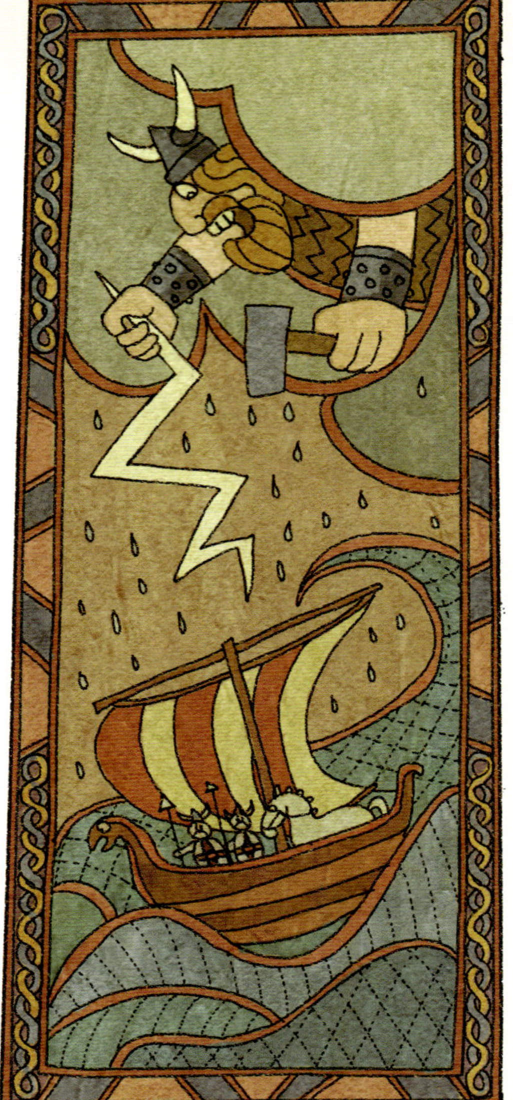
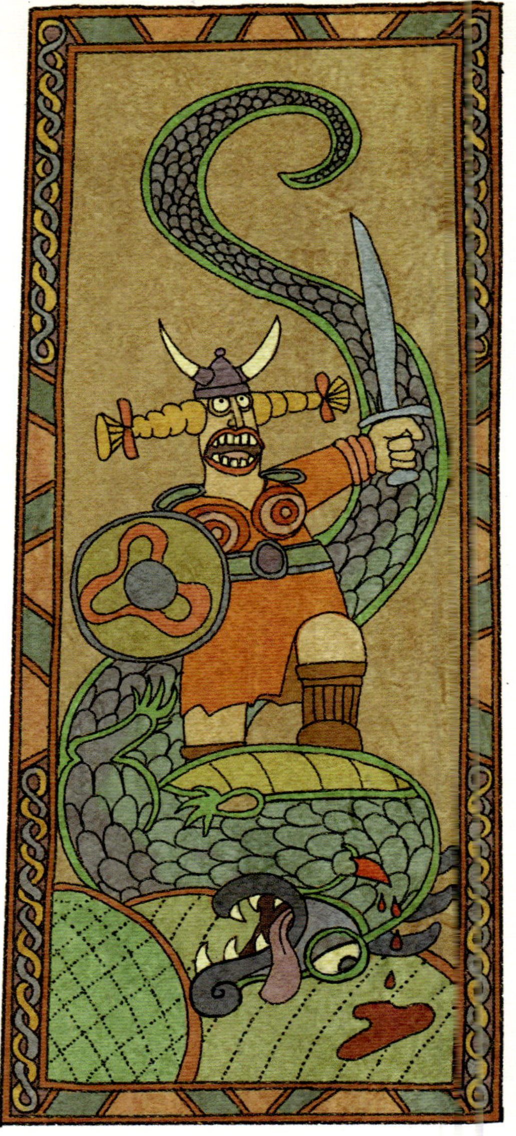
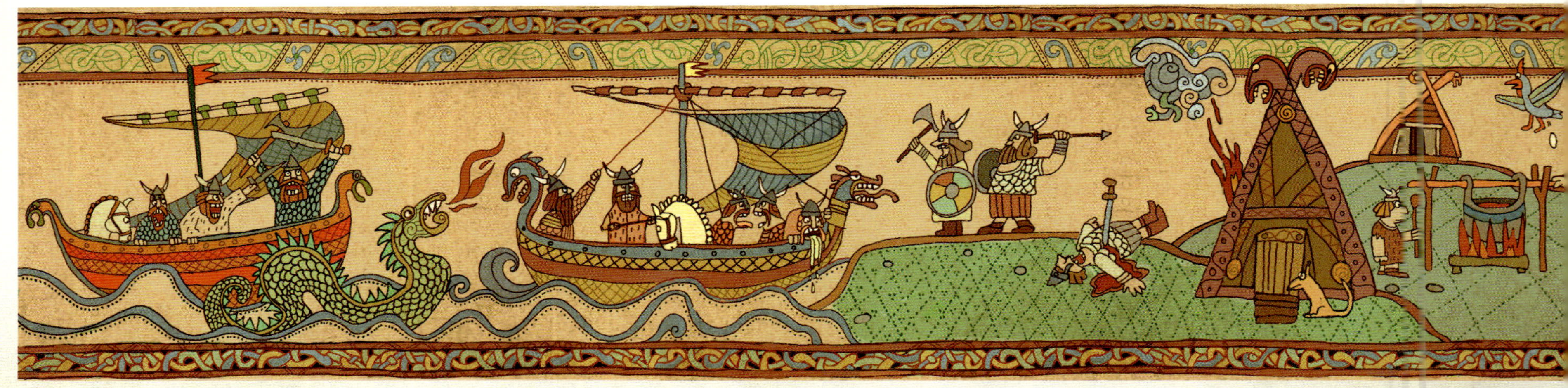

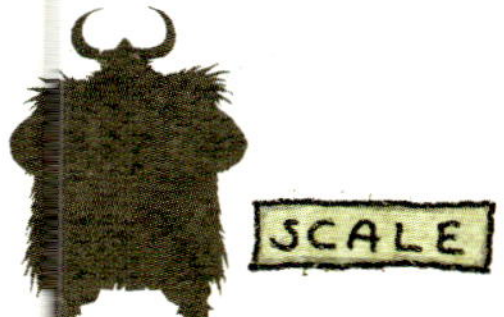

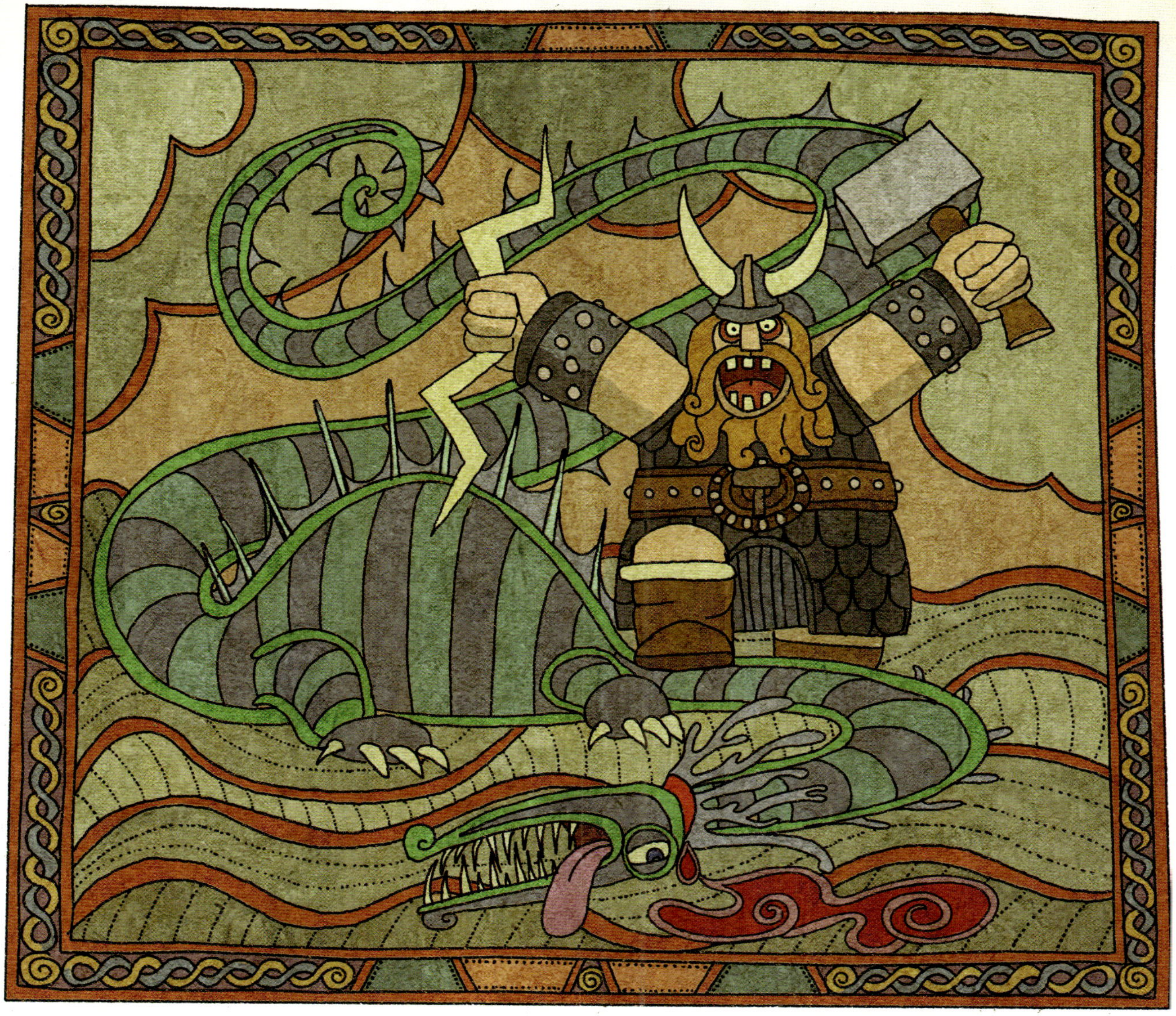

Tapestries — Kirsten Kawamura — digital paint.

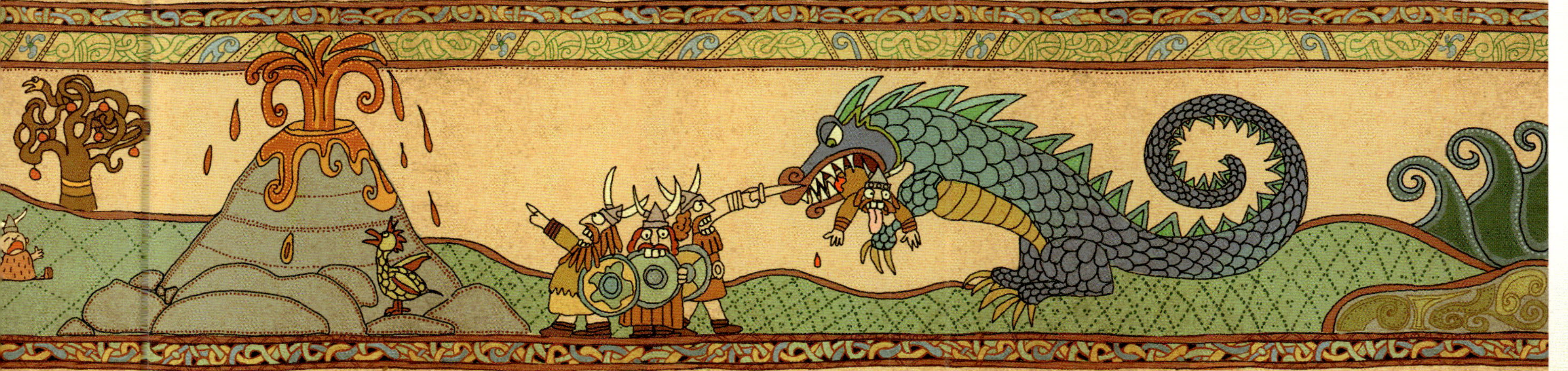

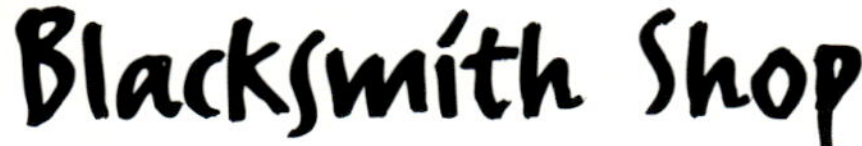

Blacksmith Shop

Great detail has gone into the blacksmith shop set as it showcases a number of important scenes in the film. "We've painted the steps to show they are well-worn, as if grime is deeply ingrained from years of muddy boots walking on them," notes Head of Surfacing Sabrina Riegel. The stairs literally sag due to thoughtful modeling efforts, and the modelers also "paid careful attention to edges of tables and corners of structures because that tells so much about how old something is, or what material it is made from," adds Modeling Supervisor Matt Paulson.

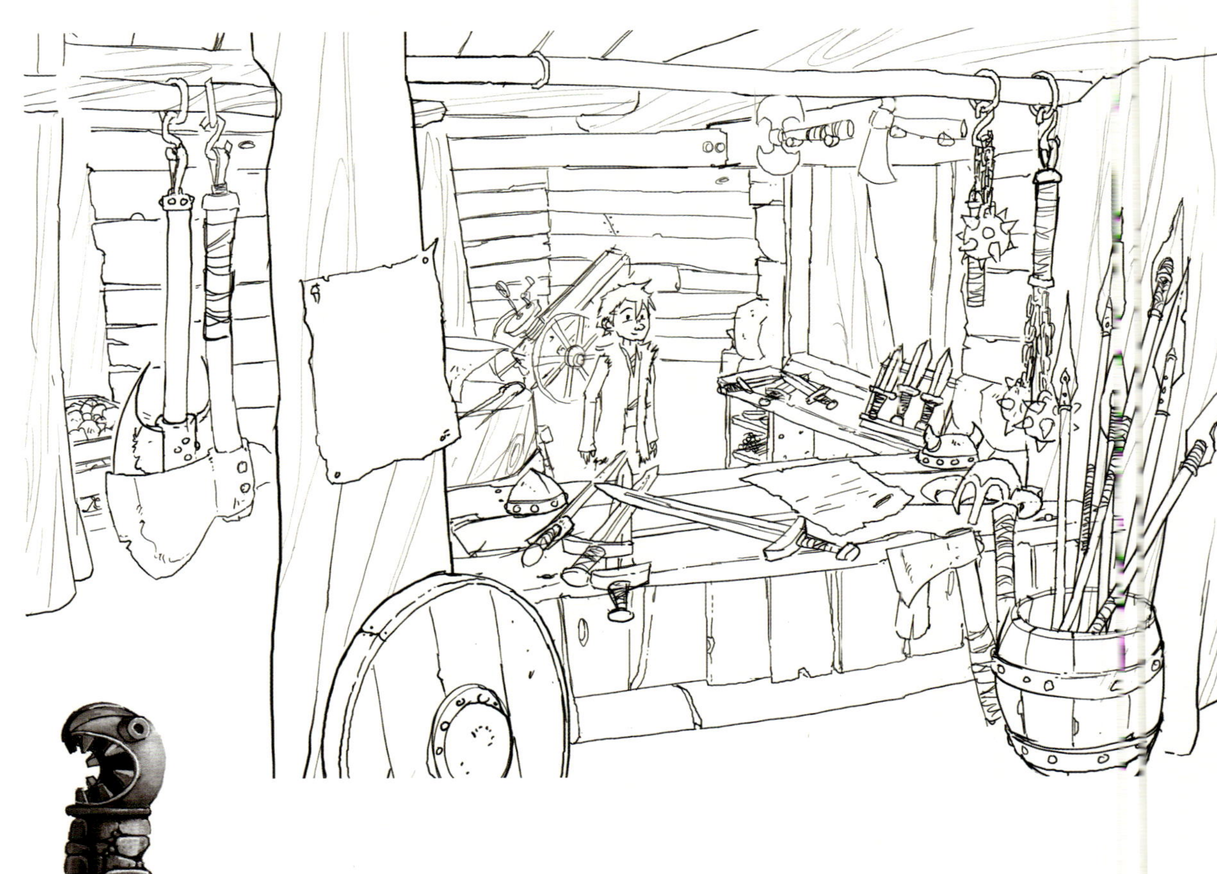

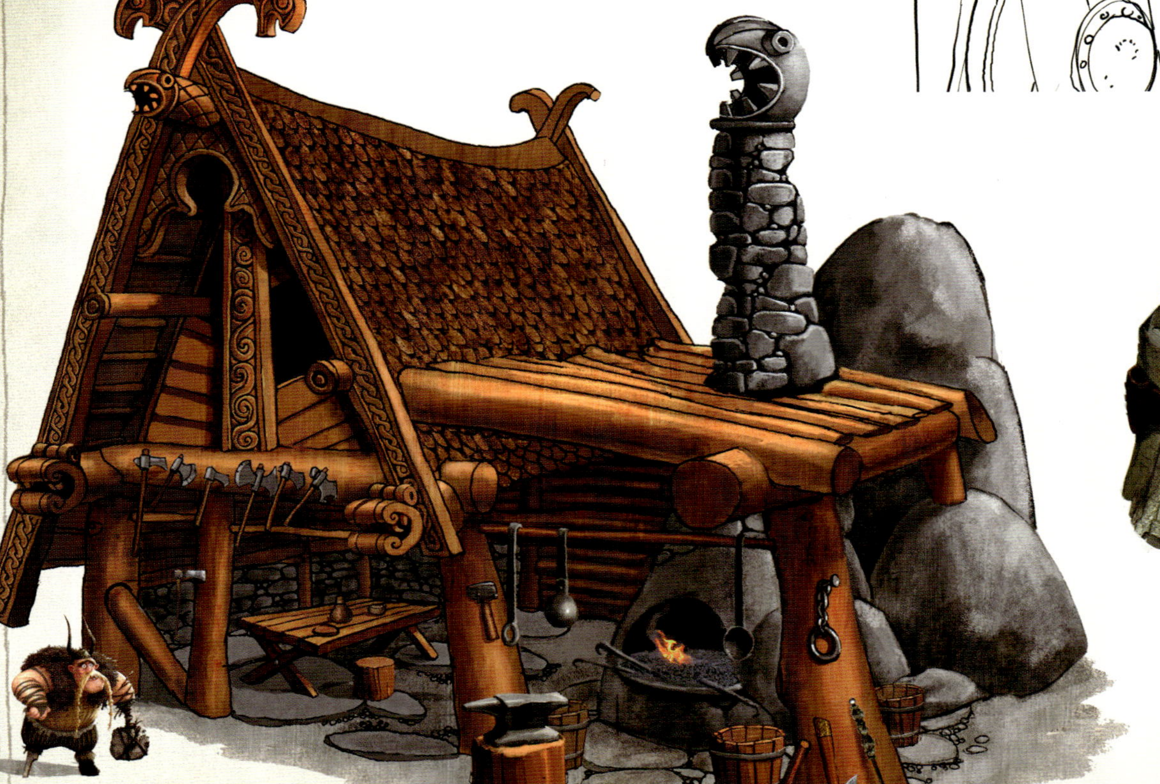

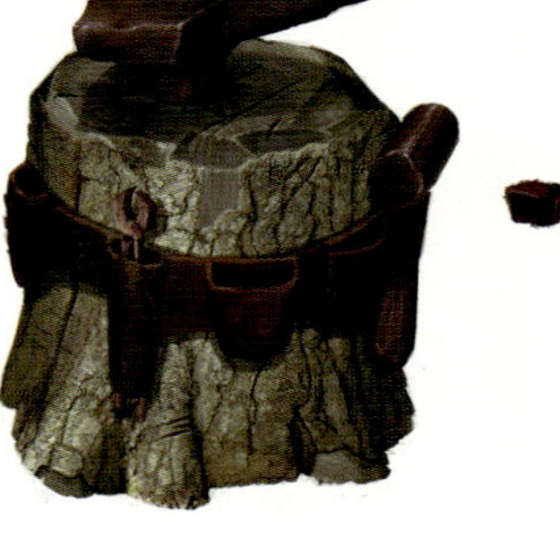

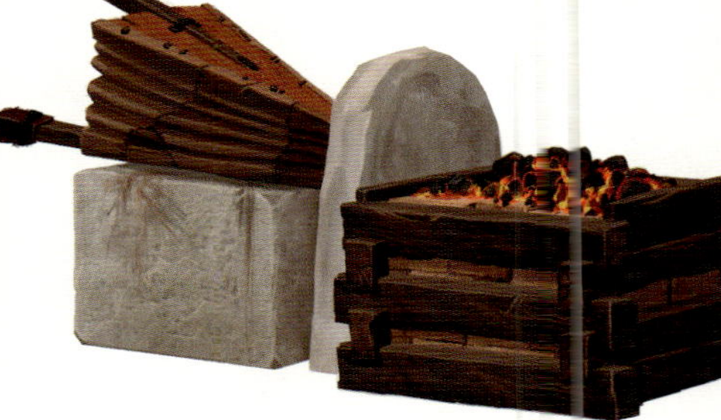

(top) **Blacksmith Shop Interior** — Mel Zwyer — digital paint.

(left) **Blacksmith Shop Concept** — Kirsten Kawamura — digital paint.

(above) **Anvil** and **Bellows** — Travis Koller — digital paint.

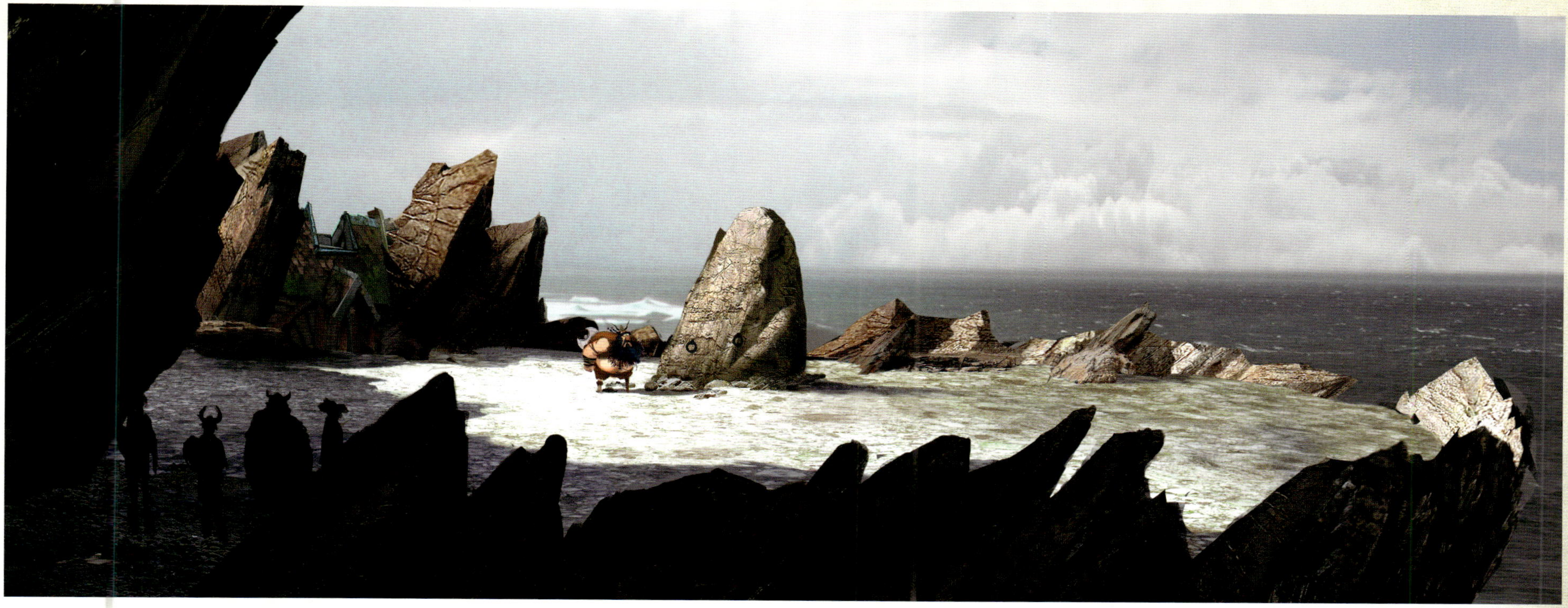

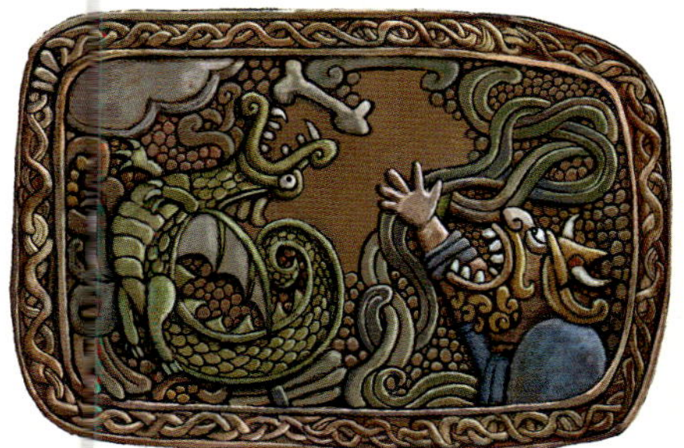

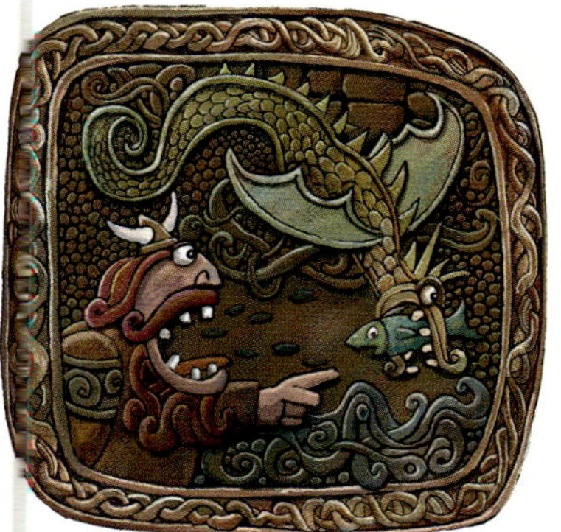

Training Grounds

The training grounds are one of the more substantial structures built by the Vikings, featuring large statues of ancestors hewn from stone to signify the strength of their tribe and the long-standing traditions of their culture. This location is the arena in which the audience learns what the Vikings think they know about dragons. "The Viking knowledge of dragons comes exclusively from brief, violent encounters in battle situations. They have practical information such as how much fire they can breathe and what their weaknesses are, as opposed to what Hiccup learns in the extended time he spends with Toothless," explains Director Chris Sanders.

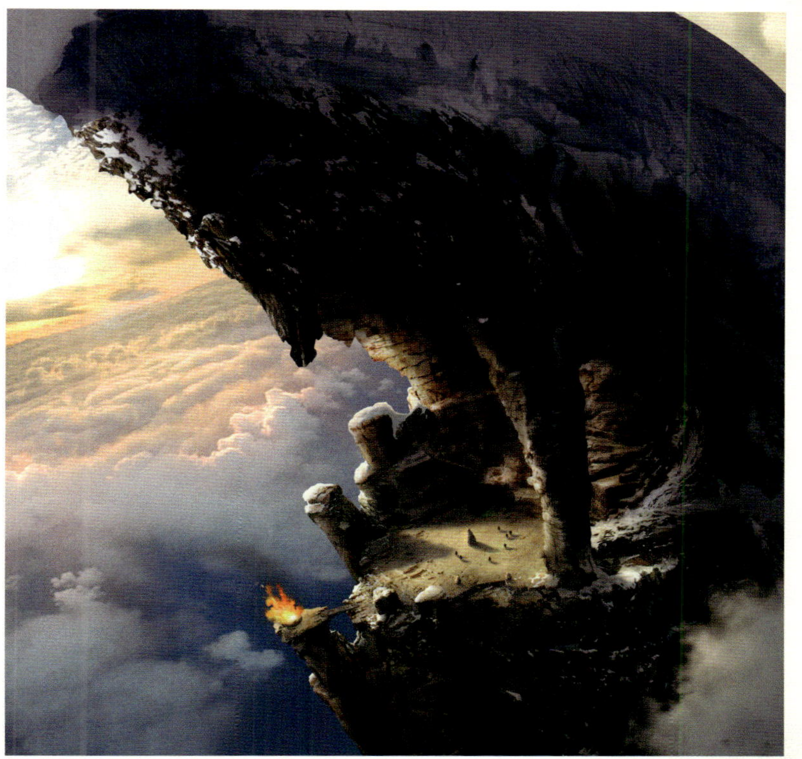

(top) **Training Ground Concept** — Mike Yamada — digital paint. (above *left)* **Training Ground Carvings** — Kirsten Kawamura — digital paint. *(above right)* **Training Ground Concept** — Pierre-Olivier Vincent — digital paint.

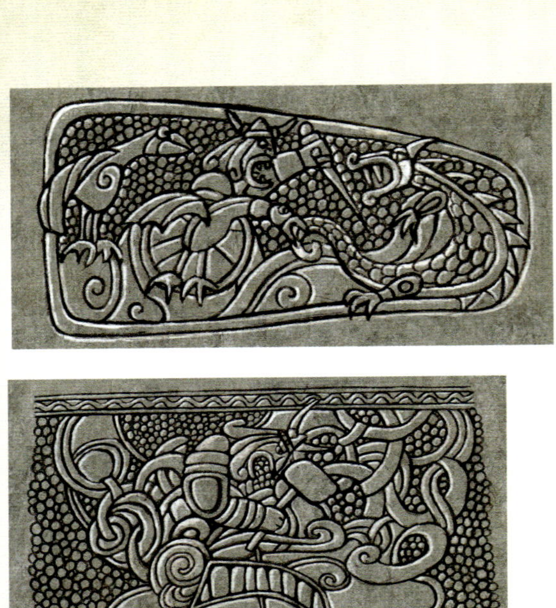

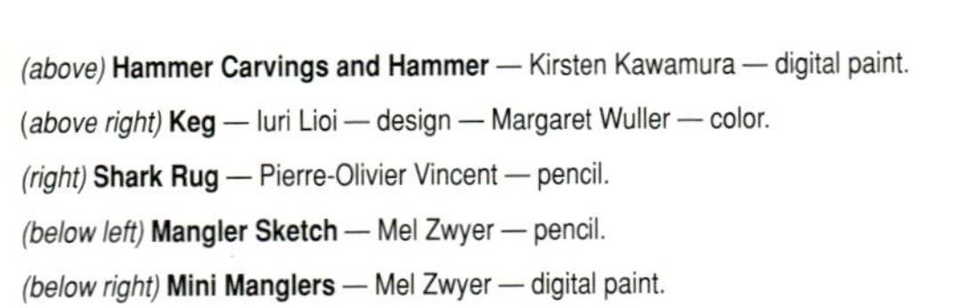

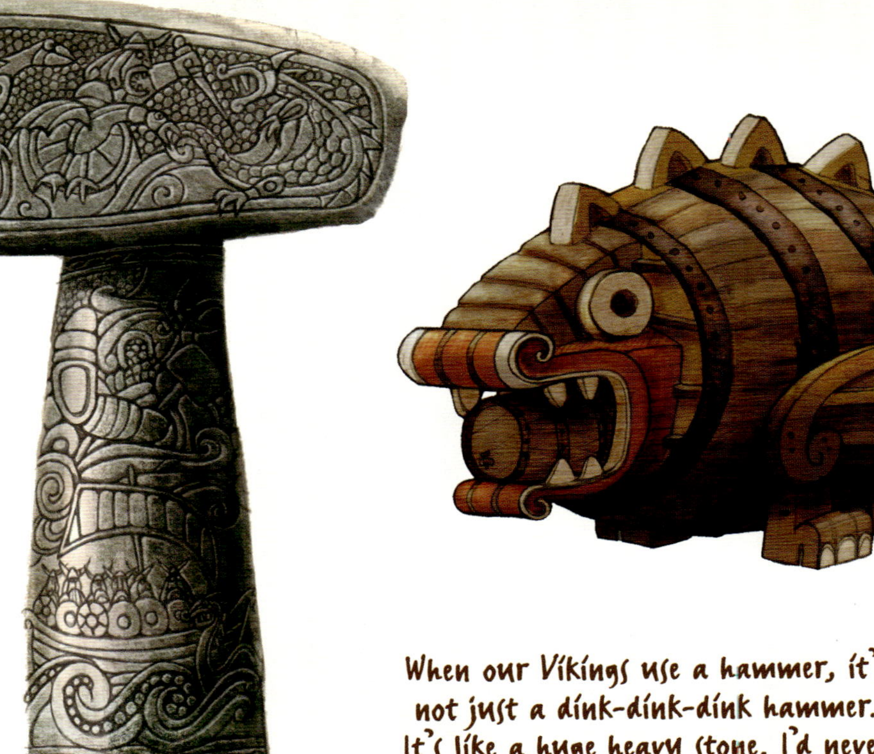

(above) **Hammer Carvings and Hammer** — Kirsten Kawamura — digital paint.

(above right) **Keg** — Iuri Lioi — design — Margaret Wuller — color.

(right) **Shark Rug** — Pierre-Olivier Vincent — pencil.

(below left) **Mangler Sketch** — Mel Zwyer — pencil.

(below right) **Mini Manglers** — Mel Zwyer — digital paint.

When our Vikings use a hammer, it's not just a dink-dink-dink hammer. It's like a huge heavy stone. I'd never even be able to lift one of those things.

—Kathy Altieri, Production Designer

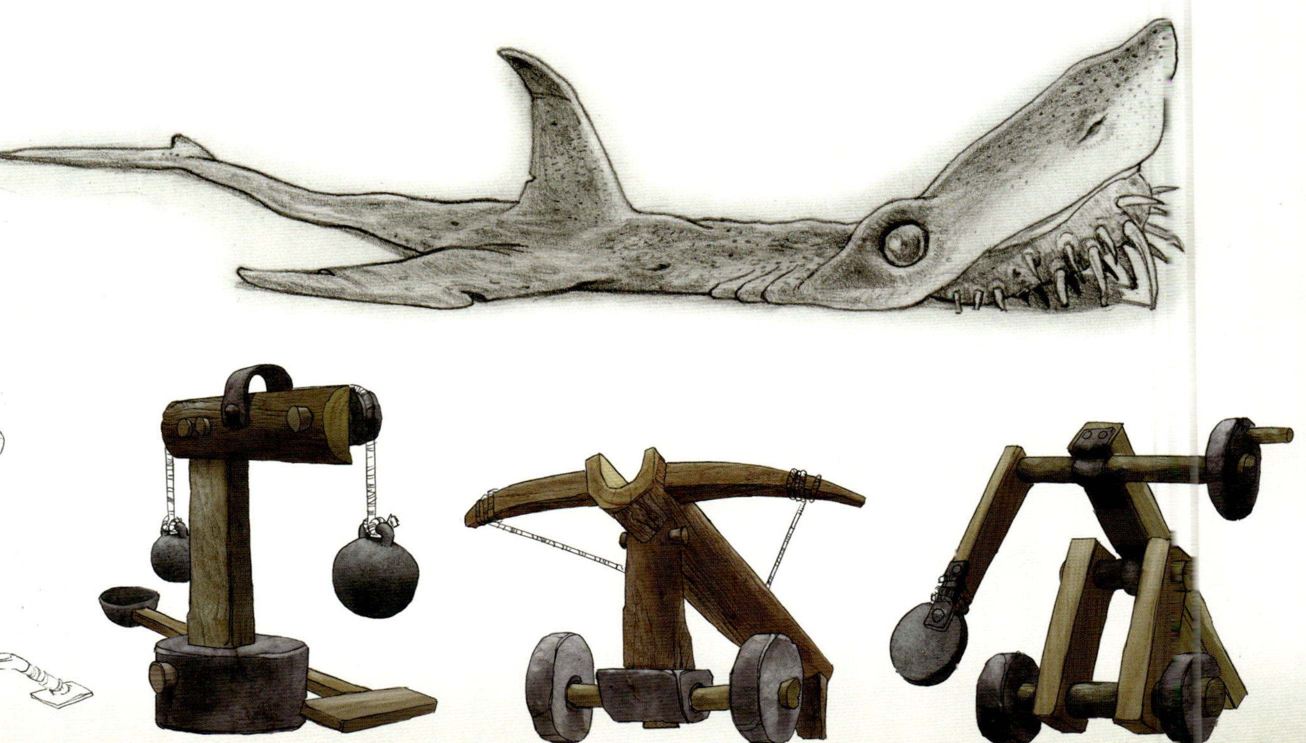

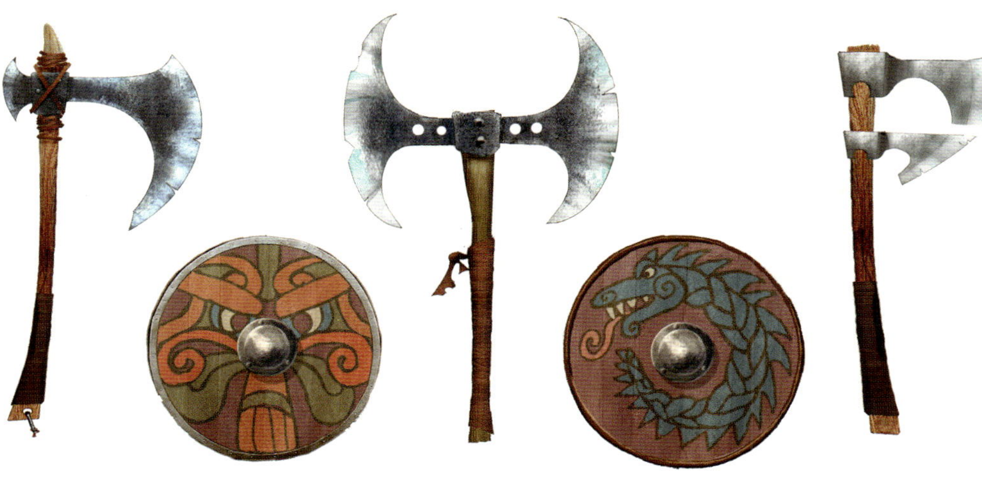

Props & Iconography

Weapons comprise a good percentage of the prop builds in the film, since Vikings are all about battling dragons. This activity requires a whole armory of shields, maces, axes, and other accoutrements. "These Vikings are not fussy craftsmen, but they are certainly enthusiastic weapons-makers. Their weapons are primitive and chunky, kind of like their brains," notes Production Designer Kathy Altieri. All props in the film appear "scuffed and stained, and nothing is new and clean," says Head of Surfacing Sabrina Riegel. "Water buckets have been sitting around getting rusty, and axes are meant to be handed down from generation to generation, so the handles are darker where hand oils and sweat have stained them over time."

With all of the props in the film, a conscious effort was made to come up with items which were a little unusual but recognizable enough to work in whatever capacity they were intended. A perfect example of this is the shark rug in Stoick's house, an idea that came to Art Director Pierre-Olivier Vincent over four years earlier in the film's development. "It's a twist on the traditional bearskin rug that hunters would have, but it expresses the overzealous aggression of the Vikings with a little bit of humor," explains Vincent. Indeed, "only a Viking would go out and pound a shark on the head just to make a rug out of it," adds Production Designer Kathy Altieri.

There are also many detailed carvings and artifacts to be found in the village. While research shows that Viking constructs were rudimentary and medieval, the film's design theory called for "imagery and architecture that reflected the intellectual simplicity of the culture through broad, simple shapes that are sturdy, caricatured, and whimsical," says Production Designer Kathy Altieri. Color choices were also a bit more bold than what traditional Viking iconography suggests, but Art Director Pierre-Olivier Vincent was inspired by the fact that "scientific studies reveal that there are pigments found on many of the great monuments of the world such as the Parthenon, proving that such structures were much more colorful at one time than they are known to be in modern culture."

WHILE THE DAUNTING Viking sculptures and the dramatic tapestries illustrate the serious legacy of the culture, there is room for a bit of humor in Meade Hall: At one time, just inside the main doors a dragon statue stood as a "stow your weapons" station, much like an oversized pincushion.

(above) **Axe Variants** — Mel Zwyer — digital paint — **Shields** — Kirsten Kawamura — digital paint.

(right) **Dragon Statue** — Mel Zwyer — digital paint.

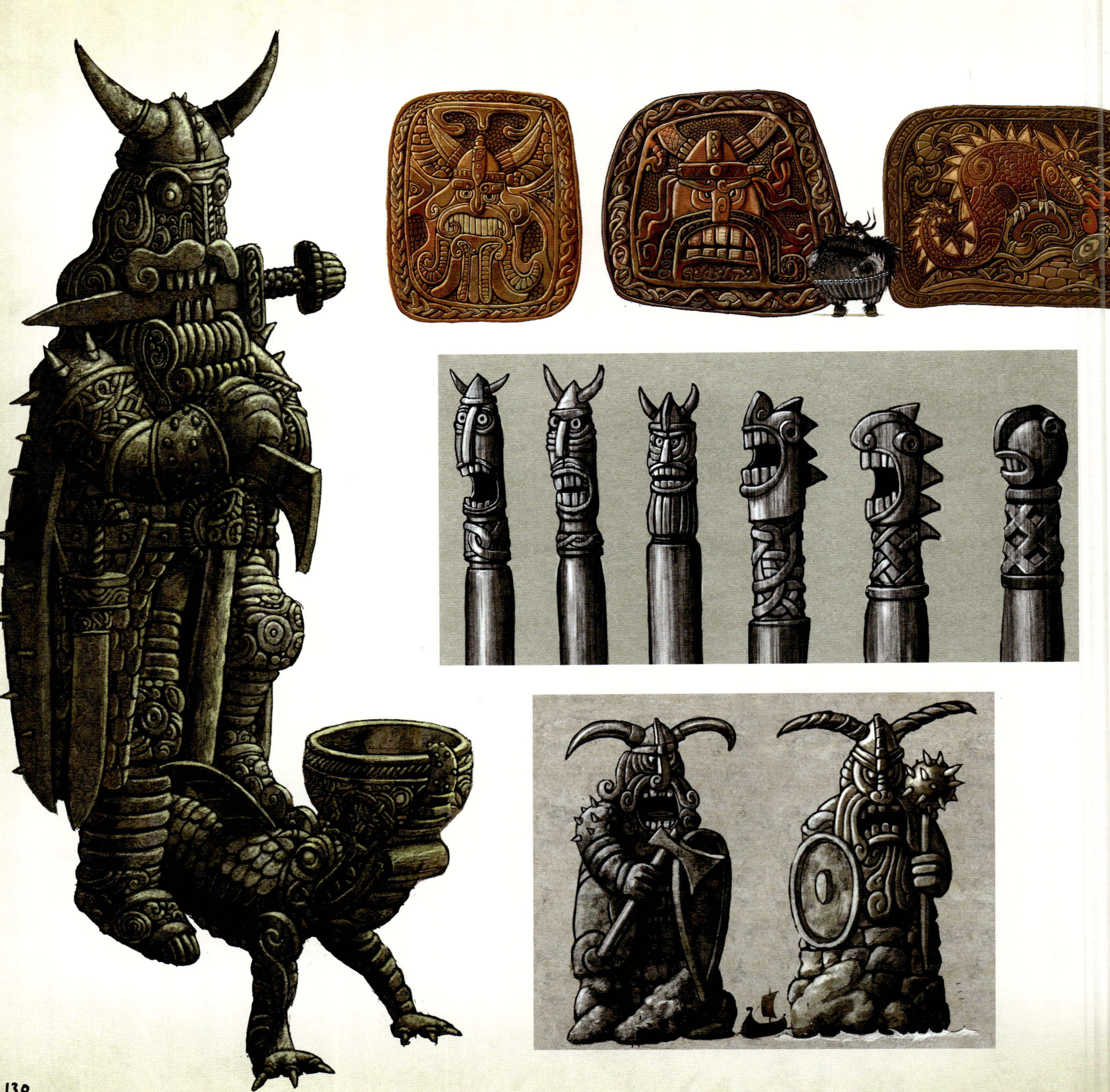

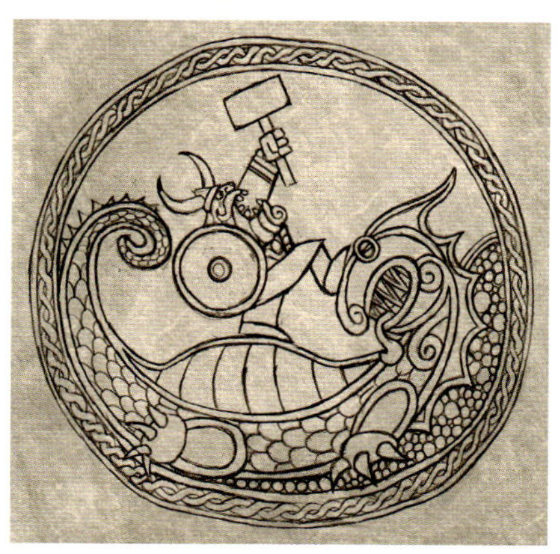

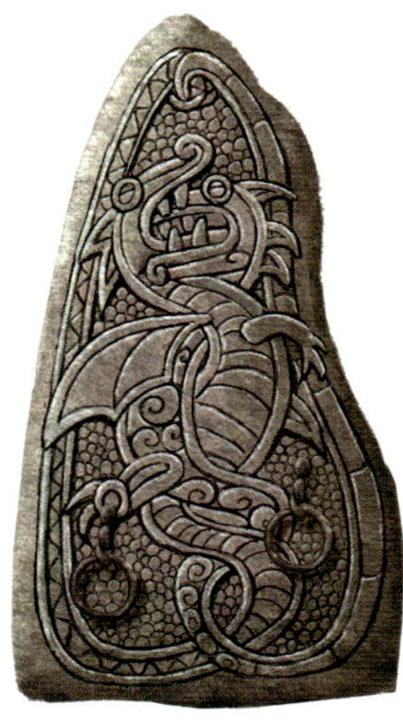

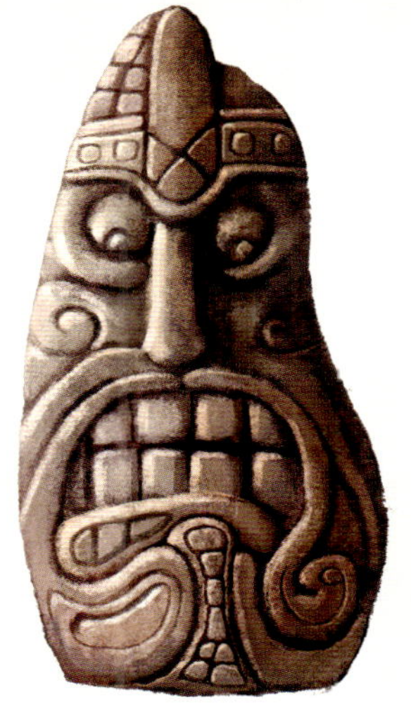

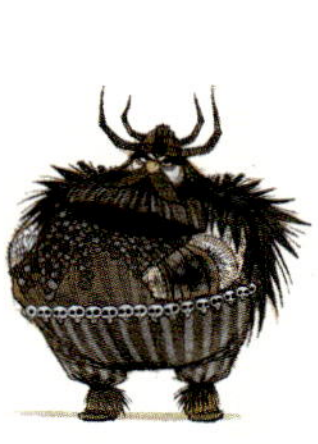

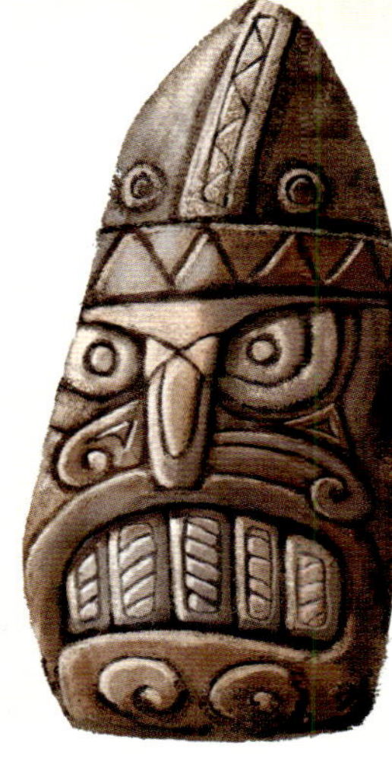

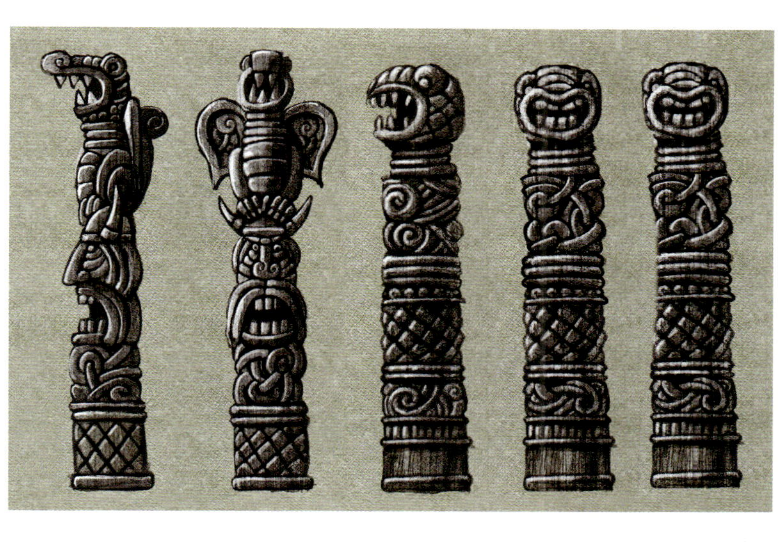

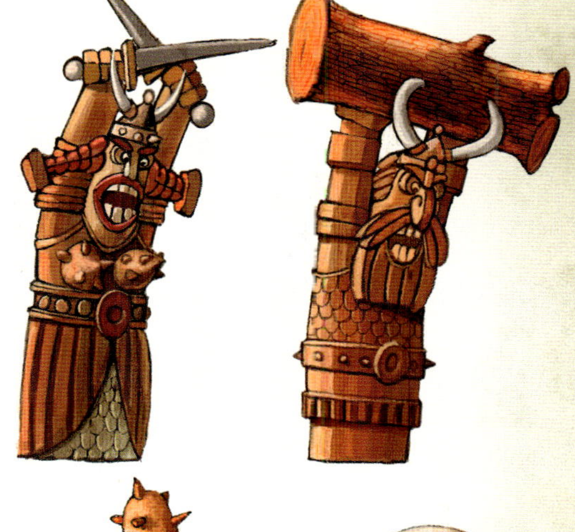

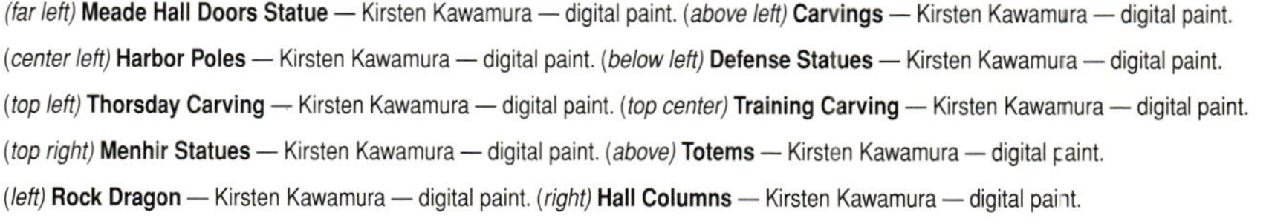

(far left) **Meade Hall Doors Statue** — Kirsten Kawamura — digital paint. *(above left)* **Carvings** — Kirsten Kawamura — digital paint.
(center left) **Harbor Poles** — Kirsten Kawamura — digital paint. *(below left)* **Defense Statues** — Kirsten Kawamura — digital paint.
(top left) **Thorsday Carving** — Kirsten Kawamura — digital paint. *(top center)* **Training Carving** — Kirsten Kawamura — digital paint.
(top right) **Menhir Statues** — Kirsten Kawamura — digital paint. *(above)* **Totems** — Kirsten Kawamura — digital paint.
(left) **Rock Dragon** — Kirsten Kawamura — digital paint. *(right)* **Hall Columns** — Kirsten Kawamura — digital paint.

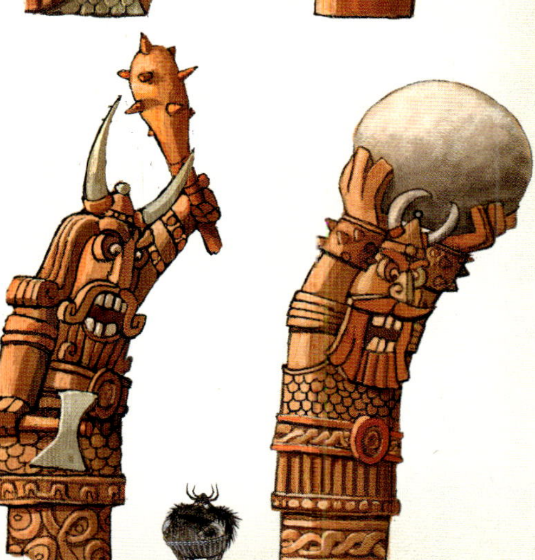

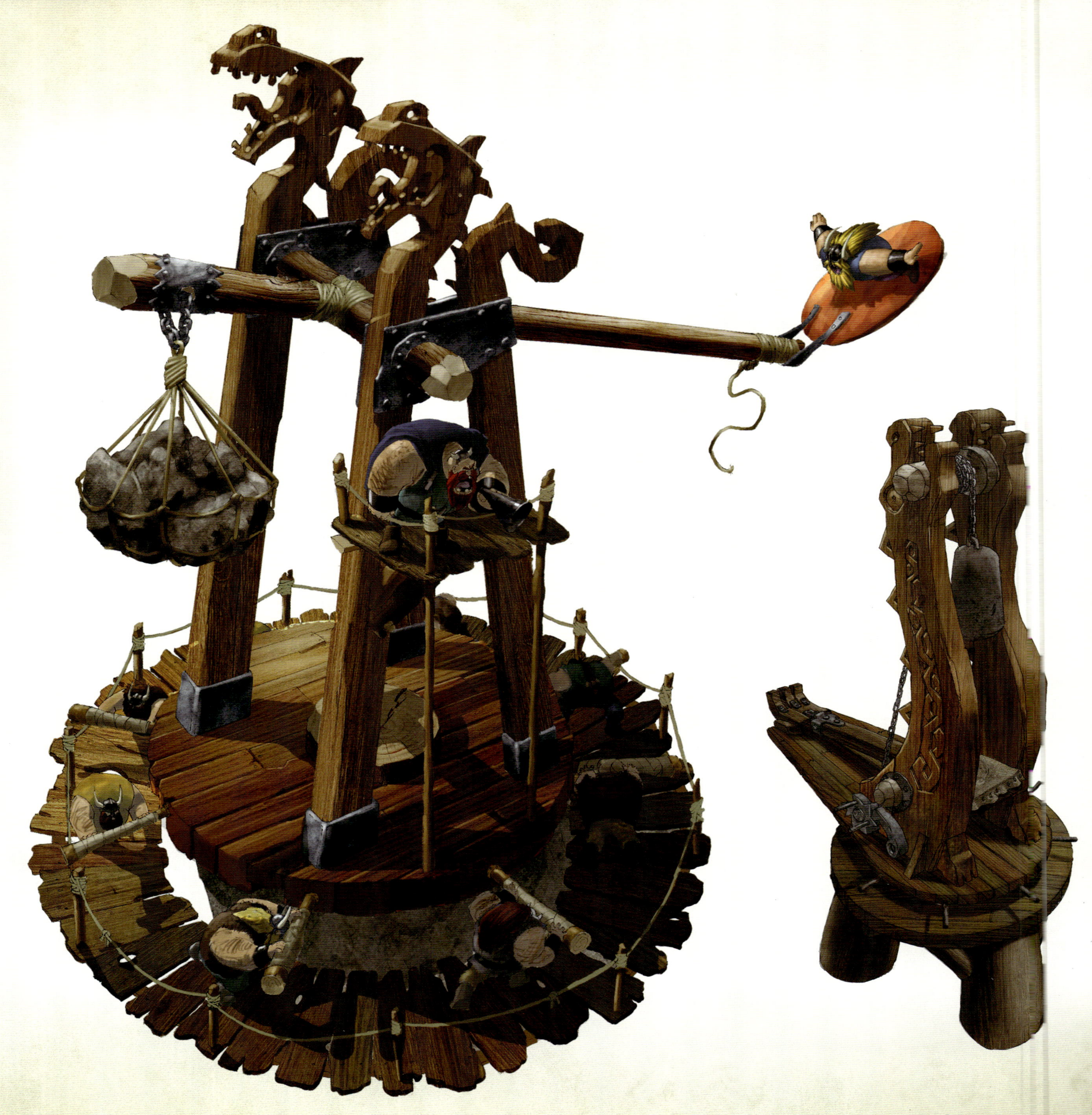

Viking Defense

Towers & Contraptions

While most shires of folklore protected themselves by constructing high stone walls along their perimeter, that defense tactic simply does not work when the enemy is airborne. "To illustrate the fact that this village is on constant dragon alert, every shot of the set is meant to include a defense tower or defense contraption," notes Art Director Pierre-Olivier Vincent.

The "screaming Viking" defense towers serve two practical purposes. Their imposing presence wards off dragons by day, standing as a perfect example of stone and scale representing the strength and intimidation techniques of the Viking people. By night they also stand as beacons along the shore by having firelight glowing in their mouths.

Catapults, slingshots, and various examples of Middle Age machinery inspired the designs of the defense contraptions, and these mechanisms are used to launch rocks (and even the occasional Viking) at their dragon targets.

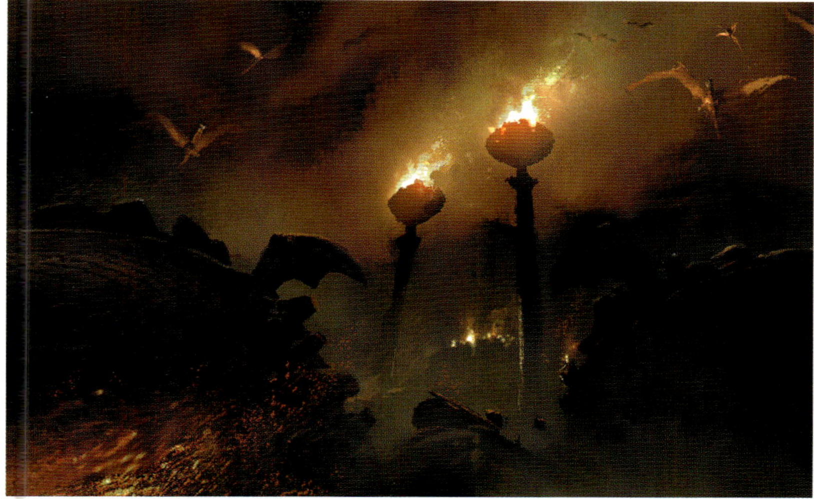

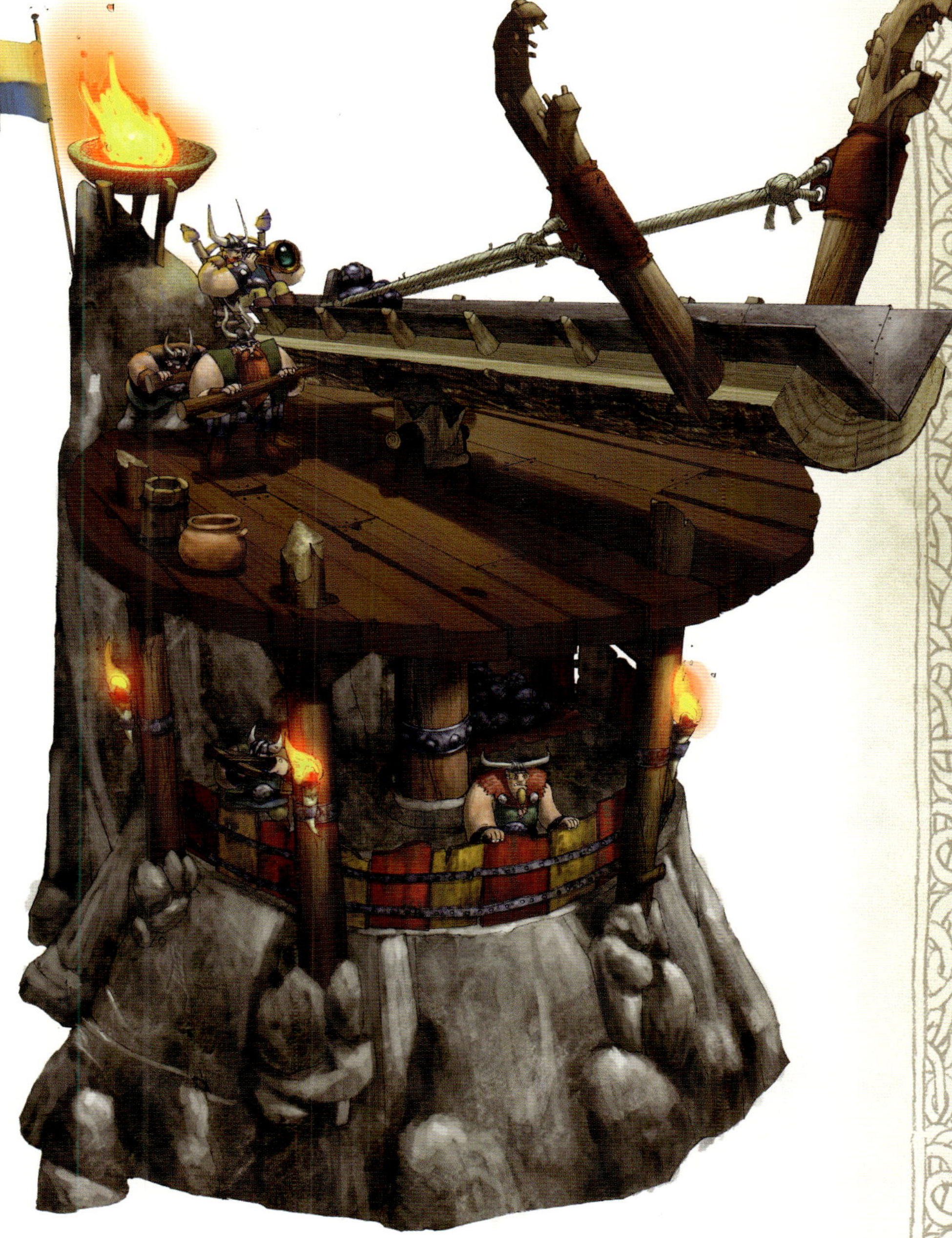

(far left) **Trebuchet Tower** — Mel Zwyer — digital paint. *(far left)* **Striker Tower** — Mel Zwyer — digital paint. (above *left)* **Braziers in Sky** — Dominique Louis — digital paint. *(above right)* **Slingshot Tower** — Mel Zwyer — digital paint.

Viking Boats

"These vessels are bigger, more aggressive, and more outrageous than actual Viking ships," notes Art Director Pierre-Olivier Vincent. To diversify the fleet in an efficient way, there are three basic boat designs and a variety of interchangeable dragon heads, tails and prows that can be added or removed," explains Modeling Supervisor Matt Paulson. Vincent's earlier boat designs were more accurate portrayals of Viking ships, complete with sail stands on each of the boats. Due to the need to accommodate character movement on the limited boat deck, however, these sail stands were removed and replaced with the more traditionally recognized hanging sail setups.

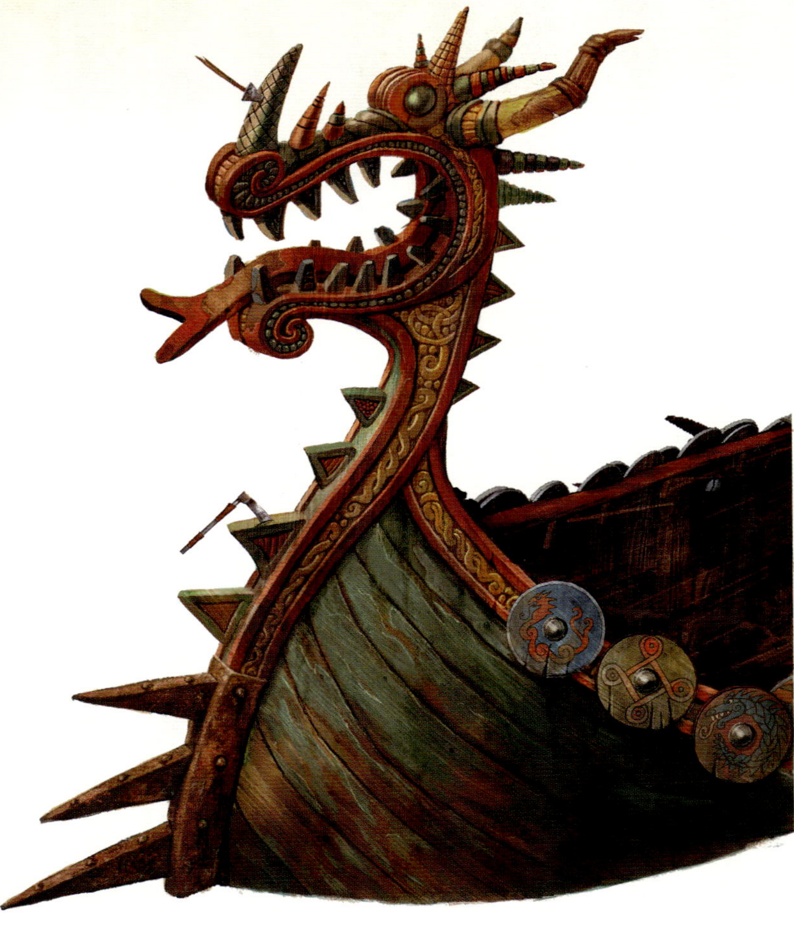

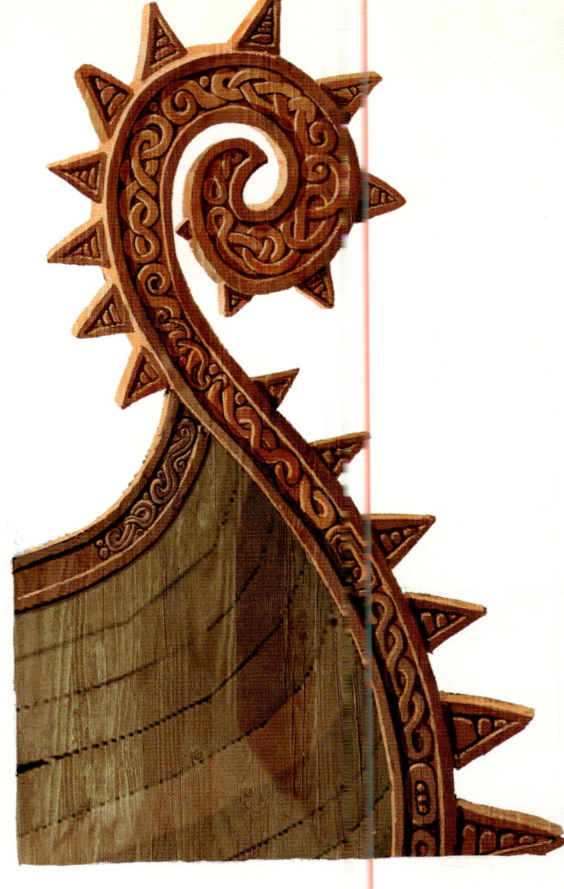

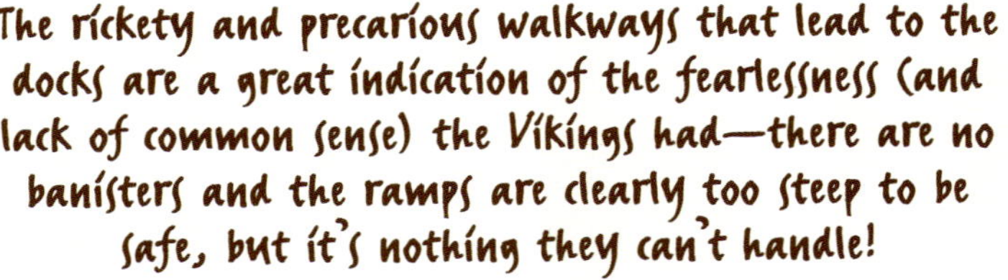

The rickety and precarious walkways that lead to the docks are a great indication of the fearlessness (and lack of common sense) the Vikings had—there are no banisters and the ramps are clearly too steep to be safe, but it's nothing they can't handle!

—Kathy Altieri, Production Designer

(above left) **Kids Boat Front** — Kirsten Kawamura — digital paint. *(above right)* **Kids Boat Back** — Kirsten Kawamura — digital paint. *(right)* **Sails** — Margaret Wuller — digital paint. *(below)* **Dragon Prows** — Nicolas Weis — digital paint. *(far right)* **Battleship Front** — Kirsten Kawamura — digital paint.

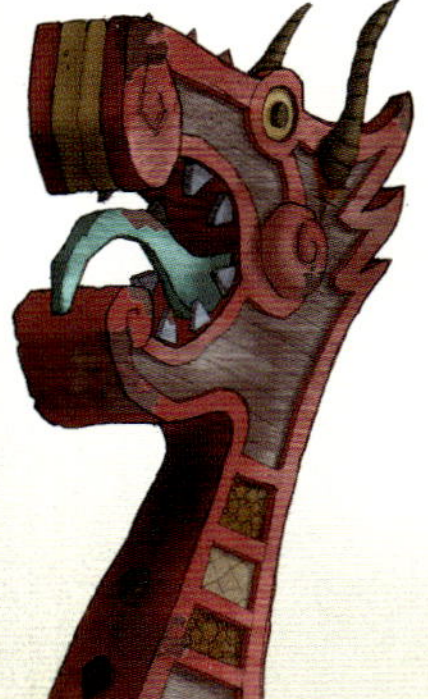
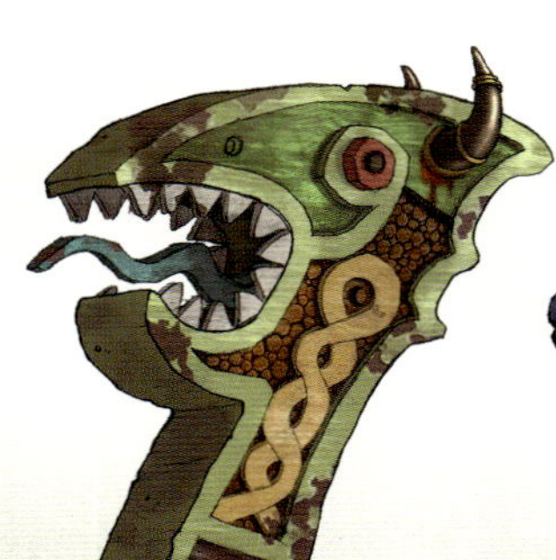
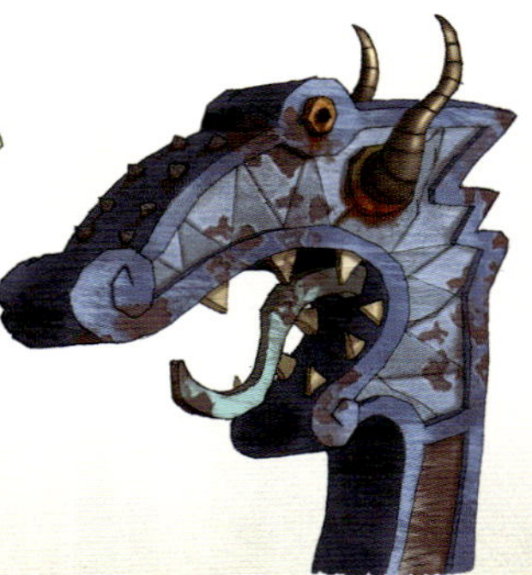
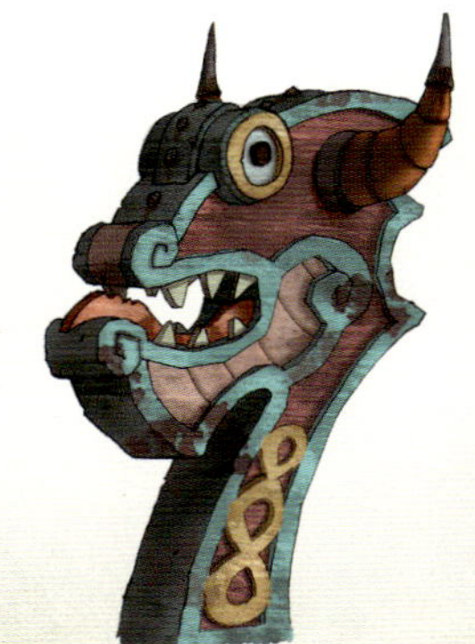
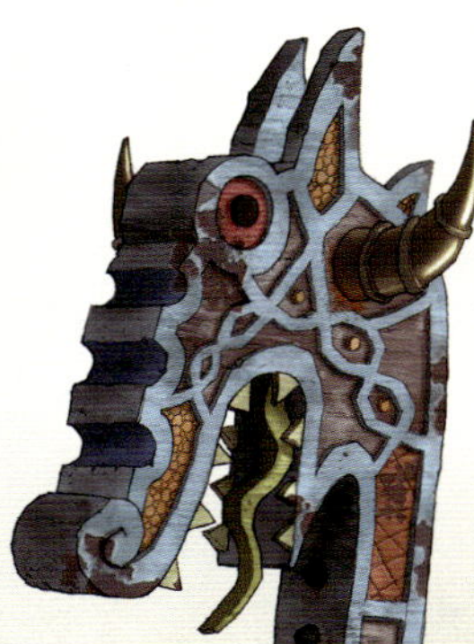
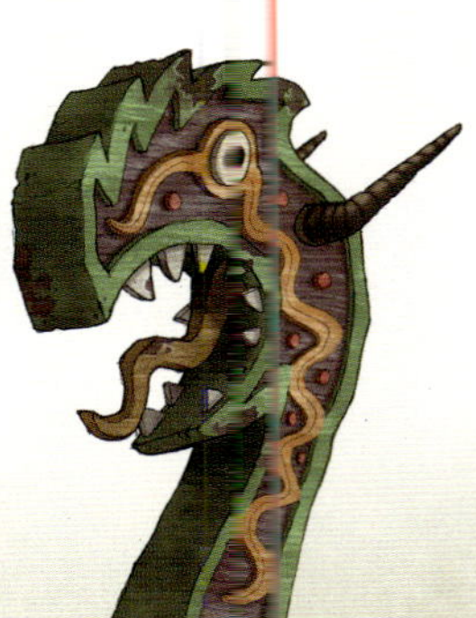

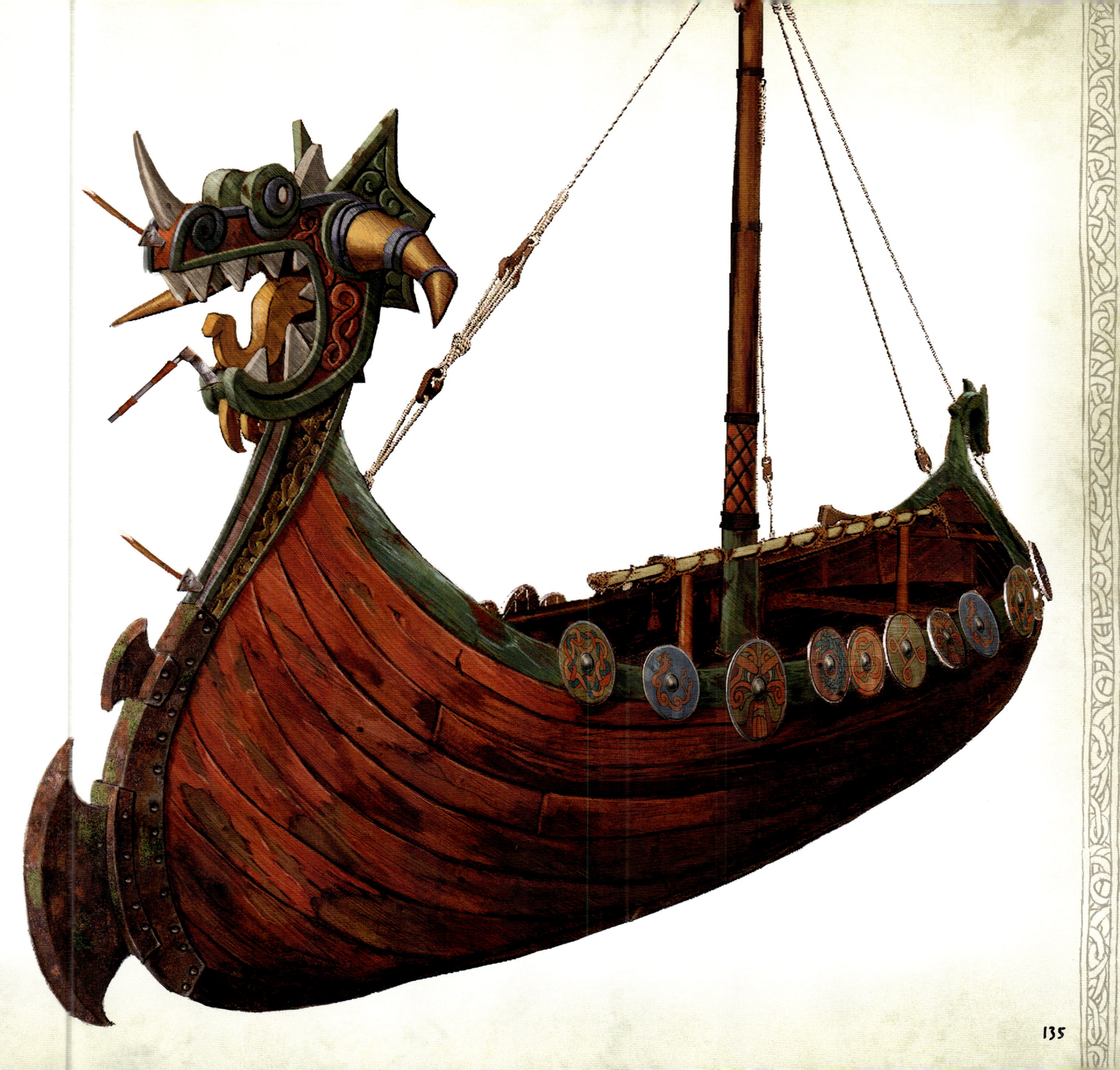

Viking Contraptions

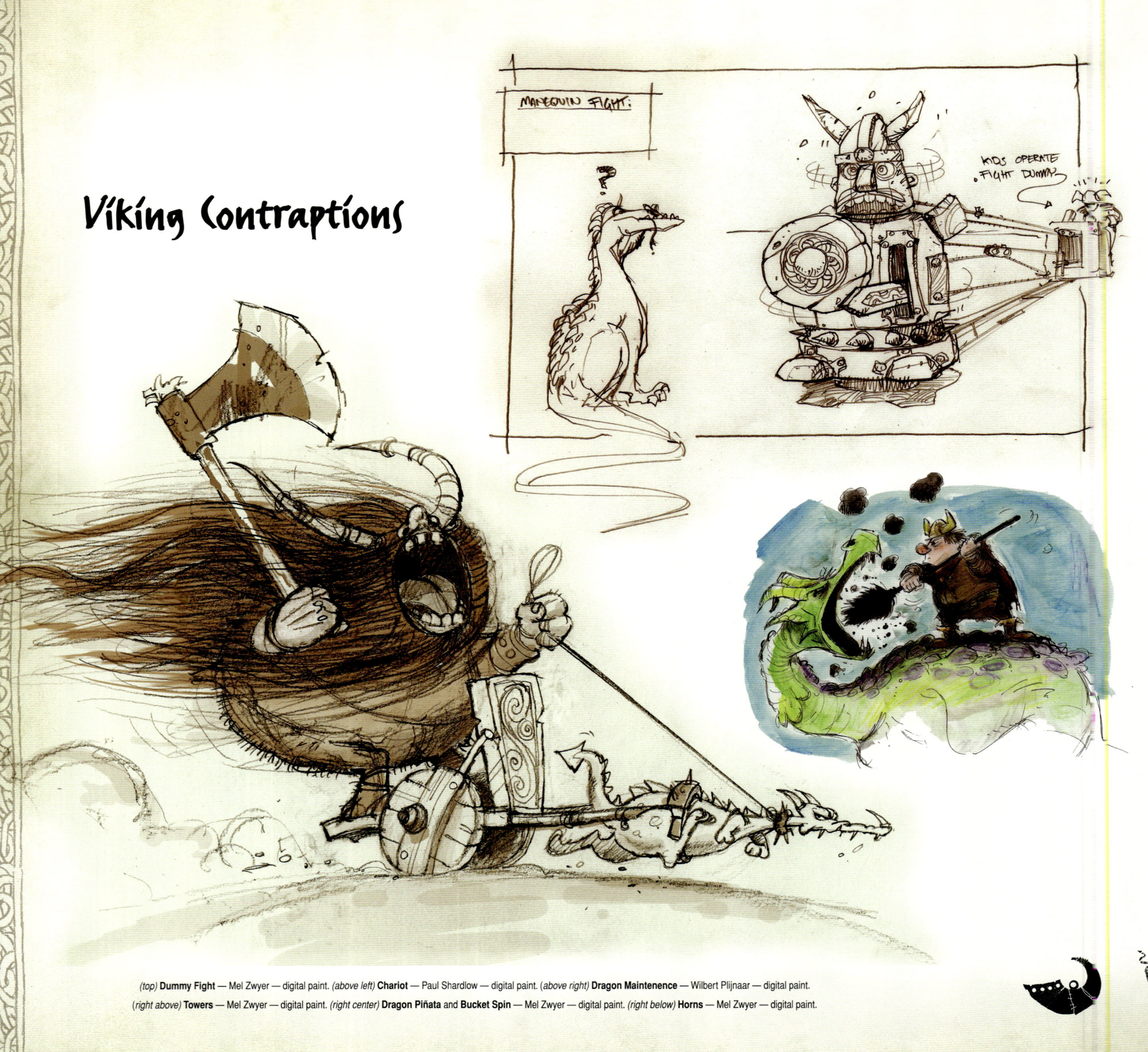

(top) **Dummy Fight** — Mel Zwyer — digital paint. *(above left)* **Chariot** — Paul Shardlow — digital paint. *(above right)* **Dragon Maintenence** — Wilbert Plijnaar — digital paint.
(right above) **Towers** — Mel Zwyer — digital paint. *(right center)* **Dragon Piñata** and **Bucket Spin** — Mel Zwyer — digital paint. *(right below)* **Horns** — Mel Zwyer — digital paint.

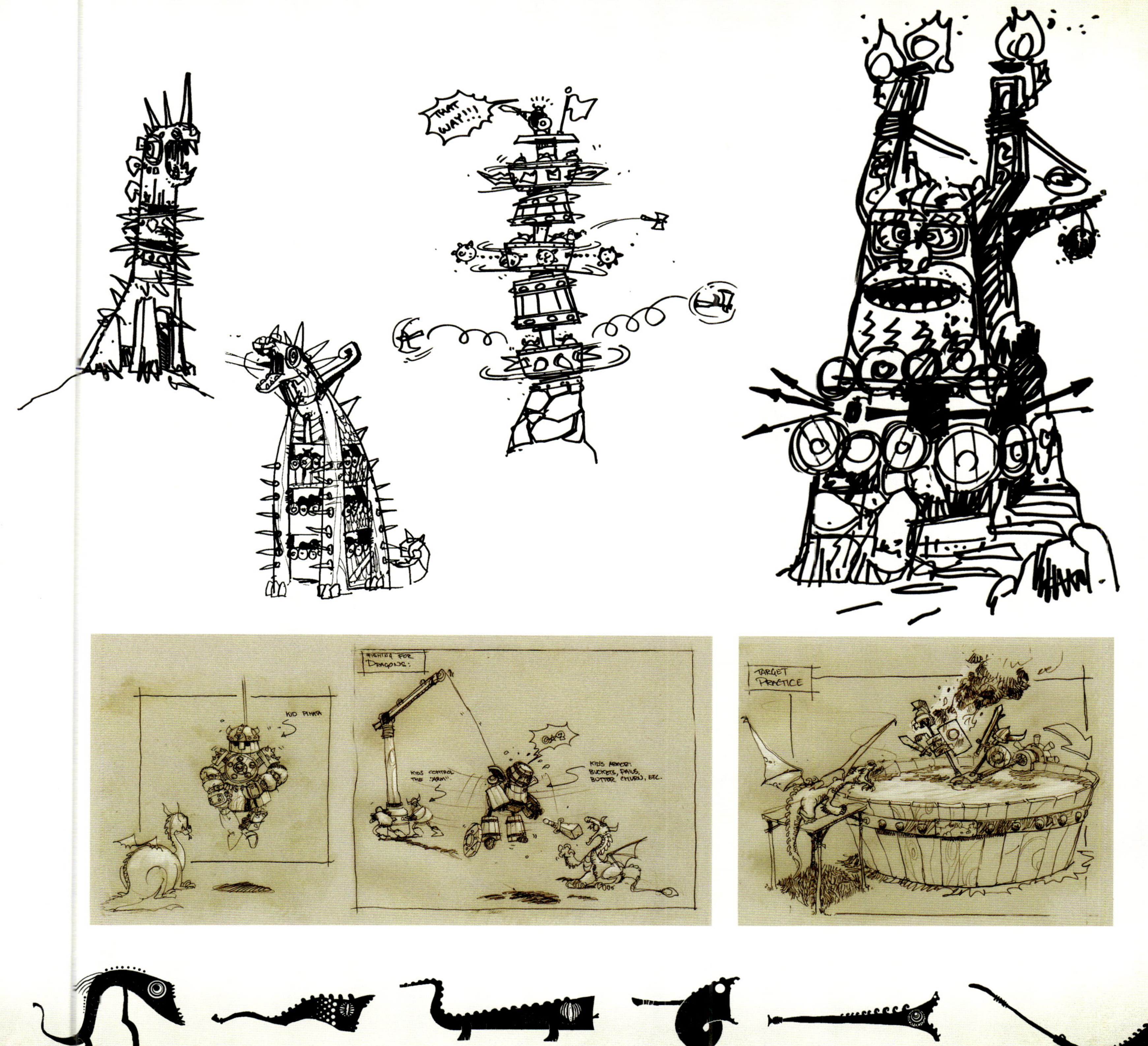
THAT WAY!!!
KID PINATA
FISHING FOR DRAGONS:
KIDS CONTROL THE "ARM"
KID'S ARMOR: BUCKETS, PAILS, BUTTER CHURN, ETC.
TARGET PRACTICE

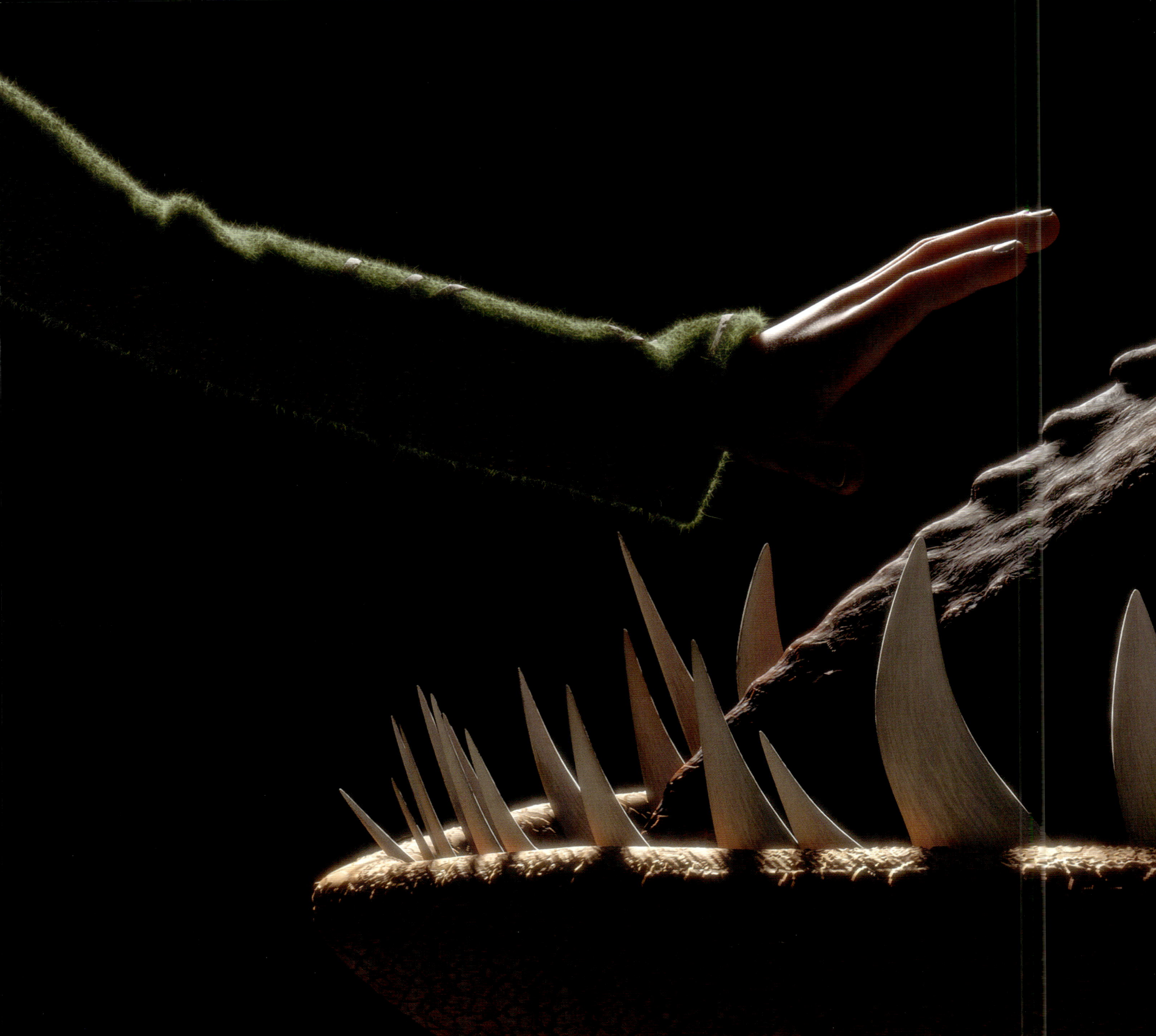

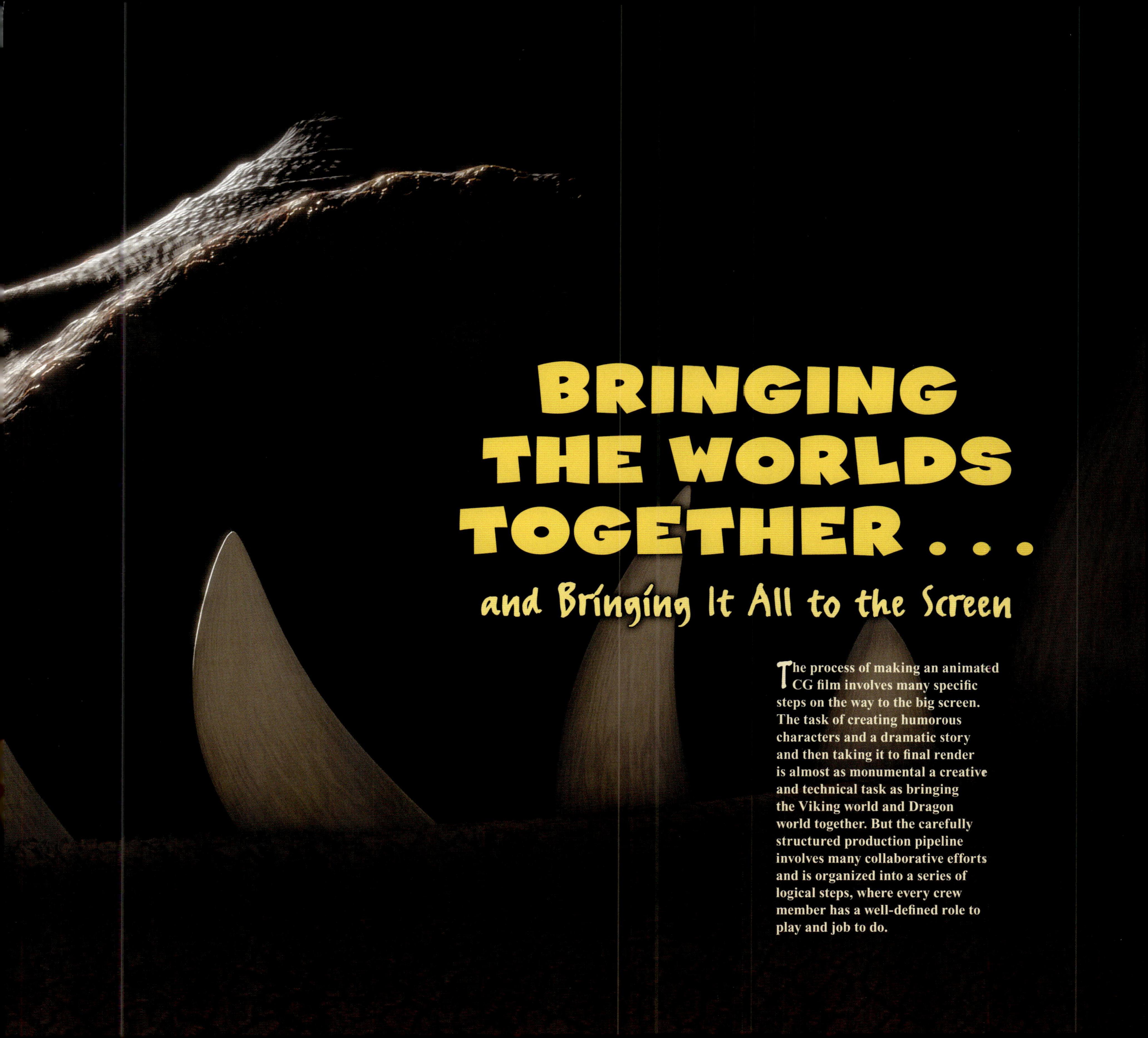

BRINGING THE WORLDS TOGETHER . . .

and Bringing It All to the Screen

The process of making an animated CG film involves many specific steps on the way to the big screen. The task of creating humorous characters and a dramatic story and then taking it to final render is almost as monumental a creative and technical task as bringing the Viking world and Dragon world together. But the carefully structured production pipeline involves many collaborative efforts and is organized into a series of logical steps, where every crew member has a well-defined role to play and job to do.

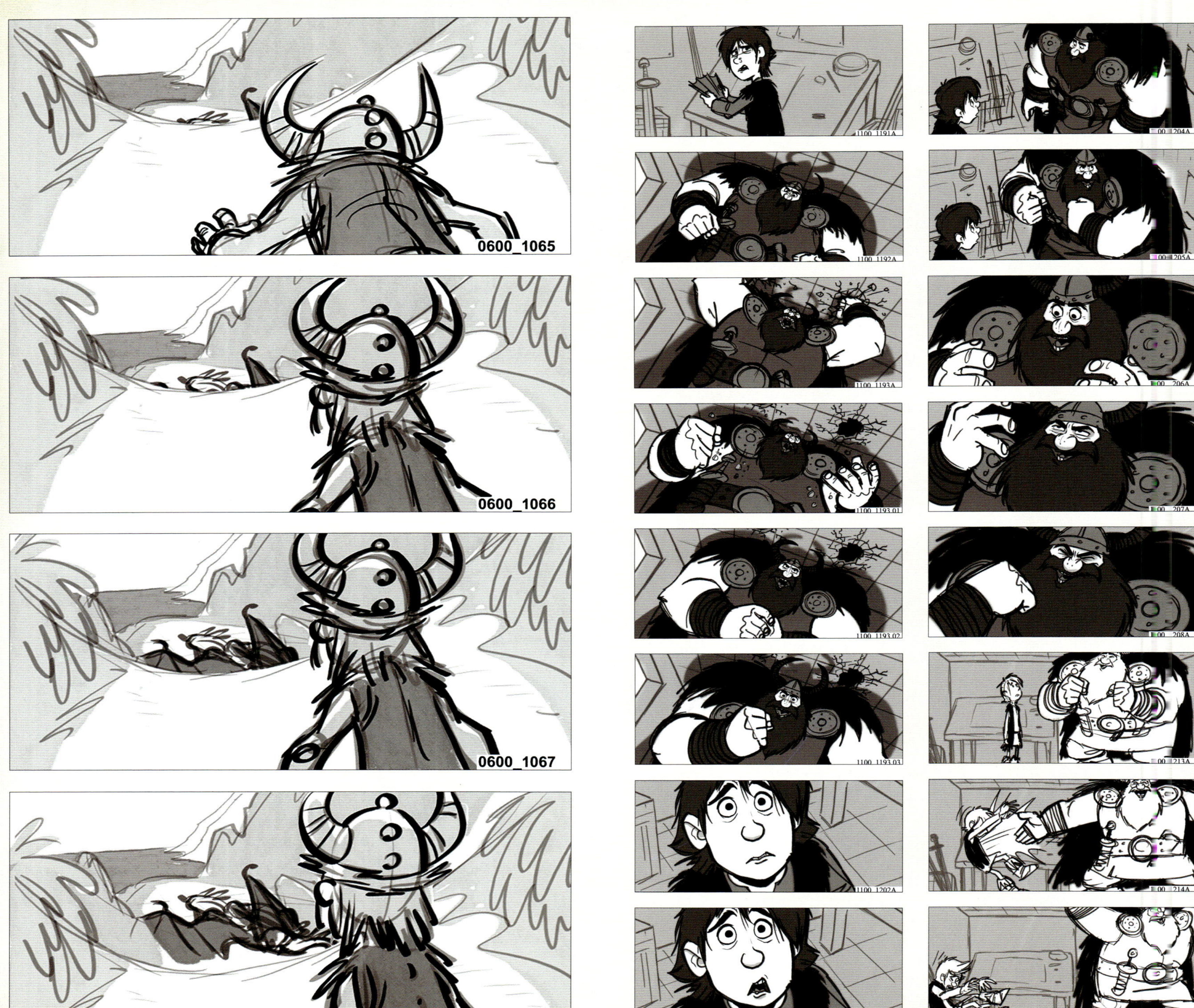
0600_1065
0600_1066
0600_1067
0600_1068

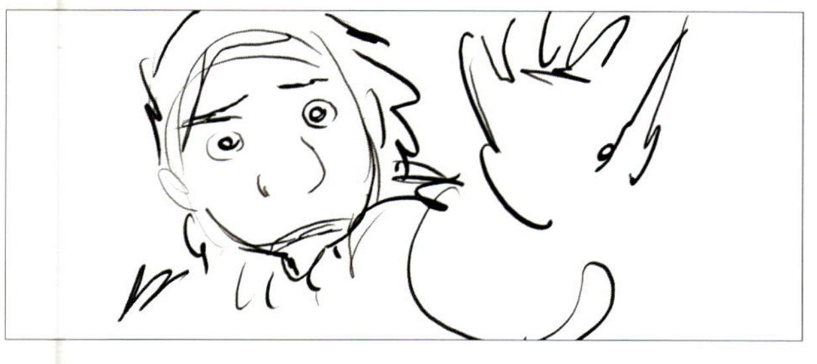
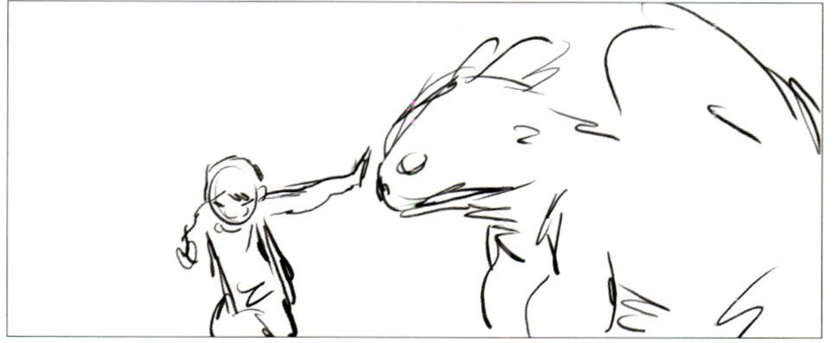
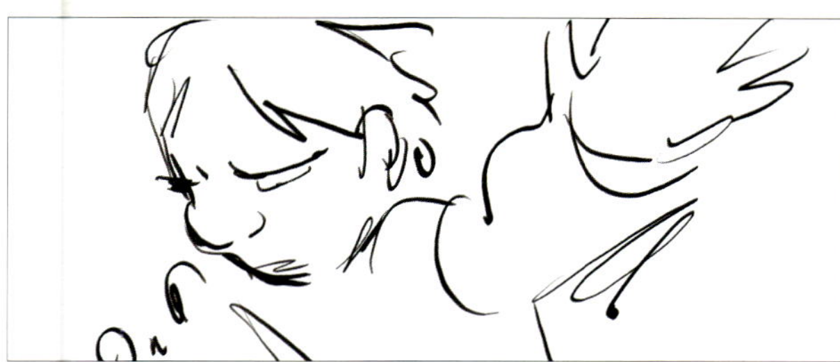
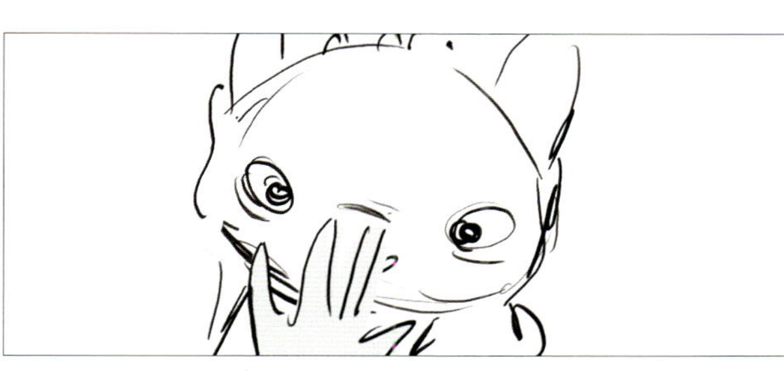
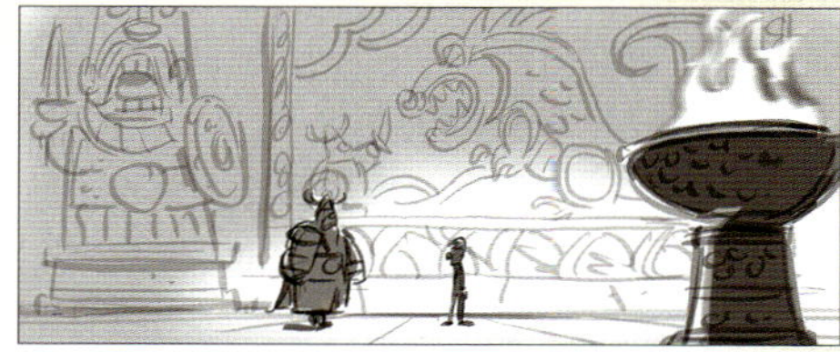
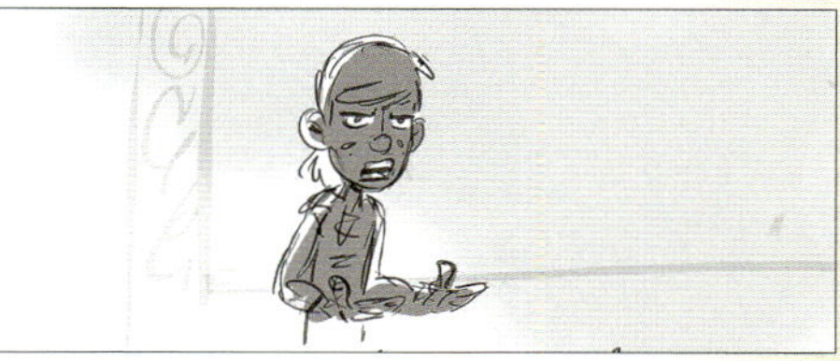
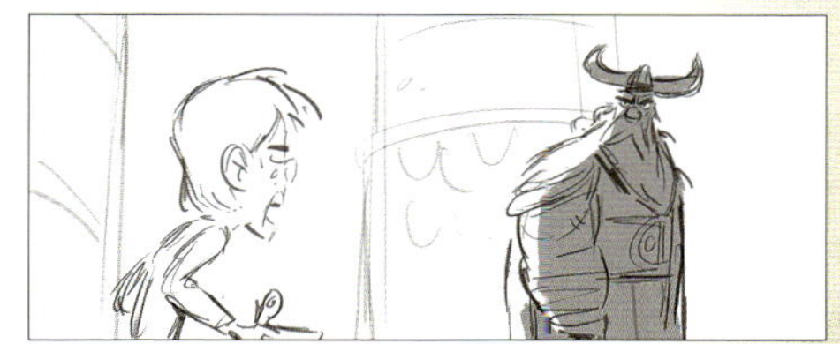
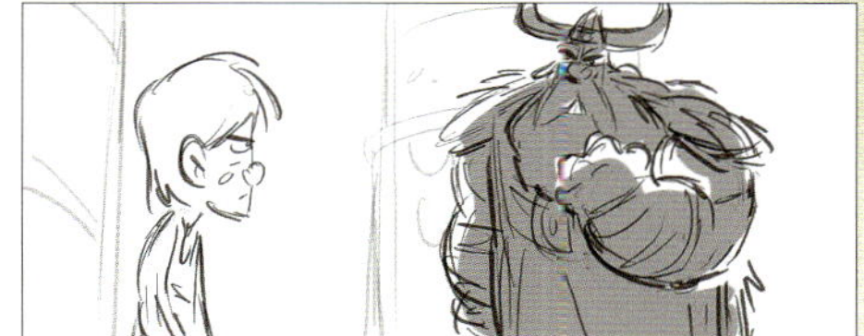
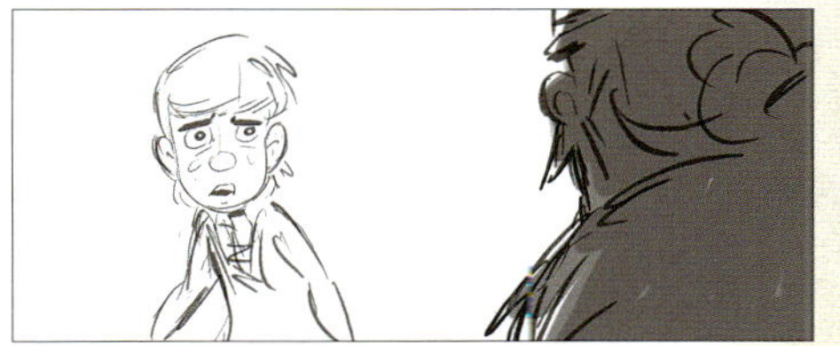
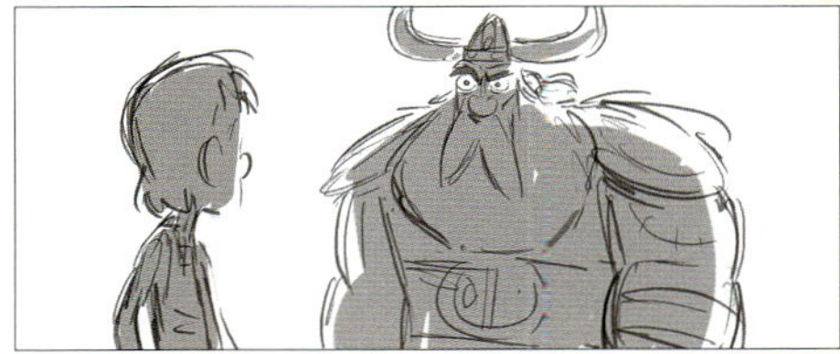
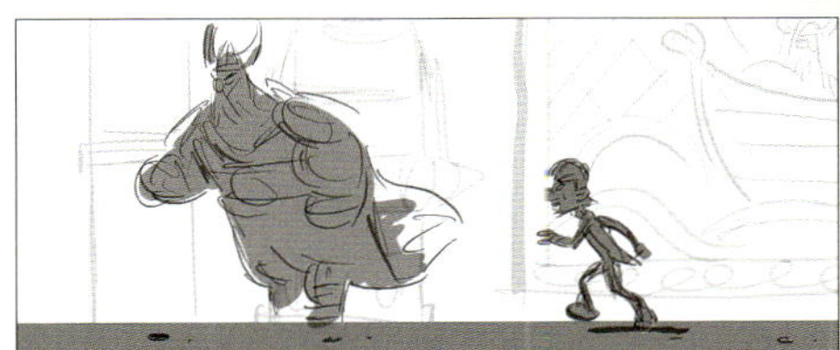

Story

The story team carries perhaps the most daunting task of a film crew: If the storyline they craft isn't solid, then everything else that appears on the screen is inconsequential. In *How to Train Your Dragon*, the story begins with the Dragons and Vikings as enemies. As in the original book, Hiccup and Toothless develop a powerful, secret relationship within this hostile atmosphere. "This dynamic gave the story an interesting act two, with a double life to follow: By day Hiccup was becoming a true Viking and by night he was consorting with the enemy," explains Director Chris Sanders. "Those two worlds are going to eventually collide—it's the nature of the structure—so it gave us a great opportunity to have something collapse in the second act, and then a big problem for Hiccup to fix in act three," notes Director Dean DeBlois.

One of the most involved efforts of the story team is to find the proper combination of drama, humor, and action. The team put great thought into developing the emotional storyline first and then letting comedic moments fall into place as long as they did not undercut the drama of a scene. "Our humor comes from the heart of the characters, their unique personalities and characteristics, more than anything," says Sanders. The way Hiccup jokes with his detractors and the way Toothless makes dragon flight even more exciting for his human riders are perfect examples of this character-based humor. Similarly, the numerous action-packed scenes of this film are not just pure entertainment opportunities; they actively move the storyline forward while giving the audience an exciting adventure along the way.

The sense of scale that was predominant in design theory for *How to Train Your Dragon* was also an important tenet for the story. "We knew we wanted a sense of 'David and Goliath' in the movie, where the smallest, least considered character of the story has to face something colossal. That is how we ended up with a physically, and metaphorically, huge dragon at the end of the movie," explains Head of Story Alessandro Carloni. Plus, it is simply rewarding to watch how Hiccup and Toothless together are much stronger than either one would have been individually in fighting the Red Death.

(previous pages) CG Still. *(far left)* **Sequence 600 "Hiccup Finds the Dragon"** — story sketch — Tom Owens — digital paint. *(left)* **Sequence 1100 "Stoick Shows an Interest"** — story sketch — Ben Ballistreri — digital paint. *(above)* **Sequence 1050 "Forbidden Friendship"** — story sketch — Tron Mai — digital paint. *(right)* **Sequence 1900 "Meltdown"** — story sketch — John Puglisi — digital paint. *(following pages)* **Sequence 2475 "Battle in the Clouds"** — story sketch — Chris Sanders — pencil.

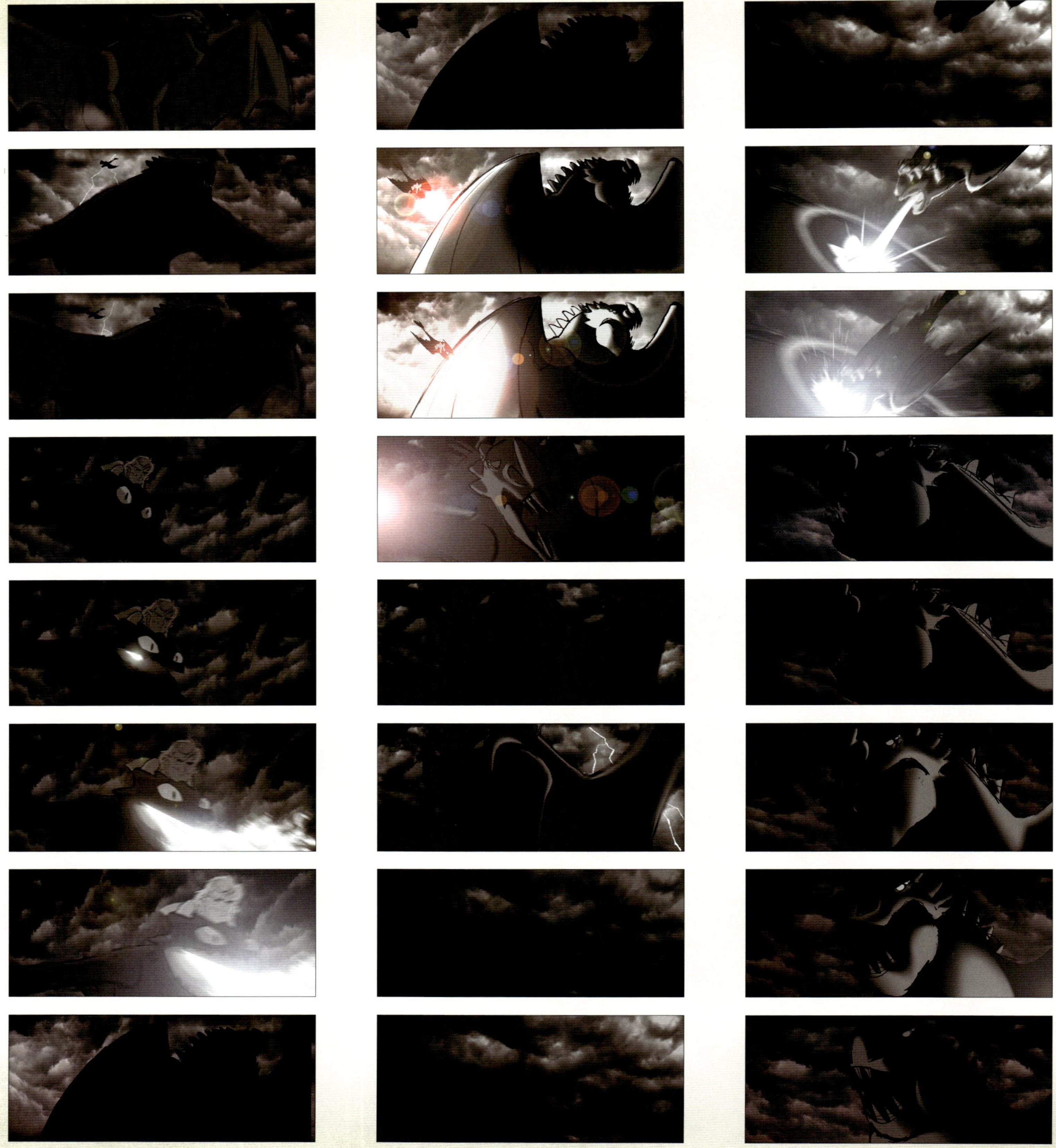

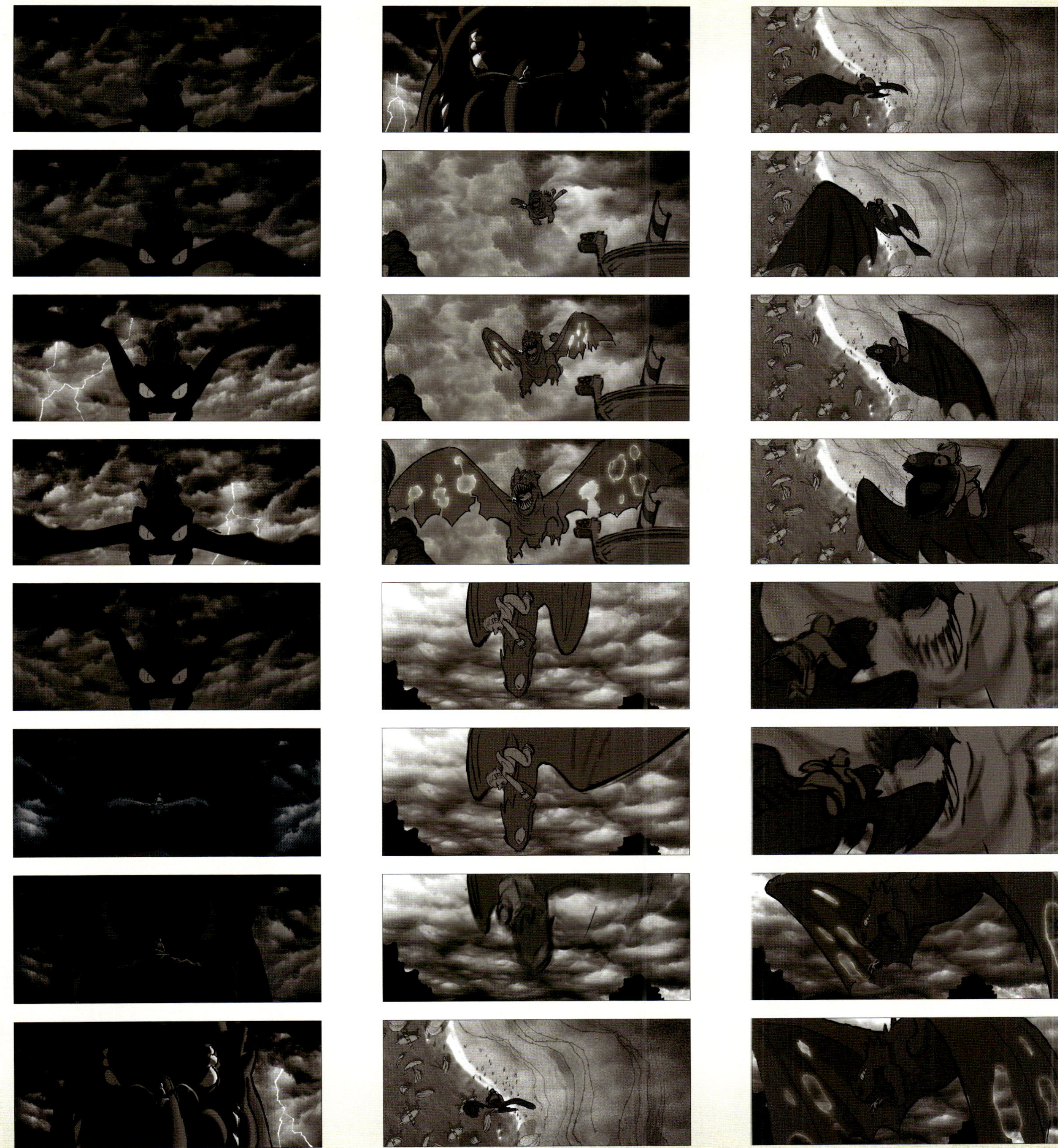

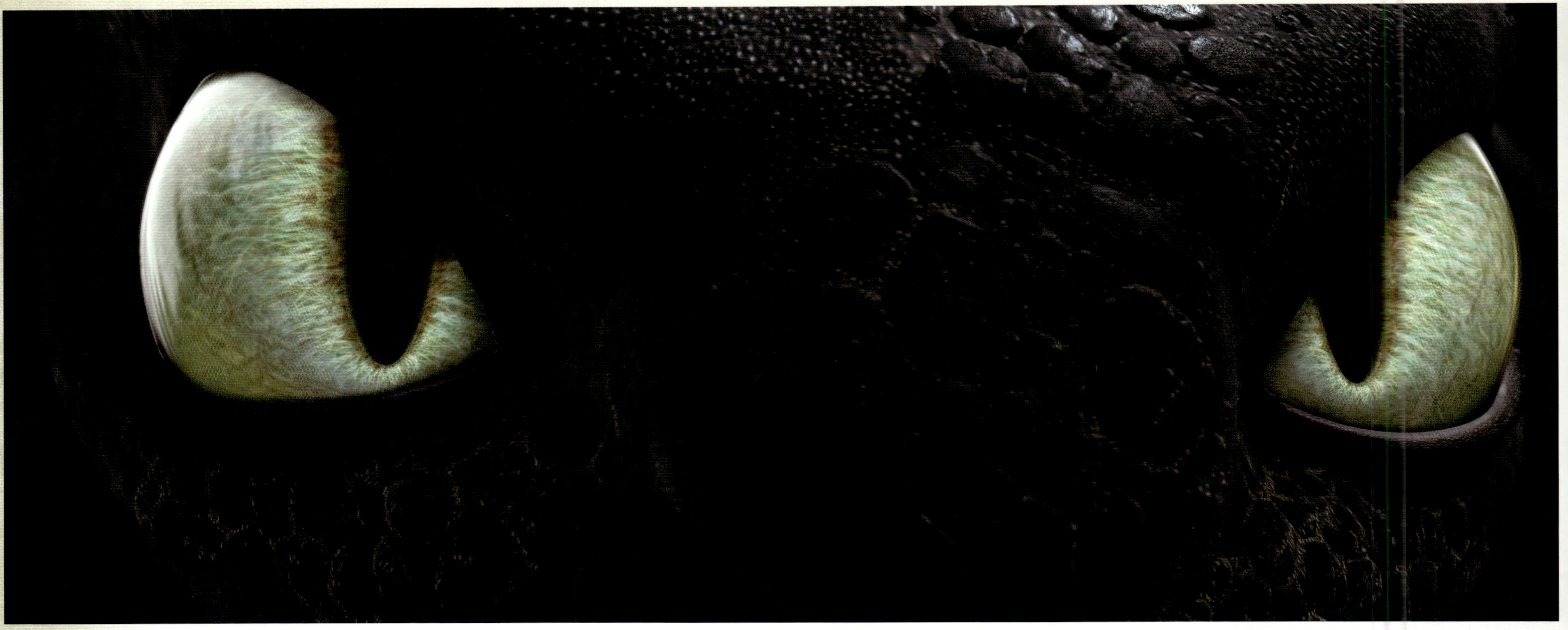

Layout, Cinematography & 3D

The layout department sets the stage for the film by placing characters and props in the modeled environments, and then turns the camera on. It is their job to use the "camera" to support the storytelling.

The cinematography in *How to Train Your Dragon* is more realistic than one might expect in the CG world, where almost any camera move is possible. "Since our film is very realistically designed, our cinematic design calls for live action–inspired camera motion to help support the strong and often serious emotions in our story," explains Head of Layout Gil Zimmerman.

The layout department also greatly affected the 3D stereoscopic experience through its set dressing decisions. "While assembling sets, we made sure to establish many levels of foliage because 3D stereoscopic filmmaking is at its best when a set gives us plenty of objects in any composition to convey that depth," adds Zimmerman.

In scenes where there is little dialogue, such as when Hiccup first sees the downed dragon in the forest, camerawork also conveys the emotional arc visually by accentuating point of view. "In this scene, we try to experience the discovery from Hiccup's perspective. For instance, in the shot where Hiccup first catches a glimpse of the dragon, we follow him with a Steadicam as if the audience is walking right alongside Hiccup. The camera travels to the ridge over Hiccup's shoulder and just captures a glimpse of the dragon before cutting away to wait for the audience to have a moment to experience the elation with him," explains Zimmerman.

(above) **Toothless Eyes** — CG still.

(right) **Hiccup Hill** — CG still.

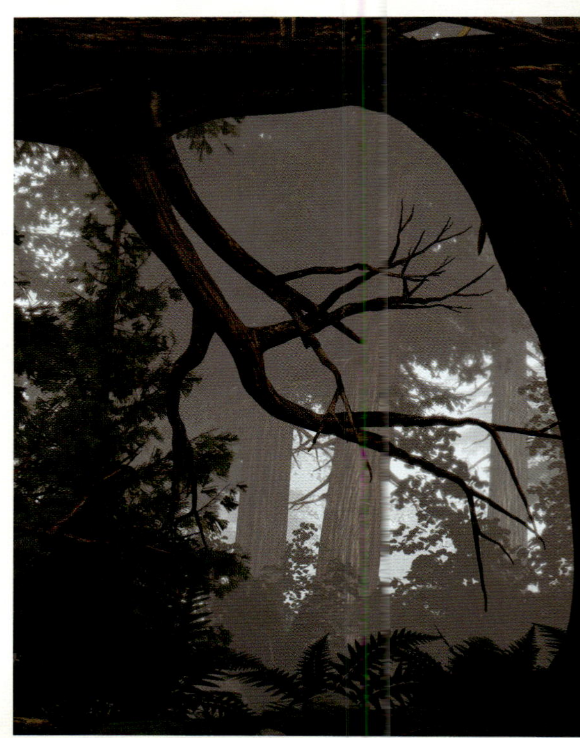

> We only accentuate the 3D stereoscopic experience in organic, story-driven moments to deliver the emotion of a scene, such as when Hiccup first reaches out to touch Toothless. We want the audience to feel that nervous excitement.
>
> —Gil Zimmerman, Head of Layout

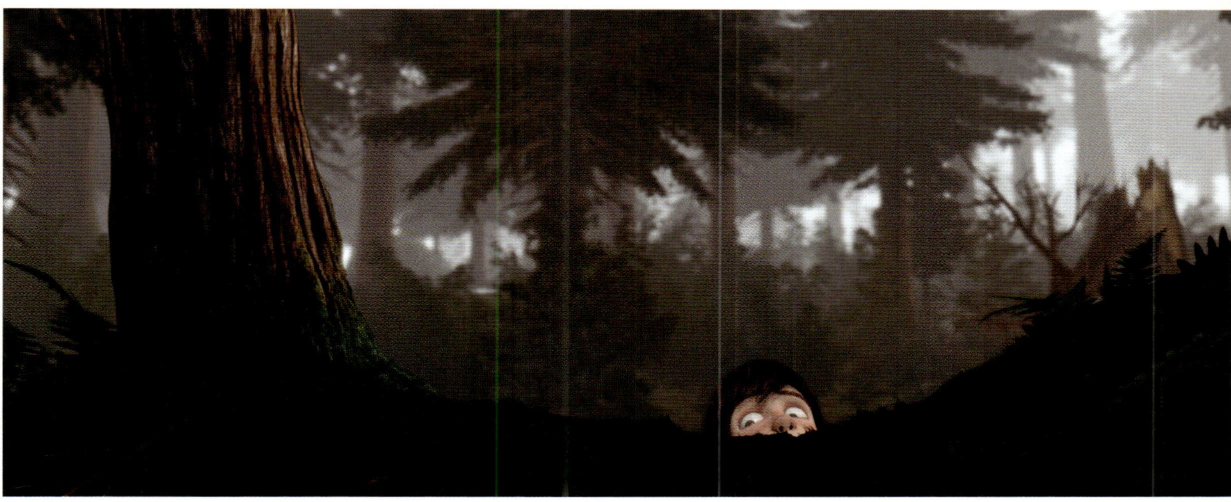

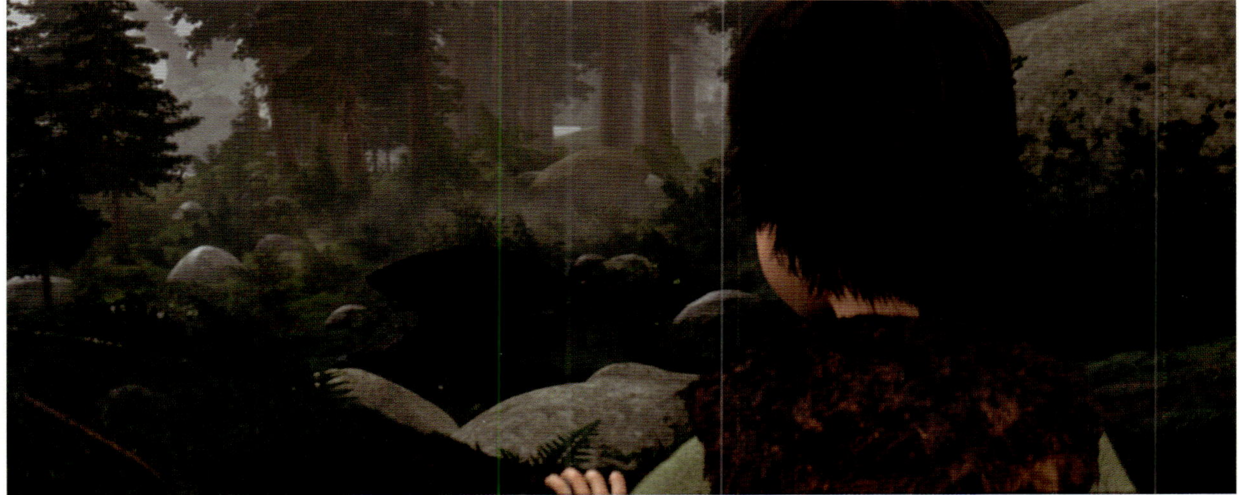

(above right) **Hiccup Peek** — CG still.
(below right) **Hiccup Back** — CG still.

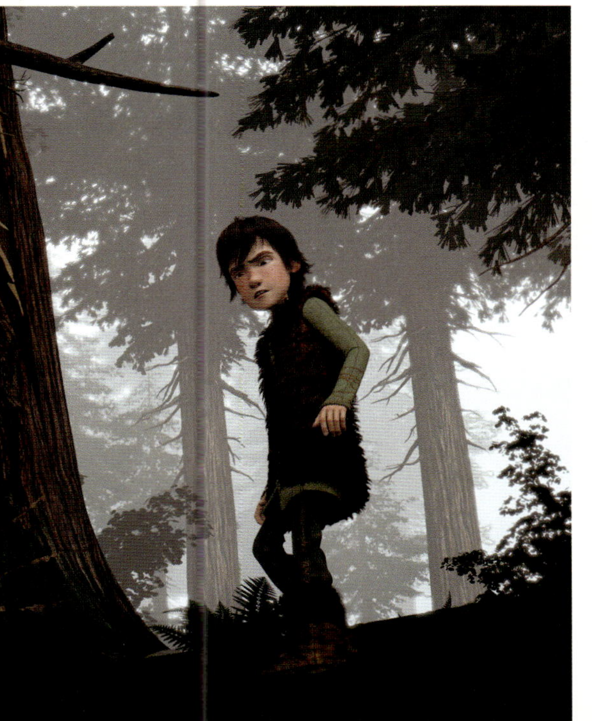

LAYOUT ADDS to the audience experience by utilizing 3D stereoscopic technology to create an emotional and sometimes physical effect in the filmgoer. "To build anxiety in the audience, we create contrast in the 3D stereoscopic depth, which generates a physical and perceptual reaction in the audience," explains Head of Layout Gil Zimmerman. "For example, as we come up to the top of the ridge, you'll notice how the two cameras are almost aligned, and the image is now essentially flat and physically easier for the audience to focus on. Then as Hiccup drops down, the cameras separate and the image becomes very dimensional, which now makes the viewer's eyes re-focus, causing a slight postural sway and increase in heart rate, which hopefully translates into the anxiety in Hiccup's point of view at seeing this dragon for the first time. The audience has the anticipation and can feel the physical excitement of the moment. It's similar to how an artist uses color in a scene or over the course of a movie, with mono-saturated looks when it's an emotional downturn and super-saturation during a big, bright, musical moment."

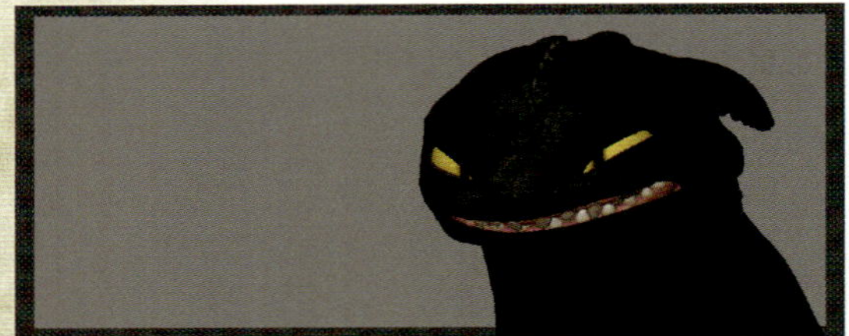

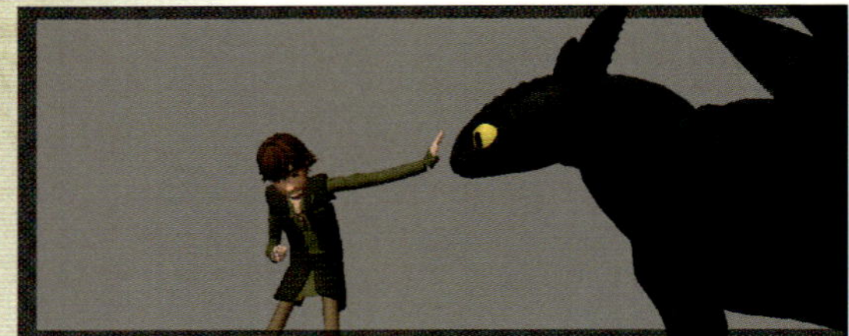

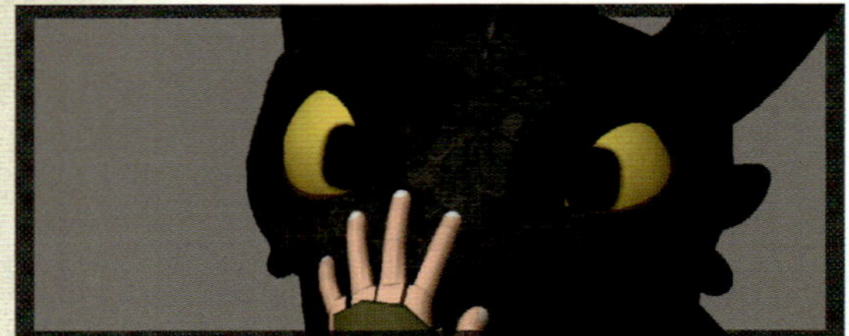

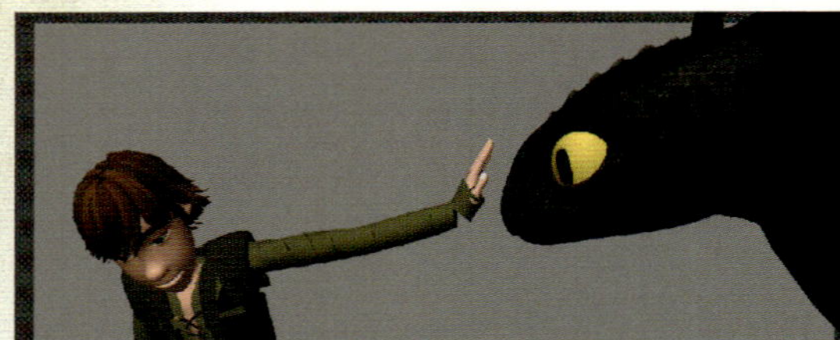

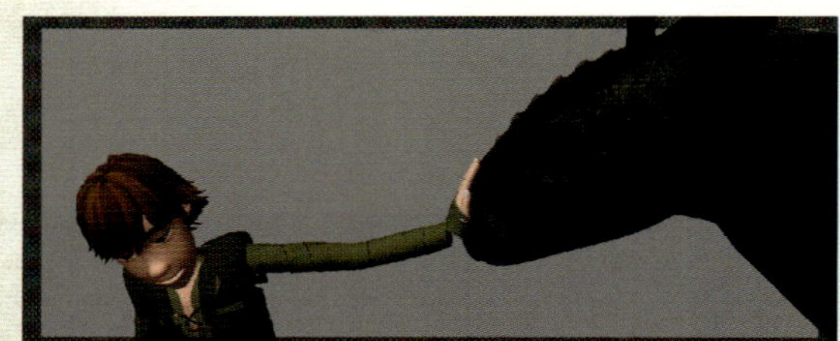

Animation & Character Effects

Animators provide the physical acting for the characters, and just like the actors providing the voices, animators think about character motivation in each scene before embarking on their portrayal. Toothless was the most challenging character to animate in *How to Train Your Dragon*, given his importance in the film and lack of verbal communication. For example, animators had to think through scenarios like "how would a wild animal act in captivity?" while working on the sequence where Hiccup first approaches the injured Toothless. "At this point in the story, we knew we needed to establish Toothless as a creature, not a personality, so we brought in an animal behavior consultant to gain some insight. She taught us that it would try to get away immediately, but for dramatic purposes, we thought that having Toothless be more nobly resigned to his fate, just laying down his neck to be killed, would be a draw for compassion from both Hiccup and the audience," recalls Head of Character Animation Simon Otto.

The animation team also spent an extraordinary amount of time and focus to get the "Forbidden Friendship" sequence right, because they knew the scene when Hiccup and Toothless first get to know one another was "the heart of the movie, and that if we failed that we would lose the audience at the end of the story," says Otto. The team studied storyboards and set up key poses for the entire sequence before assigning specific shots to animators, and they also tested the Toothless rig to see if it could handle certain inventive movements, such as sitting upright on its tail.

The character effects department is responsible for making sure that the animated characters look the way they were intended when final and all the elements are placed into the scene. In support of the action-packed animation in this film, the character effects team had to contend with numerous flying sequences, in which humans and dragons are moving at rates exceeding one hundred miles per hour. Way beyond the normal scope of making clothing and hair move naturally, the team had to believably portray the effects of having a strong wind in the characters' faces, where their clothes flutter, the hair blows around, and props, like Hiccup's cheat sheet, flap in the wind. "It's really challenging to make these things look good. The character effects team has to hit just the right blend of realistic wind, keeping the characters' hair in a pleasing shape. When they've done their job well, it makes a huge difference in the feeling of speed in the flying shots," explains Visual Effects Supervisor Craig Ring.

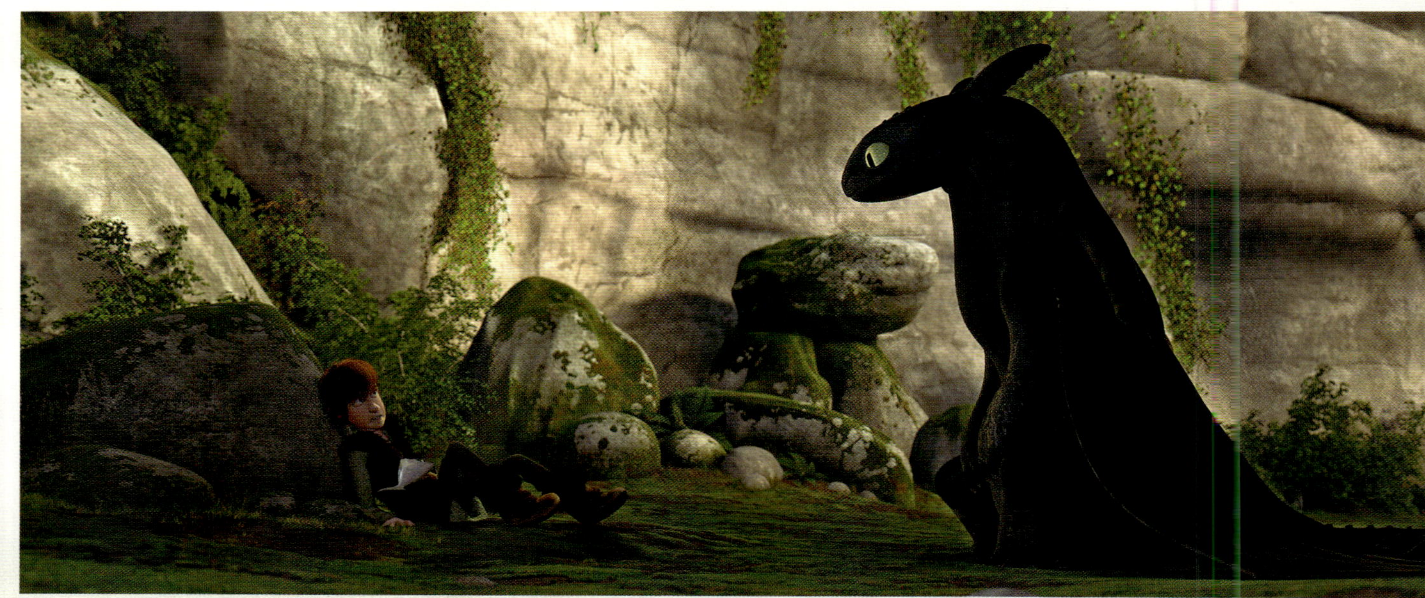

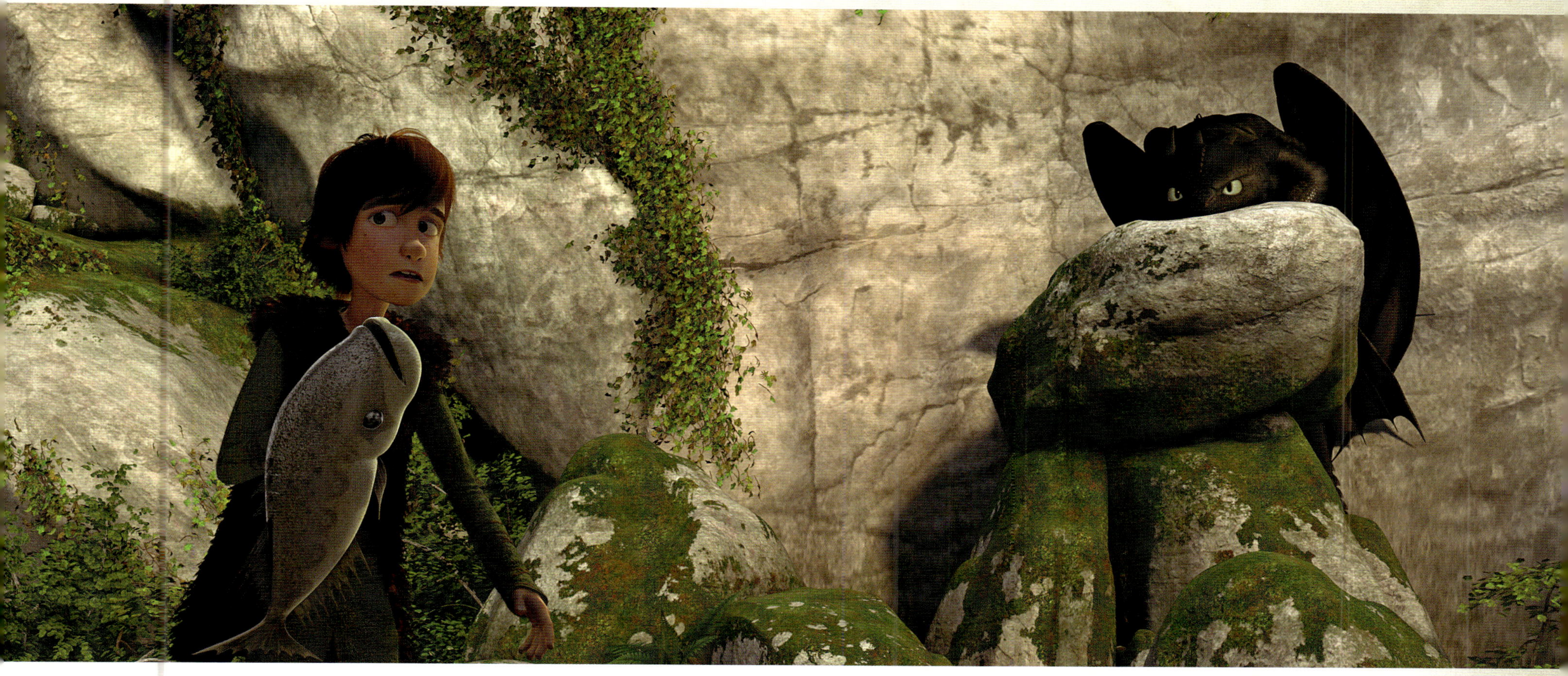

In our film's environment, stylized shapes are brought into reality by texture and light to create a sense of believability. This is also true in animation, where stylized characters are given naturalistic movements, gestures, and emotions to create that same level of perceived realism.

—Simon Otto, Head of Character Animation

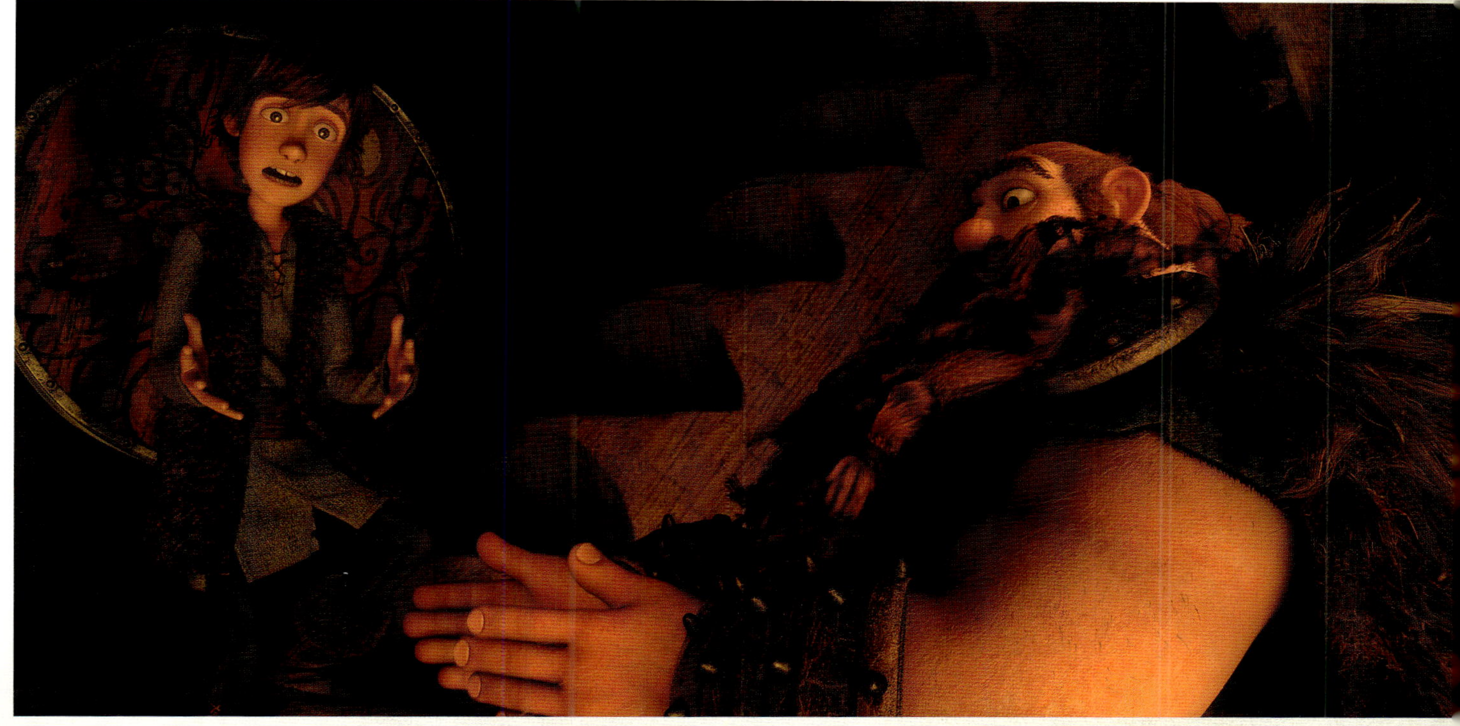

(far left) Animation Key Poses. *(left)* CG still. *(above)* CG still. *(right)* CG still.

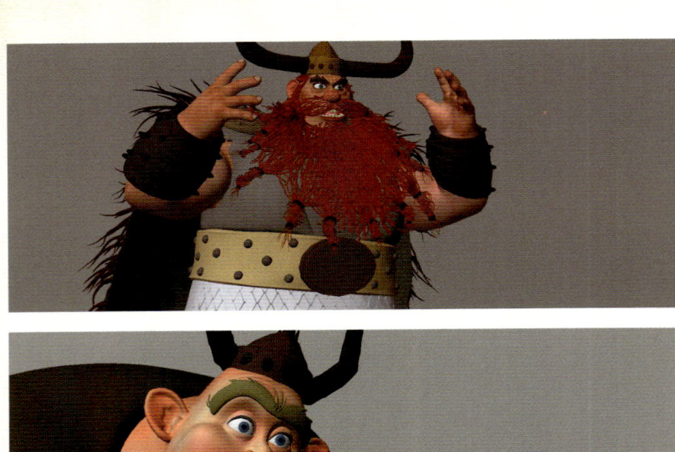

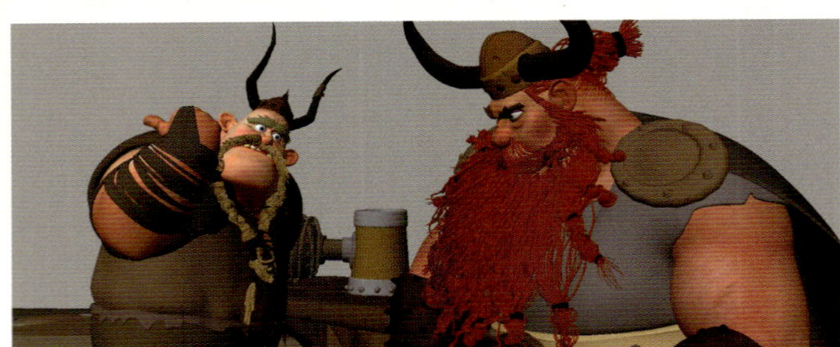

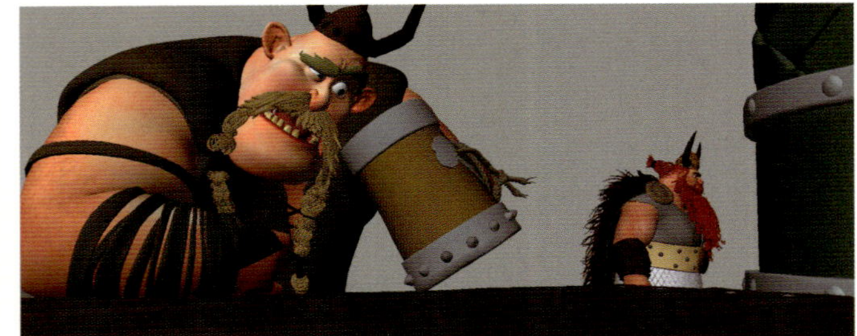

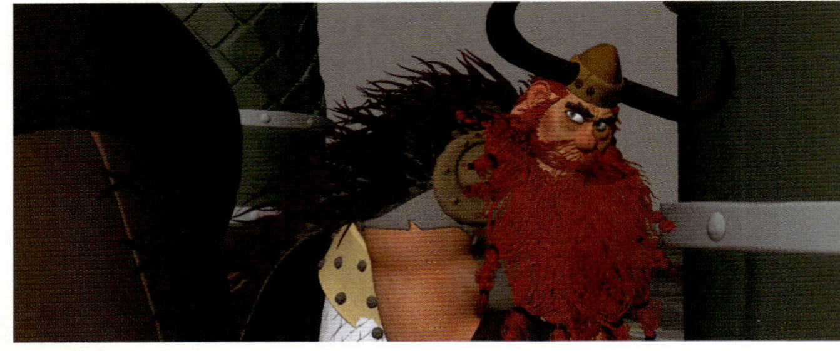

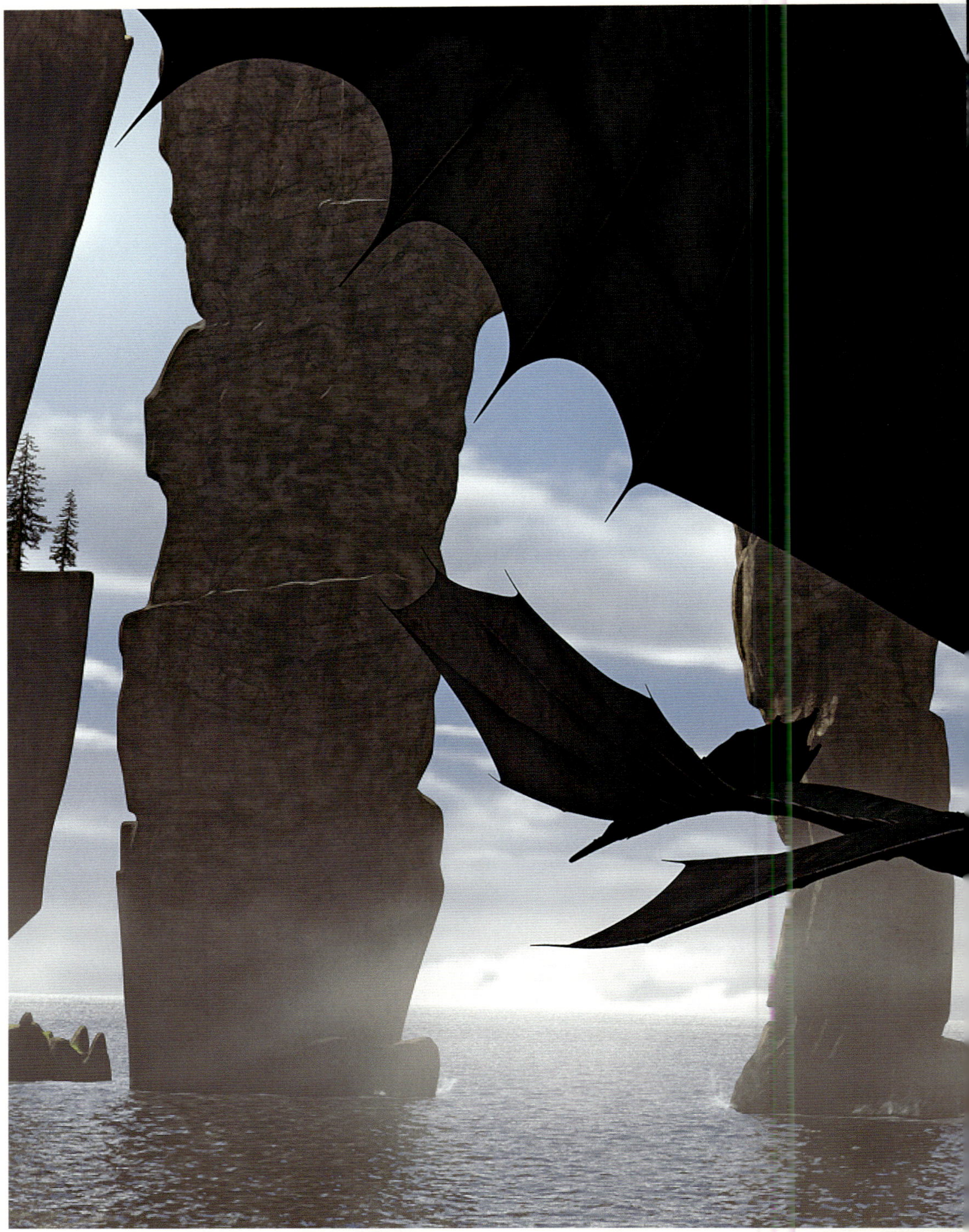

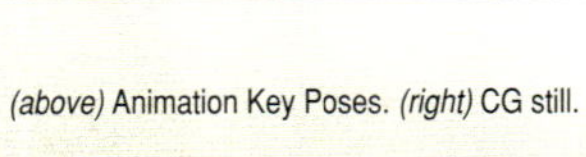

(above) Animation Key Poses. *(right)* CG still.

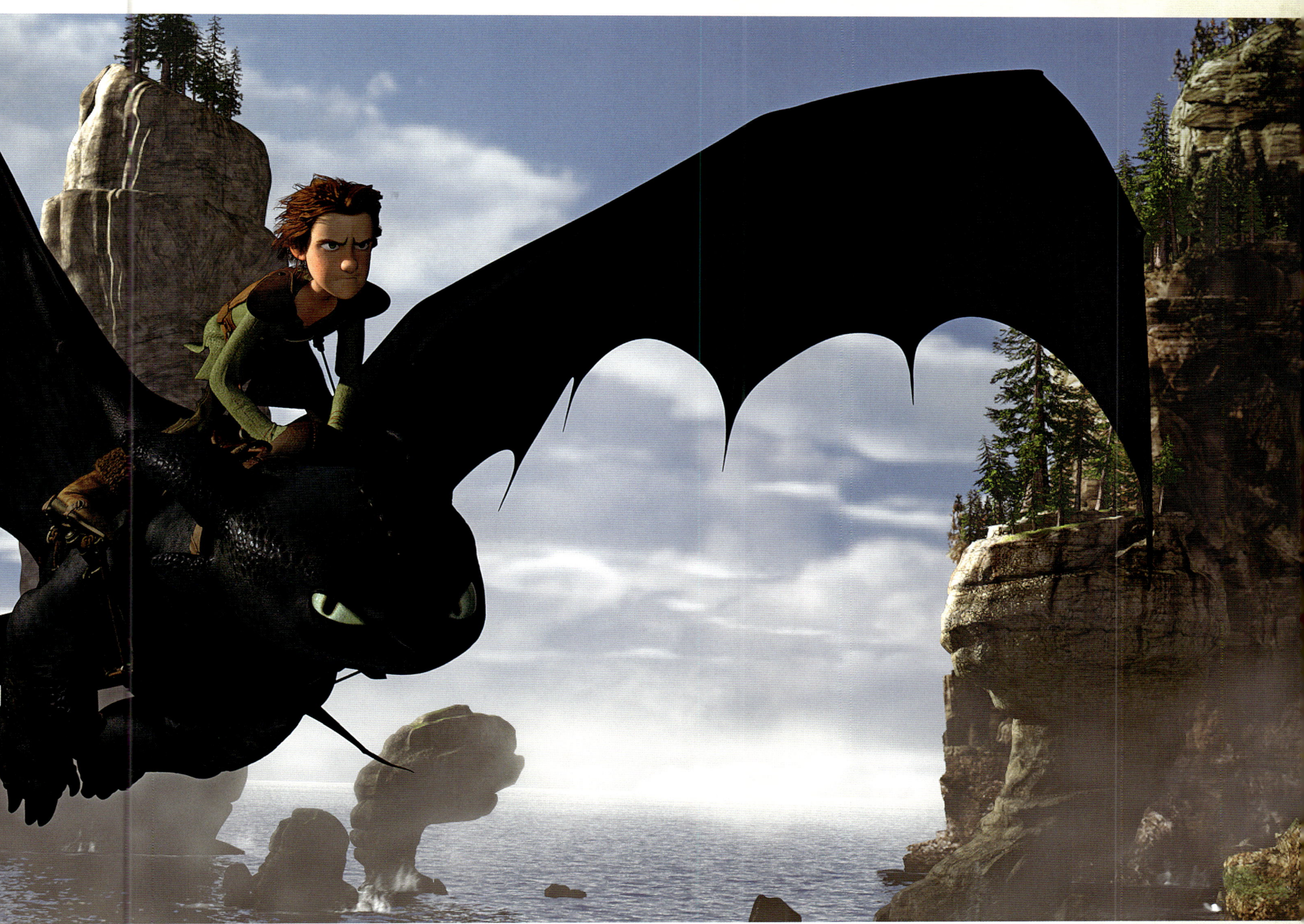

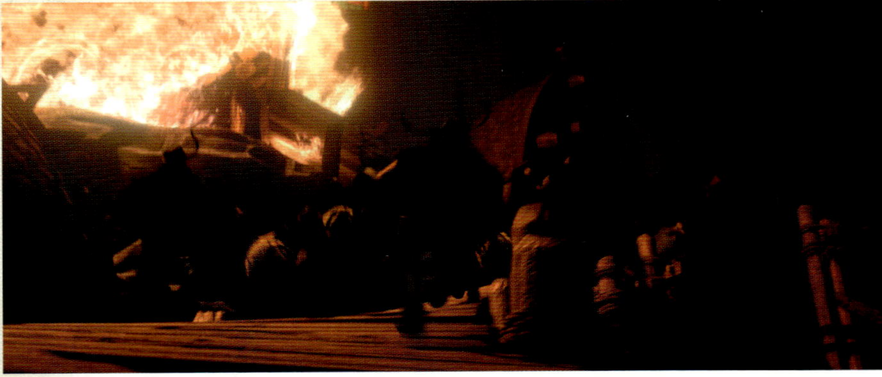

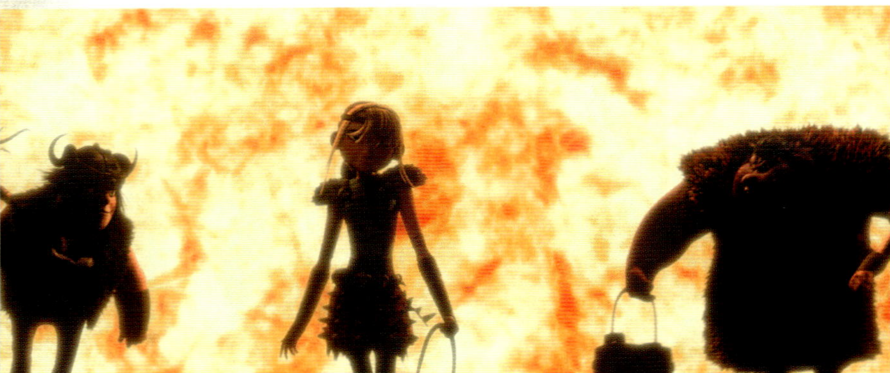

(top) CG still. *(above)* CG still. *(below)* CG still. *(below)* **Hiccup Hill** — CG still.

Effects

The effects team is charged with creating all elements with motion outside of character animation in a CG film. Considering the scale of action portrayed in *How to Train Your Dragon*, this responsibility required ambitious, focused effort. Beyond the obvious fire-breathing dragon complexities, the team was also responsible for producing complicated fire destruction, extensive rock shattering, and interactive cloud effects.

Fire-breathing dragons inflict massive fiery destruction upon their targets, so the effects team had to come up with efficient ways to ignite props and sets. The team essentially built modular fire blocks that, like snap-on toy building sets, can be stuck on a roof, boat, or tree as needed. These elements are placed thoughtfully to show fire that envelopes its host prop. "Seeing the fire interact and curl around these environments was really important. Our fire has organic-shaped emmission patterns so it can wrap around objects to create a more authentic look, which we use on all the brazers in the film as well," explains Head of Effects Matt Baer.

Dragon-induced rock shattering was another key effect. To portray the damage incurred by the Red Death smashing through a volcanic rock wall, the effects team built "cookie cutters" into the cliff wall to break it up into fragments. "First we paint seed particles all over rock models and feed thousands of them into rigid body simulators, which can

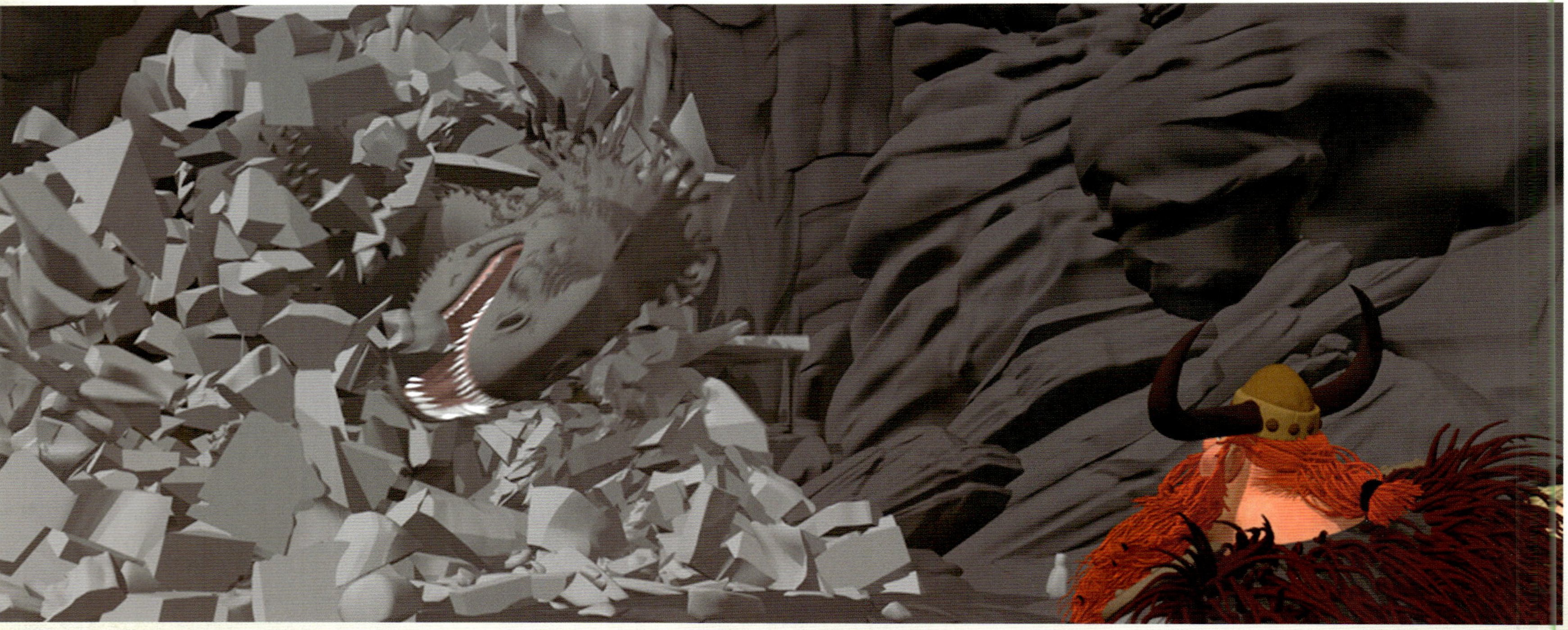

3D stereoscopic film technology brought additional challenges to our effects work. We learned that the angle of the fire to the camera was important to consider. When it was going across the camera, it looked extremely flat, like we had texture mapped a card. We now know the right balance of the angle and textural detail required to give our fire the proper depth.

—Matt Baer, Head of Effects

be layered. We then assign options such as variably sized shale rock debris, sand, or pyroclastic dust, and where each of the cracks between the pieces propagate, we blast out huge emissions of these elements," explains Baer. This effect required the development of new technology for volumetric rendering—an appropriately "ground-breaking" accomplishment for this film.

While clouds are generally made by water vapor in the sky, here they are made by the effects, lighting, and matte painting teams. In several sequences where Hiccup and Toothless fly through the clouds, simple clusters of spheres—almost like a bunch of grapes—are placed in space and then matte painters "project beautiful, detailed paintings onto them to make them look like clouds. Since the paintings exist in 3D space, as the camera moves around, they move and parallax just like real clouds do," explains Visual Effects Supervisor Craig Ring. The effects and lighting teams also fill these clouds with a glowing translucency to give a magical look to the atmosphere.

For sequences in which characters actually come in contact with clouds, the effects team created cumulonimbus clouds with which they can interact. These elements are more challenging to manage because they require varying detail: Within a single cloud, they can range from wispy to more structural, like the archways seen in the flight that Hiccup and Toothless share with Astrid. The amount of light that scatters within them must also be dialed up or down as needed, and "we achieve the desired balance of density and light by using volume rendering with custom shaders that allow us to blend from one frequency of detail to another," says Head of Effects Matt Baer.

Putting multiple effects together in shots—such as during the big battle at the end of the film, when the Red Death finally unleashes his powerful fire and the sky fills with big, napalmlike, churning smoke illuminated by fire and haze in full frame—proved to be an enormous challenge to render, based on huge file sizes. "We solved this by having two effects developers, one in the Glendale Studio and one in the Northern California PDI facility, work together to write a new render program, which we ended up using in more than one-third of our effects shots," recalls Head of Effects Matt Baer. Also, previous rendering tools would call for the layering of atmospheric elements, but in a stereographic film, such a setup would look like cards on the screen, so this new system proved important on several levels.

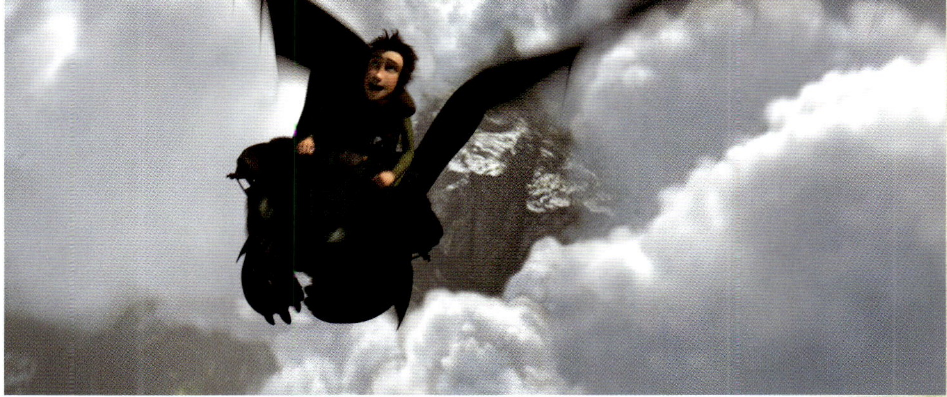

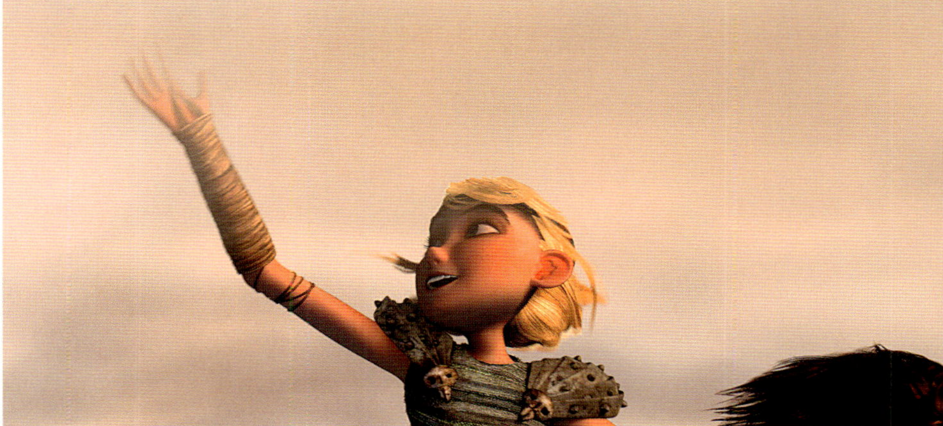

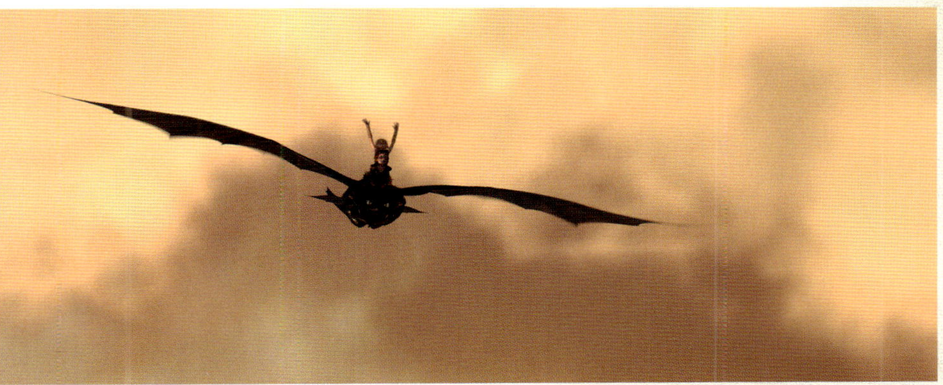

(above right) CG still. *(center right)* CG still. *(right)* CG still.

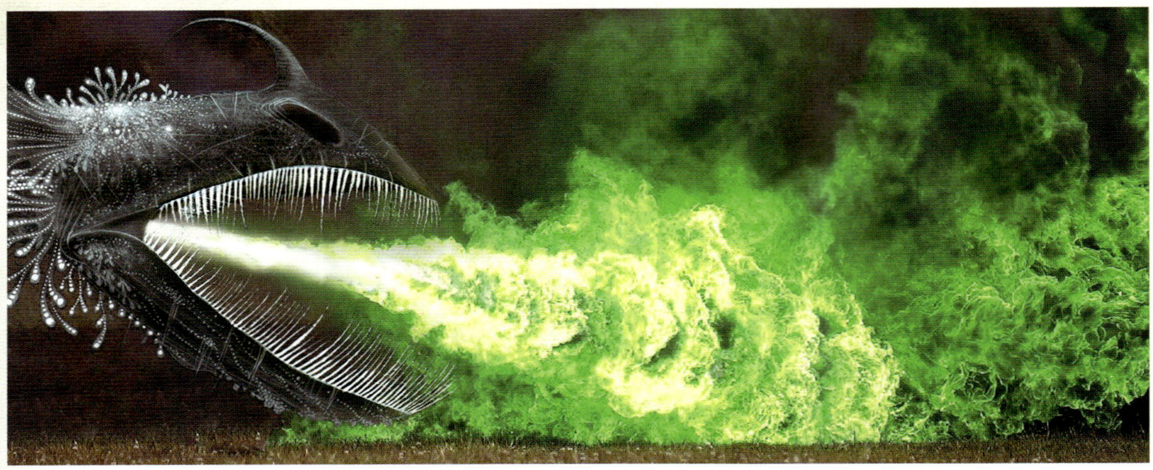

(above) **Red Death Fire** — Craig Ring — digital paint. *(below)* **The Red Death Fire** — CG still.
(bottom) **Rolling Brazier** — CG still. *(right)* **Monstrous Nightmare** — CG still.

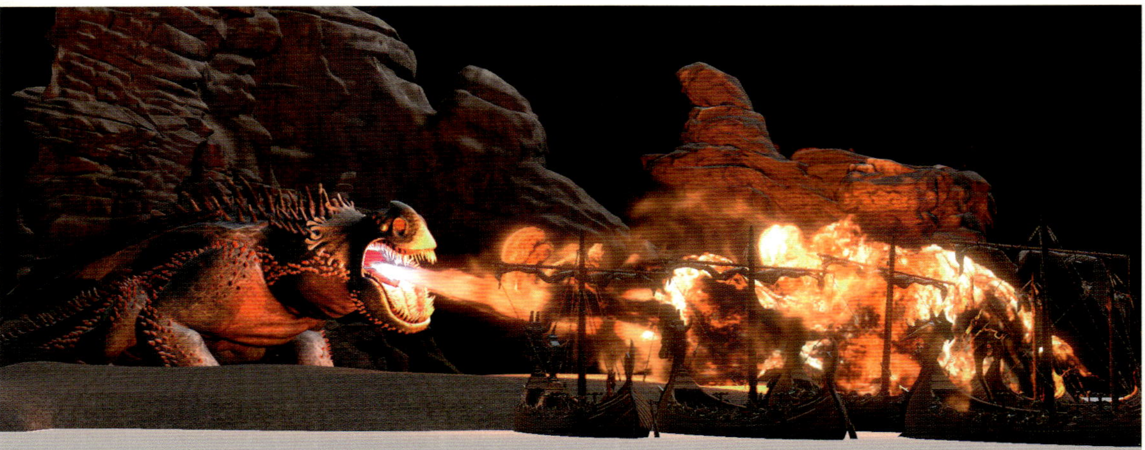

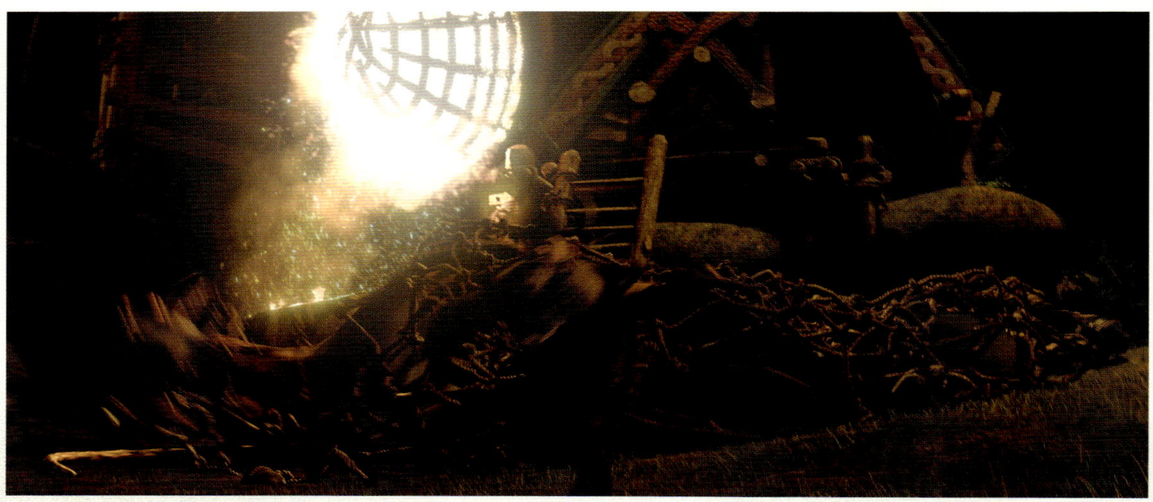

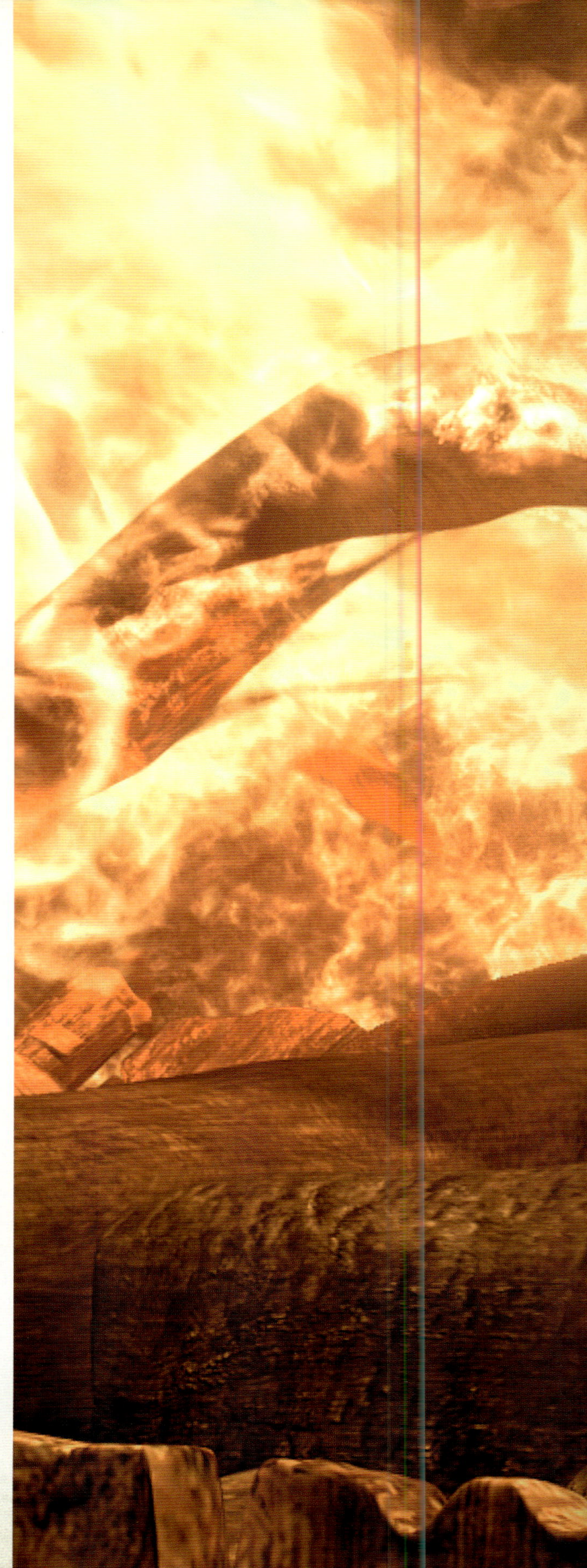

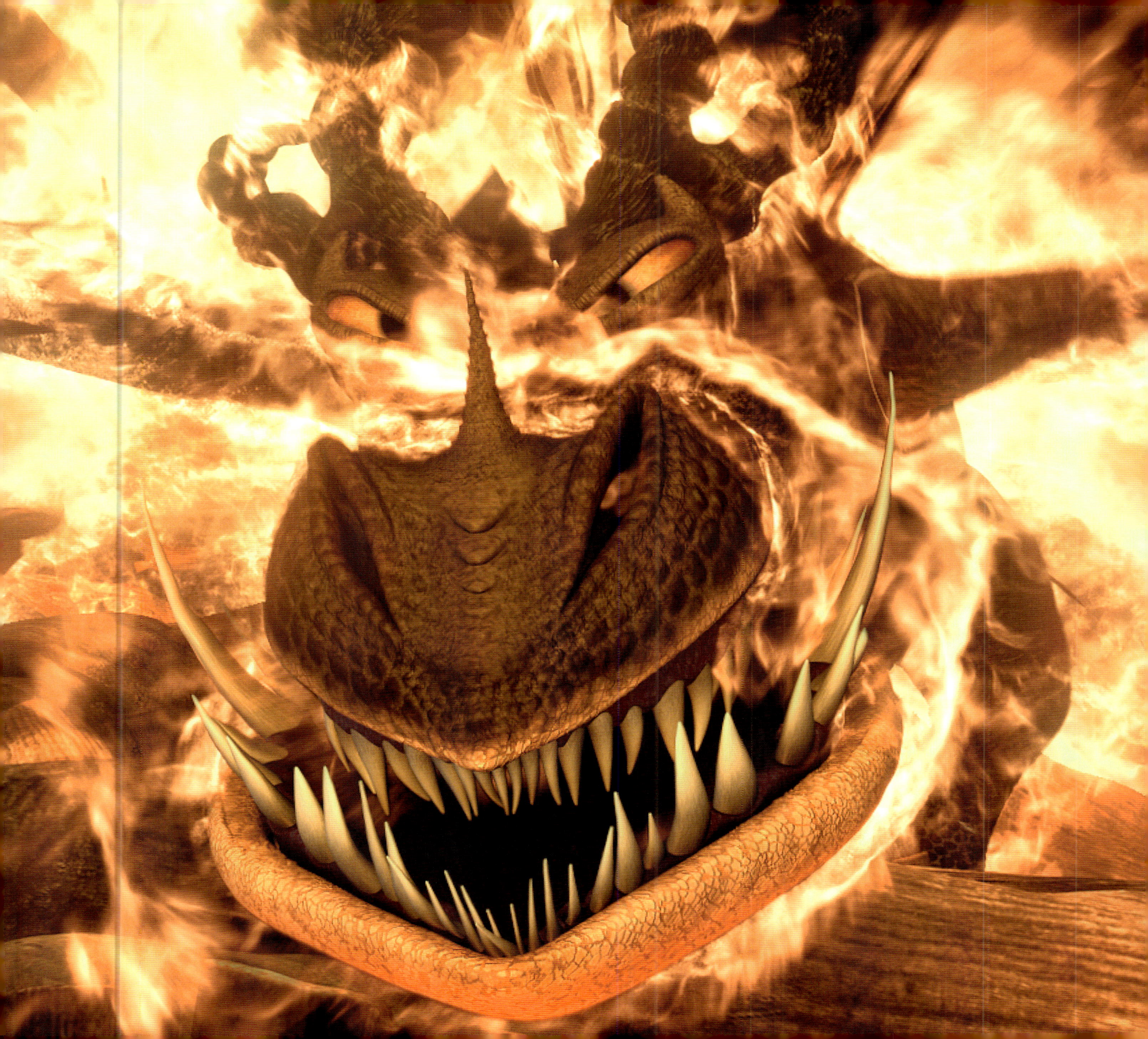

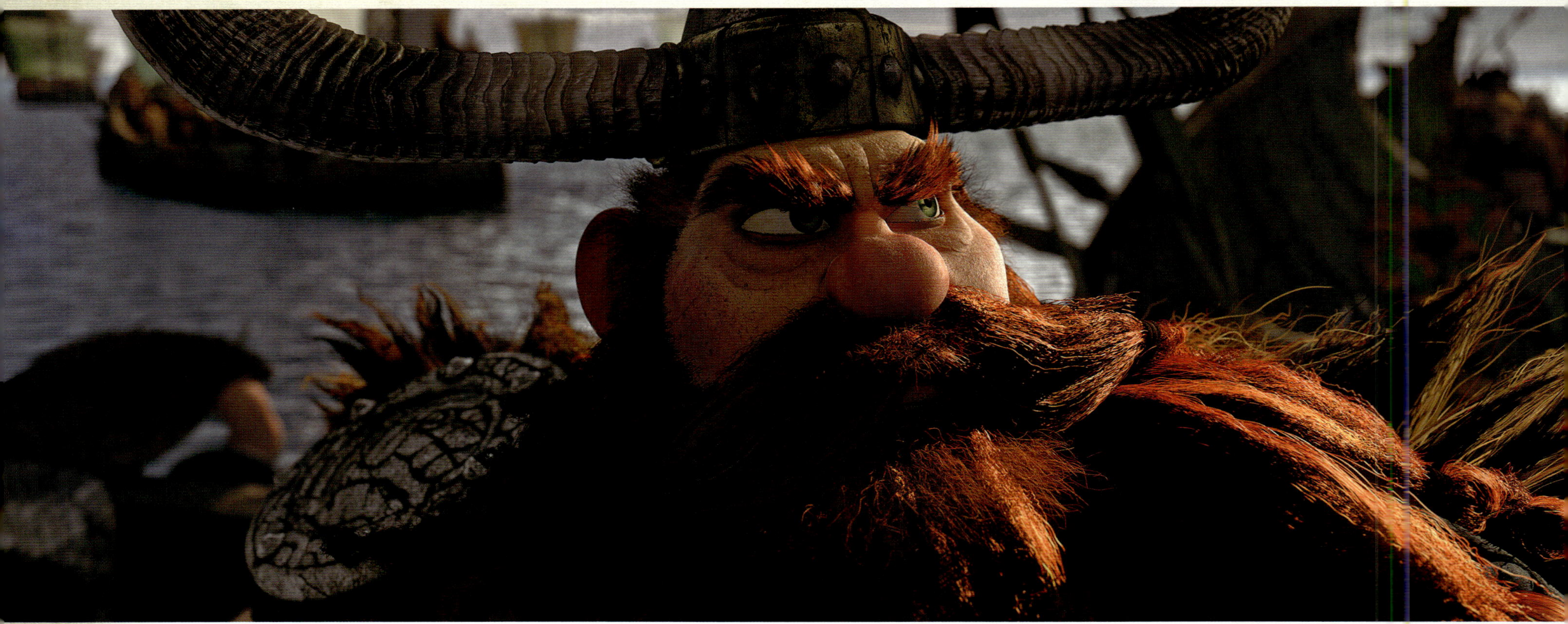

Half of the time, contrast is what gives a scene its drama. —Roger Deakins, Visual Consultant

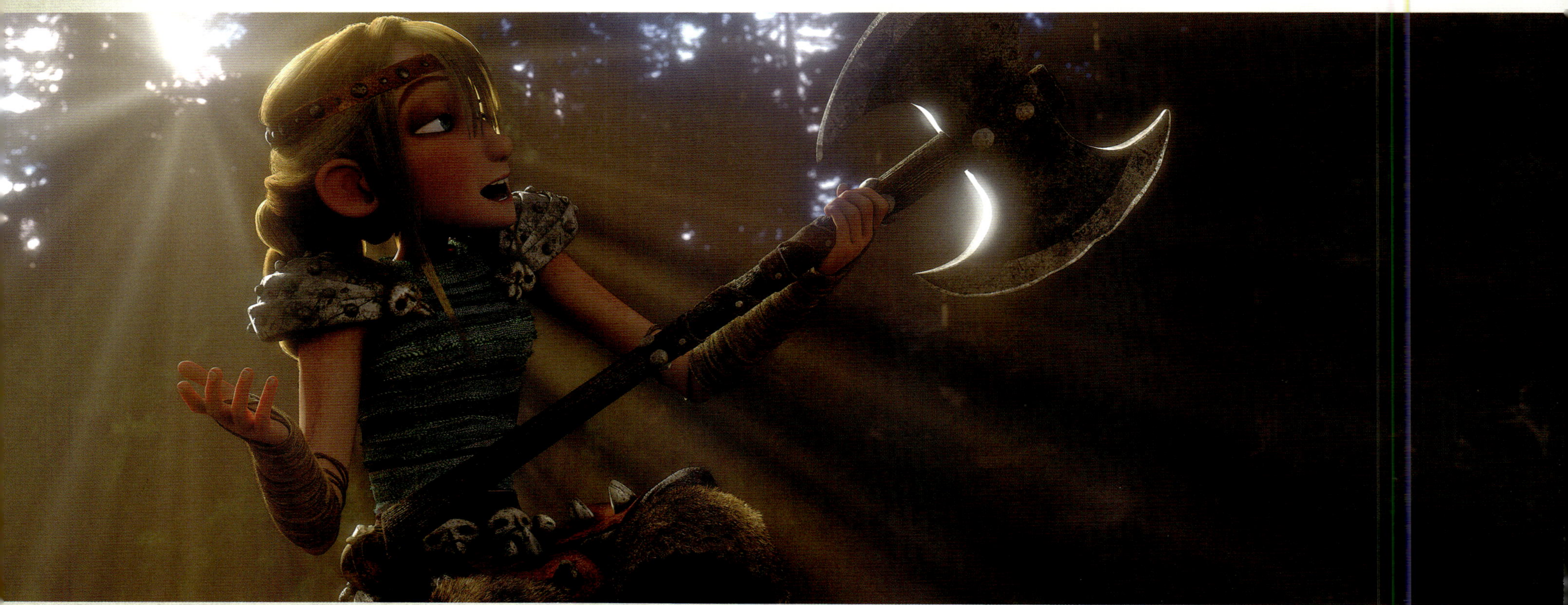

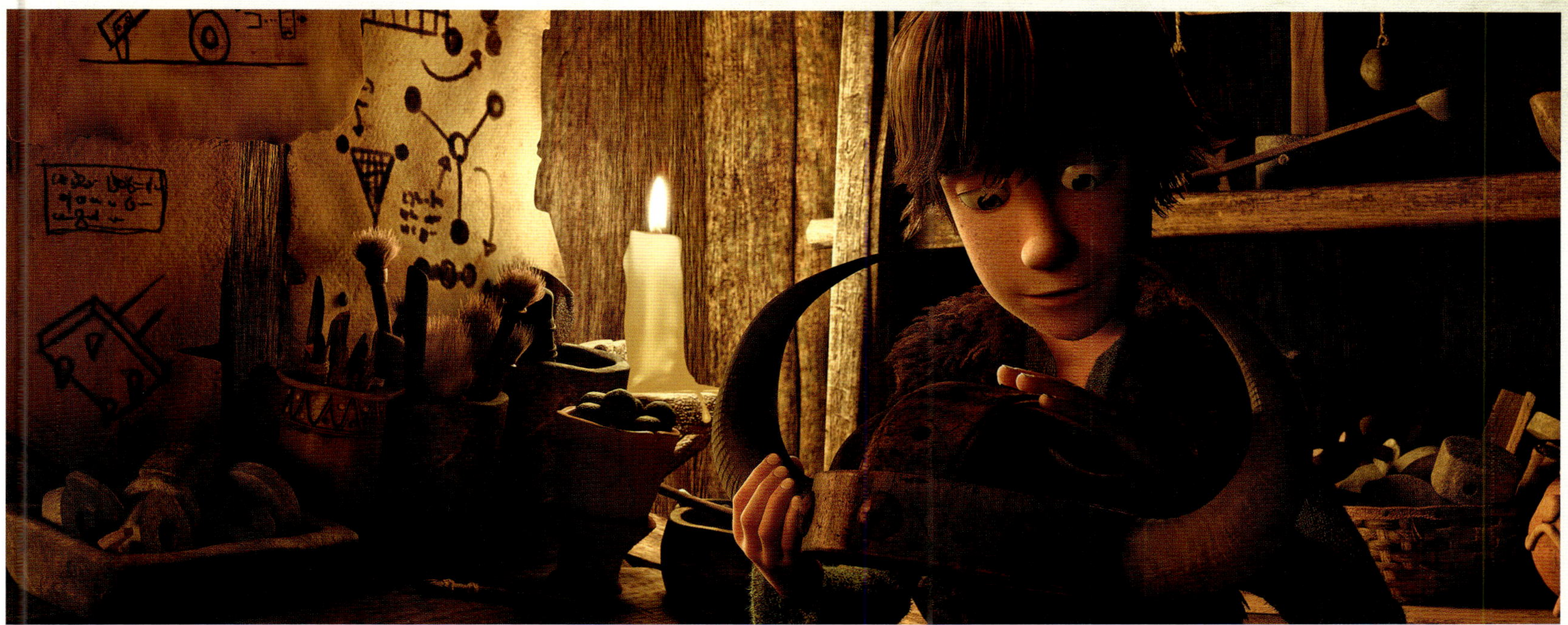

Lighting

The lighting department must deliver the directors' vision for the final look of the film by setting up proper light and shading combinations on each and every element, in each and every shot. For *How to Train Your Dragon*, Directors Chris Sanders and Dean DeBlois wanted to cast a Nordic light on their sets while playing to the drama of the story in a sophisticated style. Enter live-action Cinematographer Roger Deakins, whose work in particular on *The Assassination of Jesse James by the Coward Robert Ford* and *The Village* inspired the production. His consultation brought a vast knowledge of soft, cinematic lighting, plus a strong use of contrast, "which complements the tone of the story and gives the film a visual handsomeness," describes Production Designer Kathy Altieri.

To give a sense of just how dramatic the lighting can be, in some scenes, the only light source is little more than two small candles. This is a brave choice in the CG world, where it's tough not to show off every little detail that time was taken to design, build, and texture. "There's a balance between using naturalism and giving some creative style to it, or adding some dramatic effect to it," says Deakins, whose goal was to take light and wrap it across a form (without using a traditional rim light in the back) while still helping to deliver clear, readable character expressions.

Deakins' style of lighting involves *not* showing every single detail of what is in a shot and letting the audience create its own story about what is happening within that scene. This cognitive effort on the part of the viewer makes him more invested in the overall cinematic experience by having to actively think and feel his way through the story, subconsciously giving him a deep level of involvement with the characters. "It's the film equivalent of an impressionist painting," says Altieri.

With all the detail in our environments, it was important to keep the presentation of the characters on these backgrounds simple and clear. Roger really helped us portray how strong "simple" can be.

—Chris Sanders, Director

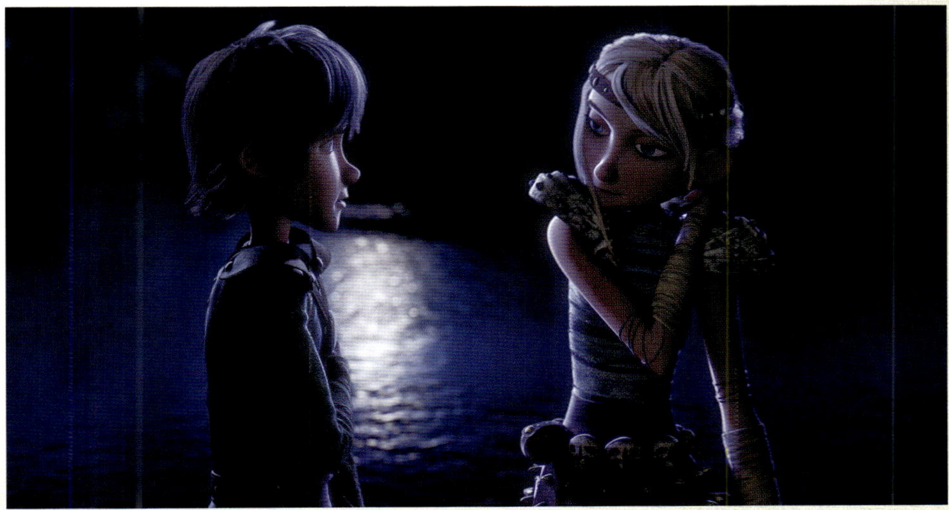

(all) CG Stills.

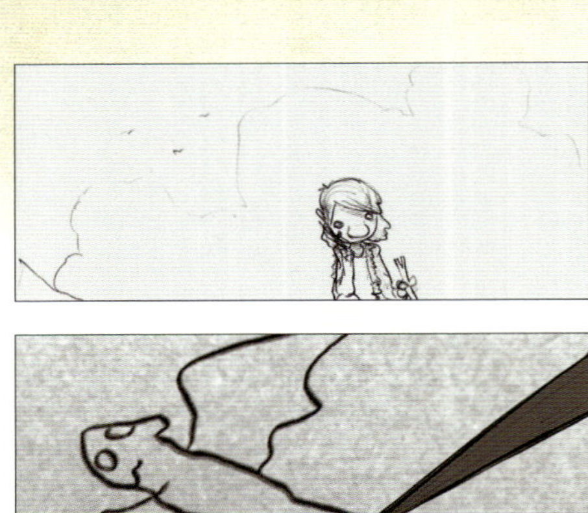
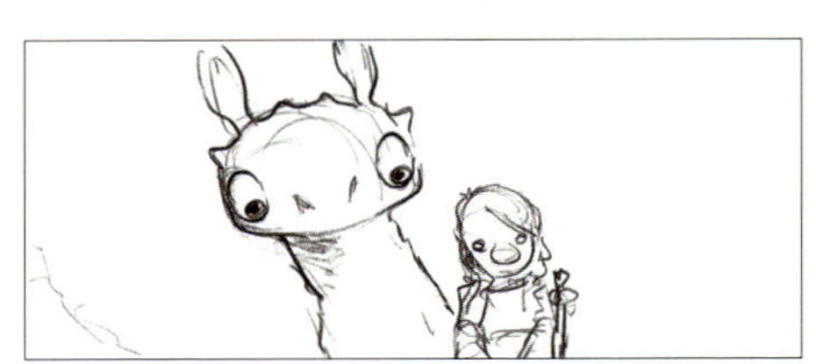
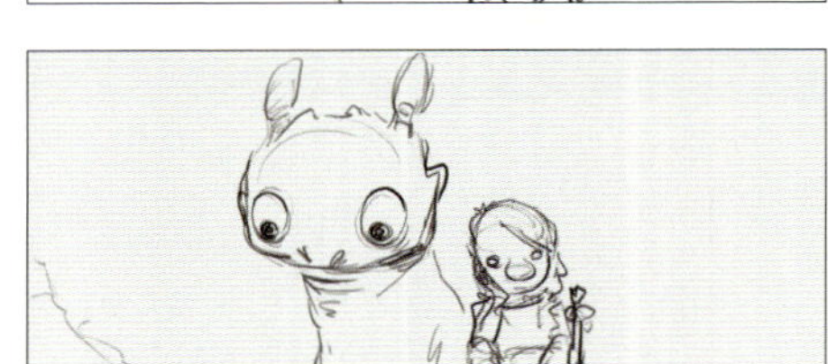
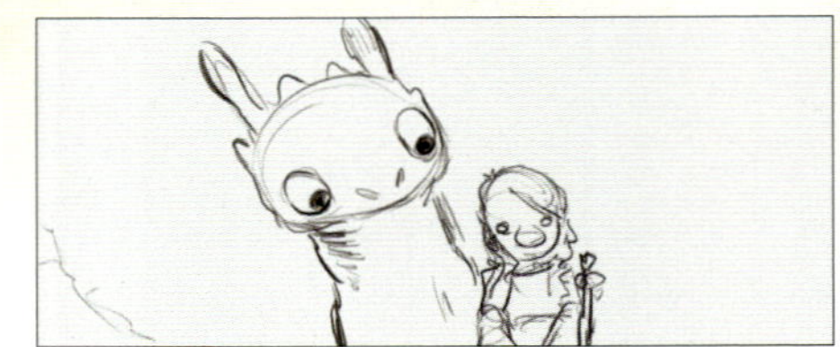
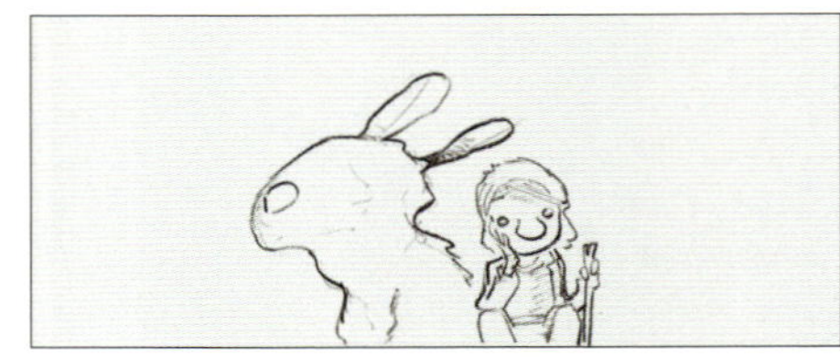
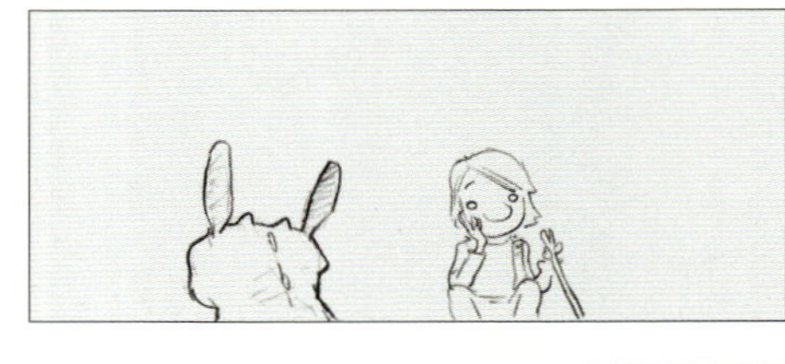
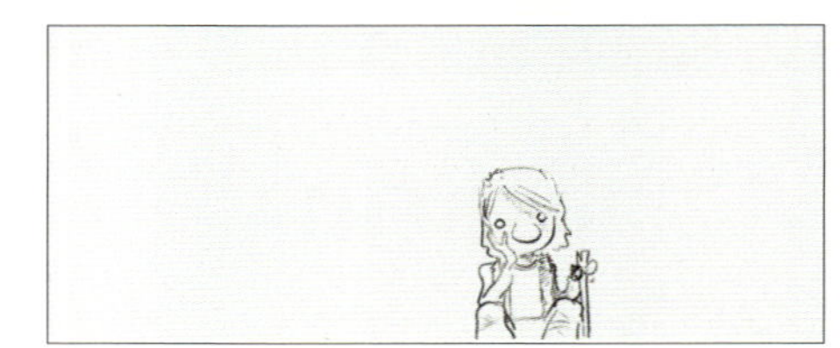
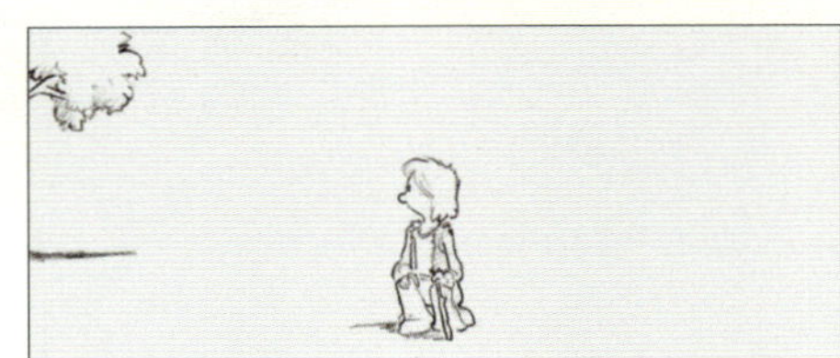
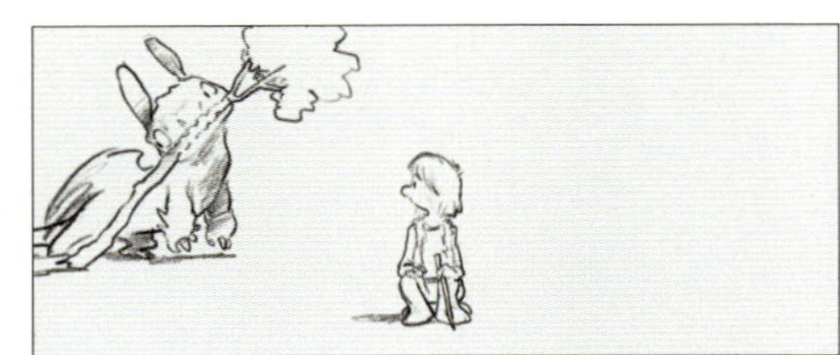
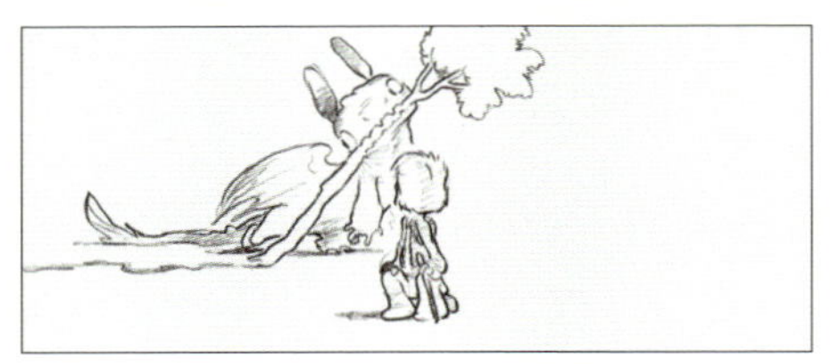
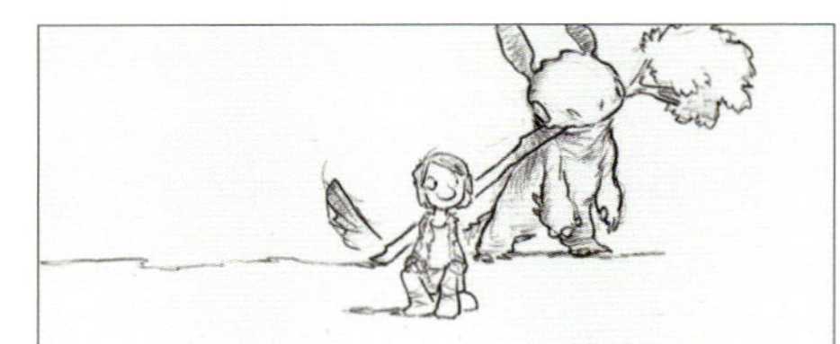

Editorial

The editorial crew has the unique advantage of seeing the film at all stages of production because nearly every department in the pipeline delivers its shots to the edit bay as it completes its work.

Perspective is perhaps the most important through-line for the editorial team to consider. When editorial cut together the sequence where Hiccup and Toothless are getting acquainted in the cove, the team was very mindful of each character's point of view, what emotion each would be feeling, and why he would be feeling such a way in each shot. Those character-based considerations inform the decisions of whether to go with two-shots, profiles, or close-ups in each moment. "It was all about discovering the idea of what it's like to go from a very tentative relationship to one that is truly joyful and fun," recalls Editor Darren Holmes.

The editorial team also had the unique opportunity to work in more of a live-action style. When Hiccup and Toothless battle the Red Death, the production took the approach that they were shooting this sequence in live-action by creating a long "master shot" which editorial then cut like a live-action team would. "We got the sense of what the storyboards were looking for, then we built basic animation and layered temporary effects, lighting, and clouds into one big Maya file," explains Head of Layout Gil Zimmerman. Next the "previs" put a variety of interesting camera moves into the shot to try to capture it cinematically. "Then it came down to editorial to let us find an organic cut, which gave the directors opportunity to find the movie instead of trying to call it out shot-by-shot much earlier in the process, as is the norm," continues Holmes. After the directors approved of the cut in editorial, the sequence went back into the production pipeline at the layout department and then moved forward through the subsequent departments like all other shots in the film.

(above and right) **Sequence 2475, Battle in the Clouds** — story sketch — Alessandro Carloni — digital paint.

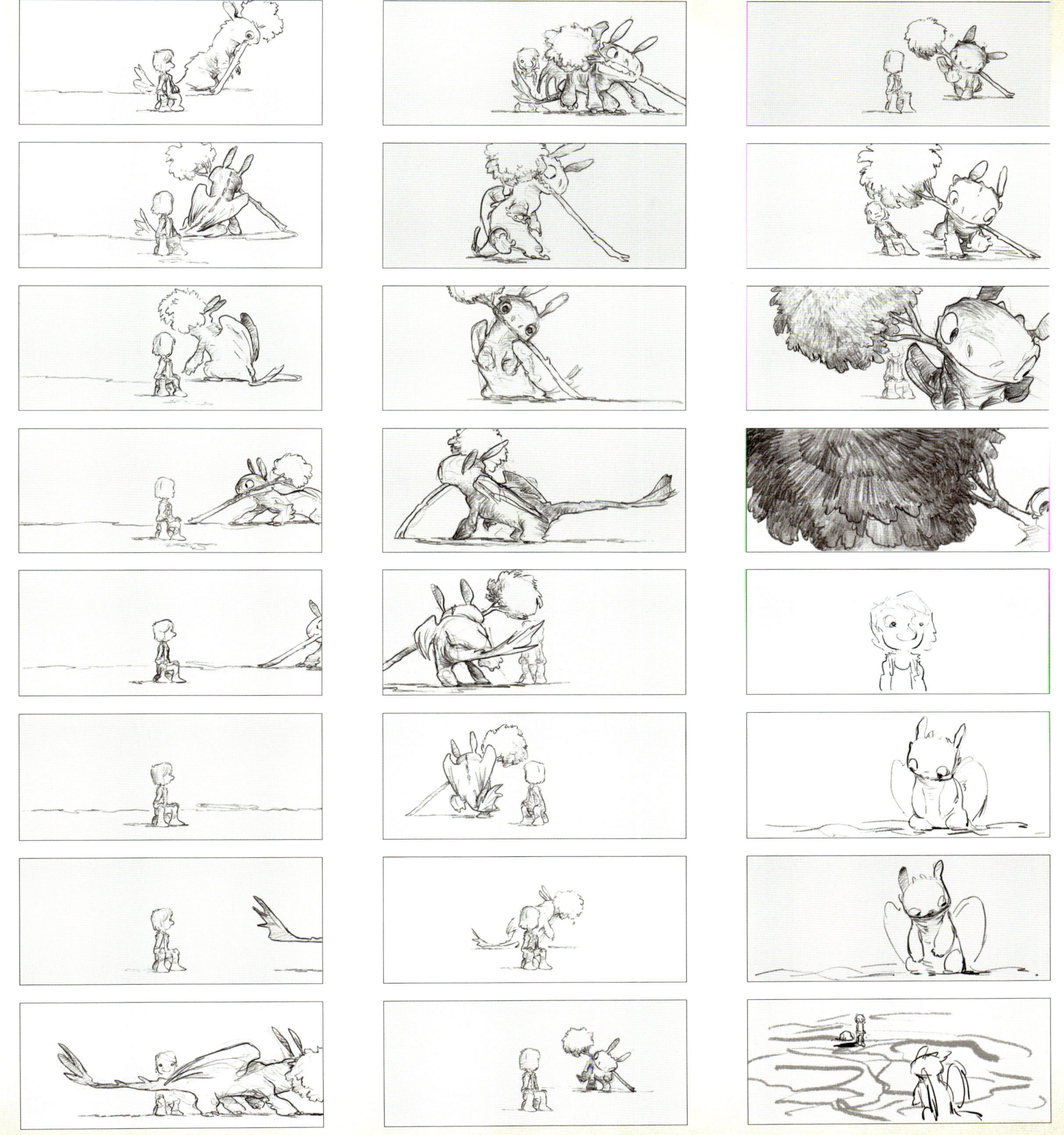

Closing Thoughts: Two Worlds, One Film

Evident from the earliest stages of visual development, there is a palpable energy to this film—a powerful mix of the rugged landscapes, the Viking spirit and the fire of dragons. It is an energy matched by that of the crew of *How to Train Your Dragon*. Just as Hiccup had the vision to reinterpret the relationship between the Viking and Dragon worlds, these filmmakers had the vision to make their story a memorable, larger-than-life experience for the audience.

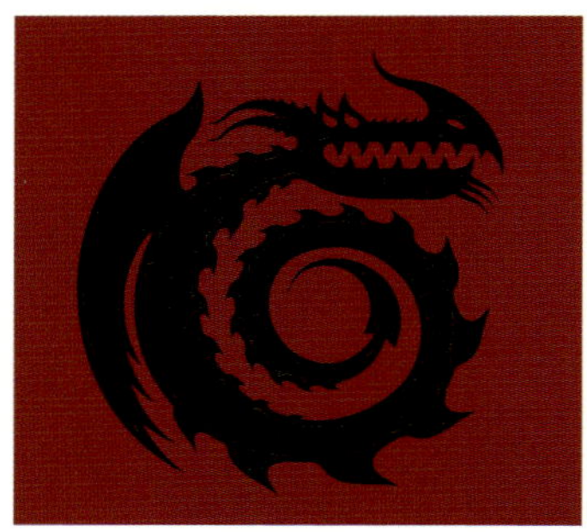

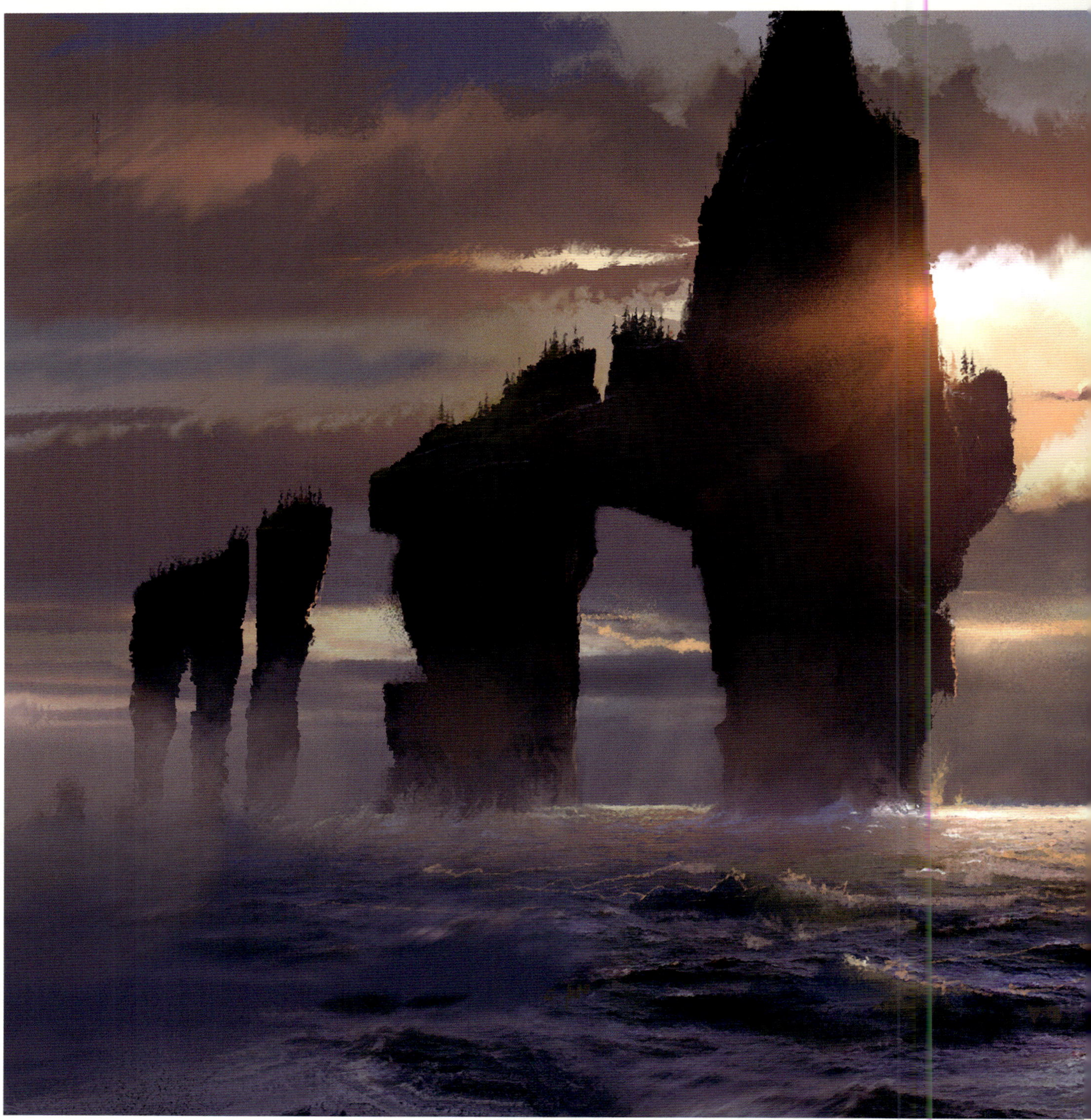

(*above*) **Insignia** — Pierre-Olivier Vincent — digital paint.

(*right*) **Cloud Key 4** — Dominique Louis — digital paint.

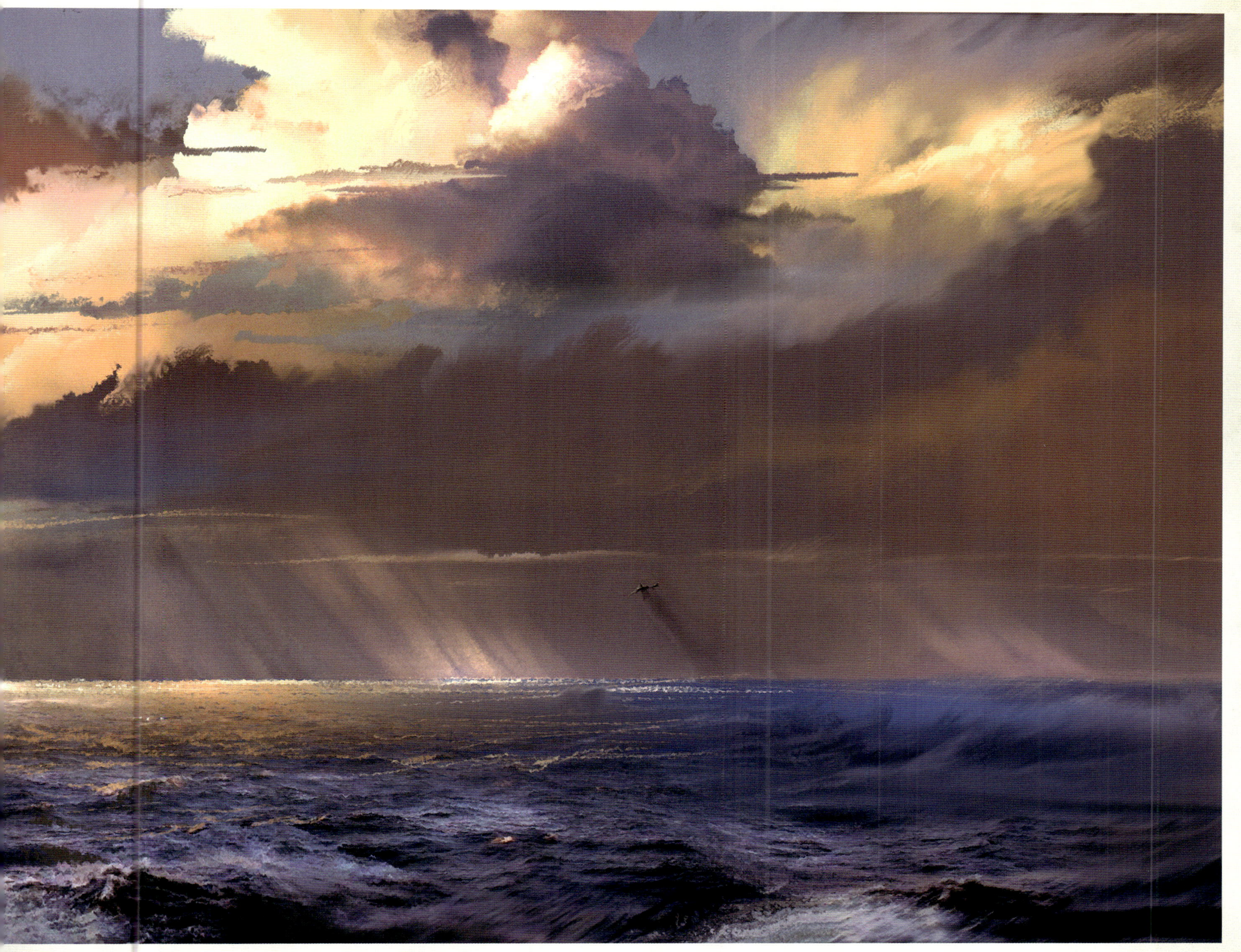

Acknowledgments

The publisher wishes to thank, first of all, the wonderful artists at DreamWorks who created *How to Train Your Dragon*, and would like to acknowledge in particular the following people for their special contributions to the book:

Cressida Cowell and Craig Ferguson for their wonderful introductory pieces.

At DreamWorks: Kathy Altieri, Bonnie Arnold, Kristy Cox, Dean DeBlois, Carolyn Frost, David Hail, Jeff Hare, Jennifer Hoskin, Chris Jefferies, Angela Park, Chris Sanders, Curtis Thompson, Vy Trinh, and Pierre-Olivier Vincent.

Special gratitude to writer Tracey Miller-Zarneke and designer Timothy Shaner.

Also to the Newmarket team, including Frank DeMaio, Keith Hollaman, Paul Sugarman, Heidi Sachner, Harry Burton, and Tracey Bussell.

—Esther Margolis, Publisher, Newmarket Press

The author wishes to thank the list above as well as the crew of *How To Train Your Dragon* for opening up their busy schedules and robust art files to make this book possible. She is thankful for the opportunity to embark on this literary adventure with such talented publishing associates as Keith Hollaman and Tim Shaner. The author dedicates this work to her family and friends for their continued love and support—especially her husband Mike, and their two little dragons, Josh & Ryan.

—Tracey Miller-Zarneke

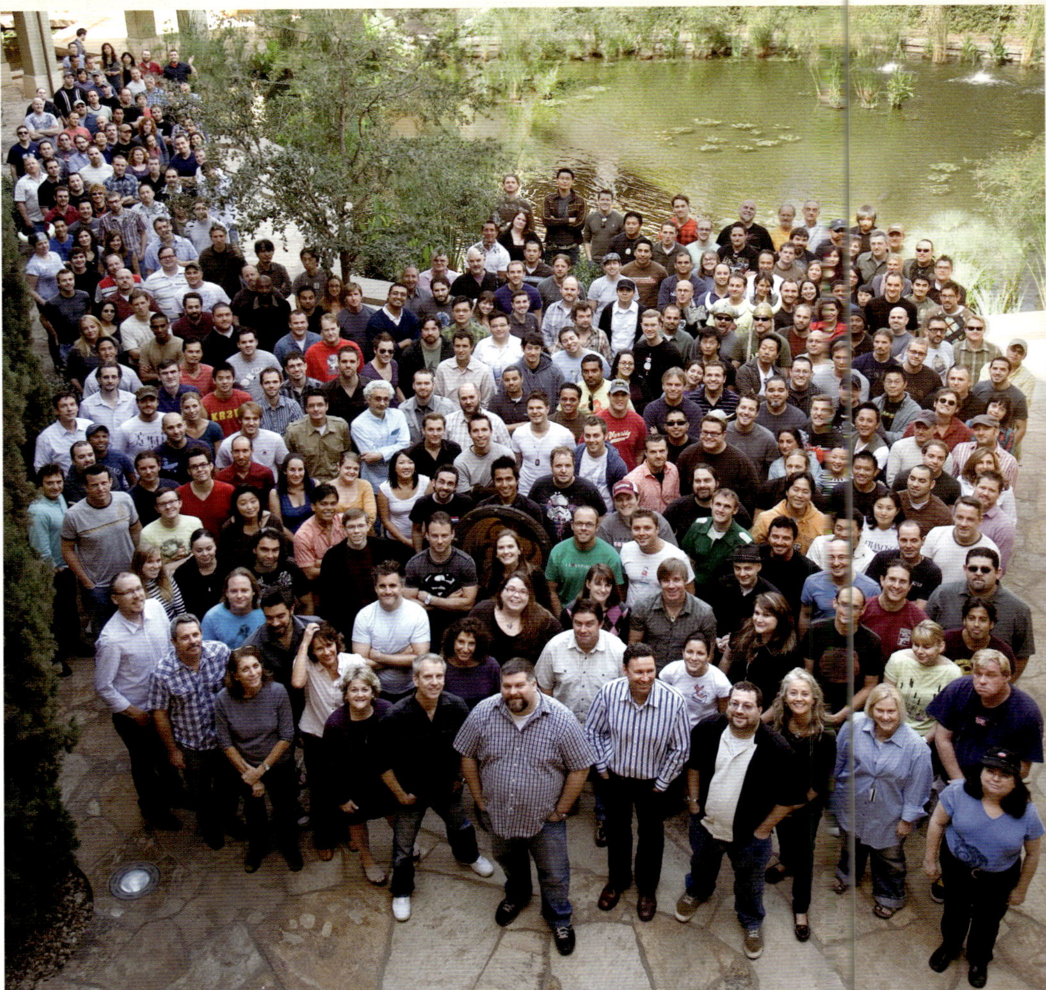

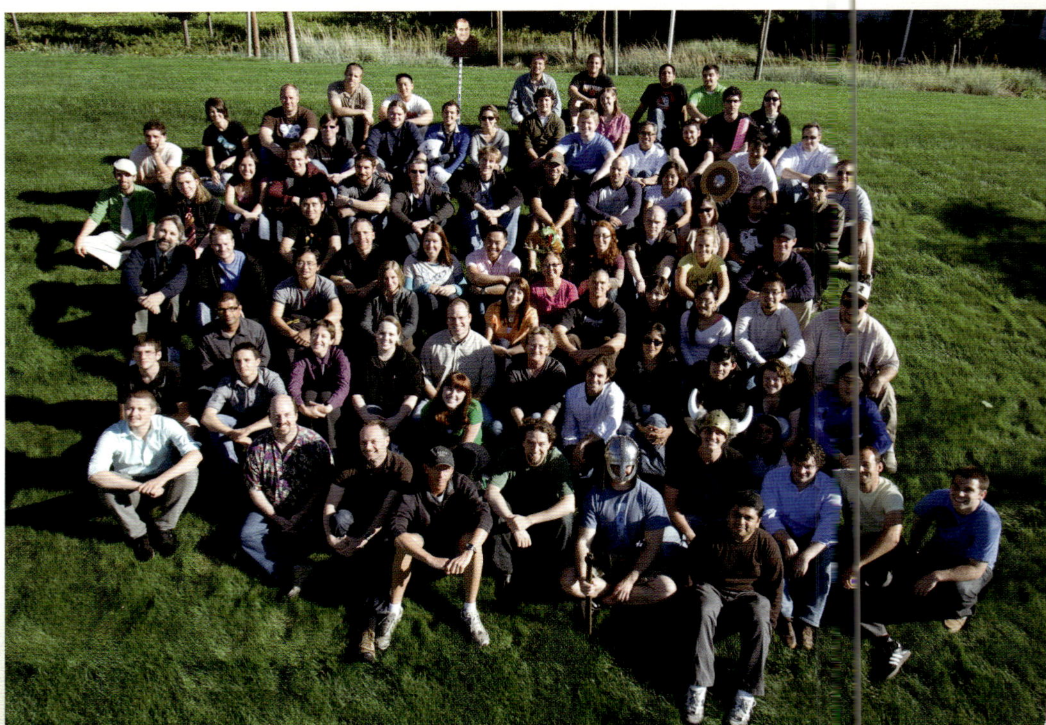

(above right) **DreamWorks Glendale Crew** — Photo — Mathieu Young.

(right) **DreamWorks PDI Crew** — Photo — Javier Solsona.